MW00774432

Poe and the Remapping of Antebellum Print Culture

Poe and the Remapping of Antebellum Print Culture

Edited by J. Gerald Kennedy and Jerome McGann

LOUISIANA STATE UNIVERSITY PRESS

BATON ROUGE

Published by Louisiana State University Press
Copyright © 2012 by Louisiana State University Press
All rights reserved
Manufactured in the United States of America
First printing

Designer: Laura Roubique Gleason
Typeface: Arno Pro
Printer: McNaughton & Gunn, Inc.
Binder: Acme Bookbinding

LIBRARY OF CONGRESS CATALOGING-IN-PUBLICATION DATA

Poe and the remapping of antebellum print culture / edited by J. Gerald Kennedy and Jerome McGann.
    p. cm.
Papers presented at a literary conference on Edgar Allan Poe held at the University of Virginia.
Includes bibliographical references and index.
ISBN 978-0-8071-5026-9 (cloth : alk. paper) — ISBN 978-0-8071-5027-6 (pdf) — ISBN 978-0-8071-5028-3 (epub) —ISBN 978-0-8071-5029-0 (mobi)
1. Poe, Edgar Allan, 1809–1849—Criticism and interpretation—Congresses. 2. Poe, Edgar Allan, 1809–1849—Knowledge—Book industries and trade—Congresses. 3. Literature publishing—United States—History—19th century—Congresses. 4. Publishers and publishing—United States—History—19th century—Congresses. 5. Literature and society—United States—History—19th century—Congresses. I. Kennedy, J. Gerald. II. McGann, Jerome J.
PS2638.P66 2013
818'.309—dc23

2012020864

Contents

Acknowledgments

The editors of this volume wish to thank MaryKatherine Callaway, director of LSU Press, for her encouragement; Margaret Lovecraft for her editorial oversight; and Stan Ivester for his deft copyediting. We also owe a debt of gratitude to the press's outside reader, Meredith McGill, for her astute suggestions for organizing and improving the volume. Charles M. "Mitch" Frye provided invaluable editorial assistance in preparing the manuscript for submission, and Barbara J. McManus of Information Technology Services at LSU offered eleventh-hour technical help. We also appreciate the work of James W. Long in creating the index. Finally, we thank Dr. Kelly Miller, formerly of the University of Virginia, for helping to organize the symposium from which this volume of essays emerged.

Poe and the Remapping of Antebellum Print Culture

Introduction

J. GERALD KENNEDY

Amid commemorations of Edgar Poe's bicentennial year, a contingent of literary scholars met at the University of Virginia to launch a collaborative research
project. While less theatrical than the restaging of Poe's burial in Baltimore, this
gathering confronted the author's anomalous, problematic position in American literary history as well as the larger, more complex question of how to remap
the burgeoning, dispersed print culture that facilitated the invention of American literature between 1820 and 1850. The Charlottesville event had been initiated
by Jerome McGann, best known for his work in Romantic and Victorian literature as well as in textual editing but more recently a herald of digital humanities
research and a converted Americanist. McGann himself proposed the trope of
"remapping" that invited participating scholars to rethink the cultural space in
which Poe operated—the extent and configuration of an emerging literary culture constructed less (it now seems) by the monumental achievements of a few
revered authors than by the accumulated compositions of "scribbling" women
and men—to repurpose Hawthorne's complaint—whose poetry and prose filled
newspapers, magazines, annuals, and books emanating from presses across the
country. Contrary to Emerson's romantic claim that "an institution is the lengthened shadow of one man," American literature emerged from the impromptu
collaboration of editors, publishers, and authors—a self-appointed literati who
in response to the opportunities of an expanding print culture produced belles
lettres for the masses.[1]

The task of figuratively remapping this phenomenon presents challenges of
its own. In a lively, deconstructive book, Denis Wood has shown how cartography—especially the sort produced before global positioning satellites—typically
performs several covert tasks in its representation of a spatial domain.[2] According
to Wood, maps "mask the interests that bring them into being" (95). They serve
unstated political or cultural purposes; they construct rather than reproduce a

world, privileging certain vantage points; they participate in the very histories they help to instantiate; they simultaneously present and suppress information through selectivity; and they embody signs and codes that subtly manipulate the entire map-reading process. Wood offers a chastening critique, and participants in the project wished to avoid a mere re-centering of antebellum print culture—famously conceived by F. O. Matthiessen in *American Renaissance* (1941) to re-volve around Emerson, Hawthorne, Melville, Thoreau, and Whitman on an axis from Boston to New York—that would position Poe at the crux of another fixed national cartography. We wished instead to remap the space of antebellum print culture horizontally, not from a top-down, hierarchical perspective that would re-inscribe literary preeminence. Poe would figure not as the unrecognized Master Genius, but rather as a shrewd, peripatetic author-journalist whose circulation in what he called "Literary America" epitomized the ploys and practices of a horizontal culture of letters sustained by proliferative redistribution.

In her illuminating study of the "culture of reprinting," Meredith McGill underscores the diffused, regional nature of U.S. literary culture and the haphazard dissemination of republished fiction and poetry.[3] Poe figures notably in McGill's account, presenting "a career charted through the heart of this culture" (151) and instancing a brilliant adaptability to the peculiar, even bizarre conditions of a largely unregulated print industry. Like many of his contemporaries (Hawthorne and Child also come to mind), Poe perceived himself as "essentially a magazinist."[4] He worked within a network of competing periodicals and contended with the vagaries of public taste as well as the "horrid laws of political economy"—the market forces so astutely analyzed by Terence Whalen.[5] But Poe was likewise enmeshed in a system built upon the unchecked reprinting of literary compositions—the unremunerated republication of what he and others regarded as their intellectual property. McGill shows how an obstinate republican faith in the free circulation of books and ideas militated against copyright protection; this was an ethos that newspaper and magazine publishers promoted to ensure their right to reprint (and profit from) virtually any published material that came their way. Literary texts thus had a life of their own, moving across the antebellum landscape from journal to journal, pragmatically re-edited to fit local needs and available column space. Sometimes editorial reformatting eliminated the authorial byline or the original print source of the material. Yet rooted in the imperatives of what Benedict Anderson has called "print-capitalism," this exploitative, inherently predatory system performed the cultural work of articulating an imagined national community.[6]

To remap literary America not by focusing on a cluster of luminaries in the Northeast but rather by reconstructing the network of relationships, authorial and institutional, within a decentralized system of distribution requires attention both to the connective and the focalizing functions of print culture. In the present collection of essays, contributors have examined the problematic conditions of both authorship and nationhood in the antebellum United States. Poe figures as an avatar of this horizontal culture of reprinting, envisioning the broad contours of the American literary world, critiquing the nascent nation, and demonstrating the recirculation of ideas and texts. From the earliest assessments of his career— literally from the infamous obituary by Rufus Griswold in 1849—the tendency to separate Poe from the American scene, to see his poetry and fiction as inherently disconnected from antebellum culture, has institutionalized a fundamental misrepresentation. Poe has figured minimally in dominant theories of American literature, we might conclude, because he scorned nationalistic themes, exposed American literary jingoism, ridiculed Jacksonian democracy, hoodwinked the reading public, and conceived nightmarish plots that conjured unwelcome racial demons. Yet as Shawn Rosenheim and Stephen Rachman demonstrated in their trend-setting collection *The American Face of Edgar Allan Poe* (1995), the author was, from the outset, immersed in and responsive to the magazine market as well as the national pressures and preoccupations it embodied.[7] He was also a man on the move, shuttling from city to city, back and forth across the Mason-Dixon line, promoting American literature while challenging literary nationalism and envisioning a transregional cohort of authors as he attacked provincial cliques and coteries. Whether operating editorially from periodicals in Richmond, Philadelphia, or New York, Poe long resisted centralized cultural authority and construed the American republic of letters as a network of *littérateurs* stretching from Maine to Georgia and from New York to Louisiana. Such a map corresponds to the actual scope of the horizontal print culture that had grown up in the United States. To represent American literature otherwise, as the achievement of a few great minds inhabiting the Boston-Concord corridor (as several literary histories of the United States have done), is to skew the literary map into a cartoon of New England provincialism.

Charting a "Literary America" that reflects the actual parameters of a culture in which texts circulated freely and authors (as well as editors) often moved from place to place, seizing new publishing opportunities, forces one to confront the messiness, complexity, and volatility of the antebellum literary world. Periodicals came and went in a hurry—James Russell Lowell's *Pioneer* (which lasted three issues) offers a famous example—and publications materialized in improbable outposts. James Hall founded the *Illinois Monthly Magazine* in the frontier town of Vandalia in 1830; in 1837–38, a biweekly magazine called the *South-Western Journal* emanated for several months from Natchez, Mississippi. In this cultural optimism, young Edward Patterson unsuccessfully urged Poe in 1849 to join him in founding a distinguished periodical in Oquawka, Illinois. Print media proliferated at a furious pace. Many civic and reform groups had their own presses, placing in circulation pamphlets, reports, and books; the temperance and anti-slavery movements, for example, promulgated hundreds of personal narratives and countless works of fiction, all circulated to awaken the conscience and raise the consciousness of a populace bent on nation building. Charles Sellers has observed that "periodicals arose to target every specialized audience—literati and farmers, doctors and lawyers, women and children, Democrats and Whigs." He estimates that between 1825 and 1850, somewhere between four and five thousand periodicals were launched, of which roughly six hundred survived at mid-century.[8] In this incredible welter of activity, an American culture of letters began to emerge.

Reprinting from periodicals spread across the national landscape. For review purposes, many newspapers received copies of weekly and monthly journals from which they routinely culled usable material, thus promulgating recirculated material to the grassroots. Regionally, newspapers also exchanged courtesy copies with each other, extending the reach of reprint practices into every town of modest size. First-hand news reports from "correspondents" circulated with viral alacrity, even though no organized system for gathering and distributing news yet existed. The circulation of literary texts followed a more leisurely and inconsistent pattern, one contingent upon unfilled page space as well as the taste of the editor who managed "selections" or "extracts." This arbitrary, irregular transmission of tales, essays, and poems privileged popular appeal over profundity, and sentiment or sensation over subtlety. Monthly magazines themselves often derived a goodly amount of material from reprinting (a few almost entirely so), and by the 1840s Poe summarized the demands of a popular audience for "Magazine Literature": "we need the curt, the condensed, the pointed, the readily diffused." Such materials responded to the "*rush* of the age," and as he well understood, rapid diffusion held the key to success for both authors and publishers in an American culture committed to the principle that the unimpeded circulation of ideas and information served the ends of a democratic republic.[9] Yet he conversely warned that the reprinting and distribution of foreign books, thanks to the lack of an international copyright law, repressed "national literature" and encouraged post-colonial subservience by disseminating a "monarchical or aristocratical sentiment" that was ultimately "fatal to democracy."[10] Poe even insisted that "in Letters as in Government we require a Declaration of Independence. Better still would be a Declaration of War."[11]

His plea for cultural self-respect did not, however, compel him to embrace popular, Jacksonian democracy or nationalistic efforts to enshrine American myths in literature. Indeed, Poe rather deliberately avoided the provincialism of U.S. historical subjects and instead practiced a poetics of dislocation, especially in fiction, that made his texts (as McGill observes) more suitable for reprinting because "strategic generality" held open "a tale's potential field of address" (157). Generic Gothic settings appealed to precisely the multiple, disparate audiences that reprinting cultivated. Yet this strategy did not imply indifference to the changing American scene; rather, it created a way to critique national life and politics by displacing them onto invented, vaguely European or Old World locales or by projecting them into apparently occult, metaphysical narratives. Sometimes, as in "The Man That Was Used Up," "Some Words with a Mummy," or "Mellonta Tauta," he delivered stinging attacks on nationalistic delusions embedded in farcical dialogue. What mattered, for Poe, was the recirculation of his writing: "to be appreciated, you must be *read*," he remarked in defense of one tale's disgusting conclusion.[12] In this regard, he embodies the very principle of a print culture predicated on popular interest and republication.

Repeatedly Poe endeavored to advance the idea of literary America—and his standing within the ranks of contemporary authors—by exploiting magazine circulation and reprinting. In the pages of the *Southern Literary Messenger,* for example, he favorably reviewed (August 1836) a government report proposing a South Seas expedition and later (January 1837) waxed enthusiastic about Jeremiah Reynolds's address to Congress hailing the benefits of such an undertaking. The latter piece appeared in the very issue featuring the opening installment of "The Narrative of Arthur Gordon Pym," an unsigned story that Poe hoped would create a clamor for its book publication by diffusing throughout the nation a thrilling and apparently authentic account of the first voyage into the extreme Antarctic region. Although the series ended with the second episode (due to the author's dismissal from the *Messenger*), Harper and Brothers eventually published Poe's novel—a hoax attributed to Pym but slyly associated with Poe—in 1838, just as the government-sponsored Wilkes Expedition was departing for the Pacific Ocean. He devised a similar scheme in 1840, shamelessly plagiarizing from

Lewis and Clark, Alexander Mackenzie, and Washington Irving (especially the recent *Astoria*) to concoct for *Burton's Gentleman's Magazine* six installments of a frontier narrative, "The Journal of Julius Rodman," serialized and promoted as "an account of the first passage across the Rocky Mountains of North America ever achieved by a civilized man."[13] Concealing his authorship, he shamelessly vaunted the pseudonymous "journal" in another periodical, *Alexander's Weekly Messenger*. But once again Poe's ouster from an editorial position interrupted the serial account, which he chose not to resume. Even so, the initial portion of this "found" narrative of a journey to Alaska (as Anna Brickhouse explains later) caused brief excitement in the U.S. State Department.

Poe's career indeed presents, from one perspective, a succession of journalistic stunts designed to convert celebrity or notoriety (he made little distinction between the two) into cultural capital in literary America. From the bogus chirographic analysis of his "Autography" series for the *Southern Literary Messenger* to his exposé on "Maezel's Chess-Player," his national cryptographic challenge on "Secret Writing" in *Graham's Magazine,* his controversial indictments of Henry Wadsworth Longfellow for plagiarism, the "Balloon Hoax" that rocked New York City on April Fool's Day, 1844, or his "Facts in the Case of M. Valdemar," which convinced readers at home and abroad that mesmerism could postpone death itself, Poe used the diffusion of a culture of reprinting to indulge in brazen, sporadic mystifications of the reading public. Having lived in Boston, New York, Philadelphia, Baltimore, Richmond, and Charleston (where he served in the army), he had an informed sense of the literary circles in each city, and however perverse or self-interested his critical opinions, he also recognized the importance to an inchoate national culture of such contemporaries as Irving, Cooper, Emerson, Willis, Sedgwick, Simms, Child, Fuller, Hawthorne, Bird, and Kirkland—from many of whom he solicited magazine pieces. Little more than a year after the "Rodman" episode, he revived his "Autography" series for *Graham's Magazine,* presuming to designate all the American literati worth knowing about—and through plaudits and gibes to suggest a controversial reevaluation.

Poe craved a panoramic vision of American letters and aimed to articulate the same in a book he planned to call *The Living Writers of America*. More fully than any of his more esteemed contemporaries, Poe grasped the inside workings of the "magazine prison-house"; and he possessed the ingenuity to manipulate an exploitative system, turning reprinting into a strategy of relentless self-promotion.[14] If he failed to achieve commercial success or professional stability, he nevertheless carved out a body of distinctive work that illustrates his oppositional relationship to both literary nationalism and regional provincialism. For roughly the last decade of his career, he was consumed by the desire to found a prominent monthly magazine that would not only feature American writers exclusively but also project a broader vision of the literary nation that asserted both cultural independence and attentiveness to the global audience.

The organization of the ten essays collected here reflects four distinct cartographic concerns. One is the configuration of a horizontal American literary culture as it existed in the 1830s and 1840s, and my own essay traces Poe's compulsion to designate the literati of the United States and to envision their affiliation in a U.S. republic of letters that transcended boundaries of region, gender, or profession. Yet this mapping of authors across an expanding national geography coincided with the publication of the first selective anthologies of American writing and thus the beginnings of a vertical charting of the literary nation, as soon reified by ensemble paintings and engravings of the leading authors of the United States. Leon Jackson also assumes an extensive, horizontal print culture but focuses on the problem of literary status in a "culture of celebrity" that derived its intensity partly from the sporadic tendency of reprinting to impose anonymity by effacing authorial signatures. In this sense his essay analyzes the structure of literary authority and the strategies for self-promotion operative in a decentered but interconnected culture. Poe's various manipulations of print media to achieve fame and offset his anxieties about social and cultural respectability (beyond those mentioned above) form the crux of Jackson's critique.

If Poe often resorted to generic Gothic settings to avoid literary provincialism, he nevertheless devoted a surprising amount of attention to the controversies of Jacksonian America. The second section of chapters reconstructs a critique often embedded in texts that initially appear disconnected from the contemporary scene, although occasionally—as Scott Peeples shows—focused explicitly on national life and politics. Betsy Erkkila reads F. O. Matthiessen's exclusion of Poe from *American Renaissance* as symptomatic of a complicated response to Poe's oppositional role as a critic of democracy, Anglo-Saxon progress, and "Manifest Destiny." She moves across the entire Poe canon, beginning with his early poetry and then decoding such anti-Jackson satires as "Epimanes" and "The Man That Was Used Up" along with a handful of other tales before concluding with *Eureka* and a postscript on Matthiessen's own "imp of the perverse." Peeples, by contrast, focuses on a specific journalistic project, Poe's "Doings of Gotham" letters, and puts these columns in the context of a new wave of American writing—fictional and reportorial—concerned with problems of urban growth in the 1840s.

Paradoxically, the "New York City letters" phenomenon on which Poe meant to capitalize reflects both the emergence of a national publishing center toward the middle of the century and the persistence of a vast, horizontal print culture still dependent upon reprinting to circulate metropolitan gossip. Jennifer Greeson portrays Poe as a cultural critic who mocked New England assumptions of cultural authority, especially as couched in the universalizing rhetoric of Emerson's essays, and she positions Poe as writing from the cultural margin—quite literally so in his "Marginalia" assaults on nationalism. Her re-reading of *The Narrative of Arthur Gordon Pym* as a mockery of New England sectionalism precedes a broader discussion of *Eureka* as a coded, satirical exposé of the way that Transcendentalism subtly fed U.S. expansionist ambition and validated California's annexation in 1848—even as individual Transcendentalists had repudiated the Mexican War.

The dissemination of Poe's work in a culture of reprinting produced unusual, even improbable lines of influence, and our next section features three very different accounts of the afterlife of his texts. Leland Person reflects on the historicity of interpretation before turning to a famous instance of Poe's transformation of U.S. historical materials. Noting that Poe's theory of the short story insists on the reader's role in the making of meaning, Person shows how "The Murders in the Rue Morgue" in effect probes (or "cruises") the reader's political and racial sensibilities by conjuring the anti-amalgamation hysteria in Philadelphia around 1840, and he demonstrates how the racist antebellum association of African Americans with apes and "animal" sexuality—an association Poe's tale exploits—has persisted to our own time in King Kong films and other imagery from popular culture. In her chapter, Anna Brickhouse reconstructs the dubious strategy of an obscure State Department librarian and translator, Robert Greenhow, who studied early documents to gather support for U.S. national interests by subverting British territorial claims in the Americas. Constructing a defense of American land claims in the Oregon country, Greenhow (possibly in collusion with Poe) cited the first installment of Poe's "Rodman" in *Burton's Gentleman's Magazine* in a government report to help confirm the priority of American exploration and discovery in the Pacific Northwest. Turning to Poe's poetry, Eliza Richards takes up the problem posed by "The Raven" and considers how its obsessive repetition soon causes the reader to anticipate the refrain and become the speaker's unwitting double. That replication also ensured the persistence of the text: assembled from elements of previous poems, "The Raven" itself proved eminently reproducible, its "recombinatory" features circulating through the public prints thanks to the many parodies and imitations thereby inspired, and it achieved its most eloquent rewriting, Richards argues, in Whitman's 1859 poem, "Out of the Cradle, Endlessly Rocking."

Our concluding section features two essays that, in very different ways, attempt to recalculate the topography of the antebellum literary world and to reconsider Poe's location within that culture. Working "by the numbers," Maurice Lee shows that even when perceived as marginal, Poe has not been neglected in American literary studies, as evidenced by statistics based on the *PMLA International Bibliography.* He then examines Poe's own quantitative characterizations of contemporary print culture as well as his efforts to calculate its perverse axioms before turning to "The Mystery of Marie Rogêt" and "The Man of the Crowd" as projections of Poe's ultimate mistrust of numerical analysis. In the concluding chapter, Jerome McGann recounts the turn in literary scholarship generally and in Poe studies specifically that has reoriented research and criticism away from narrow, author-centered models of enquiry toward a recognition of the hugely complicated discursive field—the multiple interactive networks of print media—in which all literature historically emerges. He then explains the urgent need for electronic tools and archives that will enable us to understand literary history in this expansive perspective, and he argues that Poe is a representative figure whose perambulations and perverse practices enable us to apprehend the long invisible workings of antebellum print culture.

All of the contributors to this volume have some investment in Poe studies within differing, larger engagements in nineteenth-century literary and cultural history. We see this volume as a first step toward a definitive remapping that reflects the extent, intricacy, and decentralization of print conventions and relations in the United States. Poe figures in this project not because of any assumed preeminence among contemporary literati, but because he was among the first to regard the republic of letters then emerging in the United States as a community imaginable across boundaries of region, party, and clique, and beyond differences of gender. His involvement in the magazine world and print culture, in the politics of reputation, in the problem of copyright, in the dilemma of sectionalism, in the cultural rivalries among eastern cities, and in his ceaseless promotion of "Independence, Truth, [and] Originality" in American literature make him singularly representative of the practical realities of antebellum literary production.[15] As Jerome McGann suggests, our ability to map the full complexity of antebellum print culture may well require the development of new digital methods to reproduce the fluidity of literary texts and the dynamic historical processes that occasioned them. But for now, an attention to Poe's involvement with literary America will, we hope, suggest some of the rich possibilities for emerging new forms of cultural cartography.

Notes

1. Hawthorne's complaint about the literary market having been overrun by "a d——d mob of scribbling women" appeared in his letter to William D. Ticknor, 19 January 1855, in the *Centennial Edition of the Works of Nathaniel Hawthorne* 17 (*The Letters, 1853–56*), 304. Emerson's "lengthened shadow" aphorism figures in "Self-Reliance," *Essays and Lectures*, ed. Joel Porte (New York: Library of America, 1983), 267.

2. *The Power of Maps* (New York: Guilford Press, 1992).

3. *American Literature and the Culture of Reprinting, 1832–1853* (Philadelphia: Univ. of Pennsylvania Press, 2003).

4. Poe to Charles Anthon, ca. late October 1844, in John Ward Ostrom, Burton R. Pollin, and Jeffrey A. Savoie, eds. *The Collected Letters of Edgar Allan Poe*, 3rd ed., vol. 1 (New York: Gordian Press, 2008): 470.

5. *Edgar Allan Poe and the Masses: The Political Economy of Literature in Antebellum America* (Princeton, NJ: Princeton Univ. Press, 1999), 21–57.

6. *Imagined Communities: Reflections on the Origin and Spread of Nationalism*, rev. ed. (London: Verso, 1991), 37–46.

7. *The American Face of Edgar Allan Poe* (Baltimore: Johns Hopkins Univ. Press, 1995).

8. *The Market Revolution: Jacksonian America, 1815–1846* (New York: Oxford Univ. Press, 1991), 371.

9. *Graham's Magazine*, December 1846. See J. Gerald Kennedy, ed., *The Portable Edgar Allan Poe* (New York: Penguin, 2006), 599.

10. *Godey's Lady's Book*, September 1845. See *The Portable Edgar Allan Poe*, 595.

11. *Broadway Journal*, October 4, 1845. See *The Portable Edgar Allan Poe*, 584.

12. Poe to Thomas W. White, 30 April 1835, in *The Collected Letters of Edgar Allan Poe*, 3rd ed., vol. 1, 84.

13. *Journal of Julius Rodman* in *Collected Writings of Edgar Allan Poe*, ed. Burton R. Pollin, vol. 1: *The Imaginary Voyages* (New York: Gordian Press, 1994), 521.

14. "Some Secrets of the Magazine Prison House," *Broadway Journal*, 15 February 1845. See *The Portable Edgar Allan Poe*, 579.

15. Poe to James Russell Lowell, 30 March 1844, in *The Collected Letters of Edgar Allan Poe*, 3rd ed., vol. 1: 432.

I | Locating the Republic of Letters

Inventing the Literati

Poe's Remapping of Antebellum Print Culture

J. GERALD KENNEDY

As Edgar Poe seems to have grasped from his debut as a magazinist, authors are made, not born, fashioned by a subtle process embedded in the systems of production and distribution that constitute print culture. Beyond the strange genius flaunted in his poetry and tales, Poe possessed an uncanny understanding of the power of magazines and newspapers to create cultural icons. Apart from book reviews, his various efforts to construct an idea of the literary nation and to install himself as a critical kingpin—by naming the country's principal literati, by promoting a quality periodical to feature U.S. authors exclusively, and by compiling materials for an American literary history—comprise an illuminating yet largely unappreciated dimension of Poe's achievement.

In a famous essay titled "What Is an Author?" Michel Foucault deconstructs "the author" as a cultural invention, associating the very concept with a "privileged moment of individualization in the history of ideas." Writing near the end of the twentieth century, Foucault declares the death of the author and (in a move endemic to structuralism) asserts the autonomy of the text as a play of signifiers, but he also acknowledges the historical rootedness of what he calls the "author function." Notions of authorship began in antiquity, when the Greeks revered those who gave lasting form to primal myths and narratives. But the modern concept of "the author" achieved currency much later. Foucault offhandedly remarks,

> Certainly, it would be worth examining how the author became individualized in a culture like ours, what status he has been given, at what moment studies of authenticity and attribution began, in what kind of system of valorization the author was involved, at what point we began to recount the lives of authors rather than of heroes, and how this fundamental category of "the-man-and-his-work criticism" began.[1]

But Foucault offers only provocative hints about the emergence of the author as a cultural entity, leaving to others the task of reconstructing the rise of professional authorship and the fetishizing of the man or woman of letters as a public personage. To be sure, each national culture has its own peculiar history of authorship, reflecting the spread of literacy, the rise of a middle-class reading public, the emergence of a publishing industry, the distribution of books, the proliferation of public libraries, and the commercialization of literature, which almost from the outset (as Foucault suggests) capitalized on the author's name as a trademark, the brand of a certain quality and style.

Taking up the challenge of Foucault, Martha Woodmansee has traced the modern European concept of the author to the eighteenth century, citing two instrumental cultural developments. Symptomatic of the transition from neoclassicism to Romanticism, one involves a radical rethinking of the origin of writing, a process Woodmansee illustrates by juxtaposing the aesthetics of Pope and Wordsworth. She contrasts the earlier Enlightenment model of the writer as "master of a body of rules, preserved and handed down . . . in rhetoric and poetics, for manipulating traditional materials"—a model sometimes inflected by suggestions of divine or artistic inspiration—with an emerging, Romantic conception of the poet or novelist as one who displays original genius by creating "something utterly new, unprecedented." By ascribing texts to "the writer's own genius," readers and critics "transform the writer into a unique individual uniquely responsible for a unique product." Woodmansee observes that this shift occurs within a significant historical and economic context—the transition from "the limited patronage of an aristocratic society" to "the democratic patronage of the marketplace."[2] Turning to Germany and the publishing dilemmas of Gissing, Schiller, and others, she sees modern authorship, conceived as the display of individual literary prowess, entangled in legal questions of property and copyright. To this account one might add that—apposite to the succession of European revolutions from 1789 to 1848—the emergence of the author also roughly parallels the emergence of modern nations, democratic republicanism, and the "imagined communities" bound together (as Benedict Anderson suggests) by "print-languages" and common cultural practices.[3] This juxtaposition forms the premise of Patrick Parrinder's sweeping study, *Nation and Novel*, which emphasizes the formation of collective British national consciousness, paradoxically, through solitary acts of novel-reading—and through ongoing public recalculations of the nation's leading authors.[4]

The fact that Samuel Johnson could publish *The Lives of the Poets* confident of public interest in writers of verse indicates the entrenchment of "the author" as an English cultural concept by 1781. Shortly after the turn of the next century, as William Charvat has observed, Scott, Byron, and their generation put authorship on a professional footing in Great Britain by developing lucrative arrangements with London publishers for volumes produced at regular intervals and sold to a swelling popular audience. But in the United States, conditions for professional authorship—a burgeoning publishing industry, the proliferation of literary newspapers and magazines, and an expanding middle-class readership—did not coalesce until the 1820s. Through that decade, Charvat remarks, Irving and Cooper sustained commercial success and created models of authorial prowess for an entire literary generation. Even when taking issue with Charvat on certain points, more recent studies by Michael Newbury, Leon Jackson, and David Dowling have proceeded from the assumption that literary authorship became a viable profession in the United States in the 1820s.[5]

At the close of that decade, Boston editor Samuel Kettell published *Specimens of American Poetry* (1829), the first comprehensive national anthology of verse, in effect establishing not only a canon of U.S. poetry but also a "tolerably complete list" of noteworthy poets from the colonial era to the 1820s. Working self-consciously for "the cause of American literature," Kettell assembled "biographical and critical notices" of literary men and women (preponderantly New Englanders, but not exclusively so) who produced "testimonials of talent and mental cultivation." The project sprang from the editor's chagrin that while learned acquaintances were "familiar with the details of Tiraboschi, Bouterwek, and Sismondi," they knew nothing about "the most gifted spirits of the soil where they were born and bred."[6] Kettell recognized that he was creating new knowledge by compiling a history of the nation's poetry and identifying her prominent native poets, for periodicals had barely stopped referring to American literature as an urgent yet hypothetical project. Within roughly two decades, however, editors and critics as well as painters and engravers were all vying to represent the nation's preeminent authors.

In the United States of the 1820s and 1830s—when Boston, New York, and Philadelphia were vying for preeminence as our cultural capital, when Baltimore, Richmond, and Charleston comprised the literary emporia of the Atlantic South, and when Cincinnati, St. Louis, and New Orleans represented the bustling periphery of national change—American literature was indeed a sprawling, amorphous field of discourse, loosely connected by newspapers and magazines that formed the principal sites of influence and exchange thanks to the practice of reprinting.[7] The incipient culture lacked coherence, in part because American nationhood rested upon foundational conflicts not simply unresolved but indeed not yet even explicitly acknowledged. Geographical distance and regional difference also impeded the articulation of a distinctive, representative literature worthy of global attention. A legion of would-be authors reared on Shakespeare, Milton, and Pope worked mostly in obscurity, in outposts from Portland, Maine, to Augusta, Georgia, responding to what Catharine M. Sedgwick derisively called "cacoethes scribendi," the itch to write, sometimes by producing novels or memoirs but mostly by composing poems, tales, and essays for the literary newspapers and periodicals springing up between about 1820 and the onset of the Civil War.[8] The unspoken prize was national glory, a place in the emerging American literati, the first pantheon of U.S. authors.

Goaded by Sidney Smith's famous taunt—"Who reads an American book?"— early editorial discussions of literary nationalism betrayed an underlying anxiety.[9] What made a novel, play, or poem "American" was precisely the conundrum faced by writers whose very conception of language and literature derived (with only a few exceptions) from the British tradition. As Richard Ruland has shown, calls for "originality" and cultural "independence" proliferated long before Emerson joined the chorus by admonishing young American scholars that they had "listened too long to the courtly muses of Europe."[10] Advocates demanded "materials" representative of New World experience, and reviewing Cooper's *The Spy* in 1822, W. H. Gardiner identified as apt subjects for American historical romance "the times just succeeding the first settlement" (by which he meant European colonization), "the era of the Indian wars" (as if those conflicts occupied some remote past), and "the revolution."[11] Nationhood for early advocates implied a strictly Anglo-Saxon model of history. Reflections on literary nation-building occasionally pondered the essential, or essentializing, riddle of what constituted the American nation. But no one, at this time, thought to ask the more radical question posed in 1882 by Ernest Renan: "What *is* a nation?"[12]

For inhabitants of the United States of America and its organized territories, the questions of what the American nation was—or to whom it belonged—or where, exactly, it might be located—exposed a fundamental anxiety rooted in the incongruities of the Declaration of Independence and the unprecedented happenstance of a far-flung, heterogeneous population asserting governmental independence as a modern republic before it had become a unified people, a nation. Rights of full citizenship pertained to the few; liberty and equality, the hallowed founding principles, remained highly restricted, much-contested ideals. The civic status of women, blacks (free and slave), Indians, immigrants, mulattos and métis, paupers, Catholics, Jews, and radical free-thinkers was at best ambiguous, at worst oppressive. How could there be an American literature if "America" itself were a fiction devised by an elite intelligentsia consumed by nationalism, or at least nation-envy? How could a national literature emerge from a handful of relatively small cities so scattered as to be practically oblivious to each other?

One commentator who reflected, at least briefly, on the geographical obstacles to an American literature was the poet James Russell Lowell, who wrote:

> The situation of American literature is anomalous. It has no centre, or, if it have, it is like that of the sphere of Hermes. It is divided into many systems, each revolving round its several suns, and often presenting to the rest only the faint glimmer of a milk-and-watery way. Our capital city [Washington], unlike London or Paris, is not a great central heart, from which life and vigor radiate to the extremities, but resembles more an isolated umbilicus, stuck down as near as may be to the centre of the land, and seeming rather to tell a legend of former usefulness than to serve any present need. Boston, New York, Philadelphia, each has its literature almost more distinct than those of the different dialects of Germany; and the Young Queen of the West [Cincinnati] has also one of her own, of which some articulate rumor barely has reached us dwellers by the Atlantic. Meanwhile, a great babble is kept up concerning a national literature, and the country, having delivered itself of the ugly likeness of a paint-bedaubed, filthy savage, smilingly dandles the rag-baby upon her maternal knee, as if it were veritable flesh and blood, and would grow timely to bone and sinew.[13]

Lowell's scornful image of the painted "savage . . . rag-baby," incapable of life or growth, represents what Robert Berkhofer has called "the white man's Indian," a simulacrum ironically promulgated in popular literature, often to represent what was unique about the country.[14] But what interests me most in this account is Lowell's implicit mapping of a decentered American culture with a vacuum at its core and with multiple discrete cultural systems, each revolving around different regional sites that seemed cosmically remote from the others. As I have suggested, national newspapers and magazines to some extent countered this diffusion by reprinting not just poems, tales, and essays from competing periodicals but also editorial opinions from other urban centers. And as Ronald Zboray has shown, literary peddlers and booksellers simultaneously traversed the nation by road, canal, and rail, performing another sort of cultural dissemination.[15] But as Lowell knew only too well, success in the solar system that revolved around Boston and Cambridge did not ensure national popularity. Each urban matrix nurtured provincial ideas about the nature of the nation. There was no "great central heart" of the antebellum United States from which emanated an authentic national culture.

The focus of Lowell's essay was not, however, the "anomalous" condition of American literature. Serendipitously, for my purposes, that meditation introduced his 1845 biographical sketch of Edgar Allan Poe for *Graham's Magazine*. Lowell paid tribute to Poe's "genius" as well as his accomplishments as a poet and a writer of tales. But insisting that "before we have an American literature, we must have an American criticism," he underscored Poe's role as a critic of contemporary American literature. Lowell also promulgated two biographical fabrications that Poe had evidently supplied—that he was "graduated with the highest honors" from the University of Virginia and that he fought with the "insurgent Greeks" (and presumably also with Byron, why not?)—before making his way to St. Petersburg, where his lack of a passport got him into difficulties.[16] But what Lowell failed to note about Poe, and the failure is egregious, given his opening paragraph, is that no other contemporary American literary figure worked so tirelessly or so ingeniously to overcome the anomalous disjunction of national culture and to construct an idea of American literature that transcended geographical distance and regional diversity. In the context of editorial stints in Richmond, Philadelphia, and New York, and through sojourns in Boston and Baltimore, Poe developed extended networks of literary connections and became familiar with several distinct cultures of letters. In a handful of ways, and most famously in his protracted effort to found a quality monthly journal that might feature "contributions from the most distinguished pens (of America) *exclusively*," he worked to reify a national republic of letters, diverse yet unified, whose center Poe imagined to be himself or an editorial cabal of influential writers (as he later proposed to Lowell) who would unite secretly to produce "a Magazine of high character."[17]

This one facet of Poe's cultural work as a facilitator of national literature has in fact received considerable attention, and the magisterial essay "Poe's Vision of His Ideal Magazine," by my late, esteemed colleague Lewis P. Simpson, still stands up after fifty years as a luminously concise discussion of the implications of Poe's contemplated periodical.[18] The networking aspect of Poe's travail—no less obsessive than his magazine dream—was to designate the American literati, to advance the cause of American letters by constructing a fiction of literary community.

Interestingly, during his self-guided apprenticeship as a writer of magazine tales in the early 1830s, Poe produced a mélange of mostly satirical pieces conceived as the effusions of an imaginary "Folio Club." The punning names of the members identified in Poe's introduction to the projected (but never published) volume suggest correlations between tales and writers. But what seems most revealing is the urge to invent a club, a "diabolical association" of eleven members, including the author himself, which would collectively "abolish Literature, subvert the Press, and overturn the Government of Nouns and Pronouns," by each producing and presenting, over postprandial wine, one tale per month.[19] In this fantasy of convivial insurrection, Poe's "Junto of Dunderheadism" playfully figures the author as belonging to a madcap coterie that will change the system of literary production altogether. In a curious fashion, he thus set the agenda for his later career.

When, through the intervention of John Pendleton Kennedy, Poe obtained an appointment from Thomas W. White to help edit the *Southern Literary Messenger,* one of his innovations for the February 1836 issue was a feature he called "Autography." Playing on popular familiarity with Joe Miller's *Jest Book,* a British collection of jokes and witticisms first published in 1739 but revived in many later editions, the spoof develops the fiction of an American Joseph Miller—from a family "British, but not particularly British"—walking into Poe's editorial "*sanctorum*" and protesting "a certain rascally piece of business" in the *London Athenaeum,* ascribed to Miller, in which a set of bogus letters had been sent to "several and sundry characters of literary notoriety about London" solely for the purpose of eliciting autograph replies. Miller's faux indignation at being implicated in this mischief anticipates his presentation to Poe of a bundle of letters containing "*American* autographs." These are, Miller claims, "the autographs of our principal *literati,*" and he urges Poe to publish them in the *Messenger.*[20] The joking, trivial aspect of the piece belies the audacity of the cultural coup Poe attempted to carry out: from a small city in the upper South, outside the eastern metropolitan corridor, an editorial assistant for an upstart journal was presuming to designate the "principal" writers of the entire United States. Twenty-four letters figured in the first installment, and fourteen more followed in August, bringing Poe's "Autography" to a total of thirty-eight brief, perfunctory letters from American literary figures, with facsimile signatures and concise analyses of handwriting that let Poe insert, here and there, pithy judgments about the writer's personality or literary style. As Jonathan Elmer points out, much of the humor of "Autography" lies in the seemingly inconsequential but subtly suggestive letters by which the literati respond to supposed enquiries from Miller.[21]

What seems most striking about Poe's 1836 configuration of the American literati, however, is its catholicity. In addition to such notable exponents of belles lettres as Irving, Cooper, William Gilmore Simms, and James Kirke Paulding, Poe includes five women—Lydia H. Sigourney, Catharine M. Sedgwick, Eliza Leslie, Sarah Josepha Hale, and Hannah F. Gould. But he also lists jurists, clergymen, professors, elected officials, publishers, editors, and military men. Chief Justice John Marshall, William Wirt, Judge Joseph D. Story, Captain Jeremiah Reynolds, and Mordecai M. Noah (the first culturally prominent American-born Jew) are among those honored as "literati." Even more striking is the geographical diversity of Poe's imagined great writers: he names (in addition to Story, Sigourney, Sedgwick, Gould, and Hale) renowned New Englanders such as John Quincy Adams, William Ellery Channing, and Edward Everett; New York literary notables such as N. P. Willis and William Leete Stone (alongside Irving and Paulding); distinguished Philadelphians Robert Montgomery Bird, Robert Walsh, and Matthew Carey (in addition to Miss Leslie); and a handful of litterateurs from the upper and lower South, among whom are Marshall, Wirt, John Pendleton Kennedy, Thomas R. Dew, and Timothy Flint—the last correctly identified as a resident of Alexandria, Louisiana. It was a bold stunt for a neophyte magazinist to set himself up as the arbiter of literary merit in America. But just as important, this much-neglected text also illustrates Poe's determination to conjure up a republic of letters that would defy the spatial obstacles to a national literary culture.

Poe's earliest opportunity to promote his idea of literary America collapsed, however, with his departure from the *Messenger* on January 3, 1837. But not long after moving to New York, where he sought work with one of the literary newspapers or magazines, he had a chance to revel, albeit for a single evening, in an approximate version of his imagined literary community—the Booksellers' Banquet of March 30, 1837. This grand event attracted three hundred invitees to the City Hotel, where the banquet hall was appointed with busts of Irving, Franklin, Scott, Shakespeare, and Milton. Here publishers, booksellers, and authors mingled and met; whether Poe conversed with Irving, the principal celebrity, cannot be confirmed but seems plausible. He would surely have spoken with Irving's friend James Kirke Paulding, whose work he had published and with whom he had corresponded at the *Messenger.* Poe quite possibly met one of his "Autography" nominees, Columbia professor Charles Anthon, on this occasion and likely spoke with Richard Adams Locke, whose moon hoax he had read. Others in attendance were the poets Bryant and Halleck. As Kevin Hayes has observed, some writers (like Halleck or William Leete Stone) would have been less than delighted to meet the newcomer, given his criticism of their work in the *Messenger,* but the soirée gave Poe a fresh perspective on the literary world as well as a vivid consciousness of the cultural distance between Richmond and New York.[22] Poe may have met one or both of the Harper brothers in attendance and, if he did, he surely spoke of his sea-novel-in-progress, *The Narrative of Arthur Gordon Pym*. Poe's impromptu toast to the "monthlies of Gotham" did not, however, spark a job offer from any of them. Indeed, the Panic of 1837 turned Poe's first year in New York into a nightmare, the bleakest interval in his literary career; he considered abandoning writing altogether.

But a move to Philadelphia in early 1838 opened new prospects. Quickly Poe renewed ties with Carey, Lea, and Blanchard, the publisher that had once shown interest in his "Folio Club" tales, and he developed acquaintances among Philadelphia magazinists and writers. By May 1839, he obtained an editorial job with William Burton's *Gentleman's Magazine,* and although he privately ridiculed the journal, he used the position to reestablish his authority as a critic and to extend his literary influence. A few months with Burton, though, provoked the same impatience that his labors for White had: Poe chafed at supervision by perceived nincompoops and imagined the journal he could produce on his own. He wrote a friend in September of that year: "As soon as Fate allows, I will have a Magazine of my own—and will endeavor to kick up a dust."[23] By 1840, in a move that provoked Burton to fire him, he worked up a prospectus for the *Penn Magazine,* promising "absolutely independent criticism" free from the puffery manufactured "at the nod of our principal booksellers." He also pledged to promote "the general interests of the republic of letters, *without reference to particular regions; regarding the world at large as the true audience of the author* (italics mine)."[24] Poe's determination to transcend a regional perspective implies the national cast of his "republic of letters"; yet he had no interest in promoting literary nationalism per se, which he attacked consistently as provincial in its appeal. In letter after letter to literary types and potential benefactors, he underscored his devotion to "the growing literature of the country."[25] Soon he began advocating for an international copyright law to protect "poor-devil" American authors forced to compete against pirated works by British authors. But illness and economic adversity thwarted the launch of his proposed magazine.

When Poe accepted a position with *Graham's Magazine* in February 1841, he did so with an understanding that owner George Graham would eventually aid him in publishing *The Penn*. This was a deft move on Poe's part, for Graham had money and seemed not to regard Poe's strictly literary journal as a rival to his own illustrated magazine, which had already expanded its circulation fivefold since Graham bought out Burton. Both the association with Graham and the magazine's impressive national circulation gave Poe new clout as he expanded his contacts with American authors. In June 1841, he sent almost-identical letters, we must assume, to the eight writers he and Graham had apparently selected as the ideal contingent of regular contributors to a new, high-quality magazine: Irving, Paulding, Cooper, Bryant, Kennedy, Longfellow, Halleck, and Willis. (How Longfellow reacted to the invitation of Poe—who had already attacked him in print as a plagiarist—is interesting to imagine.) Then a few months later, still buoyed by the supposition that Graham would become his business partner, Poe decided the time was right to revive—and expand—his "Autography" series. In three consecutive issues of *Graham's,* from November 1841 through January 1842, Poe presented more than one hundred signatures from, as he put it, "the most noted among the living literati of the country."[26] Portraying himself as a literary man in touch with virtually everyone, Poe claims that a "motley mass" of letters and manuscripts from "every individual in America who has the slightest pretension to literary celebrity" has supplied all the signatures he will need. The key is discrimination: "From these we propose to select the most eminent names — as to give *all* would be a work of supererogation."[27] That is, Poe takes upon himself the job of choosing the top one hundred or so American writers, for without selectivity, the whole exercise is pointless. But he mentions no principles of selection, and his choices betray a partiality for his personal acquaintances. Poe acknowledges in print three purposes in his new "Autography": to show the relationship between chirography and personality, to circulate "literary gossip," and to provide autographs for collectors. But implicitly he has another, more compelling aim: to position himself as the supreme authority on American literary eminence. As he determines the membership of the 1841 literati, Poe also indulges in more extensive critical assessments: he hails underappreciated writers and typically punctures, through censure or innuendo, the popular image of the more eminent authors. About Irving (who had, at Poe's request, provided advance praise in 1839 for *Tales of the Grotesque and Arabesque*) Poe opines that he "has been so thoroughly satiated with fame as to grow slovenly in the performance of his literary tasks."[28]

In comparison to the 1836 version of "Autography," the sequel projects, obviously, a much-expanded vision of the luminaries of American letters. The new array is once again uniquely European-American (Poe could not surmount the racial prejudices of his era) but more preponderantly masculine, with only 11 women among the 127 figures featured in the 1841 lineup. Those joining the female cohort include Emma C. Embury, Mrs. E. F. Ellet, Mrs. E. C. Stedman, and Ann S. Stephens, while Lydia Maria Child once again fails to win Poe's notice, quite possibly for her pronounced anti-slavery views. (Scorn for abolitionism presumably also compels Poe to say of Whittier, "his themes are *never* to our liking.")[29] The interregional representation remains conspicuous—Poe even cites among his literati several frontier magazinists or poets, including one John Tomlin, identified as the postmaster of Jackson, Tennessee—and this list adds several new literary personalities from the South (such as Thomas Holley Chivers), from New England (notably James Russell Lowell), and from New York and Philadelphia as well. Perhaps understandably, given the subscription base of *Graham's Magazine,* the City of Brotherly Love receives disproportionate attention, and Poe assigns to Judge Robert T. Conrad "the first place among our Philadelphia *literati.*"[30] There is a perceptible increase in critical risk-taking: whereas the young editor of the *Messenger* contented himself with a few playful jabs at such lesser lights as Theodore S. Fay and Grenville Mellen, the older Poe singles out for derision several paragons of Boston literary culture. He pointedly abuses J. G. Palfrey, the powerful editor of the *North American Review,* for insularity, narrowness, and pretentiousness; he impugns Longfellow's reputation by observing that "his sins are chiefly those of affectation and imitation — an imitation sometimes verging upon downright theft";[31] and he dismisses Ralph Waldo Emerson as an obscurantist, a "mystic for mysticism's sake."[32]

A notable new emphasis on what Poe calls the "editorial category" perhaps signals the most salient development, for he elevates to national literary prominence at least two dozen relatively obscure editors of newspapers or magazines. In five years he had acquired vast inside knowledge about the system of literary production in the United States—the very "culture of reprinting" elaborated by McGill. We must assume that Poe expanded his literati to include publishers and editors who might purchase a story, praise his work, or offer a position. How else can one account for the inclusion of J. Beauchamp Jones, Andrew McMakin, H. Hastings Weld, Ezra Holden, or Benjamin Matthias? Owners and/or editors of monthly journals—L. J. Godey, Park Benjamin, Cornelius Mathews, Graham, and Mrs. Stephens among them—also swell the ranks of Poe's literati. In the 1841 "Autography," he constructs literary America as a network of newspapers and magazines, provisioned by a contingent of mostly white male authors scattered across the land but primarily aggregated in a half-dozen cultural hubs. For a critic often preoccupied as a reviewer with cliques and coteries, Poe curiously ignores alliances in this enumeration. Nor is there any apparent logic to the order in which he presents his American all-stars. Having been criticized by E. P. Whipple for thus appointing himself (as Kenneth Silverman notes) a "literary dictator," Poe in the second installment shrugged off responsibility for his selections, claiming only "the sorry merit of the compiler"—but boasting simultaneously of the excitement aroused by the series thanks to the "piquancy" of his critiques.[33]

But the same month in which Poe's third installment of "Autography" appeared, his personal situation changed abruptly: Virginia's first pulmonary hemorrhage drove Poe to despair and triggered a drinking binge that scuttled his professional work and finally compelled him to resign from *Graham's*. Through it all, he kept alive his plan to publish a magazine and continued to work for the cause of American literature. In collaboration with his Whig friend Frederick W. Thomas, Poe maneuvered to obtain a government job in the Tyler administration—or better yet to secure Tyler's backing for a magazine that would perform both political and cultural work. In 1843 he issued a new magazine prospectus, this time calling his journal *The Stylus* and pitching it as an antidote to "the *cheap* literature of the day."[34] Poe aimed for "*individuality,*" and he intended the journal to showcase "the *true* intellect of the land, without reference to the mere *prestige* of celebrated names." Yet he also projected a series of "Critical and Biographical Sketches of American Writers," which would include "every person of literary note in America." Poe planned to disregard literary prestige in selecting works to publish but also to designate his own pantheon of notable authors through critical and biographical portraits. The magazine would feature American authors but *not* provincial, nationalistic writing: "It will support the general interests of the Republic of Letters, and insist upon regarding the world at large as the sole proper audience for the author." Poe seemed nearly poised for success in March by securing the backing of a wealthy Philadelphia publisher named Thomas Clarke, but just two weeks later the scheme "exploded" when Clarke, a temperance advocate, learned of Poe's humiliating drinking binge in Washington.[35]

In the fall, the undaunted Poe reinvented himself again, this time as a lyceum lecturer on the subject of "American Poetry." His standard address metamorphosed into an expansive discourse on "The Poets and Poetry of America" as Poe implicitly competed with his former colleague Rufus W. Griswold, editor of an 1842 anthology by that very title, for preeminence as a judge of American versifiers.[36] At the lectern Poe also had an opportunity to promote his yet-to-be-published magazine. But he had reached a professional impasse in Philadelphia, and by early 1844 he responded to an overture from a New York literary group then crusading for a national literature and an international copyright law. Cornelius

Mathews and Evert Duyckinck, publishers of *The Arcturus,* persuaded Poe to add his name to the list of notable figures who supported their cause, and they apparently urged him to move back to New York and join forces with them. In April, Poe returned to the city he had left in despair in 1838 and quickly reestablished ties to editors and publishers. He continued to entreat New Englander James Russell Lowell to collaborate with him in founding a monthly magazine of the highest quality, but he made an almost identical appeal to the Georgia poet Thomas Holley Chivers. He even sought support from Professor Charles Anthon at Columbia and finally coaxed him into providing commentary on "classical literature." By 1845, however, Poe saw an opportunity to become involved in editing the financially precarious *Broadway Journal,* where he freely expressed his opinions about literary America, especially after assuming sole proprietorship in July. His New York associates in the group calling itself "Young America" promoted a version of literary nationalism that Poe found wrong-headed, and he said so in print repeatedly, but he appreciated both their interest in his work and their support of the copyright issue. This aspect of Poe's career has been amply documented by McGill and earlier by Claude Richard, but it is worth noting that Duyckinck's effort to found a Library of American Authors—the forerunner, in a sense, of our contemporary Library of America editions—included early volumes by Poe and Hawthorne in an effort to establish an American literary canon and a roster of distinguished U.S. authors.[37]

Poe's own effort to identify the makeup of his imagined American "Republic of Letters" led him in 1846, after the collapse of the *Broadway Journal* and a messy scandal that exiled him from the principal literary salons of Gotham, to compose a series of short critical and biographical profiles that he called "The Literati of New York City." Retaining only a few scattered comments about handwriting (along with a handful of signatures appended to the first installment), Poe plunged into the genre of literary gossip, promising to disclose the private talk, as opposed to public opinion, about the great ones. His lineup of forty-one leading personalities features fourteen women, including, for the first time in such writings, Lydia Maria Child, Margaret Fuller, and Caroline Kirkland. Once more, clergymen, physicians, and scholars round out his vision of literary America; journal editors again receive special emphasis, but two in particular—Lewis Gaylord Clark and Charles Briggs—become objects of ridicule. A controversial figure himself in New York—thanks to his misadventures with the bluestockings, his attacks on the *Knickerbocker Magazine,* and other acts of journalistic irreverence or effrontery—Poe wrote to settle scores and challenge reputations. His

infamous attack on Thomas Dunn English for plagiarism and "deficiencies in English grammar" erupted into a literary war too tedious to summarize here.[38] Poe
also used the series to flatter or venerate a chosen few, among them his literary
darling, Francis Sargent Osgood, his friend Evert Duyckinck, and Freeman Hunt,
a wealthy editor whose good opinion Poe evidently craved.

But beyond the spicy comments about personalities, mannerisms, and physi-
ognomies, we should note that the "Literati" sketches also contain a scattered but
fairly detailed analysis of how the literary world operated—its rules of engagement, as it were. Addressing the problem of a dispersed and decentered culture,
Poe here significantly declares that New York has become, by 1846, the "focus"
of American literature and that "New York literature may be taken as a fair representation of that of the country at large."[39] As he does elsewhere, Poe zeroes in on
the ubiquitous practice of puffing books to gratify an author rather than evaluate
the writing. He criticizes the toadyism by which Longfellow and writers of his
ilk have secured "indiscriminate approbation" through "social position and influence."[40] He underscores the mediocrity of the *Knickerbocker* and insists on the
importance of "individuality" in the character of a periodical.[41] The worst thing a
journal editor can do, he elsewhere maintains, is attempt to strike a "happy medium" and thereby create a publication that fails to achieve either popularity or
distinction.[42] He acknowledges an earlier generation of American authors but
then questions the validity of literary reputations based upon mere precedence.
Poe complains more than once about the lack of an international copyright law
and the disadvantageous situation of American authors. In his analysis of N. P.
Willis, he deconstructs the art of literary self-promotion, suggesting that Willis
has made himself a literary celebrity by thrusting himself into the social world
and undertaking glamorous "adventures" that make him seem more interesting
than he really is.[43] In his comments on Fuller, he praises *Summer on the Lakes in
1843* and suggests that it contains even more of the "author's self" than it seems,
proposing cryptography as a metaphor for "reading" an author's "character" in his
or her books.[44] That is, Poe anticipates the sort of author-and-his-work criticism
associated by Foucault with the cultural construction of the "author" as a commodity. In his discussion of the minor poet James Aldrich, Poe analyzes plagiarism as the intuitive assimilation and unconscious forgetting of an intensely admired poetic thought or phrase, offering a complex meditation on one of his own
critical obsessions (a topic discussed by both Jonathan Elmer and Stephen Rachman).[45] He refrains from evoking the phrase "magazine prison-house," which
he coined in 1845, but his "Literati" insights allude recurrently to the economic

constraints that leave authors at the mercy of editors and that put editors in the grip of market pressures. In their entirety, Poe's ideas about authorship, originality, reputation, and success reflect the breadth and depth of his thinking about the "anomalous" situation of American literature and the predicament of U.S. authors.

During the last years of his life, Poe remained obsessed by three interrelated preoccupations: to launch *The Stylus* in order to showcase "the *true* [literary] talent of the land"; to complete and publish his critical history, *The Living Writers of America*, which would provide "a *faithful* account of the literary productions, literary people, and literary affairs of the United States"; and through these enterprises to designate, in a definitive and authoritative way, the true American literati. The January 1848 prospectus of *The Stylus,* from which the preceding quotes were derived, indicates that Poe planned to serialize in the magazine the critical history he also called *Literary America.*[46] Burton Pollin's essay on *The Living Writers of America* manuscript establishes the relation of that project to "The Literati of New York City" and shows the last draft to have been far more extensive than the surviving fragment suggests.[47] Poe's bare outline for the volume indeed teems with key insights into the peculiarities of the literary situation in the United States. To "expose the wires" that held together the system of literary production, dissemination, and reception, Poe backed away from prior claims about New York's primacy and emphasized that the "want of a great central emporium like London or Paris" doomed American literature to a "*cliquism*" exacerbated by "vast sectional animosities."[48] These prejudices resulted in a "depreciation of Southern & Western talent" and a general, partisan contamination of literary criticism. Every important city had its own cliques, among which he singled out the Boston "Humanity party" as "the most desperate." The magazines, which Poe believed to be "the best representatives of our literature," were nevertheless "for the most part, organs of *cliques.*" He regarded the tyrannical "spirit of *cliquerie*" as second only to the lack of an international copyright law in its destructive effect on American letters.

Just as significantly, Poe meant in his critical history to attack more vigorously the delusions promoted by literary nationalism. He planned to confront the "erroneous idea that there is anything very distinctive about American literature," and indeed insisted that "there should be *no* nationality" in our writing, which should rather aim for global appeal. He planned to critique the chauvinist tendencies of his "Young America" allies, especially Cornelius Mathews, and in a crucial portion of his outline, he laid out an argument to show that which is called Nationality is adverse to the Nation. We demand that nationality which will not cringe to [at] foreign opinion—but we repudiate that nationality wh. [which] wd. [would] throw off all respect for it—We do our Literature grosser wrong in over-praising our authors than the British cd. [could] possibly do in over-abusing them. We shd. [should] drop the gross folly of forcing our readers to relish a stupid book the better because sure enough its stupidity was American.[49]

This was of course the very argument broached in his 1836 Drake-Halleck review. Poe called for an anti-nationalistic nationality open—but never deferential—to foreign criticism and rigorous in its critical evaluation of American books.

Another prong in Poe's assault on the endemic obstacles to American literature was his critique of class differences and economic injustice. He believed that as a result of piracy and the lack of copyright protection, American literature was "altogether in the hands of a class proverbial for conservatism—the 'gentlemen of elegant leisure,'" who possessed the personal means to dabble in writing without much regard for fees or royalties. The very "conservatism" of this group predisposed it to an "imitativeness" that worked against the creation of a literature distinctive for its originality. The country had been taken over by an "aristocracy of dollars" that, in Poe's view, suppressed literary "genius, which, as a general rule is poor, for the reason that it seeks especially the unpurchasable pleasures." The pervasive worship of wealth and scorn for poverty directly affected one's prospects for publication: "Publishers here seldom glance at the work of a poor author, while our rich dillettanti have little trouble in getting a (of course temporary and factitious) fame."[50]

Poe intended to level the playing field for American authors generally by continuing to campaign for copyright protection, and he was determined to assign literary importance (and membership in the literati) on the basis of genuine merit, a merit based on principled criticism rather than on "wealth or social position"—or the spurious renown generated by puffery or cliquism. His ultimate aim, as Lewis Simpson rightly remarked, was "to impose order on the disorder of America's literary situation" and to establish in the process "an authoritative literary community in America" that corresponded to his idealized notion of a republic of letters.[51] Poe imagined a constellation of American authors exalted for the individuality of their achievement, and he believed himself "in [a] better condition to give the truth" about literary America than any rival by virtue of his fierce critical independence, innate genius, and direct, practical acquaintance with the multiple cultures of letters divided by "sectional animosities."[52] In his shuttling from Richmond to Boston to Baltimore to Richmond to New York to Philadelphia and back to New York, and in his labors as a reviewer and editor for four publications—as well as in his outreach activities in search of contributors, benefactors, and subscribers for his ideal magazine—Poe had come to know the landscape, the odd geography of the cultural space he inhabited, better than any other litterateur of his time.

⋞⫘⫘⪼

While Poe was accumulating authority as a literary pundit, however, a handful of enterprising anthologists helped to redefine the contours of the literary nation—or at least one of its principal domains. As we see in his 1842 review of Rufus W. Griswold's *Poets and Poetry of America,* Poe clearly understood the cultural work of anthologies; such volumes produced, he observed, a concentrated, holistic vision of poetry in the United States, countering the effects of geographical dispersion: "The public have been desirous of obtaining a more distinct view of our poetical literature than the scattered effusions of our bards and the random criticisms of our periodicals, could afford." By nature such anthologies reified national authorship, and Poe critiqued the selectivity of his putative rivals. Beginning with Kettell's *Specimens,* an exercise in "ignorance and ill taste," he identified four other anthologies from the previous "ten or twelve years": George B. Cheever's "excessively 'Common-Place'" *American Common-Place Book of Poetry* (1831), George Pope Morris's "twattle"-filled *American Melodies* (1840), William Cullen Bryant's mortifying *Selections from the American Poets* (1840), and John Keese's *The Poets of America* (1839). Despite a few kind words for Keese, Poe appraised these anthologies severely, not only in his role as self-appointed guardian of literary America but also, we learn, as one of the "omitted," invisible poets—a circumstance that may largely explain his appreciative review of Griswold's new publication, which included his work.[53]

Later notorious as Poe's nemesis and ill-chosen literary executor, Griswold, the ex-clergyman-turned-entrepreneur, parlayed his many anthologies and editions into an enviable revenue stream; his *Poets and Poetry of America* went through seventeen editions in his lifetime. Ever the opportunist, he compiled a school textbook, *Readings in American Poetry* (1843) on the heels of his poetry anthology, and in 1844 alone he published more than a half-dozen commercial volumes, including *The Poetry of Love.* Perhaps trying to solidify his own reputation as a literary authority, he brought out a sequel to his 1842 American poetry anthology, *The Prose Writers of America* (1847).[54] In the aftermath of Poe's death, he published an edition called *The Literati: Some Honest Opinions about Autorial Merits and Demerits, with Occasional Words of Personality* (1850), a shamelessly exploitative compilation of Poe's "Literati of New York City" portraits, together with his essay "The Poetic Principle," book reviews of leading authors (mostly American), the "Marginalia" squibs, and "Fifty Suggestions."[55] Griswold's contribution to the volume (apart from his editing) was the scurrilous "Memoir of the Author" that portrayed Poe as a drunken madman, but collecting his sketches and squibs created an opportunity for Griswold to promulgate a virtual guide to American literature, possibly to compete with Thomas Powell's *The Living Authors of America* (1850), a major critical effort to identify and enshrine the nation's truly preeminent authors.[56] Powell featured thirteen figures in the "first series," including Cooper, Longfellow, Emerson, Bryant, Fuller, Willis, and Poe. Oddly, Powell did not include Irving, Sedgwick, and Hawthorne, perhaps saving them for a never-published second series.

No one, in fact, really knew what the field of American literature looked like, so tenuously were authors, critics, and the reading public connected to each other by print culture and the U.S. mail, although in the years after Poe's death, efforts to capture its scope and character proliferated. One notable attempt to realize the aims of Poe's never-published *Living Writers of America* was Evert and George Duyckinck's 1856 *Cyclopedia of American Literature,* which reached back to the nation's origins in offering a comprehensive overview of American authors.[57] Their volume presented easily the most inclusive survey of the literati, though Griswold could not resist attacking the publication in the *New York Herald* (18 February 1856) and publishing as a monograph his detailed accounting of every odd authorial omission, dubious inclusion, or factual inaccuracy.

Painters too soon began to portray idealized images of literary America. In 1863, working from a drawing by Felix O. C. Darley, Christian Schussele produced an oil painting that purported to represent the most significant of the American literati in *Washington Irving and His Literary Friends at Sunnyside* (see www.theathenaeum.org/art/full.php?ID=43409). Schussele's group portrait was then featured in a well-circulated 1864 pamphlet titled *Sketches of Distinguished American Authors.* His tableau of fifteen authors—all white males—brings together several figures who never met, and the grouping incongruously conflates Irving's New York friends and acquaintances (Paulding, Halleck, Cooper, Bryant, Tuckerman, and Willis) with a Boston-Cambridge cohort that includes Emerson, Bancroft, Prescott, Holmes, Longfellow, and Hawthorne. Schussele thus ignored the anti–New England prejudices evident in Irving's writing as early as the *History of New York*. William Gilmore Simms and John Pendleton Kennedy figure, somewhat improbably, as token southerners who have infiltrated Sunnyside, although to be sure, Irving knew them both. Poe is nowhere to be seen—nor, for that matter, are many other notable figures whose writings helped to enrich and diversify American literature in the 1830s, 1840s, and 1850s. Schussele utterly excluded such notable female authors as Sedgwick or Stowe, whose work would have been well known to Irving. Thomas Oldham Barlow's 1864 engraving of Irving's so-called literary friends, based closely on Schussele's portrait, gave this configuration even wider circulation as a defining image of literary America during the late antebellum era.

Washington Irving and His Literary Friends at Sunnyside, 1864 engraving by Thomas Oldham Barlow after a drawing by Felix O. C. Darley and portrait by Christian Schussele.

An even more ambitious rendering of the literary nation went into circulation a few years later with A. H. Ritchie's engraving of *The Authors of the United States* by Thomas Hicks. Although the massive original painting (commissioned in 1857 to be nine-by-fourteen feet in size) has somehow disappeared—the *New York Times* reported in 1866 that it was put on exhibit "four or five years ago"—the engraving became widely distributed in the late 1860s or early 1870s as a premium for new subscribers to the New York *Independent*. Here we get Hicks's notion of who belonged to the American literati at about mid-century, although the image contains several anachronisms, one of which is the commingling of Poe (who died in 1849) with several minor writers who did not achieve literary recognition until the 1850s and after. Hicks was, to be sure, no literary critic, and he apparently included several lesser lights (such as George Boker) in this image simply because he had already painted individual portraits of them, either in his New York studio or elsewhere. His ensemble representation includes forty-four authors, of whom nine are women; virtually all of the figures frequented New York literary circles in the 1840s or 1850s, although the presence of several New Englanders (Emerson, Whittier, Lowell, Beecher, Channing, Bancroft, etc.) and the southerners Poe, Simms, Kennedy, and Philip Pendleton Cooke gives some sense of a broader geographical inclusivity.

The Authors of the United States, c. 1866 engraving by A. H. Ritchie, after an 1857 painting by Thomas Hicks

The positioning of Cooper as the central personality, with Bryant and Irving seated left and right at the central table, establishes a clear hierarchy of significance, although Halleck's place at the main table seems an afterthought. The figures excluded from this group portrait, which was probably executed in 1858 or 1859, seem especially revealing: Hicks omitted Child as well as Melville, Whitman, and Thoreau. Emerson appears in the right background, just over the head of Harriet Beecher Stowe (right foreground), and Hawthorne stands behind the bearded Bryant, gazing down at the floor. Hicks's juxtaposition of Hawthorne with Poe, who stands behind him in a mirroring pose, marks one of the painter's most suggestive interpretive gestures. The two writers, who apparently never met, worked in similar narrative modes using Gothicism, supernaturalism, and ambiguous symbolism. About the figure of Poe, Simpson has remarked,

> Thomas Hicks seems to have had some reservations about Poe's place in the American literary world. He depicts him wearing a black cloak, standing with his back to Hawthorne and gazing downward, withdrawn and introverted. Is Hicks merely presenting the romantic poet of popular legend, or is he trying to convey a sense of the special relationship Poe had to the world of letters, to say in effect that Poe was both of the public dominion of writers and not of it?[58]

Simpson might also have noted that Poe seems to be looking over the shoulder of the figure in front of him, Henry Wadsworth Longfellow, as if in eternal watchfulness for signs of literary larceny.

Hicks's painting, as rendered by Ritchie, incorporates many of the figures whom Poe had included in one or more of his versions of the literati—Sedgwick, Sigourney, Kennedy, Willis, Simms, Lowell, Mrs. Kirkland, Channing, Whittier, Lowell, Charles Fenno Hoffman, and others. Margaret Fuller appears just to the right of Irving, in a pose based on the likeness of her Hicks painted in Rome during the revolution of 1848.[59] Dignified as its composition may be, the collective portrait nevertheless incorporates inadvertent humor in Hicks's aggregation of authors who seem oblivious to the presence of their literary peers: with the possible exception of Willis and Oliver Wendell Holmes, who may be conversing at the foot of the stairs to the left, these luminaries stare vacantly up, down, or sideways, as if mindful of nothing so much as the pose they are striking on this formal occasion. If Cooper is giving an address, as the notes in his hand suggest, then no one is listening with any discernible interest. In fact if an open mouth implies dialogue, the entire assembly appears improbably speechless. Hicks suggests that these literati, so distant from each other geographically, likewise lack a common language that would make an exchange of literary ideas possible. At least the artist has envisioned a physically robust community of U.S. authors, carrying on the grand tradition of Shakespeare, Dante, and Goethe—whose statuary likenesses loom over this mythical confabulation—and continuing to contribute, as the volumes in the foreground attest, to the writing and publishing of American books.

Although Poe never managed to realize either his dream of founding a premier journal or of designating in an authoritative way the configuration of literary

America, his efforts to identify the literati inspired those like Hicks who in succeeding years attempted to represent the pantheon of authors most responsible
for staking a claim to American literary independence. Among the illustrious
group imagined by Hicks, Poe is the watchman, or so it seems, performing the
critical surveillance required to ascertain that everyone else present truly mea-
sures up. Hicks represents an unreal, impossible scene that denies the distances
and divisions that plagued the establishment of our literature, but it is a scene that
Poe would have appreciated, for it closely corresponds to his transcendent vision
of American literature, his cherished republic of letters.

Notes

1. Michel Foucault, "What Is an Author?" in *Textual Strategies: Perspectives in Post-Structuralist Criticism*, ed. Josué Harari (Ithaca, NY: Cornell Univ. Press, 1979), 141.

2. Martha Woodmansee, "The Genius and the Copyright: Economic and Legal Conditions of the Emergence of the 'Author,'" *Eighteenth-Century Studies* 17, no. 4 (1984): 426, 429, 430, 433.

3. Benedict Anderson, *Imagined Communities: Reflections on the Origin and Spread of National-ism*, rev. ed. (London: Verso, 1991), 44–46.

4. Patrick Parrinder, *Nation & Novel: The English Novel from Its Origins to the Present Day* (Oxford, UK: Oxford Univ. Press, 2006).

5. William Charvat, *The Profession of Authorship in America, 1800–1870* (1968; rpt. New York: Columbia Univ. Press, 1992), 29–30. Later studies of this phenomenon include Michael Newbury, *Figuring Authorship in Antebellum America* (Stanford, CA: Stanford Univ. Press, 1997); Leon Jackson, *The Business of Letters: Authorial Economies in Antebellum America* (Stanford, CA: Stanford Univ. Press, 2008); and David Dowling, *Capital Letters: Authorship in the Antebellum Literary Market* (Iowa City: Univ. of Iowa Press, 2009).

6. Samuel Kettell, ed., *Specimens of American Poetry* 1 (Boston: S. G. Goodrich and Co., 1829), iii–iv.

7. See Meredith L. McGill, *American Literature and the Culture of Reprinting, 1834–1853* (Philadelphia: Univ. of Pennsylvania Press, 2003).

8. Sedgwick satirized the contagion of sentimental authorship in "Cacoethes Scribendi," first published in the *Atlantic Souvenir* (Philadelphia: Carey, Lea, and Carey, 1830), 17–38.

9. Sydney Smith, Review of Siebert's *Annals of the United States, Edinburgh Review* 33 (January 1820): 79.

10. Richard Ruland, ed., *The Native Muse: Theories of American Literature from Bradford to Whitman* (New York: E. P. Dutton, 1976).

11. W. H. Gardiner, Review of Cooper's *The Spy, North American Review* 15 (July 1822): 255.

12. See Ernest Renan, "What Is a Nation?" in *Becoming National: A Reader,* ed. Geoff Eley and Ronald Grigor Suny (New York: Oxford Univ. Press, 1996), 42–55.

13. James Russell Lowell, "Edgar Allan Poe," *Graham's Magazine* 27 (Feb. 1845): 49.

14. Robert F. Berkhofer Jr., *The White Man's Indian: Images of the American Indian from Columbus to the Present* (New York: Alfred A. Knopf, 1978).

15. Ronald J. Zboray, *A Fictive People: Antebellum Economic Development and the American Reading Public* (New York: Oxford Univ. Press, 1992).

16. Lowell, "Edgar Allan Poe," 50.

17. John Ward Ostrom, ed., *Letters of Edgar Allan Poe*, 2nd ed. (New York: Gordian, 1966), vol. 1: 169, 265.

18. Lewis P. Simpson, "Poe's Vision of His Ideal Magazine," *The Man of Letters in New England and the South* (Baton Rouge: Louisiana State Univ. Press, 1973), 131–49.

19. Edgar Allan Poe, *Collected Works*, ed. Thomas O. Mabbott (Cambridge, MA: Harvard Univ. Press, 1969), vol. 2: 203.

20. Edgar Allan Poe, "Autography [Part I]," Edgar Allan Poe Society of Baltimore, www.eapoe .org/works/misc/autogb1.htm.

21. Jonathan Elmer, *Reading at the Social Limit: Affect, Mass Culture, and Edgar Allan Poe* (Palo Alto, CA: Stanford Univ. Press, 1995).

22. See Kevin J. Hayes, *Poe and the Printed Word* (Cambridge, UK: Cambridge Univ. Press, 2000), 45–65.

23. Ostrom, ed., *Letters of Edgar Allan Poe* 1: 119.

24. Edgar Allan Poe, *Essays and Reviews*, ed. G. R. Thompson (New York: Library of America, 1984), 1025.

25. Ostrom, ed., *Letters of Edgar Allan Poe* 1: 141.

26. Edgar Allan Poe, "A Chapter on Autography [Part I]," Edgar Allan Poe Society of Baltimore, www.eapoe.org/works/misc/autogc1.htm.

27. Ibid.

28. Ibid.

29. Edgar Allan Poe, "A Chapter on Autography [Part II]," Edgar Allan Poe Society of Baltimore, www.eapoe.org/works/misc/autogc2.htm.

30. Ibid.

31. Poe, "A Chapter on Autography [Part I]."

32. Edgar Allan Poe, "A Chapter on Autography [Part III]," Edgar Allan Poe Society of Baltimore, www.eapoe.org/works/misc/autogc3.htm.

33. Whipple quoted in Kenneth L. Silverman, *Edgar A. Poe: Mournful and Never-ending Remembrance* (New York: Harper Perennial, 1992), 169.

34. Edgar Allan Poe, "Prospectus of the *Stylus,*" Edgar Allan Poe Society of Baltimore, www .eapoe.org/works/misc/prospo10.htm.

35. Ostrom, ed., *Letters of Edgar Allan Poe* 1: 234.

36. Dwight Thomas and David K. Jackson, *The Poe Log: A Documentary Life of Edgar Allan Poe, 1809–1849* (Boston: G. K. Hall, 1987), 447. See also Rufus W. Griswold, ed., *The Poets and Poetry of America* (Philadelphia: Carey and Hart, 1842).

37. See Claude Richard, "Poe and Young America," *Studies in Bibliography* 21 (1968): 25–58; and McGill, *American Literature and the Culture of Reprinting.*

38. Edgar Allan Poe, "The Literati of New York City [Part III]," Edgar Allan Poe Society of Baltimore, www.eapoe.org/works/misc/litratb3.htm.

39. Edgar Allan Poe, "The Literati of New York City [Part I]," Edgar Allan Poe Society of Baltimore, www.eapoe.org/works/misc/litratb1.htm.

40. Edgar Allan Poe, "The Literati of New York City [Part IV]," Edgar Allan Poe Society of Baltimore, www.eapoe.org/works/misc/litratb4.htm.

41. Edgar Allan Poe, "The Literati of New York City [Part V]," Edgar Allan Poe Society of Baltimore, www.eapoe.org/works/misc/litratb5.htm.

42. Poe, "The Literati of New York City [Part IV]."

43. Poe, "The Literati of New York City [Part I]."

44. Poe, "The Literati of New York City [Part IV]."

45. Edgar Allan Poe, "The Literati of New York City [Part II]," Edgar Allan Poe Society of Baltimore, www.eapoe.org/works/misc/litratb2.htm. See Elmer, *Reading at the Social Limit*; and Stephen Rachman, "Es Lässt Sich Nicht Schreiben: Plagiarism and 'The Man of the Crowd,'" in *The American Face of Edgar Allan Poe*, ed. Shawn Rosenheim and Stephen Rachman (Baltimore: Johns Hopkins Univ. Press, 1995), 48–87.

46. Edgar Allan Poe, "Prospectus of the *Stylus*," Edgar Allan Poe Society of Baltimore, www .eapoe.org/works/misc/prospo12.htm.

47. Burton R. Pollin, "The Living Writers of America: A Manuscript by Edgar Allan Poe," *Studies in the American Renaissance* (1991): 151–200.

48. Edgar Allan Poe, "The Living Writers of America," Edgar Allan Poe Society of Baltimore, www.eapoe.org/works/misc/livingw.htm.

49. Ibid.

50. Ibid.

51. Simpson, "Poe's Vision of His Ideal Magazine," 133.

52. Poe, "The Living Writers of America."

53. Poe, *Essays and Reviews*, 550–51.

54. Rufus W. Griswold, ed., *Readings in American Poetry* (New York: John C. Riker, 1843), *The Poetry of Love* (Boston: L. Thompkins, 1844), and *The Prose Writers of America; with a Survey of the History, Condition, and Prospects of the Country* (Philadelphia: Carey and Hart, 1847).

55. Rufus W. Griswold, *The Literati: Some Honest Opinions about Autorial Merits and Demerits, with Occasional Words of Personality* (New York: J. S. Redfield, 1850).

56. Thomas Powell, *The Living Authors of America* (New York: Stringer and Townsend, 1850).

57. Evert and George Duyckinck, *Cyclopædia of American Literature*, 2 vols. (New York: C. Scribner, 1855).

58. Simpson, "Poe's Vision of His Ideal Magazine," 133.

59. We now know that Hicks was the "youth" Fuller tried to seduce in Rome just before her affair with Ossoli; the painter remained one of her closest male confidants, to whom she revealed the news of her pregnancy before entrusting him with a letter to her family in the event of her death during the revolution. See Robert N. Hudspeth, ed., *The Letters of Margaret Fuller* (Ithaca, NY: Cornell Univ. Press, 1987), vol. 4: 269–71. See also Hudspeth, ed., *Letters of Margaret Fuller* (1988), vol. 5: 66.

"The Rage for Lions"

Edgar Allan Poe and the Culture of Celebrity

LEON JACKSON

In the summer of 1846, Mary Gove made a series of visits to Edgar Allan Poe in Fordham, where they walked, talked, and debated the nature of authorship and its motivations. During one of these visits, Poe announced his absolute disdain for the opinion of others. "I write," he told Gove, "from a mental necessity—to satisfy my taste and my love of art. Fame forms no motive power with me. What can I care for the judgment of a multitude, every individual of which I despise?" Gove sought to reason with Poe, but he became agitated, and she turned the conversation to other matters. When she visited him next, however, Poe seemed to have performed a complete about-face. To the rather amazed Gove he now confessed: "I love fame—I dote on it—I idolize it—I would drink to the very dregs the glorious intoxication. I would have incense ascend in my honour from every hill and hamlet, from every town and city on this earth. Fame! glory!—they are life-giving breath, and living blood. No man lives, unless he is famous! How bitterly I belied my nature, and my aspirations, when I said I did not desire fame, and that I despised it." Gove again tried to reason with Poe, suggesting to him that perhaps his opinions varied with his frame of mind, but Poe would have none of it; his former assertions, he said, were entirely invalid, his latter the complete truth.[1]

Scholars have dedicated considerable energy to determining the extent to which Poe's desire for fame was fulfilled, documenting his contemporary and posthumous reputation through the accumulation and annotation of reviews, representations, reappropriations, and other trappings of renown. More recently, they have also sought to understand Poe's place within the contemporary American literary canon, bringing a variety of analytic tools to bear upon the materials collected by earlier scholars. Whether or not Poe is part of the canon—within, beneath, or outside of the so-called American Renaissance—is yet to be determined, although the rigor and empirical depth of recent studies move us closer

37

to a determination of his recent academic status.² What has not yet been assayed, however, is what Poe *himself* thought of fame, status, and reputation: how he envisaged his rank within the republic of letters, and how he understood the act of ranking—what I call the use of status regimes—more generally.³ Perplexing exchanges such as the ones recorded by Gove have scarcely been analyzed, and when scholars have sought to understand Poe's opinions of fame, status, reputation, and canonicity, they have tended to associate him with either one of his postures or the other—the fame-denying aesthete or the attention-seeking hack— rather than considering why Poe insisted on both and how he might have entertained them concurrently.

Poe was, in fact, obsessed by status—his own and others'—and his musings on the subject, by turns trenchant and spiteful, inform not only his critical and editorial practice, but also his fiction and poetry. It is a topic that scholars interested in Poe, as well as in the phenomenon of status, can ill afford to ignore. Rather than focusing on what modern scholars have had to say about Poe's posthumous status, then, I want to concentrate in this essay instead on how Poe understood his own—and his work's—status, especially as he encountered and was compelled to negotiate the antebellum period's many status regimes.

Poe's preoccupation with status and its many regimes, I want to argue, grew out of his experience of what sociologists call "status incongruence." Influentially theorized by Gerhard Lenski and others in the 1950s, status incongruence refers to the condition of finding oneself endowed with a demonstrably higher degree of prestige within one domain—such as income—than within another—such as cultural achievement or political privilege. Translated into categories made popular by Pierre Bourdieu, we might say that status incongruence reflects a disparity between economic capital on the one hand and social or cultural capital on the other. The nouveau riche and the genteelly poor both manifest status incongruity, while those who are born to poverty or to long-established wealth do not. Those who experience status incongruence, it is conjectured, tend to extremes of political conservatism or radicalism as they seek to address the dissonance they confront. They are often also afflicted by depression, loneliness, alienation, and poor health.⁴ Sufferers are beset still further by the rigidity of status systems in general, which tend to resist initiatives made by individuals seeking to move up the ladder of esteem. According to sociologist Murray Milner Jr., status is "inalienable," meaning that, although one can be said to possess status, what one possesses is simply the opinion of others, which one cannot alter at will; it is "inexpansible," meaning that only a proportion of a community can enjoy its benefits without the system as a whole collapsing through prestige inflation; its higher echelons are carefully regulated, through the use of elaborate and ever-changing "norms," which it is hard for those with lower status to adopt and imitate; and, lastly, it is often bestowed by association, so that those consorting with those of higher status find their stock rising, while those with lower status are kept at arm's reach. All in all, according to Milner, status systems are deeply inertial.[5]

That Poe experienced status incongruence is eminently clear. The orphaned child of poor actors, fostered but never formally adopted by a wealthy Virginia family, raised in a socially and economically elite culture, and then cast adrift, Poe's life presents an almost textbook example of incoherent social identity. Economically impoverished, culturally over-endowed, socially marginalized, and both blessed and burdened with the expectations that grew out of his childhood with the Allan family, Poe rarely felt as if he achieved what he called "the station in society which is my due."[6] Others also noted his social liminality. Recounting his only encounter with Poe, in the early 1830s, John H. B. Latrobe recalled that "[h]is figure was remarkably good, and he carried himself erect and well, as one who had been trained well.... Coat, hat, boots, and gloves had evidently seen their best days; but so far as mending and brushing go, everything had been done, apparently, to make them presentable." He added: "On most men his clothes would have looked shabby and seedy; but there was something about *this* man that prevented me from criticising his garments.... Gentleman was written all over him." A decade later, John Hill Hewitt found the same strange mix of high and low: "Though he looked the used-up man all over," wrote Hewitt, "still he showed the gentleman."[7] With his strange mix of threadbare clothes and dignified carriage, his pathos mitigated by what Latrobe could identify only as "something," and the signs of gentlemanliness written, palimpsestically, over his outward poverty, Poe literally embodied high status (erect carriage) and just as literally wore his low status on his sleeve (with clothes that had seen better days).

The result of such social dislocation for Poe, however, was less a gravitation to one or another political or social extreme than a constant oscillation between the poles of acquiescence and estrangement, engagement and resistance. His solution to the inalienability of status was to fabricate his own good opinion and spread it covertly, even while he attacked others for doing the same. His response to the inexpansibility of status was, likewise, to boost his own standing by discrediting the standing of others, even though, again, he deplored the practice in others. And while he often sought the company of those who enjoyed a higher status than he did, he routinely ran down such friends and found fault with them when no fault was to be found. Neither able to beat *or* join those whom he felt enjoyed the coherent status he was denied, Poe adopted what might be called a "beat *and* join" strategy, loving but also loathing those more fortunate than himself. As Poe—always one to make a virtue of a necessity—put it himself: "genius of the highest order lives in perpetual vacillation between ambition and *the scorn of it*."[8] Unable to resolve his sense of status incongruity, Poe spent much of his life obsessing over the status of others, toying with the figures they cut, but finding each of their roles impossible to inhabit.

Poe had available within his biological and foster families several models of what high, or at least consistent, status looked like. His paternal grandfather, David Poe, exemplified a widely held republican model of fame, based on noble but selfless sacrifice to the greater good. A quartermaster during the Revolutionary War, General Poe dipped into his own savings to pay for military supplies when needed, an act that was commended in public by Lafayette—himself widely feted—when he visited Richmond in 1824. The appeal of the military life was that it yoked loss (of individuated self and even of life) to glory, thereby obviating the power of deficit to create status incongruity. Poe referred in print to his grandfather with admiration on several occasions, and his decision to join the army must have been prompted at least in part by his desire to pursue this path to fame.[9] Poe's foster father, John Allan, modeled a different type of respectability altogether. A self-made businessman whose fiscal probity earned him as many kudos as did his income, his obituary insisted that, in Richmond if nowhere else, "none was better known, none more highly respected." In life, Allan represented a form of status that would later be championed more widely still in works such as *Lives of American Merchants, Eminent for Integrity, Enterprise, and Public Spirit* (1844) and in journals such as Freeman Hunt's *Merchants' Magazine.* It was a form of eminence based upon not only the accumulation of economic capital but still more on the symbolic capital of trust, by which one could borrow still more. To be credit-worthy was to be both creditable and credible. Yet as much as Allan encouraged Poe to "aspire, even to eminence in Public life," and much as Poe admired Hunt personally, he seemed to evince little desire to pursue commercial respectability or status, and he savaged its pretensions in "Peter Pendulum, The Business Man" (1840).[10] A third and, as we shall see, more compelling model was offered by his mother Eliza Poe, who enjoyed a substantial and bright, if brief, career on the stage. "Mrs. Poe's name is a brilliant gem in the theatric crown," wrote one pundit; "no one has received more than she of public applause." Orphaned when he was not yet three, Poe nonetheless found himself drawn in subsequent years to the form of acclaim that Eliza Poe had enjoyed, even as he recognized its complex relationship to inherited status. "[N]o earl was ever prouder of his earldom," wrote Poe of himself decades later, "than he of his descent from a woman who, although well-born, hesitated not to consecrate to the drama her brief career of genius and of beauty."[11]

Given adequate space, one might show how Poe's inconsistency-driven obsession with status and reputational regimes worked itself out through his attitudes toward the paradigms modeled by his mother, foster father, and grandfather; manifested itself in his attitude toward southern notions of honor; informed his treatment of gossip, scandal, and libel; shaped his view of blackmail; and drove his engagement with literary competitions. In this essay, however, I will confine myself to the status regime that seemed to preoccupy him most: that of literary celebrity.[12] To say that Poe was fascinated by celebrity would be an understatement of the greatest magnitude. It was a constant preoccupation. Over the course of his career, he spoke of phenomena as diverse as wines, ways of speaking, landscapes, poems, and magazines as having "celebrity."[13] Overwhelmingly, though, celebrity referred to a trait possessed by, or bestowed upon, an individual, or, perhaps, to that individual's defining trait.

In order to appreciate fully the extent to which Poe engaged with celebrity and wielded it as a tool through which to exorcise (but also exercise) his status anxieties, it is necessary both to define and situate the phenomenon. Although scholars of celebrity have sometimes worked at taxonomic and disciplinary cross-purposes, most agree that celebrity is the manifestation of a broad-ranging and widely appealing acclaim for an individual; that the relationship between a celebrity and his or her fans is profoundly mediated in each direction, so that celebrities cannot *know* their fans except as an aggregate, while fans cling to a wholly illusory sense of one-on-one (or parasocial) intimacy; that celebrity is a highly spectacular phenomenon, relying upon reproductive and especially visually mimetic technologies—such as the printing press and photography—to create this aura of intimacy; and that such technologies are deployed less often by the celebrities themselves than by cultural intermediaries such as showmen, impresarios, agents, and promoters, whose job it is to create the buzz which their clients enjoy. True celebrity, it is argued, necessarily involves mass mediation and a relentless focus on the persona—indeed the very life—of the celebrity. It is not enough to be accomplished; one must also be spoken about. Celebrities live in the limelight, and when their lives cease to be interesting, they cease to be celebrities. Sociologist Chris Rojek has elaborated upon these insights by differentiating between ascribed celebrity, which is the sort that is passed on dynastically as through peerage or monarchical succession; achieved celebrity, which is awarded to those who accomplish a socially and consensually recognized standard of excellence; and attributed celebrity, which is the fame that is generated solely through mediated promotion. Rojek, of course, would be the first to acknowledge that *all* celebrity entails the work of promotion to create aura; what differs from category to category is the degree of promotion and the degree to which it becomes possible to acknowledge it. Ascribed celebrity seems entirely natural, even divinely sanctioned, and the pomp that creates it is seen as effect rather than cause. Attributed celebrity, by way of contrast, is often understood, even by its beneficiaries, to be the product of deliberate manipulation, although it is no less efficacious for all its transience.[14]

While some scholars have insisted that true celebrity is a quintessentially modern phenomenon—"there was no such thing as celebrity prior to the beginning of the twentieth century," as one film critic bluntly puts it—it is becoming increasingly clear that the phenomena we associate with celebrity were beginning to coalesce as early as the seventeenth century. Unquestionably, it had achieved a degree of maturity by the antebellum period.[15] The rise of theatrical stars such as Edwin Forrest, and indeed of the very concept of the star; the thunderous applause that greeted Fanny Ellsler and Jenny Lind on their American tours; the crowds who thronged Dickens during his visit; the fan mail received by Longfellow, Sigourney, and others; the rise of promotional tie-ins such as Susan Warner undergarments and Uncle Tom cups, plates, and sheet music; the diffusion of cartes des visites, daguerreotypes, and prints of established authors; the popularity of behind-the-scenes exposés, such as Nathaniel P. Willis's tour biography of Lind, or Fanny Fern's roman à clef trashing of her brother Willis; and the immense success of cultural entrepreneurs such as P. T. Barnum all attest to the existence not merely of celebrities in antebellum America but also of a robust celebrity culture and a communications infrastructure able to sustain and diffuse that culture.[16]

Celebrity, by its very nature, tends to overspill national boundaries, and no author exemplified better the nature of early nineteenth-century celebrity in America than the British poet Byron. Not only his poetry but also his dress sense, his mores, and his private behavior became the topic for public scrutiny and consumption. "The most fashionable writer now in England," wrote the Philadelphia

Portfolio in 1814, "and the fashion there is always sure to be the fashion here—is Lord Byron." William Cullen Bryant concurred from the far side of the Byron craze. "But a few years ago," he wrote in 1832, "what an aping of Lord Byron exhibited itself throughout this country! . . . [A]t length every city, town, and village had its little Byron, its self-tormenting scoffer at morality, its gloomy misanthropist in song."[17] Poe's obsession with Byron is well documented. He not only purchased a volume of Byron's poems while in college, but adopted the poet's signature clothing, affected his moody personae, sketched a life-sized image of him onto the ceiling of his college dorm room, imitated his poetic style, claimed to have traveled to Greece like the poet, to fight for independence, and emulated his hero's swim of the Hellespont with his own swim up the James River.[18] And while he criticized Americans for making "fools of themselves in their fete-ing and festival-ing of Dickens," Poe himself assumed the role of fan and arranged two meetings with Dickens when the latter made his visit to America.[19]

Yet Poe was not a passive or consistent consumer of celebrity culture. He was, rather, both drawn to *and* repelled by it. He was drawn to it to the extent that it seemed to hold out precisely the kind of applause and validation he craved; he was repelled by it to the extent that it struck him as a fraudulent and unjustifiable valorization of those lacking in talent; and his vacillations were driven by his hopes and fears. When he was able, or hoped to be able, to enjoy the benefits of celebrity, he tended to endorse its premises and institutions and participate in them. When, by contrast, he felt that he was not receiving the attention he deserved, he tended to lash out at the phenomenon in its entirety. As a participant-observer, Poe makes an excellent lens through which to examine the phenomenon of antebellum celebrity culture, and because his observations were so often negative, we will begin by examining Poe's treatment of celebrity as fraud.

"Must expose the wires"

Celebrity, as Tom Mole has argued, "does not want to be understood."[20] It functions by creating a mystique of inevitability and an aura of enchanting spirituality around the otherwise socially constructed image. One of the clearest ways in which the cult and culture of celebrity were challenged, then, was through acts of revelation, exposure, and disenchantment. Such acts were easily deployed in nineteenth-century America because exposure was a practice entrenched deeply within not only the nation's residual Enlightenment epistemology but also within its still dominant republican culture, which emphasized fear of conspiracies, cabals, and covert manipulations of power. Indeed, some of the earliest critiques of celebrity in antebellum America took the form of attacks on the political cult of personality and its machinations. These were often advanced using tropes drawn from the world of puppetry, a theatrical practice that had a long history in both England and America, according to which the blithe politician was moved by his hidden agenda and by his various handlers, just as a puppet was moved on wires pulled by a hidden puppeteer.[21] Looking back on the 1830s, Henry Wikoff recalled editor James Gordon Bennett's "utter contempt . . . for politicians and wire-pullers" and lauded his "daily exposure of their manoeuvres and pretences" in his newspaper. He was not the only one so inclined. The "leading motive of those who pull the wires," jeered the *Brooklyn Daily Eagle* in an 1842 column on tariff reform, "is individual gain." Many delegates at Democratic Party state conventions, opined the *American Whig Review* in 1846, are "the merest automata moved by the wire-pullers behind the scenes," while a few years later the *Democratic Review* returned the criticism, denouncing "Whig wire pullers" for disrupting their meetings.[22] Such language translated easily from the political republic to the republic of letters. According to Poe's friend J. E. Snodgrass, "There have lived in every country and in every age a class of whom I know not how to designate— as a class—unless I style them Intellectual Wire-Pullers. . . . They, surely, are not unlike those who pull the wires attached to the *dramatis personae* of a puppet show." And while Nathaniel P. Willis promised, in 1829, to reveal "who pulls the wire to all the literary puppets," no one took the project further than Poe, who in all likelihood read Willis's trope when it first appeared in the *American Monthly Magazine,* although he might have encountered it in many other places. Seventeen or eighteen years after reading Willis's promise, Poe, planning a book on celebrity authors, reminded himself that he "must expose the wires." It had rarely been far from his mind in the intervening years.[23]

The image of the inanimate, puppet-like body brought to life by the intelligence of another was one that appealed to Poe deeply, as it did to many in his age.[24] The most literal manifestation, of course, is "Maelzel's Chess Player" (1836)— Poe's exposé of a chess-playing automaton that was operated by a hidden man manipulating pulleys and levers—and we see a fictional example in the whale-bone-and-ventriloquism-animated corpse in "Thou Art the Man" (1844). Such texts have rightly been seen as explorations of the boundary between man and machine, body and soul, culture and science.[25] The appeal for Poe was not merely metaphysical, however; it also cut directly to the heart of his understanding of celebrity, which, he believed, functioned in much the same way: like something inanimate or at least a brutally physical being manipulated by a hidden intelligence. "There are puppets enough," wrote Poe, "able enough, and willing enough, to perform in literature the little things to which we have had reference." In private he denounced several authors with this dismissive epithet.[26] The important thing in making any literary judgment, then, was to make a distinction between puppet and puppeteer.

In his explicit anatomies of celebrity, Poe made a broader and more figurative (but comparable) distinction between the "physique" of a celebrity phenomenon, by which he meant the superficial and (mostly) physical or embodied phenomena on which fans focused, and what he called its "morale," by which he meant the will, intention, or mind that lay behind it and the perception it engendered. He deployed just such a figure in discussing the celebrity of Longfellow's works, for example, asking "how much of their success may be attributed to the luxurious manner in which, as merely physical books, they have been presented to the public," and answering that "the physique has had a vast influence on the morale."[27] Poe even turned the morale/physique distinction on Willis himself, arguing that while there was *some* "morale" to his celebrity, "about two-thirds . . . of his appreciation by the public" was a matter of "physique." And he elaborates on exactly what such superficiality entailed:

> He "pushed himself," went much into the world, made friends with the gentler sex, "delivered" poetical addresses, wrote "scriptural" poems, traveled, sought the intimacy of noted women, and got into quarrels with notorious men. All these things served his purpose . . . [and] greatly advanced, if it did not establish his literary fame.[28]

This was not the first time Poe had sought to debunk Willis's celebrity on the grounds that it was merely a matter of physique. In his early story, "Lionizing" (1835), he literalized the phenomenon of physique-generated celebrity by recounting the adventures of a Willis-like protagonist—Thomas Smith—who becomes famous solely on the basis of his large nose. Using a popular nineteenth-century term for a minor literary celebrity—the lion—Poe's title emphasized process, suggesting that greatness was not recognized so much as it was fabricated, or as he put it himself in a letter to John Pendleton Kennedy, the work was to be taken as a satire on "the rage for Lions and the facility of becoming one." In the tale, accordingly, Smith pulls his nose, and his father pronounces him a genius; he follows his nose and it leads him to the fame of a salon; he turns up his nose at others and becomes notorious; and after being challenged to a duel and shooting off the nose of his rival Baron Bludenuff, he finds that he has lost his precious status for, as his father explains, "great is a Lion with a proboscis, but greater by far is a Lion with no proboscis at all." In a world in which fame can be bestowed so arbitrarily, it can just as easily be lost.[29]

At least the nose in "Lionizing" was a real one. A later story, "The Man That Was Used Up" (1839), describes another Smith, Brevet Brigadier General A. B. C. Smith, a celebrated Indian fighter—handsome, articulate, and brave; "one of the *most* remarkable men of the age"—who turns out to be made almost entirely of prostheses. While he is universally admired, without his fake legs, arms, eyes, teeth, hair, and palate, none of which is apparent to his admirers, he is nothing other than an "odd-looking bundle of something" lying on the floor. Assembled by his black servant Pompey, Smith comes to life, and as he does so he recommends to the narrator by name a manufacturer of talking dolls, who has built the "singular-looking machine" that allows him to speak. If Thomas Smith is nothing but a big nose, then A. B. C. Smith is not even that. He is a man defined almost wholly by what he lacks yet who is revered for what he seems to possess.[30]

The implication of such tales and tropes is clear enough. Celebrity, Poe believed, was a sham, a masquerade in which an illusion of vitality and validity was sustained through legerdemain, machinery, smoke, and mirrors. Sometimes, indeed, he seemed actually to refer to "The Man That Was Used Up" in his criticisms of celebrity authors. In tones that recalled his skewering of the handsome but bogus Smith, for example, Poe attacked American historian George Jones with the comment that "His qualifications are too well known to need comment. He has a pretty wife, a capital head of hair, and fine teeth."[31]

Of course, Poe's critique of the culture of celebrity went far beyond the mere observation that a celebrity was akin to a handsome puppet dancing on strings manipulated by others; he was also concerned to reveal the nature of the puppeteer and the dance he choreographed. An essay of this, or any, length cannot adequately discuss all of the ways in which Poe sought to expose and discredit those he thought were unfairly making celebrities out of non-entities. Even Sidney Moss's substantial book-length treatment of the subject—*Poe's Literary Battles*—offers only the high (or perhaps low) points of what was for Poe a career-long endeavor. Literary celebrity, Poe claimed again and again, was orchestrated by a "*clique,*" or series of cliques, who talked up their favored subjects and would "write . . . down" those who opposed them. They previewed, promoted, published, and puffed their authors, producing their works in handsome and expensive editions. They rigged competitions to help their protégés win and provided them with sinecures when they needed employment. In short, they manufactured celebrities as systematically and as readily as prosthetic makers manufactured the seemingly perfect but wholly fake Brevet Brigadier General A. B. C. Smith, as assembled by Pompey the servant.[32]

The situation was especially galling to Poe since it was, itself, an example of status incongruity in reverse. Authors wholly devoid of talent enjoyed prestige far beyond their merits while he, who was talented beyond measure, received inadequate recognition for his own work. "The fact is," Poe wrote in the final year of his life,

> someone should write, at once, a Magazine paper exposing—*ruthlessly* exposing—the *dessous de cartes* of our literary affairs. He should show how and why it is that the ubiquitous quack in letters can always "succeed," while *genius* . . . must inevitably succumb. He should point out the "easy arts" by which any one, base enough to do it, can get himself placed at the very head of American Letters. (*ER*, 1444)

Of course, Poe had been doing just this for much of his career, one of his earliest targets being Nathaniel P. Willis. So far from revealing who pulled the wires, Willis was, in Poe's opinion, one of the chief literary wire-pullers himself. Modern critics do not disagree, of course, but they tend to see things in somewhat less conspiratorial terms.[33] Scott Peeples, for example, has argued that Poe failed where Willis succeeded at least in part because Willis was able to develop a consistent and recognizable style or brand, while Poe was not. This, however, is only partly correct. While Poe was never able to establish a fictional brand, he very quickly established a recognizable *critical* brand—and, indeed, a modicum of celebrity—as an exposer of the dark secrets and private failings of others in the literary world: a revealer of the *dessous des cartes* (the underside of the cards). Starting in the mid-1830s, Poe came to be known as a "tomahawk" critic, a designation he did much—at least at first—to promote and disseminate.[34] Playing on the era's interest in what Neil Harris has called the "operational aesthetic" or fascination with the mechanics (the wires) by which hoaxes and frauds were perpetrated, Poe also set himself up as a debunker par excellence. Tales such as "The Man That Was Used Up" and "Lionizing" seem very clearly to work within the genre made famous by P. T. Barnum: the-hoax-perpetrated-then-explained. Yet where a humbug like Barnum was able to exploit the operational aesthetic in such a way as to charm and entertain his victims, Poe was able only to generate ill will and notoriety, pale imitations of the celebrity and adulation he craved. In the first phase of his career, Poe was an anti-celebrity, or at best a meta-celebrity.[35]

"HAS INVARIABLY MADE IT HIS BOAST"

For a minor squib published in a regional periodical, "Lionizing" did remarkably well. It was quickly reprinted in the *Richmond Enquirer* and the *Augusta Chronicle* and praise of it was reprinted in papers from Virginia to Pennsylvania. Yet, unsatisfied with this exposure, Poe penned several anonymous and pseudonymous reviews of "Lionizing," which he sent to newspapers in Baltimore (*Poe Log*, 157–60). It's hard to miss the irony in Poe's seeking to create a buzz about a story that so explicitly denounces effervescent and artificial celebrity. Yet as his exchanges with Mary Gove make clear, Poe vacillated wildly on the topic of fame. As much as he despised celebrity in others, he desired it for himself. Thomas Holley Chivers, for one, confirmed the ambivalence: "One of the most striking peculiarities of Mr Poe," he wrote, "was, his perfect *abandon*—boyish indifference—not only in regard to the opinion of others, but [with] an uncompromising independence of spirit. . . . Yet no man living loved the praises of others better than he did—for I remember that whenever I happened to communicate to him anything touching his abilities as a writer, his bosom would heave like a troubled sea." Or again, Evert Duycknick: "Poe was sensitive to opinion. He sought . . . as I often witnessed, with an intense eagerness the smallest paragraph in a newspaper touching himself or his writings."[36] While Poe denounced celebrity as fabrication, he attempted to fabricate celebrity for himself—producing many flattering paragraphs himself under pseudonyms—to feed his appetite for praise.

Throughout his career, Poe used his fiction, his criticism, and his image to advance a narrative that he believed would promote his celebrity. Defending the gruesome denouement of his story "Berenice" in a letter to editor Thomas Willis White in 1835, for example, he wrote: "The history of all Magazines shows plainly that those which have attained celebrity were indebted for it to articles *similar in nature—to Berenice.*" Pitching "The Mystery of Marie Rogêt" to George Roberts in 1842, he likewise suggested that on account of its timeliness it would "excite attention" (*L* 1: 57, 200). Yet Poe was caught in a double bind. Observing other authors receiving praise they did not deserve, he found it hard not to help himself to praise he felt he himself did deserve: Lacking, moreover, a clique of promoters who would do him justice, he was compelled to convert himself into a celebrity. It was the perfect—and indeed the only—way to circumvent the inexpansibility of status. His covert self-reviews were one of the first such strategies he employed.

While Poe's fictional works were, in every sense of the word, designed to create a sensation, and while in his self-reviews he sought to sensationalize them, celebrity authorship focused as much on life as on letters. The very person of a celebrity—his or her appearance, biography, and actions—became texts that observers consumed with avidity.[37] It was not enough, in other words, for Poe to write well; he needed also to live interestingly, or to be seen to do so. Much of the work Poe undertook to generate his own celebrity, then, took the form of covert self-fashioning in order to render his life as dramatic as possible.

Poe attempted this most strikingly through a series of autobiographical distortions, which he passed on to others, and which were intended to mitigate the status incongruity with which he felt himself burdened and which he believed the techniques of celebrity promotion could address. Among many other things, Poe claimed to be younger than he was, so that his earliest successes seemed more precocious; helped himself to editorial positions he had not earned and competition prizes he had not won; gave himself more time as a student at the University of Virginia and bragged of higher honors therein; and made himself the presumptive heir to the Allan fortune. Feeling underappreciated by his employers, he exaggerated the number of subscribers he brought to the *Southern Literary Messenger* and the number of pages that he wrote for *Burton's Gentleman's Magazine.* And while he acknowledged he was "the son of an actress" and, he wrote, "invariably made it his boast," he also claimed that his mother was not only "well-born" but that "no earl was ever prouder of his earldom" than he was of his parents' profession. Poe, indeed, often strove for the prestige associated with inherited status. Burdened by what he felt was a modest lineage, he informed Allan that he was a direct descendent of Benedict Arnold.[38] And, again and again, he mentioned his six-mile swim up the James River, which probably took place in 1824, when he was fifteen. Poe referred to his exploit on the James in the *Southern Literary Messenger* in 1835 more than a decade after the fact, again in 1840 in *Alexander's Weekly Messenger,* and again in 1843 close to twenty years later in the Philadelphia *Saturday Museum,* each time making the swim longer and his effort more heroic. His allusions to this adolescent exploit almost two decades after the fact had less to do with claims to physical prowess for their own sake and more to do with his attempts to draw admiring comparisons with Byron's celebrated swim of the Hellespont. "Any swimmer in 'the falls' in my day would have swum the Hellespont, and thought nothing of the matter," he bragged in 1835; while in 1843 he crowed that "Byron's paddle across the Hellespont was mere child's play in comparison."[39]

The 1843 claims appear in a lengthy biographical sketch published in the Philadelphia *Saturday Museum* under Henry Hirst's byline, but, in fact, written with Poe's cooperation, if not by Poe himself.[40] It was neither the first nor the

last time that he would write about himself in the third person in order to promote his fame. Poe's compulsive exaggerations—both third person and first—
speak to a deep-seated need to establish once and for all his claim to achieved
celebrity, even though he made such claims dishonestly and through techniques
more closely associated with attributed celebrity than with its achieved variant.
As David Leverenz puts it: "As a self-made aristocrat, Poe uses textuality to im-
prove his status while subverting the meanings of status stratification." As much
as he resented and distrusted celebrity culture with its textually generated status
markers, he deployed its most egregious strategies in the most cynical fashion.[41]

Poe was also aware of the power of images—as well as texts—to shape celebrity. Michael Deas, Susan S. Williams, and William Pannapacker have all suggested that modern critics' vision of Poe as a tortured Romantic genius have been
unduly influenced by the handful of daguerreotypes for which he sat in the late
1840s, when he was under unbearable duress. Kevin Hayes, however, has conjectured that Poe's poses in these pictures were very deliberately contrived by Poe
himself to create just such an image. While Hayes offers no decisive evidence,
such an attitude would be wholly consistent with Poe's controlling nature in general and his desire to control his status and its reception in particular.[42] Poe was
every inch the self-made man.

"The most noted among the living literati of the country"

Somewhere between his cynical criticisms of celebrity and his sincere attempts
to achieve it for himself lay two of Poe's most ambitious critical projects: his analysis of celebrity authors' handwriting, published in "Autography" (1836) and "A
Chapter on Autography" (1841–42), and his gossipy analyses of the lives of writers in "The Literati of New York City" (1846). Both of these were apparently test
runs for his full-length but never-completed volume, *The Living Writers of America,* or *American Parnassus,* which he intended to be his *summa* of celebrity status.
In each, as in the manuscript of *Living Writers,* one sees Poe's conflicted opinions
of celebrity. Autographs were a good place for Poe to begin his study of status
and ability, for like many others of his generation, he believed that handwriting
ineluctably revealed the true or veridical identity of the writer. "I am more than
half serious in all that I have ever said," he wrote in 1844, "about manuscript, as
affording indication of character. The general proposition is unquestionable—
that the mental qualities will have a *tendency* to impress the MS."[43] In each series
of "Autography," accordingly, Poe tried to get at the character of various celebrity

authors through analysis of their handwriting. Yet as a number of scholars have noted, the actual handwriting analyses are simply the occasion for other, more culturally laden, work to be undertaken.[44] The 1836 series, for example, provides a brilliant anatomy of celebrity-fan relations. Unlike the 1841–42 iteration, the signatures of 1836 were appended to a collection of fictitious letters, alleged to have been written by various authors of note, in response to bizarre missives from one Joseph Miller, a prankster with a "passion for autographs." Autograph collecting in America, as Tamara Plakins Thornton has argued, emerged in the early nineteenth century at exactly the same time that a celebrity culture began to coalesce, the collectors believing that by obtaining the signatures of their heroes and heroines they could enjoy a moment of unmediated communion with them.[45] While Poe's analyses of the signatures are singularly unenlightening, his depiction of the letters themselves reveal clearly the lengths to which celebrities were imposed upon by their fans. From among the thirty-eight letters offered, six respond to requests for written contributions, five to the receipt of unsolicited writings, three to requests for autographs, and two to uninvited feedback. The remainder reply to requests for information, or for the confirmation or denial of rumors, from the authors in question. Together, they paint a picture of celebrity authors as constantly harried by strangers claiming, or seeking to make, connections of one kind or another, and they correspond closely to what we know of celebrity-fan relationships in nineteenth-century America.[46]

The 1841–42 series, "A Chapter on Autography," did not employ a fictional frame, but it made clearer still fans' desire to get close to their heroes. As Poe himself put it in opening this series: "Next to the person of a distinguished man-of-letters, we desire to see his portrait—next to his portrait, his autograph. In the latter, especially, there is something which seems to bring him before us in his true idiosyncrasy—in his character of *scribe*." Acknowledging that the desire to collect celebrity autographs was "a natural and rational one," Poe bragged that the nature of his profession had given him collecting opportunities "enjoyed by few," the fruits of which he would share (*H* 15: 178–79). Yet as in the 1836 series, the actual analysis of handwriting was simply the occasion for Poe to do other work, the work here being that of literary nation building. As J. Gerald Kennedy observes in his chapter for this collection, the pieces on autography, as well as the later literati sketches, enabled Poe to create a *national* literary culture almost by fiat, where there had previously been only various local literary cultures.[47]

That Poe was able, in the sense used by Benedict Anderson, to "imagine" a national literary culture through his mosaic of sketches is clear; what is less clear is the extent to which he valued the national canon he "imagined." Observing that he was in possession of signatures from "every individual in America who has the slightest pretension to literary celebrity," and certainly too many to reproduce, he explained that his selection would be based on "celebrity rather than true worth." The distinction Poe makes is revealing, for while he does not suggest that "celebrity" and "true worth" are mutually exclusive, he clearly sees them as distinct—and distinguishable—qualities. Even while he presents a national literary canon based on celebrity, in other words, his analyses are also geared toward identifying a subset of the celebrity canon whose fame has been justifiably earned, and vilifying the rest. In short, even while all the worthy were famous, for Poe, not all of the famous were worthy.[48]

Sometimes, Poe's axiological project takes the form of explicit ranking. Thus Longfellow "is entitled to the first place among the poets of America," Lowell "to at least the second or third place." At other times, Poe shows how being too highly ranked can have a baneful influence. Irving, he believed, "has been so thoroughly satiated with fame as to grow slovenly in the performance of his literary tasks." Mostly, however, Poe pointed out whether a reputation was come by honestly. Joseph Chandler's "reputation . . . is deservedly high," he claimed, while Robert Walsh's "has been bolstered by a *clique,* [and] is not a thing to live." Sometimes, he claimed, a reputation could even be tarnished through dishonesty. James McHenry had been "the victim of a most shameful cabal in this country." Lastly, he drew a distinction between spurious public opinion and a more candid, and accurate, one held in private. William Leete Stone, for example, was "remarkable for the great difference which exists between the apparent public opinion respecting his abilities, and the real estimation in which he is privately held."[49]

Poe's various canonical projects evince a curious ambivalence regarding celebrity. While at times he seems to denounce the very institution of canonization as without merit, at others he engages vigorously in acts of canonical intervention, endorsing the status of some and questioning the status of others. Attempts to discredit status, as Murray Milner Jr. has argued, are rarely attacks on the system of status altogether; more often they are reflections of the inexpansibility of high status: attempts to raise one's own standing by reducing and thereby reappropriating the status of others. Editor George Graham certainly saw resentment in Poe's adjudications. "I do not know what your crime may be in the eyes of Poe," he wrote Longfellow in 1844, "but suppose it may be a better, and more widely established reputation. Or if you have wealth . . . that is sufficient to settle your damnation so far as Mr. Poe may be presumed capable of effecting it."[50] Poe wanted what others had, even as he resented their possession of it. He could neither achieve high status nor leave the desire for it well enough alone.

"ELIZA, MY DEAR—'THE RAVEN!'"

Notoriety came early to Poe, celebrity late. Although he was by no means unknown through the 1830s and became increasingly visible in the early 1840s, his fortune changed dramatically, if briefly, with the publication of "The Raven" in January 1845. As Eliza Richards demonstrates in her contribution to this volume, both the form and structure of the "The Raven" rendered it eminently repeatable, inviting reproduction and reappropriations that served to amplify Poe's repute. Recitations were offered not only by Poe but by other fans of the poem; parodies were produced; reprints flourished; and "Nevermore" became a watchword.[51] The publication of "The Raven" gave Poe his single taste of what achieved celebrity might be like. "I find my Raven is really being talked about a great deal," Poe told Elizabeth Oakes Smith shortly after its publication. For once, he was not exaggerating. Less than a fortnight after its appearance, the New York *Town* was describing it as enjoying "a wide celebrity." Still more significant an index of celebrity status was the conflation of the author with his work. When she first heard "The Raven" recited, Smith had announced: "It is Edgar Poe himself." Nathaniel P. Willis, likewise, in printing the poem, described it as full of "pokerishness." Yet more than associating Poe with the poem, people associated the poem with Poe. While hosting a party at which Poe was a guest, Dr. John Francis introduced the poet to his wife and others present with the announcement: "Eliza, my dear—'The Raven!'" Others also made the association. Meeting with two fans at his house in the 1840s, Poe told them that visitors often expected to see a raven above his own door and explained to his clearly disappointed guests that a print on the wall was not of Lenore. Poe had finally achieved his brand.[52]

For Poe, 1845 turned out to be his *annus mirabilis*. The publication of "The Raven" in January and of *Tales* and *The Raven and Other Poems* by Wiley and Putnam later in the year, control of the *Broadway Journal*, and the sensation made by the publication, at the end of the year, of "Facts in the Case of M. Valdemar" put Poe in the public's eye as never before. He was included by Thomas Dunn English in the latter's "Notes on Men of Note" series in the *Aristidean*, a series not unlike his own "Literati," and received many other tokens of celebrity status. He was invited, for example, to a wide number of parties and salons at which he was the guest of honor.[53] Fan mail began to arrive too, along with requests for autographs and for samples of his hair.[54]

Yet even as he enjoyed the kudos and attention that came from such achievements, he found his celebrity neutralized and then undermined by the notoriety he generated through his conflicts with Longfellow and his weak performance at the Boston Lyceum.[55] The very networks that had enabled the circulation of "The Raven" now became the conduits through which innuendo and criticism of Poe flowed. Insinuations of impropriety began to circulate, too, and the invitations to salons began to dry up. Not long after the publication of "The Raven," Thomas Holley Chivers saw Poe harangued by "a man standing on the steps of either a Whiskey-Shop, or a Restaurant, Spouting at the top of his voice in his praise— calling him the '*Shakespeare of America.*'" Chivers was horrified by what he took to be mockery. Poe was both drunk and indifferent. To be humiliated by hyperbolic praise was absolutely fitting for a man who could neither live with, or without, acclaim.[56]

Poe hoped to be recognized as an achievement-oriented celebrity, but he found himself, instead, regarded as what Chris Rojek calls a "celetoid": a "compressed, concentrated, attributed celebrity" or flash-in-the-pan. The coup de grâce was delivered by a writer in the *American Whig Review* slightly less than a year after it had caused a sensation by publishing Poe's "Raven" and "Valdemar." "A newspaper reputation can be made in a day," this author wrote,

> and by pickling and ordinary care may be made to last like the gravedigger's tanner, "some eight year or nine year," or it may be caught like the mesmerized M. Valdemar *in articulo mortis,* by a special conjurer six months longer, till it falls to pieces, a "nearly liquid mass of loathsome, detestable putrescence."[57]

Seeking to play string-puller to his own puppet, mesmerist to his own Valdemar, Poe had awoken to find his reputation had, indeed, fallen to pieces.

"MY LAST JEST"

In May 1849, mere months before his death, Poe published "Hop-Frog: or, the Eight Chained Orang-Outangs." The story of a crippled dwarf jester's fiery revenge on his royal tormentors, "Hop-Frog" has been commonly and very rightly read as a commentary on slavery, although whether it reflects a pro- or antislavery position remains a point of contention among scholars.[58] Compelling though I find the slave-inflected readings of this tale to be, I would like to suggest that "Hop-Frog" can just as aptly be read as Poe's loosely veiled commentary on the evils of celebrity culture. While it is true, for example, that "Hop-Frog" is a captive from a distant country, his diminutive body calls to mind less African American slaves and more the then-popular Charles Stratton—General Tom Thumb—who was being promoted by the very embodiment of celebrity manipulation, P. T. Barnum. Hop-Frog's deformity, likewise, seems to resonate little with the situation of African American slaves but powerfully with the exhibition of human oddities by Barnum. And, indeed, Hop-Frog's status as a jester—and entertainer—with a facility for proposing *"characters* . . . something novel"* (words repeated and italicized throughout the story) suggests that whatever else he might have had in mind, Poe was thinking of the way in which literary performers were exploited and manipulated by powerful cabals, just as Hop-Frog and his companion Tripetta are exploited by the king and his seven courtiers. Hop-Frog's inability to handle alcohol, finally, mirrors Poe's own closely enough that the association between author and eponymous jester becomes fairly compelling.[59] If "Hop-Frog" is, as I am proposing, a parable concerning the nature of celebrity culture, then what message, or fantasy, might it be advancing? Once again, we witness Poe's obsession with status incoherence as he depicts the "little man" struggling in a world of bloated and talentless figureheads less intelligent than he; once again, we see Poe's ambivalence about colluding with a rotten system as Hop-Frog is simultaneously bullied into staging his masquerade and yet takes on the role with gusto; and once again we see the concern with wire-pulling and puppetry literalized as Hop-Frog, with Tripetta's assistance, hoists the king and his courtiers into the air above the masqueraders and then burns them alive. Hop-Frog, the victim of larger but lesser men has turned the tables to become the man who pulls the strings. Hop-Frog's *"last jest,"* as he calls it, is a spectacle of savagery that leaves the reader suspended him- or herself between pity and disgust. And Poe, too, apparently, felt equally ambivalent. Writing to Annie Richmond to tell her that he had completed a new tale, he exclaimed "Only think of *your* Eddy writing a story with *such* a name as 'Hop-Frog'! You would never guess the subject (which is a terrible one) from the title, I am sure." Yet a month later, he wrote her again, asking "did you get 'Hop-Frog?' I sent it to you by mail."[60] Poe could neither embrace his story or suppress it, come to terms with celebrity nor renounce it. A victim of status incoherence consumed by a feeling that the respect and approval he received were less than his talents merited, he came to believe both that celebrity and its institutions might offer the only chance to elevate his status *and* that deploying the techniques of celebrity made him as mendacious as any of the lesser talents he criticized. Never able to take shelter for very long under the wing of a patron who would promote him in such a way as to bring him recognition, Poe sought to become his own showman: Pompey and Smith, Barnum and Tom Thumb, King and Jester, exploiter and exploited.

Notes

1. Mary Gove Nichols, *Reminiscences of Edgar Poe* (New York: Union Square Book Shop, 1931), 11–12.

2. Maurice S. Lee, "Poe by the Numbers: Odd Man Out?" and Betsy Erkkila, "Perverting the American Renaissance: Poe, Democracy, Critical Theory," both in this volume.

3. "Fame" and "Celebrity" are both absent from J. Lasley Dameron and Louis Charles Stagg, *An Index to Poe's Critical Vocabulary* (Hartford, CT: Transcendental Books, 1966).

4. See Gerhard E. Lenski, "Status Crystallization: A Non-Vertical Dimension of Social Status," *American Sociological Review* 19, no. 4 (August 1954): 405–13; Robert Edward Mitchell, "Methodological Notes on a Theory of Status Crystallization," *Public Opinion Quarterly* 28, no. 2 (1964): 315–25; Paul V. Crosbie, "Effects of Status Inconsistency: Negative Evidence from Small Groups," *Social Psychology Quarterly* 42, no. 2 (1979): 110–25; and Xiaotian Zhang, "Status Inconsistency Revisited: An Improved Statistical Method," *European Sociological Review* 24, no. 2 (2008): 155–68. Bourdieu's theories of capital are most succinctly summarized in Pierre Bourdieu, "The Forms of Capital," in *Handbook of Theory and Research for the Sociology of Education*, ed. J. G. Richardson (New York: Greenwood, 1986): 241–58.

5. See Murray Milner Jr., *Status and Sacredness: A General Theory of Status Relations and an Analysis of Indian Culture* (New York: Oxford Univ. Press, 1994), 29–41; Milner, *Freaks, Geeks, and Cool Kids: American Teenagers, Schools, and the Culture of Consumption* (New York: Routledge, 2004), 30–33.

6. Edgar Allan Poe to James K. Paulding, 19 July 1838, in *The Letters of Edgar Allan Poe*, ed. John Ward Ostrom (New York: Gordian Press, 1966), vol. 2: 681. References to this edition are hereinafter cited as *L* followed by volume and page numbers.

7. John E. Semmes, *John H. B. Latrobe and his Times, 1803–1891* (Baltimore: Norman, Remington Co., 1917), 562; *The Poe Log: A Documentary Life of Edgar Allan Poe, 1809–1849*, comp. Dwight Thomas and David K. Jackson (New York: G. K. Hall, 1987), 404.

8. Edgar Allan Poe, *Essays and Reviews*, ed. G. R. Thompson (New York: Library of America, 1984), 1417. References to this edition are hereinafter cited as *ER* followed by page numbers. I have explored this beat-and-join dynamic with respect to Poe's engagement with writing competitions in *The Business of Letters: Authorial Economies in Antebellum America* (Palo Alto, CA: Stanford Univ. Press, 2008), 218–30. For the original insight, I am indebted to Kenneth Silverman, *Edgar A. Poe: Mournful and Never-Ending Remembrance* (New York: Harper, 1991), 115–16.

9. On David Poe, see Silverman, *Edgar A. Poe*, 25, 197. For republican notions of fame, see Douglass Adair, "Fame and the Founding Fathers," in *Fame and the Founding Fathers: Essays by Douglass Adair*, ed. Trevor Colbourn (New York: W. W. Norton, 1974), 4–26. Poe's military career and aspirations are carefully assayed by William F. Hecker, "Introduction: Private Perry and Mister Poe," in *Private Perry and Mister Poe: The West Point Poems, 1831*, ed. Hecker (Baton Rouge: Louisiana State Univ. Press, 2005), xvii–lxvii. As Hecker shows, Poe felt as out of place in the military world as he did in civilian life.

10. Silverman, *Edgar A. Poe*, 97, 36. On biographies lauding merchants, see Scott E. Casper, *Constructing American Lives: Biography and Culture in Nineteenth-Century America* (Chapel Hill: Univ. of North Carolina Press, 1999), 89–91, 93–94. For Poe's relationship with Hunt, see Burton R. Pollin, "Poe, Freeman Hunt, and Four Unrecorded Reviews of Poe's Works," *Texas Studies in Literature and Language* 16 (1974): 305–13. David Leverenz artfully treats Poe's engagement with John Allan as an avatar of southern respectability in "Poe and Gentry Virginia," in *The American Face of Edgar Allan Poe*, ed. Shawn Rosenheim and Stephen Rachman (Baltimore: Johns Hopkins Univ. Press, 1995), 210–36.

11. Silverman, *Edgar A. Poe*, 8, 250. On Poe's mother, see Geddeth Smith, *The Brief Career of Eliza Poe* (London: Associated Univ. Press, 1988).

12. Scholars of status and celebrity have not tended to draw upon one another's works. For a rare and illuminating exception, see Murray Milner Jr., "Celebrity Culture as a Status System," *Hedgehog Review* 7 (Spring 2005): 66–77.

13. Wines: Edgar Allan Poe, *Collected Works*, ed. Thomas Ollive Mabbott (Cambridge, Mass: Belknap Press of Harvard Univ. Press, 1978), vol. 2: 101. This edition is hereinafter abbreviated as *CW* followed by volume and page numbers. Ways of speaking: *CW* 2: 342. Landscapes: *CW* 3: 1278. Poems: *ER*, 448. Magazines: *L* 1: 57.

14. A sampling of the recent works from which I draw these insights includes: Joshua Gamson, *Claims to Fame: Celebrity in Contemporary America* (Berkeley: Univ. of California Press, 1994); David Giles, *Illusions of Immortality: A Psychology of Fame and Celebrity* (New York:· St. Martin's, 2000); Chris Rojek, *Celebrity* (London: Reaktion Books, 2001); Graeme Turner, *Understanding Celebrity* (London: Sage, 2004); Ellis Cashmore, *Celebrity / Culture* (New York: Routledge, 2006); and Neal Gabler, "Toward a New Definition of Celebrity," Norman Lear Center, Annenberg School of Communication, Univ. of Southern California, 2001, www.learcenter.org/pdf/Gabler.pdf.

15. For celebrity as a twentieth-century phenomenon, see Richard Schickel, *Intimate Strangers: The Culture of Celebrity* (New York: Fromm, 1986), 31. Celebrity's seventeenth-century origins are asserted by Joseph Roach, *It* (Ann Arbor: Univ. of Michigan Press, 2007). Works that trace a recognizable culture of celebrity to the early nineteenth century in America include: Susan Barrera Fay, "A Modest Celebrity: Literary Reputation and the Marketplace in Antebellum America," Ph.D. diss., George Washington Univ., 1992; Peter Cherches, "Star Course: Popular Lectures and the Marketing of Celebrity in Nineteenth-Century America," Ph.D. diss., New York Univ., 1997; Thomas N. Baker, *Sentiment and Celebrity: Nathaniel Parker Willis and the Trials of Literary Fame* (New York: Oxford Univ. Press, 1999); Bonnie Carr, "Singular Success: Authors as Celebrities in Mid-Nineteenth-Century America," Ph.D. diss., Washington Univ., 2003; David Haven Blake, *Walt Whitman and the Culture of American Celebrity* (New Haven, CT: Yale Univ. Press, 2006); Sarah Babcox First, "The Mechanics of Renown; or, The Rise of a Celebrity Culture in Early America," Ph.D. diss., Univ. of Michigan, 2009; and Karah Elizabeth Rempe, "Intimacy in Print: Literary Celebrity and Public Interiority in Nineteenth-Century American Literature," Ph.D. diss., Univ. of North Carolina, 2009. An early and disparaging view of celebrity that traces it to the "graphic revolution" of the nineteenth century can be found in Daniel J. Boorstin, *The Image: A Guide to Pseudo-Events in America* (1961; New York: Vintage, 1992).

16. Forrest: Richard Moody, *Edwin Forrest: First Star of the American Stage* (New York: Alfred A. Knopf, 1960). Stars: Leon Jackson, "Rising Stars and Raging Diseases: The Rhetoric and Reality of Antebellum Canonization," *Prospects* 25 (2000): 159–76. Ellsler: Ivor Guest, *Fanny Ellsler* (Middletown, CT: Wesleyan Univ. Press, 1970), 104–86. Lind: P. T. Barnum, *The Life of P. T. Barnum* (Urbana: Univ. of Illinois Press, 2000), 296–343. Dickens: Sidney P. Moss, *Charles Dickens' Quarrel with America* (Troy, NY: Whitson, 1984). Fan mail: Jill E. Anderson, "'Send Me a

Nice Little Letter All to Myself': Henry Wadsworth Longfellow's Fan Mail and Antebellum Poetic Culture," unpublished essay, 2004, copy of paper in author's possession. L. H. Sigourney, *Letters of Life* (New York: Appleton, 1866), 367–80; Baker, *Sentiment and Celebrity*, 90–96. Warner: Anna B. Warner, *Susan Warner* (New York: Putnam's, 1909), 345. Stowe: Stephen A. Hirsch, "Uncle Tomitudes: The Popular Reaction to 'Uncle Tom's Cabin,'" *Studies in the American Renaissance*, ed. Joel Myerson (Boston: Twayne, 1978), 303–30. Daguerreotypes: Susan S. Williams, *Confounding Images: Photography and Portraiture in Antebellum American Fiction* (Philadelphia: Univ. of Pennsylvania Press, 1997), 41–45, 132–34. Willis, Lind, and Fern: Richard H. Brodhead, *Cultures of Letters: Scenes of Reading and Writing in Nineteenth-Century America* (Chicago: Univ. of Chicago Press, 1993), 62; Baker, *Sentiment and Celebrity*, 158–86; Joyce W. Warren, *Fanny Fern: An Independent Woman* (New Brunswick, NJ: Rutgers Univ. Press, 1992), 120–42. Barnum: Bluford Adams, *E Pluribus Barnum: The Great Showman and the Making of U. S. Popular Culture* (Minneapolis: Univ. of Minnesota Press, 1997).

17. *Portfolio* (July 1814), quoted in William Ellery Leonard, *Byron and Byronism in America* (Boston: Nichols Press, 1905), 23; [William Cullen Bryant], "Defense of Poetry," *North American Review* 34, no. 74 (January 1832): 75–76.

18. See *Byromania: Portraits of the Artist in Nineteenth- and Twentieth-Century Culture*, ed. Frances Wilson (New York: Palgrave Macmillan, 1999); Tom Mole, *Byron's Romantic Celebrity: Industrial Culture and the Hermeneutic of Intimacy* (New York: Palgrave Macmillan, 2007); and Ghislaine McDayter, *Byromania and the Birth of Celebrity Culture* (Albany: State Univ. of New York Press, 2009). On Poe's engagements with Byron, see Silverman, *Edgar A. Poe*, 30, 41.

19. Edgar Allan Poe, *Doings of Gotham*, ed. Thomas Ollive Mabbott (Pottsville, NY: Jacob E. Spannuth, 1929), 42–43; Sidney P. Moss, "Poe's 'Two Long Interviews' with Dickens," *Poe Studies* 11 (1978): 10–12.

20. Mole, *Byron's Romantic Celebrity*, 1.

21. For the deeply suspicious mentality engendered by Enlightenment epistemology and republican politics, see Gordon S. Wood, "Conspiracy and the Paranoid Style: Causality and Deceit in the Eighteenth Century," *William and Mary Quarterly*, 3d ser., vol. 39 (1982): 401–41; and James H. Hutson, "The Origins of 'The Paranoid Style in American Politics': Public Jealousy from the Age of Walpole to the Age of Jackson," in *Saints and Revolutionaries: Essays on Early American History*, ed. David D. Hall, John M. Murrin, and Thad W. Tate (New York: W. W. Norton, 1984), 332–72. On the practice of puppetry in nineteenth-century America and England and the range of resonances it engendered, see Paul McPharlin, *Puppet Theater in America: A History with a List of Puppeteers, 1524–1948* (New York: Harper & Brothers, 1949); John McCormick with Clodagh McCormick and John Phillips, *The Victorian Marionette Theatre* (Iowa City: Univ. of Iowa Press, 2004); and Scott Cutler Shershow, *Puppets and "Popular" Culture* (Ithaca, NY: Cornell Univ. Press, 1995).

22. Henry Wikoff, *The Reminiscences of an Idler* (New York: Fords, Howard, and Hulbert, 1880), 464; "Tarrif Petitions vs. Free Trade," *Brooklyn Daily Eagle*, 30 June 1842; "Political Corruption," *American Whig Review* 3 (May 1846): 463; "Political Miscellany," *United States Magazine and Democratic Review* 26 (April 1850): 374.

23. J. E. Snodgrass, "Quotidiana," *Southern Literary Messenger* 7 (January 1841): 64; Willis quoted in Baker, *Sentiment and Celebrity*, 44; Burton Pollin, "'The Living Writers of America': A Manuscript by Edgar Allan Poe," *Studies in the American Renaissance*, ed. Joel Myerson (Charlottesville: University Press of Virginia, 1991), 165. My reading of this phrase clearly differs from that of J. Gerald Kennedy, "Inventing the Literati: Poe's Remapping of Antebellum Print Culture," in this volume, which sees the "wires" as referring to what holds the literary public together. For

another example of the wire-pulling trope deployed to literary ends, see Fanny Fern, *Fern Leaves from Fanny's Port-Folio* (Auburn, NY: Derby and Miller, 1853), 327.

24. For the period's fascination with automata, see James W. Cook, *The Arts of Deception: Playing with Fraud in the Age of Barnum* (Cambridge, MA: Harvard Univ. Press, 2001), esp. 30–72.

25. See, for example, John Tresch, "'The Potent Magic of Verisimilitude': Edgar Allan Poe within the Mechanical Age," *British Journal for the History of Science* 30 (1997): 275–90.

26. Puppets: *ER*, 314, 1157; *L* 1: 193.

27. *ER*, 761. On Poe's elaborate theory of the signifying capacity of printed materials, see Leon Jackson, "'The Italics Are Mine': Edgar Allan Poe and the Semiotics of Print," in *Illuminating Letters: Typography and Literary Interpretation*, ed. Paul C. Gutjahr and Megan L. Benton (Amherst: Univ. of Massachusetts Press, 2001), 139–61. For a searching analysis of Poe's mind-body dualism, see David Leverenz, "Spanking the Master: Mind-Body Crossings in Poe's Sensationalism," in *A Historical Guide to Edgar Allan Poe*, ed. J. Gerald Kennedy (New York: Oxford Univ. Press, 2001), 95–127.

28. *ER*, 1120. On Poe's attitude toward Willis's fame—at once resentful and envious—see Scott Peeples, "'The *Mere* Man of Letters Must Ever Be a Cipher': Poe and N. P. Willis," *ESQ* 46 (2000): 125–47.

29. Poe to John Pendleton Kennedy, 11 February 1836, *L* 1: 84. *CW* 2: 177. For readings that emphasize the tale's satiric freight, see Richard P. Benton, "Poe's 'Lionizing': A Quiz on Willis and Lady Blessington," *Studies in Short Fiction* 5 (1968): 239–44; G. R. Thompson, "On the Nose: Further Speculation on the Sources and Meaning of Poe's 'Lionizing,'" *Studies in Short Fiction* 6 (1968): 94–96; and Alexander Hammond, "Poe's 'Lionizing' and the Design of 'Tales of the Folio Club,'" *ESQ* 18 (1972): 154–65. On the "lion" as a transitional form of celebrity, see Richard Salmon, "The Physiognomy of the Lion: Encountering Literary Celebrity in the Nineteenth Century," in *Romanticism and Celebrity Culture, 1750–1850*, ed. Tom Mole (Cambridge, UK: Cambridge Univ. Press, 2009), 60–78.

30. *CW* 2: 380, 386, 388. On "Used Up" as a critique of military fame, see David Haven Blake, "'The Man That Was Used Up': Edgar Allan Poe and the Ends of Captivity," *Nineteenth-Century Literature* 57, no. 3 (2002): 323–49.

31. *ER*, 642. Poe, of course, was absolutely correct in noting that physicality—along with, more generally, the visibly tangible—was central to the development of celebrity relations, and he would exploit the phenomenon in his gossipy physical descriptions of authors in "The Literati of New York City" (1846).

32. Sidney P. Moss, *Poe's Literary Battles: The Critic in the Context of His Literary Milieu* (Carbondale: Southern Illinois Univ. Press, 1969), 68–69. Moss makes clear that attacks on cliques were a career-long preoccupation for Poe.

33. See Baker, *Sentiment and Celebrity*.

34. Peeples, "'The *Mere* Man of Letters Must Ever Be a Cipher,'" 131. For "branding" as a central feature of celebrity, see Mole, *Byron's Romantic Celebrity*, 16–22. On Poe's critical brand, see Leon Jackson, "'Behold Our Literary Mohawk, Poe': Literary Nationalism and the 'Indianation' of Antebellum American Culture," *ESQ* 48 (2002): 97–133.

35. On the "operational aesthetic," see Neil Harris, *Humbug: The Arts of P. T. Barnum* (Chicago: Univ. of Chicago Press, 1973), esp. 61–89.

36. [Thomas Holley Chivers], *Chivers' Life of Poe*, ed. Richard Beale Davis (New York: E. P. Dutton, 1952), 62; Sidney P. Moss, *Poe's Major Crisis: His Libel Suit and New York's Literary World* (Durham, NC: Duke Univ. Press, 1970), xvii. For Poe's lifelong quest for approbation, see Jackson, *Business of Letters*, 218–30.

37. See, especially, Gabler, "Toward a New Definition of Celebrity."

38. For Poe's substantial and patently misleading autobiographical statements, see "Memorandum," *Complete Works of Edgar Allan Poe,* ed. James A. Harrison (New York: Thomas Y. Crowell, 1903), vol. 1: 344–46 (this text is hereinafter cited as *H,* followed by volume and page numbers); "Edgar Allan Poe," *Saturday Museum,* 4 March 1843. Falsehoods from each document traveled far. Circulation figures: Terence Whalen, *Edgar Allan Poe and the Masses: The Political Economy of Literature in Antebellum America* (Princeton, NJ: Princeton Univ. Press, 1999), 58–75. Actress: *H* 12: 186. Arnold: *L* 1: 22.

39. *L* 1: 57; Clarence Brigham, "Edgar Allan Poe's Contributions to Alexander's Weekly Messenger," *Proceedings of the American Antiquarian Society* 52 (1942): 78; "Edgar Allan Poe," *Saturday Museum.*

40. See Burton R. Pollin, "Poe's Authorship of Three Long Critical and Autobiographical Articles of 1843 Now Authenticated," *American Renaissance Literary Report* 7 (1993): 139–71.

41. Leverenz, "Poe and Gentry Virginia," 223.

42. Michael J. Deas, *The Portraits and Daguerreotypes of Edgar Allan Poe* (Charlottesville: Univ. Press of Virginia, 1989); William A. Pannapacker, "A Question of 'Character': Visual Images and the Nineteenth-Century Construction of Edgar Allan Poe," *Harvard Library Bulletin* 7 (1996): 9–24; Susan S. Williams, "Daguerreotyping Hawthorne and Poe," *Poe Studies / Dark Romanticism* 37 (2004): 14–20; and Kevin J. Hayes, "Poe, the Daguerreotype, and the Autobiographical Act," *Biography* 25, no. 3 (2002): 477–92.

43. *ER,* 1322–23. On handwriting analysis in antebellum America, see Tamara Plakins Thornton, *Handwriting in America: A Cultural History* (New Haven, CT: Yale Univ. Press, 1996).

44. See, especially, Jonathan Elmer, *Reading at the Social Limit: Affect, Mass Culture, and Edgar Allan Poe* (Palo Alto, CA: Stanford Univ. Press, 1995), 37–47.

45. *CW* 2: 262. See Thornton, *Handwriting in America,* 71–86. Ironically, Poe would pose as an autograph hunter and write a pseudonymous letter to Sarah Helen Whitman in 1848 asking for hers as a way of ascertaining whether she was still living in Providence (*L* 2: 379).

46. Unsolicited fan mail: Jackson, *Business of Letters,* 89–95, 163–64; Anderson, "'Send Me a Nice Little Letter All to Myself'"; Sigourney, *Letters of Life,* 367–80.

47. Kennedy, "Inventing the Literati," in this volume. On the enduringly local nature of literary culture in the antebellum period, see Trish Loughran, *The Republic in Print: Print Culture in the Age of U.S. Nation Building, 1770–1870* (New York: Columbia Univ. Press, 2007).

48. *H* 15: 178–79; Benedict Anderson, *Imagined Communities: Reflections on the Origin and Spread of Nationalism,* rev. ed. (London: Verso, 1991).

49. *H* 15: 191, 239, 182, 216, 188, 258, 213.

50. Milner, *Freaks, Geeks, and Cool Kids,* 87–94; *Poe Log,* 452.

51. See Eliza Richards, "Poe's Lyrical Media: The Raven's Returns," in this volume.

52. *Poe Log,* 497, 502, 496; Silverman, *Edgar A. Poe,* 238; Carroll D. Laverty, "Poe in 1847," *American Literature* 20 (1948): 165.

53. On Poe's participation in New York's salon culture, see Eliza Richards, *Gender and the Poetics of Reception in Poe's Circle* (Cambridge, UK: Cambridge Univ. Press, 2004).

54. On hair clippings as gifts creating intimacy, see Helen Sheumaker, *Love Entwined: The Curious History of Hairwork in America* (Philadelphia: Univ. of Pennsylvania Press, 2007). For a request for Poe's hair, see *Poe Log,* 637. At least six locks of Poe's hair exist in various collections, suggesting that he gave them out on occasion. See "Non-Manuscript Poe Artifacts," www.eapoe.org/geninfo/poeartfs.htm. "Berenice," in this respect, could be seen as a cruel commentary on souvenir collecting.

55. For a different reading of Poe's Lyceum presentation, see Greeson's "Poe's 1848," in this volume.

56. [Chivers], *Chivers' Life of Poe*, 57. Poe's fall from grace and involvement in a ruinous libel case is documented fully in Moss, *Poe's Major Crisis*.

57. "Literary Phenomena," *American Whig Review* 4 (October 1846): 406. For celetoids, see Rojek, *Celebrity*, 20–29.

58. For a recent and thoughtful analysis that helpfully summarizes the positions, see Paul Christian Jones, "The Danger of Sympathy: Edgar Allan Poe's 'Hop-Frog' and the Abolitionist Rhetoric of Pathos," *Journal of American Studies* 35, no. 2 (2001): 239–54.

59. *CW* 3: 1347. The one scholar to frame "Hop-Frog" by reference to Barnum is Paul Gilmore, *The Genuine Article: Race, Mass Culture, and American Literary Manhood* (Durham, NC: Duke Univ. Press, 2001), 98–124. For a convincing reading of the tale as an autobiographical allegory concerning literary production, see Scott Peeples, *Edgar Allan Poe Revisited* (New York: Twayne, 1998), 151–52.

60. *CW* 3: 1354; *L* 2: 425, 435.

II | Surveying the National Scene

Perverting the American Renaissance
Poe, Democracy, Critical Theory

BETSY ERKKILA

Nature produces only monsters and the whole question is to understand the word savages.

—CHARLES BAUDELAIRE, "New Notes on Edgar Allan Poe"

Fear, revulsion, and horror were the emotions which the big-city crowd aroused in those who first observed it. For Poe it has something barbaric; discipline just barely manages to tame it.

—WALTER BENJAMIN, "On Some Motifs in Baudelaire"

The figure of Edgar Allan Poe made F. O. Matthiessen anxious and uneasy. It was as if he feared a return of the repressed that might erode the story of America's first artistic cultural flowering that he seeks to tell in *American Renaissance: Art and Expression in the Age of Emerson and Whitman* (1941). Matthiessen's now seminal study not only named a period and defined a canon (Emerson, Thoreau, Hawthorne, Melville, and Whitman); it also set the critical, evaluative, and New England–centered terms within which future readings and interpretations of American literature would occur.

Poe did not fit within Matthiessen's explicitly nationalist design of "producing a renaissance" of mid-nineteenth-century American culture commensurate with America's emergence in the post–World War I period as a major economic and political power on the stage of the world. Although Matthiessen tells a comparative, transatlantic, and interdisciplinary story that begins in the English Renaissance with Shakespeare, Milton, and the Metaphysicals and then migrates across the Atlantic to New England Puritanism, the American Renaissance, and Henry James and T. S. Eliot in the twentieth century, his American Renaissance is at the same time an idyllic moment of specifically literary creation (1850–55) cordoned off from its pre-history in the revolutions in America, France, and Santo

Domingo in the late eighteenth century and destroyed by technology, the factory, and "rising forces of exploitation" in the post–Civil War period. Poe's presence would have disrupted this idyllic vision by exposing the terrors of revolution, technology, the factory, and the "rising forces of exploitation" that lay *inside* and not *outside* Matthiessen's American Renaissance as its underlying specter.

And yet, given the new critical protocols that underwrite the approach Matthiessen describes in his preface, "Method and Scope," a primary concern with *what* the books were "as works of art," a concentration "entirely on the foreground, on the writing itself," a focus on close reading and analysis of "masterworks," and an evaluation of these works "in accordance with the enduring requirements for great art," the exclusion of Poe seems baffling.[1] For it was Poe more than Emerson, Whitman, or any other writer in *American Renaissance* who was the first to turn away from what Matthiessen calls "belletristic trifling" to write serious literary criticism focused on "*what* books were as works of art." Poe formulated a theory of art for art's sake, he emphasized "unity of effect" as the underlying principle of both the poem and the short story, and in review after review for the *Southern Literary Messenger, Graham's Magazine,* the *Broadway Journal,* and other contemporary journals, he invented a new kind of literary criticism based on close reading, formal analysis, and aesthetic evaluation. If this critical enterprise earned Poe the nickname of "tomahawk man" among his contemporaries, through his influence on French symbolism and what T. S. Eliot called an aesthetic tradition that focuses with "increasing consciousness of language" on "*la poésie pure,*"[2] Poe reentered the American literary tradition and literary criticism during the Cold War years in the name of art for art's sake, aesthetic formalism, and the new criticism—the very "method" if not "the scope" that frames Matthiessen's study.

"The great attraction of my subject was its compactness," Matthiessen explained. "Emerson's theory of expression was that on which Thoreau built, to which Whitman gave extension, and to which Hawthorne and Melville were indebted by being forced to react against its philosophical assumptions." Emerson was "the cow from which the rest drew their milk." Matthiessen's elucidation of this "somewhat complex method" registers Poe's exclusion metatextually by treating him as a footnote to the subject of artistic and ultimately national *compactness* or unity:

> I have avoided, therefore, the *temptation* to include a full length treatment of Poe. The reason is more fundamental than that his work fell mainly in the decade of 1835–45; for it relates at very few points to the main assumptions about literature

that were held by any of my group. *Poe was bitterly hostile to democracy,* and in that respect could serve as a revelatory contrast. But the chief interest in treating his work would be to examine the effect of his *narrow but intense theories of poetry and the short story. . . .* My reluctance at not dealing with Poe here is tempered by the fact that *his value, even more than Emerson's, is now seen to consist in his influence rather than the body of his own work.* No group of poems seems as enduring as *Drum-Taps;* and his stories, less harrowing upon the nerves than they were, seem relatively *factitious* when contrasted with the *moral depth of Hawthorne or Melville.*[3]

The language of "temptation" is itself revealing, suggesting the impulses of desire and fear that drive Matthiessen's exclusion and a possible fall from American paradise into the "harrowing" reality of everyday nineteenth-century life were he to incorporate "the body" of Poe's work into his "compact" narrative. The reasons Matthiessen gives for Poe's exclusion are themselves "factitious." Poe's work, he claims, fell outside the "concentrated moment" of renaissance. But this does not prevent him from opening and indeed grounding his "renaissance" in *Nature,* Emerson's 1836 manifesto of Transcendentalism, and several other essays—"The American Scholar," "Self-Reliance," and "The Poet"—also written between 1835 and 1845; nor does it prevent him from leaping over Whitman's first edition of *Leaves of Grass,* which was published within the "half-decade" of cultural flowering between 1851 and 1855, in order to denigrate Poe's poems in comparison with the "enduring" value of Whitman's *Drum-Taps,* which was not published until the end of the Civil War in 1865. Having dismissed Poe's "narrow but intense theories of poetry and the short story," Matthiessen acknowledges (in the same sentence) Poe's transnational influence on a range of writing from "Baudelaire, through the French symbolists, to modern American and English poetry."[4]

But Matthiessen's reason for excluding Poe is "more fundamental"—and ideologically driven: "The one common denominator of my five writers, uniting even Hawthorne and Whitman, was their devotion to the possibilities of democracy," he avers. Poe, on the other hand, was an ideological outlier, "bitterly hostile to democracy." The baldness of Matthiessen's assertion that he has excluded Poe on primarily ideological grounds surprises, in part because it so completely contradicts the new critical distinction between political background and aesthetic foreground that frames his study. Having dismissed "[t]he older liberalism" as "the background from which [his] writers emerged" in order to concentrate "entirely on the foreground, the writing itself," Matthiessen nevertheless expels Poe for being insufficiently liberal, that is to say, democratic.[5]

There is in effect no room for political opposition in Matthiessen's seemingly seamless narrative of America "producing a renaissance, by coming to its first maturity and affirming its rightful heritage in the whole expanse of art and culture."[6] "Democracy" as Matthiessen uses the term is no longer a particular system of governance but the site of an ideological consensus, the universal end and truth not only of American history, but all history that would come to define the liberal consensus of the Cold War years. Matthiessen's exclusion of Poe on purely ideological grounds—and his admission that this *is* the "fundamental" cause for exclusion—is particularly ironic because it appears to mirror the very acts of totalitarian repression—under Fascism or Communism—that Matthiessen's "democracy" and American liberalism sought to oppose. Ironically, too, by excluding Poe, Matthiessen also reveals the truth of political intolerance and repression that is part of the socially and psychologically perverse counternarrative of American democratic history that Poe's writings tell.

MARGINS AND CENTERS

Walt Whitman, who attended the reburial of Poe's bones in Baltimore in November 1875, had a very different view of Poe's centrality and place in American literary history. In an account of Poe's funeral, originally published in the *Washington Star* on 16 November 1875 and later included in Whitman's *Specimen Days and Collect* (1882), Whitman confesses: "For a long while, and until lately, I had a distaste for Poe's writings. I wanted, and still want for poetry, the clear sun shining and fresh air blowing." But, he continues, "Poe's genius has yet conquer'd a special recognition for itself, and I too have come to fully admit it, and appreciate it and him." Whitman embodies his new appreciation of Poe in a dream he once had of a schooner "flying uncontroll'd" through a storm-tossed sea: "On the deck was a slender, slight, beautiful figure, a dim man, apparently enjoying all the terror, the murk, and the dislocation of which he was the center and the victim. That figure of my lurid dream might stand for Edgar Poe, his spirit, his fortunes, and his poems." In Whitman's view, Poe represented the "sub-currents (often more significant than the biggest surface ones)" of nineteenth-century democratic history. As center and victim of the nether side of the American dream turned nightmare, Poe best exemplified the "age's matter and malady" not by assent but by "contrast and contradiction" and "very often, in a strange spurning of, and reaction from them all."[7]

Whitman's relocation of Poe at the center rather than the margins of nineteenth-century American culture, his emphasis on Poe's "contrast and contradiction," and his critical reaction against his "age's matter and malady" provide the critical starting points for my own discussion of Poe and democracy. I want to argue that Poe's poems and tales are much more than expressions of personal psychology, sensational and horrific pulp written for a mass market, or mechanisms that go boo. Like Alfred Hitchcock in a later period, Poe's poems and tales sought to appeal to what he called "the critical and popular taste." Among the writers of the American Renaissance, Poe was the only writer who was fully dependent on his writing—and his craft—to make a living. In order to sell his tales, Poe self-consciously appealed to the popular taste for bone-chilling scenes of terror, excess, and violence. But as his canny satire of the sensationalist and stylistic excesses of the magazine trade in "How to Write a Blackwood's Article" evinces, Poe was a searing and at times mordantly funny critic of his age and times.

While recent work on Poe has replaced past notions of the un-American or primarily French face of Poe with an exploration of his American and sometimes primarily southern and racist sources and contexts, I want to press beyond this work to argue that in addition to being a poet and critic of his times, Poe was a moralist, a philosopher, and a metaphysician. His poems and his tales, as the French symbolists and some recent critics and theorists have recognized, were engaged in a deeply moral, philosophical, and ultimately metaphysical critique not only of the culture and politics of democracy in the Age of Jackson but of modernity and a whole view of Western progressive history grounded in Enlightenment reason, the advance of civilization, and its underlying faith, the perfectibility of man. Like Walter Benjamin, whose work on the shock effect of the city, the crowd, and modernity Poe anticipated and influenced, Poe took up the role of Benjamin's historical materialist in seeking "to brush history against the grain."[8] From "The City in the Sea," to "The Man That Was Used Up," to *Eureka,* Poe named the barbarism and violence to person, psyche, society, and world that underwrote the market revolution, the politics of democracy, and the westward march of civilization.

Poe's early poems and tales can be linked to a tradition of conservative political thought that declined during his time. Focusing on Poe's double-edged poetics of appealing to the "critical and popular" taste will show the ways that Poe's tales of what he called the "grotesque" and "arabesque" both satirize the culture and politics of democracy at the same time that they register and critique the forms of physical and psychic terror and destruction that marked the Age of Jackson. Poe's notion of the "Imp of the Perverse" is both a lens through which he critiques democratic and progressive history and a means, even more radical than

Freudian psychology, of anticipating the unconscious and the uncanny. Poe's anti-democratic, anti-progressive critique becomes more explicitly philosophical and metaphysical in his "Angelic Dialogues," and he pursues this critical strategy in his tales of detection as well as in *Eureka,* his simultaneously poetic and scientific exploration of the nature of the universe. Matthiessen himself returned to Poe in his 1948 essay in *The Literary History of the United States.* For all Matthiessen's ambivalence about Poe in his published work, the mystery surrounding Matthiessen's tragic leap to his death in 1950 might be read as a return of the repressed in the form of Poe's "Imp of the Perverse" and a "leap" into what Benjamin called "the open air of history"[9] that finally confirms by enacting Poe's dark vision of democratic and progressive history.

AESTHETICS AND POLITICS

In his preface to *The Liberal Imagination,* his influential meditation on the relation between liberalism and literature, published in 1950, Lionel Trilling reflects on the lack of any substantive conservative tradition that might force liberals to examine the weaknesses and complacencies of their position. "In the United States at this time liberalism is not only the dominant but even the sole intellectual tradition," Trilling observes. "For it is the plain fact that nowadays there are no conservative or reactionary ideas in general circulation."[10] Like Coleridge in relation to John Stuart Mill in nineteenth-century England, Poe was *the* American spokesperson for a fundamentally conservative set of political ideas that died in his lifetime, following the election of Thomas Jefferson to the presidency and what later historians have called "the Revolution of 1800."[11] In Jefferson's view, the election of 1800 signified the peaceful transition of power from the Federalists to the Democrats and thus an affirmation of the American experiment in democracy ushered in by the American Revolution. But "the Revolution of 1800" also came to signify the sovereignty of the American people in overthrowing Federalist tyranny in favor of popular democracy, and with the exception of the presidency of John Quincy Adams between 1824 and 1828, several decades of Democratic rule culminated in an expansion of the franchise among white men under Andrew Jackson, a growing valorization of the Declaration of Independence over the Constitution as the founding document of the nation, and an increasingly vocal and public appeal to the principles of individual liberty, equality, rights, and the dignity of the common man as the founding ideals of the country.

In Poe's earliest volumes of poems, *Tamerlane and Other Poems* (1827) and *Al*

Aaraaf, Tamerlane, and Minor Poems (1829), which were published during the years when Andrew Jackson came to power bearing a public rhetoric (if not reality) of democracy and the common man and an aggressive nationalist vision of westward expansion and empire, Poe set himself against the rising tide of democracy by defining a fundamentally conservative set of aesthetic and cultural values. Printed and circulated in limited editions, both volumes assert the values of poetry, beauty, and the heart against the debased and primarily didactic imperatives of the literary public sphere. Traditionally the title poem, "Tamerlane," like much of Poe's poetry, has been read as personal lyric inscription. "Poe took little from historic and dramatic sources," writes Thomas O. Mabbott, "his poem is largely a personal allegory, based on his unhappy love for his Richmond sweetheart, Sarah Elmira Royster."[12]

But as a poem that sets Tamerlane's desire for woman, love, and beauty against his "unearthly pride" and ambition for fame, conquest, and "the crush / Of empires," "Tamerlane," like other poems in these early volumes, including "Romance," "Sonnet—To Science," and "Al Aaraaf," is also an instance of the ways Poe's otherworldly aesthetics of beauty and purity also functions as a form of political and cultural critique. "I was ambitious," Tamerlane asserts, "A cottager, / I mark'd a throne / Of half the world as all my own."[13] This passage like others in the poem suggests the ways the story of Tamerlane's loss of woman and beauty through his ambitious pursuit of earthly conquest and power becomes not so much an allegory of Poe's love affair with Elmira Royster as it is a lyrical reflection on the tragedy of imperial history, especially as that history was being enacted by Andrew Jackson, whose ambitious rise to military and political power and aggressive policy of westward advance would be "consummated" by what he called "the removal of the Indians beyond the white settlements." "To follow to the tomb the last of his race and to tread on the graves of extinct nations excites melancholy reflections," Jackson observed in an address to Congress on 6 December 1830. "But true philanthropy reconciles the mind to these vicissitudes as it does to the extinction of one generation to make room for another."[14]

"Al Aaraaf," Poe's most radical experiment in pure aestheticism, anticipates in figurative and poetic form the idea of poetry as a realm of purely aesthetic experience that he would begin to define in "Letter to Mr. ———— ————," a prose introduction to *Poems of Edgar A. Poe* (1831). "A poem," Poe asserts, "is opposed to a work of science by having, for its *immediate* object, pleasure, not truth; to romance, by having for its object an *indefinite* instead of a *definite* pleasure, being a poem only so far as this object is attained."[15] Written at a time when Poe was

being disinherited from his expectations as a southern gentleman by his foster father, John Allan, "Letter" seeks to defend poetry and the poet as part of a cultural
elite—a kind of aristocracy of the mind—against both the masses and Poe's own
diminished status as the orphaned son of actors. Against "the world's good opinion," as it is represented by the democratic masses and the market, Poe sets up
what he calls "the Andes of the mind," a hierarchy of critical judgment and good
taste that rises "ascendingly" from the fools on the bottom to "a few gifted individuals" and "the master spirit," the poet, who stands on top.[16]

In *Poems* (1831), Poe also begins to accentuate three motifs that will become
increasingly important to his aesthetics, his critique of progressive history, and
his metaphysical vision: the idealized figure of woman as emblem of pure beauty,
pure love, and pure poetry in "To Helen"; fantasies of human and earthly disintegration in "Irene" (later "The Sleeper") and "The Valley of Nis" (later "The
Valley of Unrest"); and the specter of dark apocalypse in "The Doomed City"
(later "The City of Sin" and "The City in the Sea"). Like other southern writers,
Poe associated the ideal of fair womanhood—of what W. J. Cash has called "the
South's Palladium . . . Athena gleaming in the clouds"—with the social ideals and
health of southern culture.[17] "The glory of the Ancient Dominion is in a faint-
ing—in a dying condition," he wrote in 1835, in a comment that suggests the relation between the dying women of his poems and stories and increasing fears for
the health and survival of the plantation economy of the South. Virginia had become "a type for 'the things that have been,'" Poe lamented.[18] Although American critics have tended to read Poe's lyrics as forms of merely personal or perverse psychology, in Poe's 1841 angelic dialogue, "The Colloquy of Monos and
Una" (discussed below in section VI), the tone of mournfulness and the theme
of disintegration might be read as a melancholic response to the loss of a whole
way of southern life, grounded in what Poe called "the laws of *gradation*," under
the pressure of democratic and specifically northern industrial transformation.
Unlike "The Valley of Unrest," where the poet's mournfulness about "the ancient
days" is associated more generally with an "unquiet" landscape of "restlessness"
and "perennial tears"—"Nothing there is motionless"—in "The City in the Sea"
(originally "The Doomed City"), as in "The Colloquy of Monos and Una" (1841),
this melancholia is associated more specifically with the city and a hellish vision
of modern apocalypse:

> Lo! Death has reared himself a throne
> In a strange city lying alone

Far down within the dim West,
Where the good and the bad and the worst and the best
Have gone to their eternal rest.
There shrines and palaces and towers
(Time-eaten towers that tremble not!)
Resemble nothing that is ours.
Around, by lifting winds forgot,
Resignedly beneath the sky
The melancholy waters lie.

Critics have usually identified and indeed literalized the city as the legendary ruined cities of the Dead Sea, but Poe's reference to "a strange city" in "the dim
West" encodes several versions of the fall: the "dying condition" of the South
which Poe associated with the rise of industry, the city, "omni-prevalent Democracy," and the emancipation of slaves; the spiritual "doom" of America as "a city
upon a hill"; the end of human and enlightened history in the fall of the West;
and the material collapse of the universe as prophesied in Isaiah and Revelation,
whose language the poem echoes in its concluding vision of apocalypse:

But lo, a stir is in the air!
The wave—there is a movement there!
. . .
The waves have now a redder glow—
The hours are breathing faint and low—
And when, amid no earthy moans,
Down, down that town shall settle hence,
Hell, rising from a thousand thrones,
Shall do it reverence.

But while Poe echoes Biblical apocalypse, it is an apocalypse Poe-style, at once
historic doom, political jeremiad, poetic prophecy, and metaphysics.[19]

These different and overlapping nuances are evident in the changing title, content, and publication history of the poem as it moved from a more general vision
of historic doom—perhaps elicited by the social terrors of the Age of Jackson—
in "The Doomed City" of 1831, which appeared to prophesy the armed uprising
of Nat Turner, who led the bloodiest slave insurrection in history in August 1831,
only a few months after the poem was published; to the more specifically ethical
and southern jeremiad of "The City of Sin," which was published in the *Southern
Literary Messenger*, under Poe's editorship, in 1836; to a grim political judgment

against America itself in the retitled "The City in the Sea: A Prophecy," which was published in the *American Whig Review* in April 1845, along with "Some Words with a Mummy," Poe's satire of American democratic and progressive history; to the broader metaphysical reference it assumed when it was published in the *Broadway Journal* as "The City in the Sea," sans subtitle, in August 1845, at a time when Poe had undertaken the materialist critique of enlightenment philosophy, scientific empiricism, and progressive history in such tales as "Mesmeric Revelation," "The Power of Words," and "The Facts in the Case of M. Valdemar."[20] In this final printing, "The City in the Sea" reads as a chilling response to John O'Sullivan's announcement in the July 1845 issue of the *Democratic Review* that it was America's "manifest destiny to overspread the continent allotted by Providence for the free development of our yearly multiplying millions."[21] As one of Poe's most masterly poems, and one that appealed especially to the French symbolists and surrealists as an instance of *la poésie pure* in its other-worldly landscape and purely poetic language and effect, "The City in the Sea"—like "The Raven," which concludes with the specter of the Raven "sitting on the pallid bust of Pallas," and "El Dorado," which concludes with the specter of the nothingness that impels the Gold Rush and human utopian desire—reveals the ways Poe's aesthetic aspiration toward beauty is bound up with an apocalyptic vision of psychic, social, and material collapse. In other words, Poe's poems of other-worldly aspiration and seemingly purely poetic effect were also engaged in a dialectical critique of democratic and progressive history that is still *now* and *ours*.

Brushing History against the Grain

In a brilliant meditation on the cultural treasures that are the spoils of "the triumphal procession" of history, Benjamin writes:

> There is no document of civilization which is not at the same time a document of barbarism. And just as such a document is not free of barbarism, barbarism taints also the manner in which it was transmitted from one owner to another. A historical materialist therefore dissociates himself from it as far as possible. He regards it as his task to brush history against the grain."[22]

Although Poe's writings, especially his tales of the thirties, are often viewed as obscure and un-American, even in his "Tales of the Folio Club" of 1832–33, a projected collection of tales set in Germanic and other exotic settings, Poe undertook a dark and at times savagely comic critique of some of the worst excesses of barbarism, violence, and genocide that were committed under the regime of Jackson in the name of democratic progress, the will of the people, and westward advance.[23] Like Benjamin's historical materialist, in tales such as "Epimanes" (1833), "Shadow: A Fable" (1835), "King Pest the First: A Tale Containing an Allegory" (1835), and "The Man That Was Used Up" (1839), Poe brushed democratic history against the grain.

The original title of "Epimanes" foregrounds its historical subject, the mad antics of Antiochus IV, an ancient Syrian King, surnamed Epiphanes ("illustrious"), but nicknamed "Epimanes" ("madman).[24] Later entitled "Four Beasts in One; The Homo-Cameleopard" when it was published in the Broadway Journal in 1845, the tale has received only passing attention as a satire of the "the baseness of the ancient mob" and "its modern counterpart" and a parody of the contemporary taste for historical fiction set in exotic places like the Middle East.[25] But the tale has been virtually unread as a multilayered and "against the grain" satirical critique of the blood, carnage, and social terror that underlay Andrew Jackson's rise to power on the backs of the very people in whose name he ruled.

Set in the Syrian city of Antioch, 3,830 years after the beginning of the world, "Epimanes" is staged as a dialogue between a knowing narrator and a naive spectator who, with "the advantages of a modern education," takes a "peep" at tyrannical conditions in idolatrous Antioch. The story works by comic inversion. As Edward Said has argued, in the eighteenth and nineteenth centuries, the Orient emerged as the Other of the Western imperial imagination, embodying the tyranny, passion, and excess against which Western reason, enlightenment, and civilization defined itself.[26] And yet over and over, the freak antics of the mad king and his riotous people mirror the political landscape of Jacksonian America, a mirroring that Poe accentuated in 1845 when he changed the title from the more specific "Epimanes" to the more generic reign of "Four Beasts in One." Not only are the West and modernity no more civilized than the East and antiquity: the Jacksonian rhetoric of democratic progress and the westward advance of civilization notwithstanding, *nothing* has changed from past to present.

The reign of the King Antiochus, like the reign of Jackson, is a theater of the absurd. The story features a massive procession of "the rabble," along with mountebanks, philosophers, "the principal courtiers of the palace," who beat "the populace with clubs," and swarms of wild beasts both enslaved and free. All are en route to a public spectacle staged by the mad king, who is dressed as a cameleopard (giraffe), to celebrate "the massacre of a thousand Jews." Mimicking the new politics of mass entertainment, parade, and public spectacle ushered in by

the Age of Jackson, "Epimanes" may allude in particular to Jackson's inaugura-
tion on 4 March 1829 when twenty thousand people flocked through the doors
and windows of the White House to shake Jackson's hand. "Never before had an
American ceremony of state turned into such a democratic and charismatic spectacle," writes a recent historian.[27] But some who actually attended the ceremony
shared the social terror of mob rule evoked in Poe's "Epimanes." "*The Majesty
of the People* had disappeared," recalled Margaret Bayard Smith, "and a rabble, a
mob, of boys, negroes, women, children, scrambling, fighting, romping. What a
pity what a pity." To Supreme Court Justice Joseph Story, "[t]he reign of KING
MOB seemed triumphant."[28]

At the center of Poe's political satire is a critique of the destructiveness and
blood carnage that underwrote Jackson's power. Like the "gladiatorial" spectacles that sustain Antiochus's imperial rule—"perhaps the massacre of the Scyth-
ian prisoners—or the conflagration of his new palace—or the tearing down of a
handsome temple—or, indeed, a bonfire of a few Jews"—Jackson rose to power
as a military hero, known for his brutal attacks on Native tribes, his violent (and
illegal) incursion into Spanish Florida, and his triumphant defeat of the British
in the Battle of New Orleans, a bloody and ultimately unnecessary battle that left
over a thousand British soldiers wounded or dead (compared to fifty-two Americans) despite the fact that a peace treaty had already been signed.[29]

The hymn "sung by the rabble" to celebrate the fact that the king "has just fin-
ished putting to death, with his own hand, a thousand chained Israelitish prisoners" appears to burlesque the many parades, songs, encomiums, and doggerel
that hailed Jackson's victory over the British as a bloody but absolutely necessary
boost to American national pride:

> A thousand, a thousand, a thousand,
> We, with one warrior, have slain!
> . . .
> He has given us more
> Red gallons of gore
> Than all Syria can furnish of wine![30]

But the occasion of the political spectacle—"the massacre of a thousand Jews"—
also encompasses a broader critique of the ways Jackson's politics of democracy,
his celebration of American individualism, industrial and economic development, and westward advance are grounded in an essentially genocidal removal
policy of forcing Native tribes west of Mississippi, by "extermination" if necessary.

"[T]rue philanthropy reconciles the mind to these vicissitudes as it does to the extinction of one generation to make room for another," he intoned in an address to Congress on his Indian Removal policy on December 6, 1830. "What good man would prefer a country covered with forest and ranged by a few thousands savages to our extensive Republic, studded with cities, towns, and prosperous farms?" he asked.[31] Poe's literal and metaphoric allusions to the burning "of a few Jews" and "the massacre of a thousand Jews" to satirize the social horrors of Jacksonian democracy is particularly prophetic and uncanny in suggesting the continuity—what Benjamin would call the "triumphal procession" of history—that links the political usurpation of a Syrian monarch and the democratic politics of Andrew Jackson with the fascist regime and genocidal politics of Adolf Hitler.

Poe's political critique does not stop there, however. What the narrator refers to as "the noble and free citizens of Epidaphne!" are in fact dupes of the mad king. "The greatest portion [of the procession]," the narrator explains, "those especially who *belabor the populace with clubs*—are the principal courtiers of the palace, executing, as in duty bound, some laudable comicality of the king's."[32] Clubbed into subjection and abjection by the king's men, who are themselves "duty bound," the "populace" has no existence apart from the arbitrary will of the king. These courtiers "with clubs" appear to be a critique of party discipline and the workings of the Democratic Party machine during the Age of Jackson, but they are also a further chilling anticipation of state-sponsored violence in the United States and elsewhere, including Egypt and Syria in the Middle East.

Like Poe's Antiochus, "the most potent of all the autocrats of the East," Andrew Jackson and the Democratic Party machine sought to dominate all aspects of American life.[33] This imperial ambition is particularly evident in Jackson's speech vetoing the congressional bill to recharter the Bank of the United States in 1832. Presenting himself as a defender of the rights of "the humble members of society—the farmers, mechanics, and laborers" against the "rich and powerful," Jackson expanded the power of the presidency by setting himself up as an embodiment of the will of the people.[34] To the head of the Bank, Nicholas Biddle of Philadelphia, Jackson's speech had "all the fury of a chained panther biting at the bars of his cage. It really is a manifesto of anarchy . . . issued to the mob."[35] Others satirized Jackson's monarchical ambitions as an attempt to set himself up as "King Andrew the First."

For "King Antiochus" as for "King Andrew" the major threat to their political regime came not from "free citizens" but from slaves, which Poe presents in the allegorical figure of "wild beasts" domesticated by their masters. "What a

BORN TO COMMAND.

KING ANDREW THE FIRST.

King Andrew the First (1833), political cartoon depicting President Jackson
as a tyrannical king trampling on the U.S. Constitution.

terrible spectacle!—what a dangerous peculiarity!" exclaims the modern spectator on first glimpsing these animals "swarming" the city. The spectator's terrified
response associates these "wild beasts" with a similarly "peculiar institution" in
the United States and the social and psychic horrors it entails for both masters
and slaves. "Terrible, if you please; but not in the least dangerous," the narrator
hastens to assure his companion:

> Each animal . . . is following, very quietly, in the wake of its master. Some few, to
> be sure, are led with a rope about the neck, but these are chiefly the lesser or more
> timid species. The lion, the tiger, and the leopard are entirely without restraint.
> They have been trained without difficulty to their present profession, and attend
> upon their respective owners in the capacity of *men-at-arms*.

Poe underscored the "happy slave" reference in the 1836 *Southern Messenger* version and all future versions of the tale when he changed *men-at-arms* to the potentially more ominous *valets-de-chambre*. The narrator's reassurance is undermined and ironized in the very next sentence when he acknowledges (like Hegel) that the logic of slavery and the master-slave relation is resistance and insurrection: "It is true, there are occasions when Nature asserts her violated dominion;—but then the devouring of a freeman, or the throttling of a courtezan or consecrated bull are circumstances of too little moment to be more than hinted at in Epidaphne." The narrator sounds as optimistic as Jefferson, and may even mimic his famous comment on the naturalness of popular revolution in preserving democracy: "The tree of liberty must be refreshed from time to time by the blood of patriots & tyrants. It is it's [*sic*] natural manure."[36] Poe's tale derides this sublime democratic faith in blood violence as the "natural manure" and necessary ground of human freedom and progress.

Not surprisingly, given the dialectics of blood that undergirds political power in "Epimanes," the story ends with a slave insurrection. The uprising occurs at the very moment when the king is being hailed and *encored* by the populace as "'Prince of Poets,' as well as 'Glory of the East,' 'Delight of the Universe,' and 'most Remarkable of Cameleopards'" for singing his own "song of triumph":

> Who is God but Epiphanes?
> Say do you know?
> There is none but Epiphanes,
> No—there is none:
> So tear down the temples,
> And put out the sun!

The king's bathetic celebration of his "absolute power" enables Poe's political satire to also take aim at the debased taste of the democratic masses and the literary public sphere in the Age of Jackson. But he did make one concession to American—or perhaps southern—piety when he removed "Who is God but Epiphanes" from all future versions of the tale.

Poe's treatment of the slave insurrection troubles traditional distinctions between slave and master, animal and human, black and white. "The singular appearance of the cameleopard with the head of a man, has," the narrator explains, "given offense to the notions of propriety entertained in general, by the wild animals domesticated in the city." As upholders of social and anthropological purity, the "wild beasts" are in effect insulted by the impurity of the king's amalgamated appearance—his failure to maintain proper distinctions between man and beast, master and slave, homo and cameleopard. "A mutiny has been the result, and, as is usual upon such occasions, all human efforts will be ineffectual in *quelling the mob*. Several of the Epidaphians have already been devoured; but *the general voice of the four-footed patriots* seems to be for eating up the cameleopard. 'The Prince of Poets,' therefore, is on his legs, and running for his life." The narrator's references to "the mob" and "the general voice of the four-footed patriots" mimics the Jacksonian rhetoric of majoritarian democracy: "the majority is to govern," Jackson asserted in his first annual address to Congress in 1829, in words that would continue to shape the political rhetoric if not the reality of Jacksonian democracy.[37]

"The Glory of the East" outruns by a half-second his four-legged rebels, and in a further uncannily prophetic anticipation of the corruption of the modern Olympics and the sports world more generally, he is proclaimed winner of "the wreath of victory in the footrace . . . of the next Olympiad," which they "give him in advance." While the story ends happily or—depending on one's democratic view—dystopically, "Epimanes" is the first of Poe's tales to register the crisis over slavery, the fear of slave insurrection, and the pervasive violence and blood that marked democratic culture in the Age of Jackson. A little over a year before Poe began working on "Epimanes," his fear of slave insurrection assumed palpable bodily form when, in August 1831, Nat Turner led the bloodiest slave insurrection in American history in Southampton County, Virginia. The insurrection, which resulted in the death of some sixty whites, the torture and execution of scores of innocent blacks, and a widespread hysteria about the possibility of further uprisings, led to a tightening of slave laws and an increasingly vigorous defense of the institution and culture of slavery throughout the South.

"Epimanes," which Poe wrote in the early 1830s, following William Lloyd Garrison's founding of the *Liberator* in 1831, the emergence of the Abolition movement, and public debates about the future of slavery in the Virginia legislature in 1831–32, registers the widespread fear that one way or another the entire country, and not just the South, was going to be eaten alive—at least metaphorically—by the institution of slavery. Or, as Jefferson observed of the Missouri Compromise of 1820, in words that may have contributed to the imaginative conception if not the imagery of "Epimanes" and its later title "Four Beasts in One": "we have the wolf by the ear, and we can neither hold him, nor safely let him go. Justice is in one scale, and self-preservation in the other."[38]

In his searing critique of the dark side of democracy in "Epimanes," Poe anticipates many of the antidemocratic themes and terrors to which he would return not only in early tales such as "Lion-izing: A Tale," "Shadow: A Fable," "King Pest the First," and "Von Jung, the Mystific" but in later—and sometimes more politically explicit—tales such as "The Man That Was Used Up," "The Colloquy of Monos and Una," "The System of Doctor Tarr and Professor Fether," "Some Words with a Mummy," "Mellonta Tauta," and select passages of "Marginalia." "King Pest the First: A Tale Containing an Allegory" (1835; later entitled "King Pest") may be set in London during the time of the Plague, but for Poe's contemporaries its "depopulated" cityscape of "gloom, silence, pestilence, and death" might have had a more immediate historical reference to the cholera epidemic—called "King Cholera"—that killed some 3,515 people in New York City alone in 1832. "There is no business doing here if I except that done by Cholera, Doctors, Undertakers, Coffinmakers, &c.," wrote the painter Asher B. Durand's assistant of the scene of the outbreak. "Our bustling city now wears a most gloomy & desolate aspect—one may take a walk up & down Broadway & scarce meet a soul."[39]

Poe's tale combines this deathscape under siege by "the Demon of Disease" with a fairly pointed political critique of Jackson and his administration through a company of six grotesques, who masquerade as King Pest and his royal family of Pests, as they (literally) drink themselves to death in the wine cellar of an undertaker, whose district has been vacated "under pain of death." "Know then that in these dominions I am monarch, and here rule with undivided empire under the title of 'King Pest the First,'" proclaims "the president of the table," whose tall, gaunt, emaciated figure, monarchical pretensions, and royal family of pests satirizes the frontier origins and monarchical ambitions of Jackson—or "King Andrew the First" as his Whig opponents called him—and the familial and social scandals that marked his administration.[40]

But like the apocalyptic landscape of Poe's 1831 poem "The Doomed City" and the city of Antioch, which was "totally destroyed, at three different periods, by three successive earthquakes," "King Pest the First" also advances a broader and grimmer critique of progressive history, the city, technological advance, and modernity at the very heart of its political satire. The true end of their drinking ("business"), King Pest avers, in language that mocks the Enlightenment pursuit of scientific truth for the good of the world, is "to examine, analyze, and thoroughly determine the indefinable spirit" of "the wines, ales, and liqueurs of this goodly metropolis: by so doing to advance not more our own designs than the true welfare of that unearthly sovereign whose reign is over us all, whose dominions are unlimited, and whose name is 'Death.'"[41] Like King Pest the First, King

Andrew the First rules over an "undivided empire" whose true end is not democratic advance, but the end of democratic history signified by the depopulated
deathscape of New York and other parts of the country at the time of the cholera
outbreak.

The social pretense and masquerade at the heart of the political satire in "King
Pest the First" are part of a new cultural politics of the masses in the Age of Jackson that Poe satirizes in such tales as "Lion-izing: A Tale" (1835; later "Lionizing")
and "Von Jung the Mystific" (1837; later "Mystification"), in which an emergent
culture of celebrity and mystification produces personalities, reputations, and
histories (like Andrew Jackson), and writing that lacks any substance and mean-
ing.⁴² Poe's most prescient and horrific treatment of this subject is in "The Man
That Was Used Up: A Tale of the Late Bugaboo and Kickapoo Campaign" (1839),
which satirizes the Jacksonian cult of the warrior and the politics of mass mystification, at the same time that it exposes the barbarism, carnage, and dehumanizing violence that are the constitutive terms of Jacksonian Democracy. Poe's particular target is Jackson's Indian Removal policy and the Indian wars against the
Creek in Alabama and Seminole Indians in Florida, the Second Seminole War of
1835–42, and, under President Van Buren, the forced removal of some eighteen
thousand Cherokee men, women, and children from Georgia, Tennessee, and
North Carolina to Oklahoma along a Trail of Tears in which thousands died in
the winter of 1838–39.⁴³

"The Man That Was Used Up" is told from the first-person point of view by a
narrator who is himself "used up" by the mystique surrounding "that truly fine-
looking fellow, Brevet Brigadier General John A. B. C. Smith." But like "The Man
of the Crowd," the story also unfolds as a narrative of detection in which the narrator seeks to unveil the "mystery" surrounding the "singularly commanding"
presence of Smith, whose reputation as "a perfect desperado—a down-right fire-
eater" derives from his heroism and courage "in the late tremendous swamp fight
away down South, with the Bugaboo and Kickapoo Indians." Hailed as "one of
the *most* remarkable men of the age" by a public that repeats the same stock terms
of praise—"Horrid affair that," "a bloody set of wretches, those Kickapoos," "O
yes! great man!" "quite a desperado," "*prodigies* of valor," "immortal renown,"
"This is a wonderfully inventive age!"—Smith becomes the reified object and
emblem of a corrupt public sphere and the horrific workings of Jacksonian ideology as a ritual of mass mystification and robotic consent.

Like the victims of Jackson's Indian Removal policy, Smith has in fact been
literally disgorged, unmade, and unmanned in the Indian wars. He has been

reduced to "a large and exceedingly oddlooking bundle of something," an object that the narrator kicks out of the way before realizing in utter horror that "it" is in fact Smith. "He" is a collection of artificial body parts—a cork leg, arm, shoulders, bosom, wig, teeth, eyes, voice machine—that his slave, Pompey, diligently reassembles into an "object" recognizable as General John A. B. C. Smith. Having arrived at what he calls "a full comprehension of the mystery which had troubled me for so long," the narrator asserts: "It was a clear case. Brevet Brigadier General John A. B. C. Smith was the man—was *the man that was used up*." But this is a *faux* resolution that appears to close down the "mystery" of the person, the body, the human, and the post-human cyborg that is opened by Poe's tale.[44]

Moreover, the narrator appears to use only one sense of the word *used up*— the colloquial sense of being physically exhausted by hardship. The term *used up* also had a specifically American reference to someone who was thoroughly criticized or debunked in writing or conversation. Through his use of both senses of the term, Poe suggests the broader symbolic resonance of Smith not only as *a* man but *the man* who has lost a part of his humanity in the Indian wars; and *the man that was used up* by Poe himself to critique the forms of Jacksonian manliness and self-definition grounded in military violence, racial oppression, and the conquest of nature.

Critics have been baffled by Poe's "Man." Until recently much of the criticism has focused on identifying the historical antecedent for Poe's General John Smith. Possible candidates include Van Buren's vice-president, Richard M. Johnson, who was known as an Indian-killing war hero and lionized for supposedly killing Tecumseh in the Battle of the Thames River in 1813. "Rumpsey, dumsey, Colonel Johnson killed Tecumsey" became one of the campaign slogans when he ran for vice-president in 1836.[45] Other possible antecedents for Poe's "Man" include General Winfield Scott and General William Henry Harrison, who were both war heroes known for their involvement in the Indian wars. Most recently J. Gerald Kennedy has proposed that Poe's model may have been Major General Alexander Macomb, who, having led a particularly bloody war of extermination against the Seminoles, "was unquestionably the lightning-rod figure for American dismay about the Second Seminole War in mid-1839."[46]

Oddly, no one has connected Poe's general to Andrew Jackson, who had himself been so macerated by his warrior past that he had to avoid public appearances during the 1828 presidential campaign. "Although he looked like a distinguished old warrior, with flashing blue eyes and a shock of whitening steely gray hair," writes historian Sean Wilentz, "Andrew Jackson was by now [1828] a physical wreck."[47] No public political figure benefited more than Jackson from his near-mythic stature as former duelist, Indian killer, and heroic conqueror of the British at the Battle of New Orleans. But the actual person Poe is satirizing is perhaps less important than the culture of Jacksonian democracy he is critiquing: the cult of the warrior, of masculinity and national identity forged in massive blood-letting, Indian wars, racial oppression, mass mystification, and the literal disgorging of the person and humanity.

Jackson's Indian Removal policy was crucial to the realization of his democratic and national vision of economic and technological progress, westward expansion, the extension of slavery, and the dignity of (white) labor and the common man. He was "the man" whose warrior past and policy of removal reversed the Jeffersonian policy of assimilation and insisted that even assimilated Indians, including some sixty thousand Cherokee, Chickasaw, Choctaw, Creek, and Seminole inhabitants of the southeastern states, must be removed from their homes in order to make way for the advance of American civilization. These forced removals continued into the administrations of Van Buren; William Henry Harrison, himself a war hero in battles against the Indians and the British in the War of 1812; and John Tyler, who succeeded Harrison when he died of pneumonia shortly after taking office. Despite the fact that Smith, like Jackson, has been "used up" by his warrior past, he is the pitch-perfect voice of the Jacksonian rhetoric of American exceptionalism, boundless expansion, and confidence in "the rapid march of mechanical invention": "'There is nothing like it,' he would say; 'we are a wonderful people, and live in a wonderful age. Parachutes and rail-roads—man-traps and spring-guns! Our steam-boats are upon every sea. . . . There is really no end to the march of invention.'"

Like Benjamin's historical materialist, Poe's war hero as amputee and mechanical man unmasks the real historical carnage and terror underlying the rhetoric of Americans as "a wonderful people" living in "a wonderful age." The "march of invention" produces man-killers and killing machines—"man-traps and spring-guns!"—destined to occupy every sea: a cause finally for terror rather than celebration.

In "Theses on the Philosophy of History," Benjamin observes: "The concept of the historical progress of mankind cannot be sundered from the concept of its progression through a *homogenous, empty time*. A critique of the concept of such a progression must be the basis of any criticism of the concept of progress itself."[48] While Jackson's Indian Removal policy stirred humanitarian opposition during its time, until the 1980s it went uncontested by several generations of historians.

By filling the "homogenous, empty time" of American progress—"the rapid march of mechanical invention"—with the dead, mutilated, and half-dead bodies of the Indian wars, Poe's "Tale of the Late Bugaboo and Kickapoo Campaign" uncannily anticipates the work of recent historians who now read Jackson's Indian Removal policy and its horrific legacy of racism and genocide as a major failure not only of Jackson and his age but of American democracy itself.[49]

THE IMP OF THE PERVERSE

For Poe as for the Constitutional Founders, the problem of political governance was a problem of human nature. In Federalist 37, Madison explicitly comments on the potential problems posed by "the indistinctness of the object, imperfection of the human organ of conception, [and the] inadequateness of the vehicle of ideas" in the formation of human government. "The faculties of the mind itself have never yet been distinguished and defined, with satisfactory precision, by all the efforts of the most acute and metaphysical philosophers," Madison complains; "Sense, perception, judgment, desire, volition, memory, imagination are found to be separated by such delicate shades and minute gradations that their boundaries have eluded the most subtle investigations, and remain a pregnant source of ingenious disquisition and controversy."[50] The Constitution was not an unleashing of democracy or the people, but an attempt to mediate the terrors of human nature, psychology, language, imagination, and knowledge at every level.

The problems of human nature, perception, and language that Madison poses in *The Federalist Papers* are at the origins of the American Gothic as it was practiced by Charles Brockden Brown and later Edgar Allan Poe. Thus, for example, Brown's *Edgar Huntly; or, Memoirs of a Sleep-Walker* (1799), which is set at the time of the Constitutional founding, locates a distinctively American Gothic in the diseases of the mind and what he calls "the condition of our country" which he defines as "the incidents of Indian hostility, and the perils of the western wilderness."[51] Like Charles Brockden Brown's Gothic novels, Poe's Gothic tales were something more than masterly manipulations of the contemporary taste for horror and sensation in order to sell to a mass market.

Even Poe's first and most horrific exploration of monomania and psychological obsession, "Berenice," in which the first-person narrator becomes so obsessed with his loved one's teeth that he removes them from her interred but *"still alive"* body, is grounded in a mix of the social terrors of human psychology with a broader political and philosophical critique of democratic and Enlightenment history. Although the story appears to be set in the Gothic past, it originated in the deathscape of capitalist modernity, a "scandal" in contemporary Baltimore about grave robbers stealing human teeth in order to sell them to dentists.[52] Poe bet he could treat such a singular subject "seriously," and he does so by pressing "bad-taste" to the very verge of the limit in a tale that transforms the "singular" into "the strange and mystical." If the narrator appears to be a madman bent on criminal intent, he also manifests signs of human alienation and retreat from the "wretchedness" and "misery" of the world into an alternative existence of which the material trace is the one part of the body and human identity that does not die: "the many white, and glistening substances that were scattered to and fro about the floor" at the conclusion of the tale.[53]

When T. W. White, the editor of the *Southern Literary Messenger*, where "Berenice" was first published, complained that readers found the subject "far too horrible," Poe defended the tale as an attempt to appeal to the popular market for "the ludicrous heightened into the grotesque: the fearful coloured into the horrible: the witty exaggerated into the burlesque: the singular wrought out into the strange and mystical."[54] As a tale that paradoxically pushes "bad taste" to a parodic limit by burlesquing the very qualities of excess, sensationalism, and terror that appeal to a mass audience, "Berenice" provides an early horrific instance of the human perversion, male violence, and female abjection that would become part of a more explicit critique of Western philosophy, and the Enlightenment faith in reason, human agency, and historical progress in "The Black Cat" (1843) and "The Imp of the Perverse" (1845).

Poe's first theorization of "the spirit of PERVERSENESS" occurs in "The Black Cat" (1843), a tale told by an accused criminal that links the psychic and social terrors of alcoholism, male violence, slavery, animal abuse (and hanging), wife-beating, murder, and entombment in the cellar to "perverseness" as "one of the primitive impulses . . . which give direction to the character of Man." Unrecognized by philosophy, "this unfathomable longing of the soul *to vex itself*—to offer violence to its own nature—to do wrong for the wrong's sake only"—defines itself in opposition to self, law, love, and God. The narrator cold-bloodedly slips a noose around the neck of his black cat, Pluto, and hangs it on a tree because he knows "it had loved me" and in committing such a "deadly sin" he would place his "immortal soul" beyond "the infinite mercy" of God.

Whereas in "The Black Cat" the perverse instinct appears within the story as part of the narrator's defense of his sanity against the insanity of his crimes, in "The Imp of the Perverse" Poe begins with a more philosophical and broad-ranging explanation of the perverse as "an innate and primitive principle of human action" which might stand alone as a serious theoretical essay that challenges the stability of both the "cogito" and the "moral sense" and thus an entire tradition of Western rationalism, empiricism, and moral philosophy grounded in an "I" that can be depended upon to think, feel, know, and act responsibly in the world. Man is not governed by reason, morality, or the religious soul, but by "a paradoxical something, which, for want of a better term, we may call *Perverseness*":

> In the sense I intend it, it is, in fact, a *mobile* without motive, a motive not *motivirt*. Through its promptings we act without comprehensive object.... [W]e act, for the reason that we should *not*. In theory, no reason can be more unreasonable; but, in reality, there is none so strong.... [T]he conviction of the wrong or impolicy of an action is often the one unconquerable *force* which impels us, and alone impels us to its prosecution.... It is a radical, a primitive impulse—elementary.... [T]he desire to be well is not only *not* aroused, but a strongly antagonistical sentiment prevails.

What Poe defines is an unmotivated, objectless, and seemingly "unreasonable" dialectics of negation and opposition that obstructs any logical process of individual thought or historical advance, enlightened, Hegelian, or otherwise. Translated into individual action or world historical movement, Poe's "imp of the perverse" produces a dialectics not of progress but of transgression in which the rational or moral *prohibition* or "that which is *Law*" turns the taboo object or act into an "absolutely irresistible" desire.[55] This dialectics of transgression becomes the basis of Poe's tales of psychic and social terror and his simultaneously moral and philosophical critique of the perverse impulses of cruelty, arson, obsession, murder, mutilation, greed, revenge, and the will to power that in fact drive individual action and Western history from Poe's first published tale, "Metzengerstein," to "Berenice," "Ligeia," "The Man That Was Used Up," "The Man of the Crowd," "The Tell-Tale Heart," "The Black Cat," "The Imp of the Perverse," and "The Cask of Amontillado," among many others.

The reason this primordial impulse has been "overlooked" by moralists, philosophers, metaphysicians, contemporary phrenologists, and everyone else, Poe argues, is "the pure arrogance of the reason." Assuming that we know what God intended man to be and do, rather than "what man usually or occasionally did, and was always occasionally doing," we cannot understand how the primitive, motiveless workings of the perverse "might be made to further the objects of humanity, either temporal or eternal." In other words, the *a priori* assumption that God intends man and the world to advance has made it impossible to recognize a primitive and irrational perverseness that does not contribute to human self-preservation and the progress of civilization. Like the man shuddering on the brink of a precipice and longing to leap that Poe educes as an instance of the workings of the imp, humanity might be rushing toward an annihilation that cannot be prevented by intellect, or will, or thought: "To indulge, even for a moment, in any attempt at *thought,* is to be inevitably lost," Poe avers in words that brilliantly "pervert" the Cartesian foundation of modern philosophy, "Cogito ergo sum" (I think, therefore I am).

While the Princeton *Nassau Monthly* for December 1845 called Poe's tale "humbug philosophical"—and given his propensity for hoax, it could be—I want to argue that as a theory of man and as a theory of history the dialectics of perversion and contradiction that Poe propounds in "The Black Cat" and "The Imp of the Perverse" provides a more critical tool for brushing democratic history against the grain than Hegelian dialectics, the *Sapere Aude!* (Dare to Know) of Kant's Enlightenment, or the faith in irresistible progress that propelled the Age of Jackson.

As "an innate and primitive principle of human action," Poe's theory of the perverse also anticipates the Freudian unconscious and especially Freud's essay "The Uncanny" (1919). But Poe's theory of the perverse workings of human psychology was more radical and irreducible than Freud's theory of the unconscious promptings of human behavior. Whereas Freud locates the sources of human desire and "the uncanny" in the oedipal struggle between parents and children, Poe's imp is "a *mobile* without motive, a motive not *motivirt.*"[56] Like Pluto's *Doppelgänger* in "The Black Cat," the black cat with a tuft of white hair in the shape of a gallows that appears from nowhere and cannot be explained, Poe's imp of the perverse is in some sense more unhomely (*unheimlich*) than Freud's *unheimlich* (uncanny).

ANGELS OF HISTORY

Reflecting on Paul Klee's painting "Angelus Novus" in "Theses on the Philosophy of History," Benjamin writes: "This is how one pictures the angel of history. His face is turned toward the past. Where we perceive a chain of events, he sees one single catastrophe which keeps piling wreckage upon wreckage and hurls it in front of his feet."[57] This is Poe's view of history in his three angelic dialogues, "The Conversation of Eiros and Charmion" (1839), "The Colloquy of Monos and Una" (1841), and "The Power of Words" (1845). Whereas in Poe's Gothic tales the imp of the perverse becomes the instrument of both social terror and political and cultural critique, in his angelic dialogues the catastrophe of human history itself becomes the source of terror and social critique as angels regenerated into new forms of material being reflect back on the chaos and emotional suffering of the past. The dialogic form and post-apocalyptic vision of "The Conversation of Eiros and Charmion" read like a parable of the dangers of reading *with* (empathetically) rather than *against* (critically) Enlightenment and progressive history set forth in such major works of critical theory as Benjamin's "Theses Toward a Philosophy of History" (1940) and Max Horkheimer and Theodor Adorno's *Dialectic of Enlightenment* (1947).

While the world heads for catastrophe as "a *new* comet" approaches closer and closer to earth, the regime of reason and knowledge "hurled superstition from her throne," assuring "the crowd" that all is well. This confidence in reason and progress collapses into pure terror as the inhabitants of earth realize that they lack the scientific and historical knowledge to understand what is happening: "We could no longer apply to the strange orb any *accustomed* thoughts," Eiros tells Charmion. "Its *historical* attributes had disappeared. It oppressed us with a hideous *novelty* of emotion." "Thus ended all," Eiros concludes, as the atmosphere explodes into an "all-devouring" combustion in accord with "the biblical prophecies." Like Benjamin's emphasis on the need "to blast open the continuum of history" as a means of redeeming the world, Poe's science fiction tale envisions fiery apocalypse as the only hope.[58]

Poe's most explicit criticism of the political and aesthetic failures of his time occurs in "The Colloquy of Monos and Una," a tale that bears a particularly prescient and possibly formative relation with the critical theorists of the Frankfurt School. Speaking from a regenerated state of being beyond death, Monos's "weird narrative" of "man's condition" before "our dissolution" anticipates the work of Benjamin, Adorno, and Horkheimer in its critique of Enlightenment and progressive history, the will to dominate nature and human nature, and the drive to epistemological mastery seeded by fear of the unknown. "One or two of the wise among our forefathers," Monos remembers, "had ventured to doubt the propriety of the term 'improvement,' as applied to the progress of our civilization." Anticipating the distinction Benjamin would make between "progress in the mastery of nature" and "in men's ability and knowledge" and "the progress of mankind itself," which is in fact "the retrogression of society," Monos notes that occasionally "some vigorous intellect" urged "our race to submit to the guidance of the natural laws, rather than attempt their control" because "each advance in practical science" was in fact "a retrogradation in the true utility." But, Monos observes, these "noble exceptions from the general misrule served but to strengthen it by opposition." "The great 'movement'—that was the cant term—went on," he concludes, in words that critique both the triumphal westward advance of Jacksonian democracy and the "progress" of human history as "a diseased commotion, moral and physical."[59]

Like Horkheimer and Adorno, Poe linked the political failure of the Enlightenment with cultural decline. In "Monos and Una," however, Poe's aesthetics, and the decline of beauty and taste, are also linked with a particularly southern and racially inspired critique of "omni-prevalent Democracy," capitalist industry ("huge smoking cities arose" and "leaves shrank before the hot breath of furnaces"), and the "ravages" of "[t]he fair face of Nature." "Man grew infected with system, and with abstraction" and "enwrapped himself in generalities," Monos complains. "Among other odd ideas, that of universal equality gained ground: and in the face of analogy and of God—in despite of the loud warning voice of the laws of *gradation* so visibly pervading all things in Earth and Heaven—wild attempts at an omni-prevalent Democracy were made."

If Poe's vision is essentially conservative, hierarchical, and agrarian in its fear of democracy, the mob, the city, and modernity, the Frankfurt School theorists are radical, egalitarian, Marxist, and revolutionary in their embrace of the cause of the oppressed and the liberation of the masses from the structures of capitalist and class dominance. And yet despite these fundamental differences, both Poe and the Frankfurt School theorists locate the problem in the human desire to master all knowledge. In "Monos and Una," Poe in effect rewrites biblical genesis from a "philosophic" rather than a religious point of view, finding "the mystic parable that tells of the tree of knowledge, and of its forbidden fruit, death-producing, a distinct intimation that knowledge was not meet for man in the infant condition of his soul."

For Poe the solution to the problem of knowledge is not more reason and more facts: it is cultural and aesthetic. Through Monos, he begins to formulate his notion that "the poetic intellect—that intellect which we *now* feel to have been the most exalted of all" might have led the world to "those truths which to us were of the most enduring importance." These higher "truths" cannot be accessed directly through reason or intellect; they can "only be reached" metaphorically and symbolically "by that *analogy* which speaks in proof-tones to the imagination alone, and to the unaided reason bears no weight." "And these men—the poets—living and perishing amid the scorn of the "utilitarians,"

Monos remembers, "these men, the poets, pondered piningly, yet not unwisely, upon the ancient days" of simple wants and "deep-toned happiness, holy, august and blissful days, when blue rivers ran undammed, between hills unhewn, into far forest solitudes, primaeval, odorous, and unexplored."

The destruction of this golden age of the past—perhaps paradise, or America as New World paradise, or the plantation South—is, Poe suggests, due to "the perversion of our *taste,* or rather . . . the blind neglect of its culture in the schools." "[I]t was at this crisis," Monos explains, "that taste alone—that faculty which, holding a middle position between the pure intellect and the moral sense, could never safely have been disregarded—it was now that taste alone could have led us gently back to Beauty, to Nature, and to Life."[60] Here Poe, the so-called *aesthete* and avatar of *pure poetry,* imagines a more powerful social role for the poet than the Marxist critical social theorists.

But significantly, he also aligns himself with what we now think of as Adornian critical theory at several points. Like Adorno's *Aesthetic Theory,* Poe emphasizes the aesthetic autonomy of art by giving it a "truth" content, but this content is not finally metaphysical or transcendental: it is mediated by the social world and thus can only be "reached" metaphorically and accessed by the imagination. For Poe, as for Adorno, music has a crucial role to play in cultivating a taste for beauty, or as Plato argued, in "making the man *beautiful minded.*" Like the Frankfort theorists, Poe also attributes the failure of human history to the failure of "mathematical reason" and the "intemperance of knowledge" as opposed to what Pascal called "the sentiment of the natural." "But, for myself," Monos confesses, in an epigrammatic phrase that resonates with the later social theory of Benjamin and Adorno, "the Earth's records had taught me to look for widest ruin as the price of highest civilization."

Like Benjamin's vision of a "leap in the open air of history" as the only means of arresting the continuum of knowledge and history, Poe imagines that "the infected world" can only be regenerated through death and post-apocalyptic revivification "for the redeemed, regenerated, blissful, and now immortal, but still for the *material,* man." Cited by Benjamin in a note "On Some Motifs in Baudelaire" as a "mystical" account of the experience of "bliss" beyond death when "the empty passage of time" is "rid of its horrors," "The Colloquy of Monos and Una,"—like "The Conversation of Eiros and Charmion" and "The Power of Words," in which language itself assumes material form in the infinite pulse of creation—finds Poe outmaterializing Benjamin and historical materialism itself in imagining a "purely sensual" rebirth into eternal life.[61]

POE AS GOD

Poe's "The Colloquy of Monos and Una" was published in 1841, only a few months after the publication of his first detective story, "The Murders in the Rue Morgue."[62] Like Poe's angels, Dupin reads against the thought structures of the time. The wisdom of the Prefect in "Murders of the Rue Morgue" is "all head and no body": "He denies what is and explains what is not."[63] Dupin combines the ratiocinative power of the scientist with the imaginative power of Poe's poet to analyze what is and imagine what might be. Although the term *detective* did not exist in English when Poe published his first tale of detection, as his "The Man of the Crowd" (1840) suggests, the practice of reading what is artfully concealed as both occupation and act is a product of the epistemological crisis called forth by the spectacle and terrors of the modern city, and the conditions of anomie, alienation, darkness, crime, and mystery that the urban metropolis came to represent.

Not surprisingly, Benjamin was the first to read Poe's "The Man of the Crowd" as both an "x-ray picture of a detective story" and a penetrating critique of the "shock" effect of the city, commodity culture, and the frantic pursuit of sensation called forth by the deadening atomization and mechanization of city life.[64] Unlike the urban *flâneur* of "The Man of the Crowd," however, who ends by mirroring the manic behavior of the old man he shadows throughout the tale and who cannot finally read the mystery of the "dark crime" he sees in *"the man of the crowd,"* the detective genre as Poe invented it both exposes the horrific violence, crime, and danger of the modern city and makes its mysteries legible—at least in theory—through the ratiocinative imagination of the detective, C. Auguste Dupin.

But as Poe recognized, his detective tales worked best when Dupin unraveled mysteries that Poe himself invented for what he called "the express purpose of unraveling."[65] In "The Mystery of Marie Rogêt" (1842–43), which is set in Paris but based on the actual and sensationalized death of a young woman that took place in New York City, Poe had to fictionalize the actual crime in order to give it the motive, cause, and legibility it lacked historically. While Dupin's fictionalized detection gave the semblance of resolution, the mystery of the real death was never solved. But it is here at the "mystery" of the real that Poe's detective stories ask to be read as something more than pulp fiction produced and marketed for the *faux* thrills of a mass audience. As in "Marie Rogêt," in which the *ordinary* rather than *outré* nature of the crime leads Dupin to combine imaginative intuition with mathematical analysis—to *calculate upon the unforeseen* in accord with the principles of "true philosophy" and "modern science"—Poe's tales of detection carry on the social and philosophical critique of the limits of human reason. They also beckon toward a broader poetics and metaphysics of detection that animate Poe's poetic inquiry into the "mystery" of the universe in "Eureka: A Prose Poem" (1848).

In "Eureka" poetry merges with prose, the poet with the scientist, and beauty with truth in what Poe calls "An Essay on the Material and Spiritual Universe." "I design to speak of the *Physical, Metaphysical, and Mathematical—of the Material and Spiritual Universe:—of its Essence, its Origin, its Creation, its Present Condition and its Destiny,*" Poe announces at the outset. But despite the scientific, philosophical, and finally religious nature of his "Book of Truths," Poe insists in the Preface: "it is as a Poem only that I wish this work to be judged after I am dead." It is "for the Beauty that abounds in its Truth" that Poe wants his experimental prose poem as cosmogony to be valued.[66]

Poe begins with a letter found in a bottle, which is dated 2848. Like his fictions that harbor political and philosophical critique, this futuristic letter satirizes the "*deductive or à priori* philosophy" of Aries Tottle (Aristotle) and the "*à posteriori or inductive*" philosophy of Hog (Bacon) in an effort "to relieve the people of the singular fancy that there exist *but two practicable roads to Truth.*" By associating his philosophic critique with the founding language of "rights" and "self-evident truths," Poe's philosophical satire doubles as a political satire of the Declaration of Independence and the foundationless founding of American democracy. Setting Aristotle's "axioms, or self-evident truths" against "the now well understood fact that *no* truths are *self*-evident," the letter critiques the notion "that the Aristotelian and Baconian roads are, and of right ought to be, the sole possible avenues to knowledge."

Beyond the empirical and transcendental paths to truth is the other way of intuition, poetry, the soul, and what Poe's letter writer calls the imaginative "guess" or "leap." "[T]rue Science," he asserts, "makes its most important advances—as all History will show—by seemingly intuitive *leaps.*" The "true thinkers" are "men of ardent imagination," like the Keplers and Laplaces, who "'speculate'—'theorize'" at the same time that they pursue "*Consistency*" as the analogical ground of "*Truth.*" Even Newton's law of gravity, he argues, "the most momentous and sublime of *all* their truths," was deduced from the laws of Kepler, and these laws Kepler "*guessed*": "Yes!—these vital laws Kepler *guessed*—that is to say, he *imagined* them." Poe's imaginary letter ends with a paraphrase of Kepler's "prophetical and poetical" and "ever-memorable words" in the Proem to Book V of *Harmonice Mundi* (1619), words that Poe echoes in the Preface to his own "prophetical and poetical rhapsody" as he makes Kepler the model and muse of his poet as metaphysician.[67]

Poe's attempt to conjoin the poetics of the imaginative guess, the intuition of soul, with the principle of consistency or the analogical approach to the universe that marked the natural theology and scientific inquiry of his time makes the prose-poetic metaphysics of *Eureka* experimental, strikingly original, prophetic, and—one might add—true. Poe argues that God originally created simple Matter "from his Spirit, or from Nihility." The Universe is created through the force of spirit, electricity, revulsion and differentiation within a limited space, and then the Universe is annihilated as matter and drawn by attraction and gravity back to its original unity in God. Poe first makes this argument deductively, and then inductively through Newton's law of gravity, but at each stage of his argument— both to conceive of God creating Matter in the utmost state of *Simplicity* and to conceive of all Matter returning to God—he needs to appeal to "an irresistible Intuition" and the imagination of his readers in suggesting that "Attraction and Repulsion are the *sole* properties through which we perceive the Universe." Poe's metaphysical strategy is poetic: "I *prove* nothing. . . . I design but to suggest—and to *convince* through the suggestion."[68]

Dedicated to the nineteenth-century scientist Alexander von Humboldt, *Eureka* draws on the scientific work and theory of his time, including Newton's law of gravity and La Place's nebular hypothesis, but whereas they described the laws, Poe seeks to discover the principle—the secret—behind these laws. And it is here that the scientist, detective, and poet come together in making the "imaginative leap" that is crucial to the quest for the mystery of the universe. "Now, I have elsewhere observed," Poe writes, either identifying himself with Dupin or Dupin with the narrator of *Eureka,* as he cites Dupin's observation in "Murders in the Rue Morgue" that it is by "protuberances above the plane of the ordinary—that Reason feels her way, if at all, in her search for the True." "I leap at once to *the* secret," Poe asserts, when the apparent contradiction between the radiation of matter through space and "equable distribution" leads him to realize that the universe is "in a state of *progressive collapse.*"

The perfect analogue for the universe as Poe imagines it is a perfectly constructed poem or short story with one caveat: perfect plots cannot be constructed by finite beings: "The plots of God are perfect. The Universe is a plot of God; and thus, "*the Universe* . . . is but the most sublime of poems." Finally, however, despite the dream of endless revolution "of all orbs of the Galaxy," Poe declares in words that wittily rearticulate the Declaration of Independence in a vision of political, philosophical, and cosmic collapse, "the revolutionary processes in question do, and of right ought to, come to an end." Through this "state of *progressive collapse*," Man "ceasing imperceptibly to feel himself Man . . . will recognize his existence as that of Jehovah." Or as Poe explains in a concluding note: "That God may be all in all, *each* must become God." While this might appear to be a return to Emerson or Whitman, this is a materialist return to original unity that takes place beyond rather than within the human world. In *Eureka,* Poe's aesthetics of beauty, his critique of modernity, and his moral and philosophical vision become part of a cosmogony that envisions, in a final leap of poetic imagination, a post-human "Life" beyond death "within the *Spirit Divine,*" and "a hope—that the processes we have here ventured to contemplate will be renewed forever, and forever, and forever."[69]

MATTHIESSEN'S LEAP; OR, THE RETURN OF POE'S IMP OF THE PERVERSE

In 1938–39 Matthiessen had a nervous breakdown that blocked his work on *American Renaissance.* Like the irrational impulse to leap from a precipice that drives Poe's "Imp of the Perverse," Matthiessen was haunted by the recurrent fantasy of jumping out of a window, a fantasy that was bound up with his fear of losing his lover, Russell Cheney, who was twenty years his senior. "I cannot die because it would kill Russell," he wrote at the time of his breakdown. "And to keep from jumping I must cast out this fear of Russell's death. Many times for these past weeks I have felt possessed with a devil. I pray now for strength of nerve and courage to resist the temptation of violent unreason." Matthiessen's love affair with Cheney enabled him "to shake off" what he called his "damnable deathwish," complete *American Renaissance,* and establish himself as a founding figure in the field of American literary studies.[70]

A few years after Cheney's death in 1945, Matthiessen undertook a major reassessment of Poe in a chapter for Robert Spiller's *Literary History of the United States* (1948), a crucial volume in defining American literature as a distinctive field of study. Entitled simply "Edgar Allan Poe," on the surface at least the essay appears to mark a significant about-face in Poe's American reception. "The notion has sometimes been advanced," Matthiessen acknowledged, that Poe may be "more 'representative' than Emerson or Whitman of ordinary Americans." "In opposition to the romantic stress on the expression of personality, he insisted on the importance, not of the artist, but of the created work of art. He stands as one of the very great innovators in American literature," Matthiessen concluded.

"Like Henry James and T. S. Eliot, he took his place, almost from the start, in international culture as an original creative force in contrast to the more superficial international vogue of Cooper and Irving."[71]

Oddly, Matthiessen's conclusion is not borne out by the body of the essay, in which he appears to swing wildly between an effort to acknowledge Poe's originality, intelligence, and international fame and a perverse desire to reduce Poe's imaginative creation to a case study, a dark and maniacal reflex of his "psychological insecurity," "high-strung liability to dipsomania," "overwrought nervous system," and southern provincial "prejudices." While Matthiessen acclaims Poe's proto-modern "literary method" for shifting critical attention away from the artist to the work of art itself, in paragraph after paragraph he collapses Poe's art into his biography, which he reads through the warped lens of Rufus Griswold's scathing ("Ludwig") obituary of Poe. In his Preface to *Tales of the Grotesque and Arabesque,* Matthiessen writes, "Poe raised the crucial issue when he maintained that their 'terror is not of Germany, but of the soul.' Upon the reader's felt acceptance or rejection of the truth of that statement seems to depend whether he regards Poe's work as mainly *a meretricious fabrication* or as a *compellingly imaginative creation*" (my emphasis). For all his conscious intentions, Matthiessen's imp continues to reject Poe as a "meretricious" fabricator outside "the main currents of American thought" as if his very survival, in a world without Cheney and in the terror-ridden landscape of Cold War America, depended upon it.[72]

And it did. On 1 April 1950 (April Fool's Day), F. O. Matthiessen leapt to his death from a twelfth-floor window of the Manger Hotel in Boston. He was forty-eight years old. In the hotel room he left his keys, his glasses, his fraternity emblem, and a note that read: "How much the state of the world has to do with my state of mind I do not know."[73] While the reasons for his suicide remain a mystery, the uncertainty that Matthiessen expresses about the relation between his suicidal state of mind, "the state of the world," and his decision to leap to his death might be linked with his ambivalent response to Poe in his public and published work.

Matthiessen's tragic leap to his death evinces a return of the uncanny workings of Poe's imp of the perverse in the form of the same "temptation of violent unreason," "possess[ion] by the devil," and "damnable deathwish" he had to repress in order to complete his *American Renaissance,* from which, not coincidently, Poe had to be exorcised. The irony is that whereas Matthiessen's suicidal leap appears to enact a final identification with Poe's more terror-ridden vision of American democracy, Poe appears to have been looking forward to his marriage to his boyhood sweetheart and his life-long dream of establishing his own magazine when he died his own mysterious death in Baltimore on 7 October 1849. "The truth is, I have a great deal to do; and I have made up my mind not to die till it is done," he wrote to Nathaniel P. Willis, in words that Matthiessen himself cited in his essay on Poe to elucidate "the amount and variety of work [Poe] still managed to accomplish" in his "last years."[74] In taking his own life, Matthiessen appears to have been driven to act *perversely* not only against his Catholic faith, which forbids suicide, but against his "devotion to the possibilities of democracy," which was "the common denominator" of his *American Renaissance* and his life-long struggle against Poe's darker angel of history.

Notes

1. F. O. Matthiessen, "Method and Scope," *American Renaissance: Art and Expression in the Age of Emerson and Whitman* (1941; London: Oxford Univ. Press, 1968), vii, ix, xi.

2. T. S. Eliot, *From Poe to Valéry* (New York: Harcourt Brace, 1948), 26.

3. Matthiessen, *American Renaissance,* xii (my emphasis).

4. Ibid., xii.

5. Ibid., ix.

6. Ibid., vii.

7. Walt Whitman, "Edgar Poe's Significance," *Whitman: Poetry and Prose,* ed. Justin Kaplan (New York: Library of America, 1982), 873–74, 872, 873.

8. Walter Benjamin, "Theses on the Philosophy of History," *Illuminations: Essays and Reflections,* ed. Hannah Arendt (New York: Schocken Books 1969), 257.

9. Benjamin, "Theses," 261.

10. Lionel Trilling, *The Liberal Imagination: Essays on Literature and Society* (1950; New York: New York Review Books, 2007), xv.

11. Washington Irving and James Fenimore Cooper also shared to some extent Poe's apprehensions about popular democracy.

12. Thomas Ollive Mabbott, *The Collected Works of Edgar Allan Poe,* ed. Thomas Ollive Mabbott, 3 vols. (Cambridge, Mass.: Harvard Univ. Press, 1969–78), vol. 1: 24. Hereafter cited as *CW.*

13. *CW* 1: 55; 2: 57.

14. Quoted in John M. Blum, Edmund S. Morgan, Willie Lee Rose, Arthur M. Schlesinger Jr., Kenneth M. Stampp, and C. Vann Woodward, eds., *The National Experience: A History of the United States to 1877* (New York: Harcourt Brace Jovanovich, 1981), 232.

15. Edgar Allan Poe, *Essays and Reviews,* ed. G. R. Thompson (New York: Library of America, 1984), "Letter to B——," 11. Subsequent references to this edition will be cited as *ER.*

16. *ER,* 5. Poe's ongoing commitment to these values is seen in the major aesthetic essays, "The Poetic Principle" and "The Rationale of Verse," of his last years, and in his desire to establish an independent magazine, entitled the *Penn Magazine* in 1840 and later the *Stylus,* for which he was seeking funds when he died.

17. W. J. Cash. *The Mind of the South* (New York: Knopf, 1941), 86.

18. Edgar Allan Poe, "An Address on Education," *The Complete Works of Edgar Allan Poe,* ed. James A. Harrison, 17 vols. (New York: Kelmscott Society, 1902): 8: 119.

19. *CW* 2: 610; 1: 195–96, 201; 2: 610; 1: 202.

20. The publication history of the poem that would eventually be best known as "The City in the Sea" is recounted in *The Complete Poems of Edgar Allan Poe*, ed. J. H. Whitty (New York: Houghton Mifflin, 1911), 218.

21. John L. O'Sullivan, "Annexation," *Democratic Review* 17 (July 1845): 5.

22. *Illuminations*, 256–57.

23. "Tales of the Folio Club" is the title Poe gave in 1833 to a never-published collection of stories that included "Metzengerstein," "Epimanes," and "Lionizing."

24. Mabbott, ed., *CW* 2: 117, 118.

25. Ibid., 117; Scott Peeples, *Edgar Allan Poe Revisited* (New York: Twayne, 1998), 32; see also Daniel Royot, who describes the tale as "an allegory of Jacksonian democracy [that] addresses the issues of propaganda and mob rule" ("Poe's Humor," in *The Cambridge Companion to Edgar Allan Poe*, ed. Kevin J. Hayes [New York: Cambridge Univ. Press, 2002], 64).

26. *CW* 2: 121. Edward Said, *Orientalism* (New York: Vintage, 1979).

27. *CW* 2: 123–24. Sean Wilentz, *The Rise of Democracy: Jefferson to Lincoln* (New York: W. W. Norton & Co., 2005), 312.

28. Margaret Bayard Smith, *First Forty Years of Washington Society in the Family Letters of Margaret Bayard Smith*, ed. Gaillard Hunt (New York: F. Ungar Publishing Co., 1965), 295; Justice Story cited in Eric Foner, *Give Me Liberty! An American History*, 2 vols. (New York: W. W. Norton, 2006), vol. 1: 303. In his famous 1832 message to Congress vetoing the Bank, Jackson presented himself as the defender of "the humble members of society, the farmers, mechanics, and laborers" against "the rich and powerful" ("President Jackson's Veto Message Regarding the Bank of the United States; July 10, 1832," in Documents in Law, History, and Diplomacy (avalon.law.yale.edu/19th_century/ajveto01.asp). To his opponents, like John Quincy Adams, he was "King Andrew the First" who gained power by whipping up the passions of "King Mob."

29. *CW* 2: 123. Sean Wilentz, *The Rise of American Democracy*, 173–75, 324–27; see also Kenneth Stampp, who writes: "The Battle of New Orleans was the last engagement of the war—in fact, it was fought two weeks after a treaty of peace had been signed. But it helped sweeten the bitter taste of the defeats and disappointments of the previous two and a half years, and it launched Andrew Jackson, the Hero of New Orleans, on his dazzling career" (*National Experience*, 185).

30. *CW* 2: 125.

31. In *National Experience*, 232.

32. *CW* 2: 126, 123 (italics mine).

33. Ibid., 126. "Party machines, headed by professional politicians, reached into every neighborhood, especially in cities," writes Foner, *Give Me Liberty!* 1: 322.

34. "President Jackson's Veto Message Regarding the Bank of the United States; July 10, 1832," in Documents in Law, History, and Diplomacy, avalon.law.yale.edu/19th_century/ajveto01.asp.

35. Cited by Wilentz, *The Rise of American Democracy*, 371.

36. *CW* 2: 123. Letter of Thomas Jefferson to William Smith from Paris, 13 November 1787, in *Thomas Jefferson: Writings*, ed. Merrill D. Peterson (New York: Library of America, 1984), 911.

37. *CW* 2: 127; italics mine. *State of the Union Address of Andrew Jackson* (Middlesex, UK: Echo Library, 2009), 9.

38. *Writings of Thomas Jefferson*, ed. Paul Leicester Ford, 12 vols. (New York: Putnam, 1905), 10: 157–58.

39. Cited in John Noble Wilford, "How Epidemics Helped Shape the Modern Metropolis," *New York Times*, 15 April 2008, www.nytimes.com/2008/04/15/science/15chol.html. New York City was worst hit, but the epidemic spread to other parts of the country, including Philadelphia, Baltimore, where Poe was living at the time, and Richmond.

40. *CW* 2: 242, 250, 247. See Wilentz, who describes the "political slanders" circulated by the Adamsites even before the election of 1828, including charges that Jackson was "a bigamist," his wife "an adulteress," his mother "a common prostitute," and his father "a mulatto" (*The Rise of American Democracy*, 306).

41. *CW* 2: 121, 250.

42. See Foner, who writes: "By 1840, the mass democratic politics of the Age of Jackson had absorbed the logic of the marketplace. Selling candidates and their images was as important as the positions for which they stood" (*Give Me Liberty!* 1: 335).

43. The Kickapoos were involved in the wars in Florida; "Bugaboo" is Poe's fictive name, suggesting the fictive nature of Indian "terror" invented to justify stealing their land.

44. *CW* 2: 378, 380, 382, 386, 389.

45. William Whipple, "Poe's Political Satire," *University of Texas Studies in English*, 35 (1956): 81–95. On Johnson and Tecumseh see Wilentz, *The Rise of American Democracy*, 448.

46. On General Winfield Scott, see Ronald T. Curran, "The Fashionable Thirties: Poe's Satire in 'The Man That Was Used Up,'" *Markham Review* 8 (1978): 14–20; and Daniel Hoffman, *Poe Poe Poe Poe Poe Poe Poe* (Garden City, NY: Doubleday, 1972: 196–99. On Scott and Harrison, see Richard A. Alekna, "'The Man That Was Used Up': Further Notes on Poe's Satirical Targets," *Poe Studies/Dark Romanticism* 12 (December 1979): 39. For J. Gerald Kennedy's excellent work of critical and historical contextualization, see "Unwinnable Wars, Unspeakable Wounds: Locating 'The Man That Was Used Up,'" *Poe Studies/Dark Romanticism*, 39–40 (2006–7): 77–89. For a rich discussion of "Man" in relation to questions of race, masculinity, and national identity, see Robert A. Beuka, "The Jacksonian Man of Parts: Dismemberment, Manhood, and Race in 'The Man That Was Used Up,'" *Edgar Allan Poe Review* 3, no. 1 (Spring 2002): 27–44.

47. According to Wilentz, Jackson was almost toothless; he had an irritation in his lungs from a bullet caught in one of his duels; he had another bullet lodged in his arm which caused osteomyelitis; he had rheumatism in his joints and constant headaches; he had a "near total collapse of his health in 1822 and 1825," and "for the rest of his life, he enjoyed few days completely free of agony," 301. See also Robert V. Remini, *Andrew Jackson and the Course of American Freedom, 1822–1832* (New York: Harper and Row, 1981), 1–3, 91–92.

48. *CW* 2: 381; Benjamin, *Illuminations*, 261 (my emphasis).

49. See Wilentz, *The Rise of Democracy*; Michael P. Rogin, *Fathers and Children: Andrew Jackson and the Subjugation of the American Indian* (New York: Knopf, 1975); and Ronald T. Takaki, *Iron Cages: Race and Culture in Nineteenth-Century America* (New York: Knopf, 1979).

50. Madison, "Federalist 37," *The Federalist Papers* (New York: New American Library, 1961), 229, 227.

51. Charles Brockden Brown, *Edgar Huntly; or, Memoirs of a Sleep-Walker* (New York: Penguin, 1988), 3.

52. On the stealing-teeth scandal as a source for "Berenice," see Mabbott, in Poe, *CW* 1: 207, and footnote.

53. In the 1845 and 1850 versions: "the thirty two small, white, and ivory looking substances that were scattered to and fro about the floor." In these later versions the emphasis appears to be on the human teeth themselves as material trace of the spirit world beyond death rather than the white substance. For a reading that illuminates the tale's emphasis on the "resurrection" of the body, see Joan Dayan: "The Identity of Berenice, Poe's Idol of the Mind," *Studies in Romanticism*, 24 (Winter 1984): 491–513.

54. Poe to Thomas W. White, April 30, 1835, *Letters* 1: 57–58.

55. *CW* 3: 852, 1220, 1221, 852.

56. *CW* 3: 1219, 1220, 1223; Mabbott, in Poe, *CW* 3: 1217n, 1220.

57. *Illuminations*, 257.

58. *CW* 2: 459, 461; "Theses," *Illuminations*, 262.

59. *CW* 2: 609–10; *Illuminations*, 259–60.

60. *CW* 2: 609–10.

61. Ibid., 611–13. Benjamin, "On Some Motifs in Baudelaire," *Illuminations*, 199–200n14.

62. According to Mabbott, "Murders" was completed in manuscript in March 1841 and published in *Graham's Magazine* in April 1841 (18: 166–79); "The Colloquy of Monos and Una" was published in *Graham's* in August 1841 (19: 52–55). *CW* 2: 526, 606.

63. *CW* 2: 568.

64. Benjamin, "Paris of the Second Empire," *Charles Baudelaire: A Lyric Poet in the Age of High Capitalism*, trans. Harry Zohn (London: NLB, 1973), 48.

65. Poe to Philip Pendleton Cooke, August 9, 1846, *Letters* 2: 328.

66. Poe, *Edgar Allan Poe: Poetry and Tales*, ed. Patrick F. Quinn (New York: Library of America, 1984), 1261, 1259; subsequent references will be cited as *PT*.

67. *PT*, 1263–64, 1269–70.

68. *PT*, 1277, 1283, 1288.

69. *PT*, 1293, 1347, 1342–43, 1348–49, 1346.

70. *Rat & the Devil: Journal Letters of F. O. Matthiessen and Russell Cheney*, ed. Louis Hyde (New York: Alyson Books, 1988), 254.

71. Matthiessen, "Edgar Allan Poe," in *The Literary History of the United States*, 3 vols., ed. Robert Spillers et. al. (New York: Macmillan, 1948), 342.

72. Matthiessen, "Edgar Allan Poe," 330. For a rich and probing analysis of the relation between Matthiessen's fantasy of "defenestration," his conclusion of *American Renaissance* with the figure of Whitman's "Man in the Open Air," the emergence of the American national security state, and his suicide, see Donald E. Pease, "Negative Interpellations: From Oklahoma City to the Trilling-Matthiessen Transmission," *boundary 2* 23, no. 1 (1996): 1–33.

73. Harry Levin, *Memories of the Moderns* (New York: New Directions, 1982), 219.

74. Poe to Nathaniel P. Willis, December 30, 1836, in *Letters* 2: 339; Matthiessen, "Edgar Allan Poe," 336.

"To Reproduce a City"

New York Letters and the Urban American Renaissance

SCOTT PEEPLES

Traditional formulations of the American Renaissance locate its occurrence al-most exclusively in New England, most famously on Emerson's "bare common" or Thoreau's Walden Pond, but nearly always either "in nature" (on the mast-head of the Pequod, for instance) or a small town (Concord, Salem, Andover) where the past speaks louder than the future. Whitman, of course, is the excep-tion in F. O. Matthiessen's pantheon, but for all his celebration of the urban and the modern, Whitman is just as easily regarded (and taught) as a voice "grow-ing outdoors, / [enamour'd] Of men that live among cattle or taste of the ocean or woods."[1] Another obvious exception—canonical despite his exclusion from *American Renaissance*—is Poe, an author more associated with enclosed spaces than with open, natural environments that invite transcendence. Poe, like most popular writers of his time, was a city dweller throughout his career, as reflected in a large portion of his writing, from the Dupin tales and "The Man of the Crowd" to the comic stories "The Spectacles" and "The Business-Man" to "The Literati of New York City" and the miscellanies in the *Broadway Journal.* Following David S. Reynolds's *Beneath the American Renaissance,* scholarly interest in mid-nine-teenth-century literature has expanded to include sensational and subversive lit-erature associated with the city, as well as Poe's representation of it.[2] Still, more attention needs to be paid to Poe's less canonical urban texts and the mid-cen-tury literature of urbanization generally, not just as a counterpoint to Transcen-dentalism but as a predominant concern of antebellum American culture and literature. Poe, specifically his series "Doings of Gotham," illuminates one par-ticular phenomenon within that literature, the popularity of informal journalistic sketches of New York City life in the early 1840s. "New York Correspondents"—including Poe as well as Nathaniel Parker Willis, Lydia Maria Child, and George G. Foster—responded to the constant and seemingly chaotic change that sur-rounded them by creating textual cities of the future in their own images.

New York's rise as the nation's economic and cultural capital is one of the most dramatic developments of the antebellum period. Having established itself as the national financial center in the wake of the American Revolution, the city saw unparalleled economic growth after the opening of the Erie Canal in 1825 made it the hub of commercial traffic.[3] Meanwhile, largely as a result of German and Irish immigration, the city's population soared from 123,706 in 1820 to 312,710 in 1840 to 813,669 in 1860.[4] Consequently, lower Manhattan became increasingly crowded while the urban frontier moved rapidly northward. Less than 10 percent of the population resided above Fourteenth Street in the early 1830s, but by the end of the 1850s more than 50 percent did. Developers snatched up available land, building on what had previously been green space and creating no new parks (until Central Park was established in 1857) as the grid expanded.[5] Fire and water—particularly the Great Fire of December 1835 and the construction of the Croton Waterworks, which began in 1837—changed the physical and social landscape as well: the fire and subsequent rebuilding frenzy "touched off a pell-mell flight of the wealthy" northward, according to historians Edwin G. Burrows and Mike Wallace.[6] The new mansions were outfitted for running water, provided by the system of aqueducts, tunnels, and pipes from the Croton River.[7] The introduction of north-south rail transportation in 1831, combined with ever-increasing omnibus traffic, changed the pace of city life and made simply crossing the street a new adventure.[8]

Both foreign and domestic observers of antebellum New York expressed amazement at the chaotic energy and rapidity of change in the city. Fanny Kemble described the city in her journal (published in 1835) as "an irregular collection of temporary buildings, erected for some casual purpose, full of life, animation, and variety, but not meant to endure for any length of time."[9] As for the buildings that did endure, their use was likely to change with the city's demographics. "He who erects his magnificent palace on Fifth Avenue to-day," predicted Henry Philip Tappan, "has only fitted out a future boarding-house, and probably occupied the site of a future warehouse."[10] May 1, the annual "moving day" when leases turned over and tenants flooded the streets with all their belongings, seemed to epitomize New York; the very fact that such a large percentage of the city's inhabitants lived in boardinghouses signified a population conditioned to transience. "The streets are alive with business, retail and wholesale, and present an aspect of universal bustle," wrote Isabella Bird in *The Englishwoman in America.* In the words of Lady Emmeline Stuart-Wortley in 1849, "Nothing and nobody seem to stand still for half a moment in New York."[11]

On one hand New York was exceptional: no established U.S. city was grow-ing this quickly, had such a high percentage of foreign-born residents, or was as cosmopolitan. On the other hand those very qualities made it the *most* American city, where national trends were anticipated or intensified, so that to comprehend New York—if one could—was to comprehend America's future.[12] In the preface to his 1837 book *A Glance at New York*, Asa Greene attributes to the entire nation the pace of change that will quickly make his book obsolete: "[T]he changes, tak-ing place in every part of the United States, being confessedly such as to outstrip the rapidity of modern printing, no reader, it is supposed, can be so unreasonable as to expect that those facts, which have been written respecting the condition of any part of this country to-day shall come out of the press equally facts respect-ing its condition to-morrow. It should not surprise him, therefore, to find some little variance between Truth and Type in the following pages."[13] A decade later, in his series *New York in Slices*, George G. Foster would claim that "every powerful nation must have one intellectual centre, as every individual must have a brain, whose motions and conceptions govern the entire system. In the United States, New York is that centre and that brain."[14]

New York's rise as a center of print culture played a significant role in making it the nation's "brain"; the fact that so many visitors and residents were publish-ing their impressions established Gotham as a textual space, an idea or perhaps a set of competing ideas, descriptions, and printed responses to the physical city. Greene alludes to the variance between "Truth and Type" as a result of constantly changing Truth, but we might also take his distinction to suggest a more funda-mental variance between the brick-and-mortar (and wooden) city and the vir-tual—or textual—city. The sources quoted above attest to the emergence of the metropolis-as-text, examined at length by David Henkin in his book *City Reading*. Henkin quotes Nathaniel Hawthorne's 1836 editorial commentary on an illustra-tion, published in *The American Magazine of Useful and Entertaining Knowledge*, of Coffee House Slip on Wall Street: "[T]he mere shadowy image of a building, on the frail material of paper . . . is likely to have a longer term of existence than the piled brick and mortar of the building."[15] In this passage Hawthorne, an "Ameri-can Renaissance" writer with little connection to New York, recognized not only the ephemeral status of buildings but also the importance of the city as repre-sented in periodicals such as the *American Magazine*, acknowledging the alter-nate—but not entirely separate—existence of what Henkin calls the "paper city." Ultimately Henkin is less concerned with texts and printed images representing the city than he is with the new and expanding uses of print and "public reading" in antebellum New York; his work suggests that New Yorkers quite literally *read* the city, which was covered in printed material ranging from signs painted on buildings to "bills" posted on any available wall space to newspapers to visiting cards to paper money. But, as the Hawthorne quote illustrates, the physical city was simultaneously written *on* and written *about*; in both ways it was coming to be understood primarily through the medium of print. Newspapers in particular became "a central site in the city's public sphere and, moreover, a dominant force in the construction of the city as what Benedict Anderson has called an 'imagined community.'"[16]

As it did for so many other transplants, New York might have represented for Poe a chance to make a new start for a writer-editor frustrated by the lack of forward progress in his career. It has never been clear exactly why, in April 1844, Poe moved from Philadelphia back to New York (where he had lived for about a year in 1837–38), but Arthur Hobson Quinn's suggestion that "it was the atmosphere of the growing metropolis . . . rather than any specific advantage" makes sense.[17] Poe's letter to Maria Clemm, written the morning after his arrival with Virginia, attests to his optimism as well as his anxieties. He rhapsodizes over the bounteous feasts presented to them at their boarding house: "Last night, for supper, we had the nicest tea you ever drank, strong & hot—wheat bread & rye bread— cheese—tea-cakes (elegant) a great dish (2 dishes) of elegant ham, and 2 of cold veal, piled up like a mountain and large slices—3 dishes of the cakes, and every thing in the greatest profusion. No fear of starving here." Unless he runs out of money, of course. There are eight references to prices, buying, and borrowing in this relatively brief letter, suggesting that finances were a source of friction between Poe and Muddy and that the decision to move to New York was a calculated gamble that Poe believed would pay off if he could remain frugal and sober: "We have now got 4 $ and half left. Tomorrow I am going to try & borrow 3 $—so that I may have a fortnight to go upon. I feel in excellent spirits & have'nt drank a drop—so that I hope so[on] to get out of trouble."[18]

Poe lived in Manhattan for the next two years, moving across the Bronx River to Fordham in 1846. A renter like most New Yorkers of his time, he had at least five different residences in those two years: from the boarding house, he moved the family to the "Brennan Farm" in what is now the Upper West Side; they moved back to the city proper in early 1845 and relocated at least two more times before the end of the year.[19] During the pivotal, hectic period in Manhattan, Poe published fifteen new stories—more than any comparable period of his career— but also contributed dozens of reviews, editorials, notices, and announcements to the *Evening Mirror* and the *Broadway Journal.* He experienced the radical turns of fortune that characterized the nation's cultural and financial center: he became a celebrity upon the publication of "The Raven" in early 1845, gained control of his own periodical, and then struggled and failed to keep it alive as his reputation faltered. Having grown up in Richmond, the third largest city in the South, and having worked in what he famously called the "magazine prison-house" there as well as Baltimore, New York, and Philadelphia, Poe could certainly appreciate the relationship between print culture and city life.

Probably just before moving from Philadelphia to New York in April 1844, Poe arranged with Eli Bowen, the nineteen-year-old co-editor of the *Columbia Spy,* a modest weekly published in Columbia, Pennsylvania, to contribute weekly columns on life in the Metropolis. Unfortunately, little can be known about how Poe came to this arrangement with Bowen; but the *Spy* promoted Poe in the weeks before it began publishing "Doings," noticing the "Balloon Hoax" within days of its appearance in the *Sun* and reprinting Poe's most recent story, "A Tale of the Ragged Mountains," from *Godey's.*[20] With the publication of the first installment on May 18, Bowen included this introduction:

> Edgar A. Poe, Esq., well known to the Literary public as an eminent scholar and distinguished critic, we are pleased to announce to our readers, will, in future, be a regular contributor to the Spy. Besides other matters, he will furnish us with a weekly "Correspondence" from the City of New York, where he has taken up his residence for the present.[21]

Bowen's introduction reminds us that, despite the success of "The Gold-Bug," Poe's reputation prior to the publication of "The Raven" was stronger as a scholar and critic than as a poet or fiction writer. And the announcement that he will write a "Correspondence"—capitalized and in quotation marks—may be read as an expectation that readers would recognize that term as a specific genre within periodical writing.

Which it was. In February 1844, the New York *Herald* griped about the sudden popularity of the form: "It seems that the various leading papers, in many of the States and large cities throughout the Union, do not think their newspaper arrangements complete, unless they have a 'New York correspondent,' who furnishes them with the fiddle-faddle, chit-chat, and other small balderdash, which can be picked up on Broadway, at the bar-rooms, lobbies of the theatres, and other places of public resort in this Babylon."[22] With obvious self-interest, the short-lived *Magazine for the Million* defended what the *Herald* dismissed as a shallow fad, by way of introducing their own series, "Everybody's New York Correspondence" by Giles Scroggins, that same month: "It is a very natural thing that papers in every part of the Union should find their most attractive matter to be a correspondence from the city of New York. . . . In some cases these letters are copied back into our own [New York] papers; and in one instance, of a widely circulated weekly, they prove its most interesting feature." (The editor goes on to encourage "our newspaper contemporaries at a distance" who lack their own New York correspondents to reprint Scroggins's correspondence.)[23] By 1844, the "New York Letters" format was indeed flourishing. The Washington *National Intelligencer* had published a series of widely reprinted New York letters by "E.B." in the late 1830s, and the *Southern Literary Messenger* had attempted a similar series in 1839 (which was revived more successfully in 1848, lasting well into the 1850s). Then in the early 1840s a variety of periodicals—from the *Charleston Mercury* to the *Cincinnati Gazette* to the *New England Weekly Review*—featured dispatches from New York, written in first-person (though the writers were frequently anonymous) and describing personal encounters with the hustle and flow of city life.[24] Growing up alongside, even slightly anticipating, city mystery novels such as George Lippard's *The Quaker City* (1845) and Ned Buntline's *Mysteries and Miseries of New York* (1848), the "Letters from New York" subgenre thrived in a period when New York's transformation fascinated both its own inhabitants and readers throughout the United States.

When the *Herald* referred to the popularity of "chit-chat" and the *Magazine for the Million* cited the "most interesting feature" of a "widely circulated weekly," both were almost certainly referring to the New York letters of Nathaniel Parker Willis, who as editor of the *New Mirror* regularly reprinted his own "Chit-Chat of New York," written for the *National Intelligencer* in 1843–44. Willis had pioneered the genre of periodical travel dispatches in the early 1830s with a series of gossipy, voyeuristic letters from Europe. In the early 1840s he wrote New York letters for the satirical weekly *Brother Jonathan,* then moved his column to the *National Intelligencer* (which *Brother Jonathan* occasionally reprinted as "Things in New York," alongside other series such as "The Architects and Architecture of New York" and the satirical series "Life in New York" by "Jonathan Slick"). The *New Mirror,* edited by Willis and George Pope Morris, not only reprinted his correspondence for the *Intelligencer* but also published a few installments of another Willis series entitled "Daguerreotype Sketches of New York," soon replaced by his equally Gotham-centered "Jottings," not to mention a number of other writers' impressions under titles such as "Sketches of the Metropolis." Expanding on the concept, the *Mirror* also frequently published "correspondence" from writers in Europe and other parts of the United States.

In short, as editor and writer, Willis is the central figure in the development of periodical travel sketches in mid-nineteenth-century America, but in the early 1840s he and others adapted the form to write from an insider's perspective about New York. Already known as a gossipy, esoteric writer, Willis made little effort to analyze the city or comment on political matters. He made clear in the headnote to the first installment of his "Sketches of New York" that, like a daguerreotypist, his goal was to capture the "surface of things in this city."[25] Furthermore, whether writing for the *Mirror* or the *National Intelligencer*, Willis seems to assume an audience familiar with New York, providing no geographical or social orientation. Consider, for instance, this description of the City Hall Park fountain:

> I chanced to look down upon the Park while the ground was covered, and I wished that the Common Council might see it with my eyes, for the fountain was playing beautifully in a basin of spotless white, which, if exactly imitated in marble, would be better worthy of that radiant column than the mingled mud and greensward that commonly surround it. I have been surprised to notice the complete satiety of public curiosity to this superb object. A column of water, fifty or sixty feet high, is continually playing in the most thronged thoroughfare of the city, and it already attracts as little attention as the trees in the Park, or the liberty-cap on Tammany Hall.[26]

As this passage suggests, seeing the city through Willis's eyes is the purpose of the "daguerreotype sketches," but he presumes that his readers have already seen it with their own eyes. Willis often seems to be teaching his readers to appreciate the physical beauty of the urban environment: referring to the snow's melting a week later, he writes, "Much as nature loves the country, she opens her green lap first in the cities."[27] Similarly, the entries in his earlier series for the *National Intelligencer* almost invariably began with a discussion of the weather. Of course, the weather is not always good, but his preoccupation with it reminds his readers that such simple, physical pleasures and frustrations as those that come with the changing seasons are conversation openers for New Yorkers just as they are for everyone else, an element of cozy familiarity in a place typically depicted as chaotic and foreign. While acknowledging—indeed, chronicling—New York's constant change, Willis's persona (somewhat like Whitman's a decade later in "Crossing Brooklyn Ferry") sees and celebrates a city that maintains its beauty and its essential character.

As T. O. Mabbott surmised when the "Doings of Gotham" series was discovered in 1928, Poe's tone "is largely . . . intended to be like that of the most popular light journalist of the day, N. P. Willis" (xvii). Without question, Poe was thinking about Willis at the time he was writing for the *Spy:* he introduced himself to Willis in a letter dated May 21, 1844, three days after the publication of the first "Doings" installment.[28] Probably in an effort to win Willis's favor, Poe references him in three of the seven installments, even quoting two entire poems (Willis was the only poet so honored). Though the resemblance fades over the course of "Doings of Gotham," in the first letter Poe is clearly imitating Willis's breezy style of journalism:

> It will give me much pleasure, gentlemen, to comply with your suggestions and, by dint of a weekly epistle, keep you *au fait* to a certain portion of the doings of Gotham. And here if, in the beginning, for "certain," you read "*un*certain," you will the more readily arrive at my design. For, in fact, I must deal chiefly in gossip—in gossip, whose empire is unlimited, whose influence is universal, whose devotees are legion; —in gossip, which is the true safety-valve of society—engrossing at least seven-eighths of the whole waking existence of mankind. (23)

The emphasis on gossip, the elevated language ("epistle," "*au fait*"), and the rhetorical apology for his own lack of serious purpose evoke Willis's trademark persona. By the end of the first letter, Poe even praises the same park fountain Willis described in the *Mirror,* comparing it favorably to the one at the old Bowling Green on lower Broadway. Poe never achieved, or perhaps never really sought, that kind of consistency or intimacy with his audience that defined Willis's career, but "Doings of Gotham" seems like an attempt to emulate (and perhaps parody) Willis.[29] Along with his editorial miscellanies in the *Broadway Journal* (September 1845–January 1846) and "The Literati of New York City" (June–October 1846), "Doings" presents Poe as a literary gossip columnist. And yet he's ultimately not very gossipy: he reports on the furor over the publication of a book defaming James Gordon Bennett, the reaction to his own "Balloon Hoax," the popularity of Morris and Willis, a small scandal involving the Kentucky poet William Wallace, the misplaced (in Poe's opinion) excitement over Edward Bulwer's visit to New York in the wake of Dickens's tour, and so on. But amidst these reports from literary New York are random comments on foot races (he's unimpressed), raree shows, architecture, political campaigns, blue laws (he's against them), the "space-penetrating" Frauenhofer telescope, the presidential campaign, the Wilkes Expedition to the South Pole, and the grisly murder case of Polly Bodine.

Having just moved from Philadelphia, Poe makes occasional references to his recent home, but he neither declares nor implies any moral judgment on New York through these comparisons, other than to point out that Gotham is generally dirtier than its rival. Poe remarks significantly on the rapid pace, and particularly the pace of *change,* in New York:

> A day or two [ago] I procured a light skiff, and with the aid of a pair of sculls (as they here term short oars, or paddles) made my way around Blackwell's Island, on a voyage of discovery and exploration. The chief interest of the adventure lay in the scenery of the Manhattan shore, which is here particularly picturesque. The houses are, without exception, frame, and antique. Nothing very modern has been attempted—a necessary result of the subdivision of the whole island into streets and town-lots. I could not look on the magnificent cliffs, and stately trees, which at every moment met my view, without a sigh for their inevitable doom—inevitable and swift. In twenty years, or thirty at farthest, we shall see here nothing more romantic than shipping, warehouses, and wharves. (40–41).

Here we have Poe not slouched over a writing desk, not wearing that worried look as he takes the drink that will lead to three days' debilitation, not hovering over Virginia's sick bed, but paddling a little boat, looking up and enjoying the scenery, even lamenting the inevitable loss of natural beauty. Whether or not Poe really took time out to paddle on the East River and contemplate the transformation of his environment, he was comfortable adopting the persona of someone who did. Poe seems to have known that this sort of excursion, these sorts of observations – on the changing cityscape, the destruction of anything old—and even the semi-detachment of a journalist who can appreciate what is being lost as the city changes and grows were conventions of the "New York Correspondence."

"The city is thronged with strangers," Poe writes in his second letter, "and everything wears an aspect of intense life" (31). Poe likely moved on May 1, experiencing first-hand the day's notorious chaos, to which he alludes in his first letter:

> We are not yet over the bustle of the first of May. "Keep Moving" have been the watchwords for the last fortnight. The man who, in New York, would be so bold as not to peregrinate on the first, would, beyond doubt, attain immortality as "The Great Unmoved"—a title applied by Horne, the author of "Orion," to one of his heroes, Akinetos, the type of the spirit of Apathy. (24)

Not surprisingly, given Poe's socially conservative outlook, he seems sympathetic to the mythical "Great Unmoved" amidst the constant motion of New York. He praises the "unspoiled" parts of the city—foreshadowing Whitman, he refers to it by the aboriginal name "Manahatta" —and descries "improvement." He describes the "shanties of the Irish squatters" as "picturesque," and laments the impending doom of old wooden mansions: "The spirit of Improvement has withered them with its acrid breath," he writes. "Streets are already 'mapped' through them, and they are no longer suburban residences, but 'town-lots.'" Elsewhere he laments that "[i]n some thirty years every noble cliff will be a pier, and the whole island will be densely desecrated by buildings of brick, with portentous *facades* of brown-stone, or brown-*stonn,* as the Gothamites have it" (26).

Poe is particularly distressed by new architectural developments in Brooklyn, which he describes in his fifth letter: "I know few towns which inspire me with so great disgust and contempt" (59), mainly because of the new style of houses being built there: "What can be more silly and pitiably absurd than palaces of painted white pine, fifteen feet by twenty?" (59) In Poe's "The Business Man," Peter Proffitt had attempted to make a living building shanties next to fashionable new palaces, enticing his neighbor to pay him to move his "eyesore";[30] the Poe of "Doings of Gotham" clearly prefers the "eyesore," as he condemns the architects of "Brooklynite 'villa's" to hell: "I really can see little difference between putting up such a house as this, and blowing up a House of Parliament, or cutting the throat of one's grandfather" (60). He's not terribly enamored of Brooklyn's street vendors, either. They make life noisy, as does inferior stone pavement, to which Poe has the solution:

> Of the stereatomic wooden pavement, we hear nothing, now, at all. The people seem to have given it up altogether—but nothing better could be invented. We inserted the blocks, without preparation, and they failed. Therefore, we abandoned the experiment. Had they been Kyanized, the result would have been very different, and the wooden causeways would have been in extensive use throughout the country. . . . In point of cheapness, freedom from noise, ease of cleaning, pleasantness to the hoof, and, finally, in point of durability, there is *no* equal to that of the Kyanized wood. But it will take us, as usual, fully ten years to make this discovery. In the meantime, the present experiments with unprepared wood will answer very well for the profit of the street-menders, and for the amusement of common-councils—who will, perhaps, in the next instance, experiment with soft-soap, or sauer-kraut. (61–63)

Like the "skiff" passage quoted above, this one—from which I've quoted selectively in the interest of length—might stump some readers who think they know Poe when they see him. Did Poe really care this much about street paving? Almost a year later, in the *Broadway Journal,* he would again hold forth on the subject, not merely reprinting the long paragraph quoted above but expanding his claims on behalf of Kyanized wooden pavement. The gossipy, Willis-inspired style of the first letter quickly gives way to the voice of a stodgy and somewhat cranky old-timer. Here and throughout most of "Doings of Gotham," Poe presents himself not as the new arrival that he was but as a curmudgeonly Knickerbocker.

By contrast, Willis's celebration of Gotham is rarely dampened, but he does give a sobering account of a police-escorted visit to Five Points, as if duty-bound to follow the path set by Charles Dickens in *American Notes.* His description is consistent with Dickens's and others', registering the requisite shock at the sight of extreme poverty: "I did not dream that human beings, within reach of human aid, could be abandoned to the wretchedness which I there saw—and I have not described the half of it, for the delicacy of your readers would not bear it, even in description. And all these horrors of want and abandonment lie almost within sound of your voice, as you pass Broadway!"[31] He recovers his enthusiasm for Gotham quickly, however. Immediately after his description of Five Points, he compares New York to Boston, reinforcing the association of the latter with Puritanism and tradition, the former with individualism and experimentation: "Every eye in Boston seems to move in its socket with a check—a fear of meeting something that may offend it—and all heads are carried in a posture of worthy gravity, singularly contagious." New York is to Boston as rice—"boiled to let every grain fall apart" —is to mush: "Every man you meet in our city walks with his countenance free of any sense of observation or any dread of his neighbour. . . . Boston has the advantage in many things, but a man who has any taste for cosmopolitism would very much prefer New York."[32]

Willis was invoking a well-established contrast—New York's upper class was itself split between "Yankees" from New England and "Knickerbockers" of Anglo-Dutch and Huguenot ancestry—in which Boston represented the American past and Gotham the future.[33] In August 1841, Lydia Maria Child, newly arrived from Boston, made the same contrast a starting point for her highly regarded series of letters published in the New York–based *National Anti-Slavery Standard,* which she edited from 1841 to 1843. If Willis provided the prototype, Child's New York letters represent the pinnacle of the form: no other writer of the period described so much of the city or had such a keen eye for the implications of what she saw. Written ostensibly to her friend, the Boston lawyer and abolitionist Ellis Gray Loring, the letters are of course directed more widely to the *Standard's* potential readership, an attempt to broaden the appeal of the anti-slavery periodical.

In the earlier letters particularly, she compares New York to Boston, her home, but she seems to have quickly adopted the more brightly lit and less tradition-bound Gotham. She prefers the Battery to the Common, describing the former like an intoxicated tour-guide: "The city lamps surround you, like a shining belt of descended constellations, fit for the zone of Urania; while the pure bright stars peep through the dancing foliage, and speak to the soul of thoughtful shepherds on the ancient plains of Chaldea." Like Willis, Child offers readers a slightly de-familiarized, appreciative way of seeing the city, as her description moves from night to day: "But if you would see the Battery in all its glory, look at it when, through the misty mantle of retreating dawn, is seen the golden light of the rising sun!" From that vantage she sees emblems of the past in sailing ships and of the present in steamships: "In that steamer, see you not an appropriate type of the busy, powerful, self-conscious Present? Of man's conquering outward Force; and thus making the elements his servants?" Child, inveterate reformer though she is, does not protest the enslavement of the natural elements: the steamers, like New York itself, represent not just the present but the future, which she believes is bright. Even so, Child clings to some vestiges of the past, as in her first letter, when she passes street musicians, and complains that Boston has banned "these tuneful idlers," who "are to the drudging city, what Spring birds are to the country." Although she associates street-organs and bag-pipes with the past, she notes that it is the more modern city of New York that preserves them: "The world has passed from its youthful, Troubadour Age, into the thinking, toiling Age of Reform. This we may not regret, because it needs must be. But welcome, most welcome, all that brings back reminiscences of its childhood, in the cheering voice of poetry and song!"[34]

Typically, an individual letter begins with a visit to a specific locale or a chance encounter or incident; then Child reflects and expands upon the impression the experience had upon her, what it means socially, politically, or spiritually. And always, she maintains an intimate tone, alluding frequently and self-consciously to the philosophy and writing style that define her persona in the *Letters*. "I have lost the power of looking merely on the surface," she writes, in contrast with Willis, forecasting her method of *starting* with surface observations before delving into their implications for the future of the city and civilization generally (10).

Of course, Child's reform impulses drive her descriptions of poverty and injustice throughout the series as well. In Letter 2, she decries the slaughter of dogs ("at the rate of three hundred a day" in the summer of 1841 [15]), in Letter 28 the plight of match-girls, in Letter 29 the condition of prisoners on Blackwell's Island.

And in Letter 14 she describes one of the prototypical modern urban encounters, an inert body on the sidewalk:

> As I turned into the street where God has provided me with a friendly shelter, something lay across my path. It was a woman, apparently dead; with garments all draggled in New-York gutters, blacker than waves of the infernal rivers. Those who gathered around, said she had fallen in intoxication, and was rendered senseless by the force of the blow. They carried her to the watch-house, and the doctor promised she would be well attended. (62)

Though Child expresses sympathy for the woman, her description is straightforward and unemotional; neither she nor the crowd expresses alarm. The incident affects her enough that she considers staying indoors, but that proves to be only a passing thought. Indeed, her next ramble takes her to a pauper's burying-ground, where she looks into an open trench: "there I could see piles of unpainted coffins heaped one upon the other, left uncovered with earth, till the yawning cavity was filled with its hundred tenants" (65). Child finds that in New York, as in Poe's "City in the Sea," Death looks gigantically down. In an earlier letter, she had remarked that "Life is a reckless game, and death is a business transaction. Warehouses of ready-made coffins, stand beside warehouses of ready-made clothing, and the shroud is sold with spangled opera-dresses" (44). She does not need to state outright that human life is cheapened when the sight of a half-dead woman collapsed on the sidewalk is unremarkable, when coffins are stacked up in a potter's field and "death is a business transaction." In fact, the anonymous city breaks down the belief in the autonomous self as she contemplates this modern, impersonal way of death, sounding surprisingly like one of Poe's narrators:

> There is something impressive, even to painfulness, in this dense crowding of human existence, this mercantile familiarity with death. It has sometimes forced upon me, for a few moments, an appalling night-mare sensation of vanishing identity; as if I were but an unknown, unnoticed, and unseparated drop in the great ocean of human existence; as if the uncomfortable old theory were true, and we were but portions of a Great Mundane Soul, to which we ultimately return, to be swallowed up in its infinity. (44)

Child banishes the thought from her mind, and in doing so she responds as city-dwellers must: acknowledging their own anonymity, then denying it, even imagining themselves to be more honest than others for having even temporarily confronted the fact that they are unrecognizable as unique selves. She tries to laugh it off with a Thoreauvian quip, finding it "wiser to forbear inflating this balloon of thought, lest it roll me away through unlimited space, until I become like the absent man, who put his clothes in bed, and hung himself over the chair; or like his twin-brother, who laid his candle on the pillow and blew himself out" (44).

This essential tension in *Letters from New York*—between the depersonalizing environment of a "world of strangers" and the progress toward an age of empathy and love in which Child fervently believes—plays out in her depiction of immigrant groups and African Americans as well. Like most reformers of her time, Child held condescending, even racist views of ethnic Others, and for better and worse this racializing became part of her larger philosophy of human progress.[35] After a visit to a synagogue, she writes admiringly of Jewish rituals but stresses that Jews themselves mistake the past—which, to her, they represent—for the present and future: the effect of the synagogue "was strange and bewildering; spectral and flitting; with a sort of vanishing resemblance to reality; the magic lantern of the Past" (24); "I look upon the Future with active hope, and upon the Past with loving reverence," so "the scene would have strongly excited my imagination and my feelings, had there not been a heterogeneous jumbling of the Present with the Past" (25). After describing the dress and movements of "the Priest," she summarizes the visit: "I had turned away from the turmoil of the Present, to gaze quietly for a while on the grandeur of the Past; and the representatives of the Past walked before me" (25). Later in the letter, as if to drive the point home, she compares Jews to a man who lights a lamp in order to read before the sun comes up but keeps it burning well into the day, not having noticed the change that has rendered the lamp unnecessary (27).

Child's description of the Irish is equally condescending but more favorable in regard to her beliefs about human progress. "I love the Irish," she writes. "Blessings on their warm hearts, and their leaping fancies! [Thomas] Clarkson records that while opposition met him in almost every form, not a single Irish member of British Parliament ever voted against the abolition of the slave trade; and how is the heart of that generous island now throbbing with sympathy for the American slave!" Irish opposition to slavery did not cross the Atlantic, and in fact racist violence by Irish against Blacks would reach a horrific climax in the Draft Riots two decades later;[36] but in December 1842, Child sees the Irish and Africans as allies in bringing about a new age: "Not in vain is Ireland pouring itself all over the earth. Divine Providence has a mission for her children to fulfil [*sic*]. . . . The Irish, with their glowing hearts and reverent credulity, are needed in this cold age of intellect and skepticism" (151). The same, she claims, is true of the African diaspora and women's widening "field of action." "All these things," Child claims, "prophesy of physical force yielding to moral sentiment; and they all are agents to fulfil what they prophesy. God speed the hour" (152). Confronted, then, with the multicultural stew of 1840s New York, Child takes a view nearly opposite to those who posited a racial hierarchy or sounded the alarm against the genetic pollution of immigrants; instead, she looks hopefully toward a future in which the earth is dominated by the Irish, Africans, and women.

Despite her confrontations with urban poverty and injustice throughout the *Letters*, Child finds symbols of hope in uniquely urban scenes and rituals. On her walk home from the despairing trip to the graveyard, she stops to look at the reflection of multi-colored lights from a shop window in puddles of water in the street: "It was like poetic thoughts in the minds of the poor and ignorant; like the memory of pure aspirations in the vicious; like a rainbow of promise, that God's spirit never leaves even the most degraded soul. I smiled, as my spirit gratefully accepted this love-token from the outward" (63). In the final letter (as they appeared in book form), Child remarks on Moving Day with a mixture of awe and distaste:

> May-day in New York is the saddest thing, to one who has been used to hunting mosses by the brook, and paddling in its waters. Brick walls, instead of budding trees, and rattling wheels in lieu of singing birds, are bad enough; but to make the matter worse, all New-York *moves* on the first of May; not only moves about, as usual, in the everlasting hurry-scurry of business, but one house empties itself into another, all over the city. (176)

Moreover, she notes that this phenomenon, once a function of leases and a fluctuating housing market, has taken on a life of its own as a ritual; like Poe remarking on the oddity of "Great Unmoved," she quotes a neighbor who would be "ashamed" not to move on May 1. But, as is typical for her, Child turns moving day into a positive image of progress, dismissing her own criticism as a "foolish, whining complaint." After all, "Man is moving to his highest destiny through manifold revolutions of spirit; and the outward must change with the inward. . . . The old fisherman, who would have exterminated steam-boats, because they frightened the fish away from the waters where he had baited them for years, was by no means profound in his social views, or of expansive benevolence" (178). In stark contrast with Poe, Child's belief that spiritual progress accompanies or parallels the development of the city—whether that development takes the form of the mixing of races or the reinvention that comes with moving to a new residence—trumps her fears regarding more immediate social consequences of urbanization.

Child's *Letters* found an even wider audience when she collected them for a book, published initially at her own expense, in 1843: *Letters from New-York* went through eleven printings by 1850. Meanwhile, she moved her letters series to the *Boston Courier* and collected these later installments as *Letters from New York, Second Series,* in 1845.[37] That same year, George G. Foster, who would later publish the bestselling *New York in Slices* (1849) and *New York by Gaslight* (1850), contributed a brief series entitled "Letters from Broadway" to *The Harbinger,* the weekly publication of the Fourierist Brook Farm Phalanx. If Poe's initial model was Willis, Foster's was Child, the reformer who had effectively blended social commentary with wonder and playful, sometimes light-hearted description. "What of all this flashing surge, —this never-ceasing whirl of crash and clamor, with which the great car of life rolls on, —that tells aught but its own paltry story? What veins of golden light, darting beneath the troubled surface, herald the yet unrisen day?"[38] So begins Foster's first letter, in a style that clearly evokes Child. After describing the heterogenous crowd, Foster's first letter recalls watching workmen wave from the spire of the new Trinity Church, which introduces reflections on the wastefulness of the church's enormous cost, money that could be better spent easing the suffering of New York's poor. His next stop is a funeral procession for Andrew Jackson; after criticizing the hypocrisy of better-dressed mourners, he focuses on the music played at the procession:

> It was scientific to a very high degree,—warm, fresh, gushing with eloquent sentiment,—it spoke the yet unformed aspirations of the national heart. We are a musical people; we are to be a music and beauty-creating people; our destiny it is to cherish all forms of the Beautiful, and to develop the Fine Arts to a point of perfection, in the closer union of critical excellence with unexhausted inspiration, never yet seen on this earth.[39]

Like Child, Foster enlarges a moment of music appreciation into a vision of national destiny, implicitly one linked to the triumph of Fourierism in this case. The difference, in this passage, is Foster's formation of a national character; Child, as we have seen, was more likely to de-emphasize nation and link "racial" or ethnic characteristics to *human* progress. But Foster's series reinforces the impression that New York—not the Brook Farm Phalanx—is the real harbinger of change, the place where something like a national character or future society might be perceived.

At the beginning of his third "Letter from Broadway," Foster promotes *The Harbinger* by suggesting that the magazine is gaining popularity in Gotham:

> At the theatre, in hotels, on steamboats, in the picture-gallery, every where,—common-place conversation is often interrupted by a discursive discussion of some topic in the Harbinger; and thus are the people becoming gradually familiarized to the presence of that which they will at last have the courage to examine. Last night I heard a fashionably dressed man and woman, on their way to the Alhambra, engaged in a most deep and earnest discussion of the *practicability* of Association [Fourierist communal living]. Eloquent truths and fitly spoken, came to me between the waves of omnibus-rattle and villainous cigar-smoke! Is this not something?[40]

This passage reveals the presumption that New York is enemy territory for Brook Farmers—no surprise—and suggests that Foster's column was literally a dialogue-opener between the two worlds. The incongruity Foster sees between the "truths" of Fourierism—in another letter he refers to the Brook Farm Phalanx as "devoted . . . to the noble cause of humanity" —and the environment represented by omnibuses and cigars sets him further apart from the reform-minded Child: Foster's hope is for propagating revolutionary truth rather than fighting specific injustices or taking gradual steps toward egalitarian goals. Accordingly, his responses to life in Gotham tend toward cynicism and hyperbole: the influence of fashionable women is "more pernicious than that of the great moral sores that fester around the heart of society" and fashion itself is "a broad, deep, all-pervading curse . . . productive of every evil, every social calamity!"[41] Elsewhere he satirically argues that the logic of capital punishment should be extended to judges and juries: "They surely should be killed as well as the other murderers!"[42] And in the last letter of the series, he rails against political corruption and the "annual farce called 'Municipal Election,'" telling readers that "You have worked hard for these men, and they are not ungrateful—they are immediately going to work hard—for themselves."[43]

In *New York in Slices* and *New York by Gaslight*, Foster would greatly expand his attack on corruption and economic injustice, retaining from the letters format the voice of a guide to the city while aiming for the comprehensiveness of Child's volume. By 1849 and 1850, when these books were published, city-mysteries fiction had sensationalized the social consequences of rapid urban development and population growth, clearly influencing Foster. *Slices* opens with the declaration, "A great city is the highest result of human civilization," as Foster explains that "it is only in a large city, where some hundreds of thousands combine their various powers, that the human mind can efficiently stamp itself on every thing by which it is surrounded—can transmute the insensible earth to a fit temple and dwelling place for immortal spirits."[44] But in the next paragraph he hears the "groans of the victims hourly choked and thrust down beneath the wave" of "money, gain and traffic," destined for "'the night's Plutonian shore'" (of all places). If that weren't Gothic enough, Foster soon warns readers to "stop your nose! The horrible stench of poverty, misery, beggary, starvation, crime, filth, and licentiousness that congregate in our Large City, of which we were just now so boastful, as being the highest work of human mind and genius, comes reeking round the corner, and in a moment we shall stand by the very rotting skeleton of City Civilization."[45] But despite this sensational beginning, *Slices* settles into a generally sober tour of the city, or at least a "balanced" assessment, with scathing attacks on mock-auctions and prostitution, appreciative chapters on public markets and eating houses, and mixed reviews of journalists and Bowery B'hoys. *Gaslight* is more thoroughly Gothic, presenting New York after dark as a labyrinthine world inhabited by prostitutes and con men, effectively merging the city mystery with the "New York Letters" form.

The New York Letters of Willis, Poe, Child, and Foster—all published in the first half of the 1840s—present a spectrum of responses to the phenomenal growth of the city. Willis celebrates the physical beauty of the urban landscape and the amusements of the "upper ten-thousand" (though he's not completely blind to the plight of the underclass); Poe laments the constant change, the unseemly new architecture and inadequate pavement; Child focuses most of her attention on marginalized and economically distressed segments of society but embraces the general current of change and maintains hope for the future; and Foster, while focusing on the same social problems as Child, offers little hope for reform, implicitly arguing for Fourierist utopian revolution in *The Harbinger*, later offering a proto-muckraking exposé in the *Tribune*'s *Slices* and *New York by Gaslight*. Poe's letters, it turns out, are the most staid of the bunch—but the fact that Poe, so often seen as rebelling against trends and cutting his own path through the field of American literature, attempted this form, even imitating Willis in doing so, provides evidence for the vogue of "New York Letters" during that relatively brief period.

Furthermore, reading "Doings of Gotham" against other New York Letters series deepens our appreciation for how enmeshed Poe was in the network of New York journalism, and the small world that that phrase describes. Poe certainly knew Foster: he included him in his 1841 "Chapter on Autography"; as editor of *Graham's,* he published four of Foster's poems; and at one point he considered Foster a potential partner for his never-realized "Stylus" magazine. Their mutual associates included Rufus Griswold, Foster's lifelong friend with whom he lived when both men were in their teens; Thomas Dunn English, one of Poe's bitterest rivals with whom Foster co-edited the *John-Donkey,* a magazine that repeatedly mocked Poe as a crazed alcoholic in the late 1840s; and William Burton, Poe's former employer and co-editor, whose identity Foster temporarily stole, a crime for which he was jailed.[46] Poe's relationship with Willis is better known: Poe worked for Willis from October 1844 to February 1845 at the *Evening Mirror,* where in January 1845 Willis published "The Raven" with great fanfare (and in advance of the *American Review,* to whom Poe had sold the poem); Willis solicited funds for Poe and Virginia in December 1846 (much to Poe's embarrassment) and defended his former employee's character in Rufus Griswold's first edition of Poe's works (1850). Poe had less contact with Child, but he gave her an appreciative if somewhat cold entry in his "Literati of New York City" in 1846. Child and Willis crossed paths throughout their careers, most notably when Child, in 1861, edited Harriet Jacobs's *Incidents in the Life of a Slave Girl;* Willis, who employed Jacobs as a domestic and baby nurse for almost twenty years, appears in *Incidents* as Mr. Bruce. If Foster did not know Willis and Child personally, he certainly knew their work and knew them by sight, for he describes both of them in *New York in Slices:* Child in the "Literary Soirees" chapter, where she seems "uneasy and restless"; Willis, a "human julep, composed of spirits and sugar, with a pungent flavor of the mint," sighted in a chapter on Delmonico's.[47] Coincidentally, just two weeks before Foster began "Letters from Broadway," *The Harbinger* included both a reprint of Willis's sketch of Five Points and a review of Child's *Letters from New York, Second Series.*

The *Harbinger*'s reviewer, John S. Dwight, declares that "it takes all the humanity, all the sincerity, the faith, the buoyancy, the freedom, the spirituality, the ideality, and the reality of a Mrs. Child, to reproduce a city."[48] Dwight recognizes not only Child's virtues but also the intent of her project, to *reproduce* a city. Thanks to Bruce Mills's 1998 edition of *Letters from New-York* and the inclusion of excerpts in the *Heath Anthology of American Literature,* Child's *Letters* series is now well known among nineteenth-century Americanists, though it is still hardly one of the canonical classroom "Renaissance" texts. Even less canonical is the subgenre to which Child's letters and Poe's "Doings of Gotham" belong: reproducing the city through journalistic letters was the project of more than a dozen writers for newspapers and magazines in the late 1830s and 1840s. In turn, these familiar New York letters were themselves part of a larger project of creating (not merely reproducing) the idea of Gotham, the "textual city" that expanded and changed as quickly as the brick-and-mortar metropolis, serving as a synecdoche for the future—of the United States, of civilization itself. All of them seemed to experience the combination of exhilaration and frustration described by Asa Greene, that the social and physical landscape they were trying to capture in print was changing too fast even for periodical publication. Reading these letters, then, one can better understand what Poe was up to in "Doings of Gotham." More important, one can better appreciate the "shock of the new" that New York presented to Americans in the mid-nineteenth century and the range of responses it evoked.

Notes

I would like to thank Mike Duvall, Julia Eichelberger, Leon Jackson, and Maurice Lee for their helpful advice on this essay.

1. Walt Whitman, "Song of Myself," *Leaves of Grass: Comprehensive Reader's Edition*, ed. Harold W. Blodgett and Sculley Bradley (New York: New York Univ. Press, 1965), 41 (lines 255–56).

2. David S. Reynolds, *Beneath the American Renaissance: The Subversive Imagination in the Age of Emerson and Melville* (New York: Knopf, 1988). See also Dana Brand, *The Spectator and the City in Nineteenth-Century American Literature* (Cambridge, UK: Cambridge Univ. Press, 1991); Wyn Kelley, *Melville's City: Literary and Urban Form in Nineteenth-Century New York* (Cambridge, UK: Cambridge Univ. Press, 1996); and Betsy Klimasmith, *At Home in the City: Urban Domesticity in American Literature and Culture, 1850–1930* (Hanover, NH: Univ. Press of New England, 2005).

3. Kenneth T. Jackson and David S. Dunbar, eds., *Empire City: New York through the Centuries* (New York: Columbia Univ. Press, 2002), 102.

4. Campbell Gibson, "Population of the 100 Largest Cities and Other Urban Places in the United States: 1790 to 1990," U. S. Census Bureau, www.census.gov/population/www/documentation/twps0027/twps0027.html (accessed June 25, 2009).

5. David M. Henkin, *City Reading: Written Words and Public Spaces in Antebellum New York* (New York: Columbia Univ. Press, 1998), 33.

6. Edwin G. Burrows and Mike Wallace, *Gotham: A History of New York City to 1898* (Oxford, UK: Oxford Univ. Press, 1999), 600.

7. Eric Homberger, *The Historical Atlas of New York City* (1994; rev. ed., New York: Henry Holt, 2005), 82.

8. Burrows and Wallace, 565.

9. Bayrd Still, *Mirror for Gotham: New York as Seen by Contemporaries from Dutch Days to the Present* (New York: Fordham Univ. Press, 1994), 99.

10. Still, 127.

11. Still, 159–60, 143.

12. According to historian William R. Taylor, for instance, New York is both "unique and representative . . . outlandish, crazy, but somehow typical" (qtd. in Joanne Reitano, *The Restless City: A Short History of New York from Colonial Times to the Present* [New York: Routledge, 2006], 31).

13. Asa Greene, *A Glance at New York* (New York: A. Greene, 1837), v–vi.

14. [George G. Foster], *New York in Slices: by an Experienced Carver* (1849; Ann Arbor: Michigan Historical Reprint Series, n.d.), 63.

15. Henkin, 27.

16. Henkin, 122.

17. Arthur Hobson Quinn, *Edgar Allan Poe: A Critical Biography* (1941; Baltimore: Johns Hopkins Univ. Press, 1998), 405.

18. John Ward Ostrom, Burton R. Pollin, and Jeffrey A. Savoye, eds., *The Collected Letters of Edgar Allan Poe* (New York: Gordian Press, 2008), vol. 1: 437–38.

19. Dwight Thomas and David K. Jackson, *The Poe Log: A Documentary Life of Edgar Allan Poe* (Boston: G. K. Hall, 1987), 463–64; *Collected Letters*, vol. 1: 518, 533–35; Kenneth Silverman, *Edgar A. Poe: Mournful and Never-ending Remembrance* (New York: HarperCollins, 1991), 243.

20. Edgar Allan Poe, *Doings of Gotham,* ed. Jacob E. Spannuth and Thomas Ollive Mabbott (1929; rpt. Folcroft Library Editions, 1974), 121. Subsequent references are to this edition. In the autumn of 1848 Poe corresponded with Bowen again, seeking some kind of partnership or support for "the establishment of a Magazine" and agreeing to write a "Correspondence" for the Miner's Journal of Pottsville, PA (*Collected Letters* 2: 704–5). Poe sent Bowen a manuscript copy of "The Raven," which Bowen conveyed to Dr. Samuel A. Whitaker in Phoenixville, PA, on 25 September 1848, saying that he had received it two days earlier (Thomas and Jackson, 757–58).

21. Poe, *Doings,* 121.

22. "New York Letter Writers," Editorial, New York *Herald,* February 28, 1844: 1A.

23. Giles Scroggins, "Everybody's New-York Correspondence," *Magazine for the Million* 1 (February 17, 1844): 12.

24. A search on the *American Periodicals Series* database yields other examples from 1844–45, including the *Lowell Offering,* the *Christian Reflector,* and the *New York Observer and Chronicle.*

25. [Nathaniel Parker Willis,] "Sketches of New York," *The New Mirror* 1 (May 13, 1843): 85.

26. [Willis,] "Sketches," *The New Mirror* 1 (May 13, 1843): 85.

27. [Nathaniel Parker Willis], "Daguerreotype Sketches of New York," *New Mirror* 1 (May 20, 1843): 105.

28. Thomas and Jackson, 462.

29. Scott Peeples, "'The *Mere* Man of Letters Must Ever Be a Cypher': Poe and N. P. Willis," *ESQ: A Journal of the American Renaissance* 46 (2000): 125–47.

30. On August 2, 1845, Poe published, in the *Broadway Journal,* a revised and expanded version of his sketch "Peter Pendulum, the Business Man," not only shortening the title and changing the narrator's name but also adding six paragraphs and making dozens of small revisions. The fact that Poe took this much interest in the story, rather than simply dumping a lightly revised text into the *Journal,* suggests that on Broadway in 1845 he saw a heightened relevance for its satire of the business world and descriptions of comically exaggerated petty swindles.

31. [Nathaniel Parker Willis], "Daguerreotype Sketches of New York," *New Mirror* 1 (May 20, 1843): 103. For more on Dickens's influence on other writers' depictions of Five Points, see Hans Bergmann, *God in the Street: New York Writing from the Penny Press to Melville* (Philadelphia: Temple Univ. Press, 1995), 115–33.

32. [Willis,] "Daguerreotype Sketches of New York," *New Mirror* 1 (May 20, 1843): 103.

33. Burrows and Wallace, 454–56.

34. Lydia Maria Child, *Letters from New-York,* ed. Bruce Mills (Athens: Univ. of Georgia Press, 1999), 11. Subsequent references are to this edition.

35. For more on Child's racial views and philosophy, see Carolyn L. Karcher, *The First Woman of the Republic: A Cultural Biography of Lydia Maria Child* (Durham, NC: Duke Univ. Press, 1994).

36. See, for instance, Leslie M. Harris, *In the Shadow of Slavery: African Americans in New York, 1626–1863* (Chicago: Univ. of Chicago Press, 2004); and Iver Bernstein, *The New York City Draft Riots: Their Significance for American Society and Politics in the Age of the Civil War* (New York: Oxford Univ. Press, 1991).

37. See Karcher, 310–11.

38. [George G. Foster,] "Letter from Broadway," *The Harbinger* 1 (July 12, 1845): 72.

39. [Foster,] "Letter from Broadway," *The Harbinger* 1 (July 12, 1845): 73.

40. [Foster,] "Letter from Broadway," *The Harbinger* 1 (August 9, 1845): 134.

41. [Foster,] "Letter from Broadway," *The Harbinger* 1 (July 26, 1845): 104.

42. [Foster,] "Letter from Broadway," *The Harbinger* 2 (January 10, 1846): 73–74.

43. [Foster,] "Letter from Broadway," *The Harbinger* 2 (May 2, 1846): 327.

44. *New York in Slices*, 3.

45. *New York in Slices*, 4.

46. Stuart M. Blumin, "George G. Foster and the Emerging Metropolis," *New York by Gas-Light and Other Urban Sketches*, ed. Blumin (Berkeley: Univ. of California Press, 1990), 28–29, 36–37, 41–42. See also George Rogers Taylor, "Gaslight Foster: A New York 'Journeyman Journalist' at Mid-Century," *New York History* 58, no. 3 (1977): 297–312.

47. *New York in Slices*, 62, 74.

48. [John S. Dwight,] Review of *Letters from New York, Second Series,* by L. Maria Child, *The Harbinger* 1 (June 28, 1845): 41.

Poe's 1848

Eureka, the Southern Margin, and the
Expanding U[niverse] of S[tars]

JENNIFER RAE GREESON

> No astronomical fallacy is more untenable, and none has been more perti-
> naciously adhered to, than that of the absolute *illimitation* of the Universe
> of Stars.
>
> —Poe, *Eureka*

Edgar Allan Poe's last major work, *Eureka,* is many things at once. Among others,
this "Essay on the Spiritual and Material Universe" is a metaphysical inquiry into
the nature of human knowledge, and a quasi-scientific treatise on the developing
field of cosmology. My reading in this essay, however, focuses upon *Eureka* as a
satire in which Poe not only engages the language of abstract, theoretical inquiry,
but also remains firmly grounded in the political turmoil of his day. Indeed, adding a reading of *Eureka* as satire to the other ways of reading it reveals a deeper
level of import in the overall work of this complicated essay. Through his com-
pounding of the language of scientific and philosophical inquiry with the language of politics, Poe investigates the extent to which "spiritual" discourses of
objective, impartial Truth may underwrite quite "material" programs of imperial
dominion. To read *Eureka* as a satire is to see in it not only an essay on "the Universe," but also a critique of the real-world uses of the category of "the Universal."

As with any satire, uncovering the satirical dimensions of *Eureka* involves
excavating the context in which Poe wrote it. In the broad realm of U.S. political history, the most obvious context for Poe's essay is that of the U.S.-Mexican
War of 1846–48, the time during which the popular clamor of "Manifest Destiny" reached fever pitch and seemed to realize its ultimate goal. Poe gave the
lecture that was the basis for *Eureka* in February 1848, just three weeks after the
Treaty of Guadalupe-Hidalgo was finalized, ceding California and the present-
day U.S. Southwest to the United States. And Poe cemented the relays of his "universal" treatise with the march of continental expansion when he chose the title

for its published version. He titled the lecture simply "The Cosmogony of the Universe," but by the time he sent the manuscript to press in July he had retitled it "Eureka." In these months, Poe was in close contact with Bayard Taylor, who was serving as the *New York Post* correspondent in California, and thus it is probable that he would have been aware of the gold rush–inspired association of "eureka"—"I have found it"—with that newly acquired territory.[1] By the summer of 1848, a preliminary seal for the future state of California had been designed with the word "eureka" over the top as a motto. Titling anything "Eureka" at this moment was tantamount to titling it "California," naming it for that site at which the United States borders had at last reached continental scale.

A second satirical vector of *Eureka* is revealed when we place the essay in the more local context of Poe's other writing in the last years of his life—in particular, his literary criticism from late 1844 on. During these years in New York, Poe increasingly self-identified as a southerner, an identity that allowed him to express, under the aegis of sectionalism, animus against what he saw as a Boston-centered Transcendentalist hegemony in U.S. letters—a hegemony that he believed privileged political stances over aesthetic achievement, and promoted authors on the basis of their geographical identity rather than their creative genius.[2] In his most direct criticisms of the Boston Transcendentalist writers in the mid-1840s, Poe vociferously protested what he called their "frantic spirit of generalization," their tendency toward universalizing local and personal experience and perspective.[3] Reading *Eureka* in the context of this sectionalist vein of Poe's criticism, we notice that he opens *Eureka* with an extended parody of Ralph Waldo Emerson's defining 1843 *Dial* essay, "The Transcendentalist," in which Emerson had put forth one of his most direct statements of universalizing as method:

> His thought,—that is the Universe. His experience inclines him to behold the procession of facts you call the world, as flowing perpetually outward from an invisible, unsounded centre in himself, centre alike of him and of them. . . . From this transfer of the world into the consciousness, this beholding of all things in the mind, follow easily his whole ethics.[4]

Emerson had proposed that elite New Englanders discerning themselves as the "centre" of the "Universe" represented a triumph of "Idealism" over "Materialism." Poe, in his "Essay on the Material *and* Spiritual Universe," on the other hand, insisted that this "Idealism" worked in the service of, rather than replacing, "Material" aims.[5] By writing a treatise on "our legitimate thesis, *The Universe*," in an over-the-top version of what he elsewhere terms "the tone Transcendental,"

Poe was indicting the Boston "Frogpondians"—as he elsewhere termed Emerson and his circle, emphasizing the smallness of their ostensible metropolis of New England compared to the loudness of their voices.[6] *Eureka* proposes, among other things, that the Transcendentalists wrongly are taking the New England ground on which they stand to be the center of the universe; that they are refusing to see a relativity in their geographical position; and that they self-righteously are assuming that the rest of the world surveyed from the Bostonian mountaintop (in Emerson's phrase, "any hill-side around us") should conform to their parochial and self-aggrandizing agenda.[7]

In other words, reading *Eureka* as a satire reveals to us that the sectionalist vector in Poe's criticism—his anger at being marginalized by the Boston literary establishment—corresponded temporally to an unprecedented peak of expansionist sentiment in U.S. culture more broadly. In bringing together the political fields of sectionalism and expansionism, Poe's culminating "treatise on the universe" offers us a different approach to the political, philosophical, and aesthetic categories of "the American 1848," a moment when domestic and expansionist concerns tellingly overlapped. As a satire, Poe's *Eureka* seeks to expose how the category of the universal generated in New England Transcendentalism provides both form and ideology for a rising American Empire—how the self-centering spirit of universalization bears a real geopolitical consequence that is being revealed in the heat of U.S. expansion.[8] This is a claim counterintuitive to much that we know about the actual political alignments of Transcendentalist icons— we think of Thoreau's night in jail, or Emerson's assurance that acquiring Mexico would "poison" the United States. Yet if Poe's "Cosmogony of the Universe" embodies, at least on one level, his attempt to push Transcendentalist "rant and cant to that degree of excess which inevitably induces reaction," it provides us with an instructive lesson in how the language of the universal may be appropriated for the hierarchical programs of empire.[9]

This paradoxical situation had been evolving in antebellum U.S. letters for some time. Indeed, the most famous image in Emerson's early Transcendentalist writings—the "transparent eyeball" of *Nature* (1836)—is a figure of vanished dominion: "I am nothing; I see all." This dream of an absolute, singular, and omniscient subjectivity, which cannot itself be perceived or objectified, long has been identified as the first published statement of "Emerson's doctrine of the

Oversoul."[10] More recently, scholars have found the "transparent eyeball" formulation exceptionally enabling to Jacksonian expansion, authorizing the expansion itself while simultaneously exempting it from the criticisms leveled at the imperial projects of European nations.[11] Turning to the passage from *Nature,* we perceive that Emerson generates the crucial new image out of a rhetorical relay with sectional—southern—markers.

> In the woods is perpetual youth. Within these plantations of God, a decorum and sanctity reign, a perennial festival is dressed, and the guest sees not how he should tire of them in a thousand years. In the woods, we return to reason and faith. There I feel that nothing can befall me in life,—no disgrace, no calamity (leaving me my eyes), which nature cannot repair. Standing on the bare ground,—my head bathed by the blithe air and uplifted into infinite space,—all mean egotism vanishes. I become a transparent eyeball; I am nothing; I see all; the currents of the Universal Being circulate through me; I am part or parcel of God. The name of the nearest friend sounds then foreign and accidental: to be brothers, to be acquaintances, master or servant, is then a trifle and a disturbance. I am the lover of uncontained and immortal beauty. In the wilderness, I find something more dear and connate than in streets or villages. In the tranquil landscape, and especially in the distant line of the horizon, man beholds somewhat as beautiful as his own nature.[12]

The apotheosis of centralized subjectivity at the center of the passage is bracketed by invocations of the Plantation South and the Slave South, respectively. It is generated out of a specific sort of engagement with undeveloped land: and while "woods" and, particularly, "wilderness"—the other terms Emerson uses for this land in the passage—are historically resonant enough words in New England writing, the crystallizing term here is "plantations of God." This locution takes us back to the foundational Puritan plantations of New England's colonization (Plymouth Plantation, Massachusetts Bay Colony, Rhode Island and Providence Plantations), but by 1836 Emerson also evokes over a half-century of the southern plantation as primal other for the United States.

Ascending out of this simultaneity of selfness and otherness, identity with and opposition to the "plantation"—which flexible term also acts as an index of American history from colonialist contact to the sectionalist present—the "transparent eyeball" emerges to obviate relationship entirely. Now Emerson contextualizes the need to obliterate reciprocality by invoking the modern Slave South of his own moment; he descends from the mountaintop of God-stature via a degenerating progression of social relationships that reads as the demise of Republican ideals under industrialization. "To be brothers, to be acquaintances, master or servant, is then a trifle and a disturbance": he moves from fraternal egalitarianism, to noncommittal impersonality, to the anti-republican power extremes inevitably based upon slavery. While he dismisses this devolution as "a trifle" in the aftermath of achieving absolute subjectivity, he has quite deliberately constructed it as "a disturbance" to his readers. Across the passage, he directs their eyes from the invigorating Plantation South of the colonial past, to the deflating Slave South of the industrial present, and then finally to promised resolution in what might seem the subjugated South of a recuperated U.S. imperial future: "the distant line of the horizon," the promise of unlimited territorial dominion, radiating out so far as the central I/eye may will it.

It makes sense that Emerson would produce the abstract image of unilateral subjectivity, at this historical moment, by cycling through historical incarnations of the South. The founders had assumed that U.S. expansion across the continent would defuse, by diffusing, different forms of strife within the body politic—conflicts between regions, classes, races. Instead, since the Missouri Compromise of 1820, westward expansion had fed the rise of North/South sectionalism, as political leaders from the two regions squared off over whether slavery would be legal or outlawed in the new states that were being carved out of western lands.[13] Central to ordering this rapidly enlarging United States, from Emerson's geographical perspective, was re-mastering its Slave South—for this modern South had broken out of its proper peripheral relation to the national center and was, in renegade fashion, attempting to magnify rather than to ameliorate the national sin of slavery.[14]

Without the perceived challenge from and antagonistic response to this expansionist Slave South, indeed, it is hard to imagine how "New England Transcendentalism"—as it was called in Emerson's day and still is in our own—could have come into being. The term itself is plainly oxymoronic: what could be considered to be transcendent about so small and so particular a locality?[15] Rather than transcending place, the body of writing produced by Emerson in the years before the Civil War inscribes it as a silent norm, as a universal center. By 1851, Emerson was explicitly positing Massachusetts as the Western analogue of London on the imperial globe. "Massachusetts is little," he allows, but consider "Massachusetts in all the quarters of her dispersion"—the small state as controlling center of a vast, subordinate periphery. Just as "every Roman reckoned himself at least a match for a Province," and just as "every Englishman . . . in whatever barbarous country . . . represents the art, power and law of Europe," so should every Harvard man "carry the like advantages into the South."[16] This unilateral authority of the tiny center over a vast and limitless periphery—"the farthest South, and the uttermost West"—is mandated by universal and natural law: "Every nation and every man bows, in spite of himself, to a higher mental and moral existence." Emerson's appeal to higher law, though, is provoked by a quite down-to-earth, indeed debasing, statute: this is his first address on the Fugitive Slave Law of 1850, which he protests chiefly because it has caused "this royal position of Massachusetts" to be "foully lost." Sectionalist maneuvering in Congress, compromise between sections, the election of slaveholding presidents from the southern states: the politics of the day are confusing the natural, universal geographic order of things—the dominance, in the age of Empire, of the center over its periphery. "It is confounding distinctions," Emerson protests, "to speak of the geographic sections of this country as of equal civilization." The paradox is profound, and difficult to assimilate: arguing against slavery is not necessarily arguing for universal liberation and equality. Rather, an emancipationist program may exist comfortably alongside, and possibly even bolster, a system of hierarchy and domination on other bases and by other means—as the contemporaneous case of British West Indian emancipation was demonstrating in the 1830s and 1840s.[17]

New England Transcendentalism, as Emerson was developing it between 1836 and 1851, did a breathtaking end-run around the sectionalist stand-off in U.S. letters—the back-and-forth of Industrial North and Slave South, wage slavery and chattel slavery. Most southern partisans failed to comprehend the power of this new universalism, and simply dismissed Transcendentalist writers as obfuscating and possibly unhinged. But Poe grasped the potential "materialist" ends of the new "idealist" aesthetic from quite early on. Following on the heels of Emerson's *Nature*, Poe's only novel, *The Narrative of Arthur Gordon Pym* (1838), reads as a sort of hallucinatory incarnation of Emerson's "transparent eyeball." Claiming to be a found document from the United States Exploring Expedition of 1836–38—a real mission of unprecedented global scope that had been charged with circumnavigating South America, touching on Antarctica, and ending in the Pacific Northwest—Poe's novel insistently maps the domestic sectional conflict onto the seemingly limitless global appetite of nascent U.S. imperialism.[18] The title page of the book emblematizes this imperial drive in U.S. culture as the journey of an emigrating New Englander—"Arthur Gordon Pym *of Nantucket*," the absurdly specific, tiny center—into a sublimely infinite realm for his global domination, to the South and "STILL FARTHER SOUTH."

Poe's novel, though, proceeds according to what we might apprehend as a southern imperial imaginary: from his perspective, the very structure of

nineteenth-century empire originates in the white-over-black binary of racialized slavery, and his quasi-science-fiction novel of exploration unfolds a radical
white/black polarity between antagonistically posed civilized explorers and savage others.[19] The brutal, openly race-obsessed progress of Pym "STILL FARTHER
SOUTH" ends abruptly with a "shrouded human figure, very far larger in its proportions than any dweller among men" with skin "of the perfect whiteness of the
snow," whose appearance abruptly cuts off the Nantucketer's narration. Critics
have tended to interpret this whiteness *ex machina* as Poe's endorsement of an
absolute white supremacy, but in the final "Note" with which he ends the novel,
an unidentified authoritative narrator dismisses the accounts of both "Mr. Pym"
and his "editor," "Mr. Poe," to reveal that the ultimate meaning of the tale is to be
found in its literal subtext: in buried writing Pym has discovered, but mis-recog-
nized as non-literate, in chasms below the earth during his southern expedition.
These writings, the authoritative narrator explains, are in the Arabic, Egyptian,
and Ethiopian languages—a revelation that stems equally from Poe's fascination
with theories of the African origins of knowledge, and from his southern insight
that strains from Africa underwrite both U.S. culture and the very existence of
the nation on the face of the earth.

As Poe spins something like a narrative of New England sectionalism projected outward onto a global South in *The Narrative of Arthur Gordon Pym,* he
shadows the story of imperial dominion with an ever-present possibility of revolt,
of an uprising of the ostensible "savages" Pym encounters—of a further turning,
as Jefferson had styled it in his *Notes on the State of Virginia* in 1785, of the wheel of
American revolution.[20] By contrast, the singularity of Emerson's contemporaneous "transparent eyeball" admits of no such challenge from below. To transcend
the "littleness" of Massachusetts, Emerson was locating universal Truth there.[21]
The stakes of this Transcendentalist endeavor, and Poe's proleptic critique of it,
became particularly urgent by 1845, when slaveholding North Carolinian President James K. Polk pursued the annexation of Texas, ultimately wresting the entire U.S. Southwest from Mexico and extending the borders of the nation at last
to their prophesied span, from sea to shining sea.[22]

Poe's ultimate 1848 satire on New England Transcendentalist universalism stems
from his prior sense of the internal geographic centralization of U.S. literary culture, and his own alienation from that center. It has been proposed that Poe's

writings of the mid-1840s should be read as "regional debate"—though Poe was not exactly engaging in a two-sided give-and-take with the Bostonians.[23] Instead, he conducted an oblique and sporadic criticism of their cultural dominance from the literary periphery of the United States; the newspaper of the Transcendentalist utopian community Brook Farm called it in 1845 "a certain *blackguard* warfare against the poets and newspaper critics of New England, which it would be most charitable to impute to insanity."[24] Poe's sense of his exclusion from a New England–based national literature generated its own expressive form, his aptly titled "Marginalia": fragmentary philosophical, aesthetic, and critical insights that he published, several to a number, in several different periodicals between November 1844 and his death. Whereas many writers of the era kept private accounts of fleeting insights and responses to their reading, and indeed often mined such private journals for material to be worked into structured, developed, synthesized essays—both Emerson and Thoreau come immediately to mind—Poe argued for the appropriateness of his fragments standing on their own. In his introductory installment of the "Marginalia" in the *Democratic Review*, published within weeks of Emerson's "Emancipation in the British West Indies," Poe explained that

> [p]urely marginal jottings ... have a distinct complexion, and not only a distinct purpose, but none at all; this it is which imparts to them a value. ... In the marginalia, too, we talk only to our selves; we therefore talk freshly—boldly—originally— with *abandonnement*—without conceit—much after the fashion of Jeremy Taylor, and Sir Thomas Browne, and Sir William Temple, and the anatomical Burton, and that most logical analogist, Butler, and some other people of the old day.

He conceptualizes his "Marginalia" as a perverse form, paradoxically worth printing and reading for their lack of utility ("[no purpose] at all") and their racialized, outré stature ("distinct complexion"). The names he cites here further define the fragmentary and momentary form as befitting the *marginalized* author writing in opposition to a dominant culture that threatens or ignores him: assembling a list of luminaries of seventeenth-century England, royalists who wrote under restraint and duress during Cromwell's regime, Poe implies the southern sectionalist branding of New Englanders as fanatic, censoring Puritans.

It is tempting to see Poe in his "Marginalia"—his most consistent project over the last five years of his life—developing a self-identifying "southern" critique that itself transcends a simple pro-South sectionalism. To flip through the collected "Marginalia" is to experience a dizzying and multidirectional array of fugitive assaults on the accepted categories of mid-nineteenth-century national thought. To quote just one example from late 1846, this is Poe's argument—conducted entirely in one stand-alone paragraph in *Graham's Magazine*—for renaming the United States of America "Appalachia." He decried delays in adopting

> a name for our country. At present we have, clearly, none. There should be no hesitation about "Appalachia." In the first place, it is distinctive. "America" is not, and can never be made so . . . unless we can take it away from the regions which employ it at present. South America is "America," and will insist upon remaining so. In the second place, "Appalachia" is indigenous, springing from one of the most magnificent and distinctive features of the country itself. Thirdly, in employing this word we do honor to the Aborigines, whom, hitherto, we have at all points unmercifully despoiled, assassinated, and dishonored. . . . The last, and by far the most truly important consideration of all, however, is the music of "Appalachia" itself; nothing could be more sonorous, more liquid, or of fuller volume, while its length is just sufficient for dignity.

The range of disruptive forays in this compact paragraph is stunning: Poe veers from an indictment of the imbecility of present nationalist culture (not even having settled on a name for the country); to an exposure of U.S. cultural imperialism (as the United States attempts to claim "America" at the expense of the rest of the hemisphere); to a re-centering of the nation on a southern landform ("indigenous" Appalachia, "one of the most magnificent and distinctive features of the country"); to a resurrection of the crimes against "the Aborigines" upon which the nation is (and continues to be, in its expansion) based; to Poe's authoritative claim to his own superior aesthetic taste.[25] Unlike the southern sectionalist plantation romances, the "southern" critique in Poe's "Marginalia" is not pro-anything. He does not offer one system or affiliation (Slave South) in place of or as an indictment of the other (Industrial North). Rather, his "Marginalia" are *anti*-systematic: conceived of by Poe as a materially and politically forced response to his cultural marginalization, the form becomes an alternative mode of inquiry that refuses the universalization, the catalogue impulse, and the generalization that he sees as hallmarks of the New England–centered dominant culture.

Reading the "Marginalia" then makes all the more striking Poe's divergent tactics in the writing of *Eureka*—which, according to his correspondence, he felt was a culminating work in a campaign he'd been waging.[26] Rather than writing in a form that opposes system, in *Eureka* Poe writes into being a system of superlative, indeed absurd, scale: "I design to speak of the *Physical, Metaphysical and Mathematical—of the Material and Spiritual Universe:—of its Essence, its Origin, its Creation, its Present Condition and its Destiny"* (*PT,* 1261). *Eureka* is a theory of everything: one hundred and fifty pages long with no breaks or subdivisions, it proceeds in a tone of breathless and unflagging intensity, communicated with exclamations, ejaculations, italics, and dashes; and Poe claims that his treatise is *"abundantly sufficient to account for the constitution, the existing phenomena and the plainly inevitable annihilation of at least the material Universe"* (*PT,* 1277). As this passage hints, the overarching system of the universe that Poe proposes in *Eureka* involves a central point from which matter has been radiating outward since its original "constitution"; but the expansion cannot go on forever, and inevitably the limits will rush back upon the center and the universe will collapse. Critics who have tried to treat *Eureka* as Poe's serious attempt at scientific writing have gone so far as to allege that he predicts the Big Bang Theory, but it seems clear that he is using metaphor to predict something much more down to earth: the rise and fall of a compulsively expanding American Empire that has been doomed by its "constitution" to begin with.

Throughout *Eureka,* Poe invokes the language of political theory in general, and U.S. founding documents in particular, as resolutely as he does the language of cosmology, and this political language tends to focus on the problems of centralization: the problem of the one and the many ("This constitution has been effected by *forcing* the originally and therefore normally *One* into the abnormal condition of *Many"*) (*PT,* 1278); the problem of divisibility ("[An atom is] absolutely unique, individual, undivided, and not indivisible only because He who *created* it, by dint of his Will, can by an infinitely less energetic exercise of the same Will, as a matter of course, divide it") (*PT,* 1277); and the problem of identifying universal precepts upon which a nation may be organized ("[Aristotle] started with what he maintained to be axioms, or self-evident truths:—and the now well understood fact that *no* truths are *self*-evident, really does not make in the slightest degree against his speculations") (*PT,* 1263).[27] This coincidence of political theory and cosmology around the issues of centralization and collapse seems intimately related to Poe's conceptualization of his own position, as a southerner, as part of the vast peripheral expanse being organized ideologically by emanation from Boston.

Poe goes to some lengths to alert readers that *Eureka* is a satire. He subtitles it "a Prose Poem" when the very idea of a "prose poem" is anathema to his entire body of poetic theory. He dedicates the volume "with very profound respect" to Alexander von Humboldt, who recently had completed his seven-volume

Kosmos; Emerson had just lauded Humboldt for his "intrepid generalizations," and Poe repeats that praise in the body of the text—"his generalizing powers have never, perhaps, been equaled"—though from Poe, of course, this is no praise at all.[28] And when readers didn't seem to get the joke right away, Poe peeled off the first tenth of *Eureka* and published long passages of it nearly verbatim in *Godey's Lady's Book,* as the short story "Mellonta Tauta," an absurd letter from the future authored by a Transcendentalist bluestocking named "Pundita" who ends up falling into the Atlantic when her motorized dirigible deflates.[29] This willful debasing of his presumably elevated treatise continues to puzzle critics who take *Eureka* at face value as a serious scientific and metaphysical work, but "Mellonta Tauta" seems clearly calculated to addend overt national sectionalist and expansionist political markers to Poe's more subtle and extended satire of New England Transcendentalist method, which had gone over the heads of his audience.

In many ways Poe's entire performance of *Eureka* seems a continuation of what he called his "Boston hoax" of late 1845. This is the famous episode in which Poe was invited, on the heels of the popular success of "The Raven," to read at the Boston Lyceum for the first (and only) time; and rather than reading from his current work, he read a long, rambling version of a poem he had written as a teenager, and then mocked his Boston auditors in the magazine he was editing at the time, the *Broadway Journal,* for having no better discrimination than to applaud him wildly. "We do not, ourselves, think the poem a remarkably good one:— it is not sufficiently transcendental. Still it did well enough for the Boston audience—who evinced characteristic discrimination in understanding, and *especially* applauding, all those knotty passages which we ourselves have not yet been able to understand" (*ER,* 1087). Considering, especially, that Poe first presented *Eureka* as a much-hyped ultra-Transcendental lecture on the Boston model, he seems to hope for a similar con with his 1848 treatise, getting close enough to the method and language of New England Transcendentalism that he will fool his quarry into taking him seriously, which would be the most damning critique of all, "deliver[ing them] up to the enemy bound hand and foot." (As he preens at one point in *Eureka,* "I am proudly aware that there exist many of the most profound and cautiously discriminative intellects which cannot *help* being abundantly content with my—*suggestions.*") Colin Dayan has suggested that Poe's bad behavior in the original Boston Hoax was provoked by Emerson's "Emancipation in the British West Indies," published a few months earlier—that Poe was exercised by Emerson's hypocrisy in "condemn[ing] slavery while continuing to restrict blacks to the status of objects: recipients of the charity of white men who continue to be masters."[30] (If we imagine Poe reading it, Emerson's Godlike injunction to his political opponents—"Creep into your grave; the universe has no need of you"—stands out as well.)[31] Explaining his hoax in the *Broadway Journal,* Poe wrote that his aim had been to "open the eyes [of the Bostonians] to certain facts which have long been obvious to all the world except themselves—the facts that there exist other cities than Boston—other men of letters than Professor Longfellow—other vehicles of literary information than the 'Down-East Review'" (*ER,* 1097). This last term is Poe's preferred name for the powerful Boston-based journal the *North American Review,* a name that, like "Frogpondians," he coined to mock the continental ambition of what he saw as a parochial publication.

As the U.S. borders reach that continental scope—their natural expanse, according to the ideology of Manifest Destiny—Poe raises the question of limits prominently in *Eureka.* While his readers presumably take his subject, the universe, to be infinite, they are in error, he informs us at the outset. To be more precise, "in speaking of what is *ordinarily* implied by the expression, 'Universe,' I shall in most cases take a phrase of limitation—'the Universe of Stars.'" What Poe means by this phrase, he explains, is the extent of the universe conceivable from the vantage point of earth, and he argues that it has been a fundamental error to "consider the Universe of Stars coincident with the Universe proper," to assume "that, were it possible for us to attain any given point in space, we should still find, on all sides of us, an interminable succession of stars." Of course, "Universe of Stars," which he uses, capitalized, throughout *Eureka,* abbreviates to "U.S."; and the fallacious fantasy Poe describes of being able to "attain any given point in space" and still find oneself surrounded by "stars"—*states,* the stars being added so rapidly to the U.S. flag at mid-decade—this fallacious fantasy takes the United States to be infinitely expandable and able to absorb everything else that exists.[32] "No astronomical fallacy is more untenable," Poe writes, "and none has been more pertinaciously adhered to, than that of the absolute *illimitation* of the Universe of Stars" (*PT,* 1327).

Why is mistakenly conceiving of the United States as universal such a "pertinacious" problem for Poe? Comprehending the universe, asserting the universal, he insists, requires a hierarchical relationship between a perceiving center—the site where stand the people making the definitions and observations of totality—and an objectified, totalized surround. He visualizes this structural inequality inherent in the very conceptualization of the universal in specifically geographical terms—first along the vertical, and then as a sort of regional chronotope from center to periphery.

Our thesis admits a choice between two modes of discussion:—we may ascend or descend. Beginning at our own point of view—at the Earth on which we stand . . . it is clear that a descent to small from great—to the outskirts from the centre (if we could establish a centre)—to the end from the beginning (if we could fancy a beginning) would be the preferable course. (*PT*, 1271)

With the parenthetical asides, Poe stresses the dubiousness with which he regards such a centralized, specifically located production of the universe—"the Absolute," "the All-in-All"—and he describes setting oneself up as the center that defines all that surrounds it in two equally satirical ways. On the one hand, there's the will-to-God-stature not unfamiliar from Emerson's writings of the period: "The plots of God are perfect. The Universe is a plot of God. . . . As our starting-point, then, let us adopt the *Godhead*. . . .*We should have to be God ourselves!*" (*PT*, 1276). And on the other hand, there is the Frogpondian pundit on his Bostonian mountaintop:

He who from the top of Aetna casts his eyes leisurely around, is affected chiefly by the *extent* and *diversity* of the scene. Only by a rapid whirling on his heel could he hope to comprehend the panorama in the sublimity of its *oneness*. But as, on the summit of Aetna, *no* man has thought of whirling on his heel, so no man has ever taken into his brain the full uniqueness of the prospect.

The Transcendentalist who believes the world to "flow perpetually outward from a center in himself" should check his local footing: he is standing atop an active volcano in his own industrializing, urbanizing Northeast—an uncertain ground that impairs his ability to "comprehend the panorama" of the expanding United States "in the sublimity of its oneness" (*PT*, 1261).

Poe throughout *Eureka* raises a series of challenges to those "monomaniac[ally] grasping at the infinite," those who would set themselves up as an impossible center and presume to define the terms of the impossible universal (*PT*, 1342). Can the universalizers comprehend that "we have reached a point from which we behold the Universe of Stars as a . . . space interspersed, *unequably*, with *clusters*," and that "the equability of distribution will diminish in the ratio of the agglomerative processes"—in other words, that geographical inequality proceeds in proportion to modernizing centralization, realizing Emerson's "uneven country" (*PT*, 1324–25)? Can they acknowledge the unavoidable limitation of their individual perspectives? "It may be said that no fog of the mind can well be greater than that which, extending to the very boundaries of the mental domain, shuts out even those boundaries themselves from comprehension" (*PT*, 1275). Can they come to see their localized geographical perspective as relative, not necessarily affording them a full comprehension of the "outskirts" of the universe far from their own location? "Those who maintain the existence of nebulae, do *not* refer the nebulosity to extreme distance; they declare it a *real* and not merely a *perspective* nebulosity" (*PT,* 1321). And finally: can they recognize the base desire for commodities and profit underlying their supposedly Transcendental moral, intellectual, and scientific exertions? The perpetual expansion of the Universe of Stars, Poe theorizes, occurs always in the tropics, as systems, planets, and suns continually throw off matter into space from "the equatorial regions" (*PT,* 1308). This insertion of terrestrial tropicality into his cosmological metaphor emphasizes the relays between the domestic South, already possessed by the United States; the hemispheric American South presently being acquired; and the colonized southern sites around the globe, to which U.S. imperial ambition will, presumably, turn next. Poe intensifies these relays in "Mellonta Tauta," the *Godey's Lady's Book* story, in which he has "Pundita" enumerate commodities ranging from India rubber and silk to cotton and watermelon as essential to explaining her philosophical stance.[33]

Ultimately, Poe's southern critique of the methods of New England Transcendentalism was met with incomprehension and, mostly, indifference. He had hoped that the success of *Eureka* would at last enable him to establish a magazine in one of the middle states that could truly pose a challenge to the hegemony of Boston—a magazine through which he imagined creating a peripheral print community of "well-educated men . . . among the innumerable plantations of our vast Southern & Western Countries," and thereby "support the general interests of the Republic of Letters with "a national as distinguished from a sectional literature."[34] (Six months before the publication of *Eureka,* by contrast, Emerson had written the Editors' Address for a new Boston periodical designed to speak for an "energetic race" commanding "a considerable fraction of the planet"; the periodical was titled, unironically, the *Massachusetts Quarterly Review.*)[35] Poe's hope in *Eureka* for an efficacious deflation of the rising ideology of an exceptional American empire—his assurance that "regard[ing the thing] from the proper point of view . . . and in the true direction" would reveal its errors and costs—proved unfounded. A few months before his death he asked, rather drearily, "What have we Americans accomplished in the way of Satire?"[36] And more famously, in a letter to his mother-in-law: "I have no desire to live since I have done 'Eureka.' I could accomplish nothing more."[37]

So the apocalyptic ending of Poe's *Eureka* is borne out. Though he warns that the unchecked expansion of the Universe of Stars causes it to exist "in a state of progressive collapse," Poe predicts that expansion to be unstoppable, precisely because it is authorized by its previous success: "Because on the confines of this Universe of Stars we are, for the moment, compelled to pause. . . . [I]s it right to conclude that, in fact, there *is* no material point beyond that which we have thus been permitted to attain?" He asks this rhetorically, and then goes on to claim "an analogical right" to ever-further expansion: "Have we any ground whatever for visions such as these? If we have a right to them in *any* degree, we have a right to their infinite extension." It is ultimately this "analogical principle" that describes the connection between what Poe sees as the abjection of the U.S. South before the cultural hegemony of New England Transcendentalism, and the terms under which U.S. expansion across the continent (and beyond) is being ideologically assimilated into national discourse. Which brings us to the more obvious resonance of his title, one likely on Poe's mind as well: "eureka" is Archimedes' cry of discovery when he runs from the bath having discovered the principle of displacement. Poe's *Eureka* is, indeed, a study of displacement—a study of the projection of a sectional struggle for dominance out onto formerly Mexican territory—an inquiry into the extent to which a cultural register developed to keep the South in its place *within* the nation is proving infinitely exportable out onto the globe.

Notes

This essay is adapted from Greeson, *Our South: Geographic Fantasy and the Rise of National Literature* (Cambridge, MA: Harvard Univ. Press, 2010), 145–50, 159–68.

1. On Poe's contact at this time with Taylor—whose travel books Poe was reviewing positively and defending from attack, and from whom he was seeking publication opportunities—see Arthur Hobson Quinn, *Edgar Allan Poe* (New York: Appleton-Century, 1941), 567–601.

2. Poe's "southernness" and "darkness" made him marginal to the nineteenth-century nationalist literary canon as constructed by critics such as Vernon L. Parrington and F. O. Matthiessen; more recent critics such as Colin Dayan, Teresa Goddu, and Terence Whalen usefully have interrogated the extent to which "southernness" as a category glosses or interacts with more complex negotiations of race, gender, class, region, and nation in considering Poe's work. (In a related vein, John Carlos Rowe and Maurice Lee have identified Poe's "southernness" as a synonym for white supremacy.) In an important intervention, J. Gerald Kennedy has reminded us that Poe's geographical identity in the mid-1840s was shifting rather than stable, and that he focused as much as any other major author of the period on issues of broader national ideology and identity ("'A Mania for Composition': Poe's *Annus Mirabilis* and the Violence of Nation-Building," *American Literary History* 17, no. 1 [Mar. 2005]: 1).

3. Colin [Joan] Dayan tracks Poe's "critical read[ing] of the transcendentalist ideologies of his time" in *Fables of Mind: An Inquiry into Poe's Fiction* (New York: Oxford Univ. Press, 1987). On Poe's approach to "generalization": he not only hailed Humboldt as a great generalizer in the

dedication of *Eureka*; Poe also explicitly defended "generalization"—as a "speculative" or "theoretical" approach to facts versus the "bigoted" dogmatism of scientists—in a letter misaddressed to one "George E. Irbey" on 29 February 1848, in which he summarized the lecture that he was revising as *Eureka*, and enclosed yet another prospectus for the magazine for which he continued to seek funding, *The Stylus*.

4. Ralph Waldo Emerson, "The Transcendentalist," *The Complete Works of Ralph Waldo Emerson*, "Concord" ed. (Boston: Houghton, Mifflin, 1903–4), vol. 1: 334.

5. Emerson opens "The Transcendentalist" with the proposition that "as thinkers, mankind have ever divided into two sects, Materialists and Idealists" (1: 329), and goes on to define and contrast these sects. I use the authoritative text of *Eureka* established by Roland W. Nelson, in Poe, *Poetry and Tales*, hereafter cited parenthetically as *PT* (New York: Literary Classics of the United States, Inc., 1984). The "letter from the future" Poe introduces in the opening page of *Eureka* ridicules "the singular fancy that there exist *but two practicable roads to Truth*" (*PT*, 1263) and goes on to identify these schools as those of the "Hogs and Rams" (*PT*, 1269).

6. *PT*, 1271. Jerome J. McGann points out that Poe's use of the term "Frogpondian," which mocks the anti-epic scale of the Frog Pond on Boston Common, could also be cued to Byron's derisive use of the term "Lakist" to describe the school of Wordsworth and Coleridge.

7. Emerson, "The Young American," *Complete Works* 1: 384.

8. Although almost any critic who has written about *Eureka* has remarked that at least certain dimensions of it seem wildly out of keeping with Poe's stated aesthetic and philosophical stances, only Harriet R. Holman has suggested, in two incisive short articles that anticipated a more extensive reading, that *Eureka* is a full-out satire ("Hog, Bacon, Ram, and Other 'Savans' in *Eureka*," *Poe Newsletter* 2, no. 3 [Oct. 1969]: 49–55; "Splitting Poe's 'Epicurean Atoms': Further Speculation on the Literary Satire of *Eureka*," *Poe Studies* 5, no. 2 [Dec. 1972]; 33–37).

9. Poe on Carlyle in the "Marginalia" of April 1846, published in the *Democratic Review*. I use the Library of America edition of Poe's *Essays and Reviews*, hereafter cited as *ER* (New York: Literary Classics of the United States, 1984), 1393.

10. Emerson, "Notes," *Complete Works* 1: 403.

11. *Complete Works* 1: 406. Eric Cheyfitz, *The Trans-Parent: Sexual Politics in the Language of Emerson* (Baltimore: Johns Hopkins Univ. Press, 1981); John Carlos Rowe, *At Emerson's Tomb: The Politics of Classic American Literature* (New York: Columbia Univ. Press, 1999), esp. 19–22; Howard Horwitz, *By the Law of Nature: Form and Value in Nineteenth-Century America* (New York: Oxford Univ. Press, 1991).

12. *Complete Works* 1: 9–10.

13. For the classic account of expansionism and sectionalism in the first half of the century, see Albert K. Weinberg, *Manifest Destiny: A Study of Nationalist Expansionism in American History* (Baltimore: Johns Hopkins Univ. Press, 1935), esp. 160–223.

14. On southern sectionalist imperialism see Robert E. Bonner, *Mastering America: Southern Slaveholders and the Crisis of American Nationhood* (New York: Cambridge Univ. Press, 2009), and Sean Wilentz, *The Rise of American Democracy, Jefferson to Lincoln* (New York: W.W. Norton, 2005), esp. 547–667.

15. In a similar vein, but writing brilliantly about another 1845 text, David Kazanjian suggests that what Marx paradoxically called "Yankee universality" in fact "names [an] imperial articulation of U.S. citizenship, [an] interpenetration of the domestic and the foreign that marks the emergence of U.S. imperialism" (*The Colonizing Trick: National Culture and Imperial Citizenship in Early America* [Minneapolis: Univ. of Minnesota Press, 2003], 223).

16. "Address to the Citizens of Concord on the Fugitive Slave Law," *Complete Works* 11: 211–13.

17. Robin Blackburn, *The Overthrow of Colonial Slavery, 1776–1848* (London: Verso, 1988), esp. 459–68 and 519–49.

18. The expedition was documented copiously by its commander, Charles Wilkes (*Narrative of the United States Exploring Expedition During the Years 1838, 1839, 1840, 1841, 1842*, 5 vols. [Philadelphia: Lea and Blanchard, 1845]).

19. Dana D. Nelson reads this national/imperial overmapping in *Pym* as Poe's critique of Emerson: "In *Nature*, a confident Ralph Waldo Emerson observes of "man" (presumably western, European) that 'one after another, his victorious thought comes up with and reduces all things, until the world becomes at last only a realized will.' *Pym* exposes the process by which colonial knowledge achieves this exclusive 'realized will.' As Emerson aptly suggests, it succeeds only by reduction: both in its willful blindness and in its attempt to repress cultural/narrative heterogeneity" (*The Word in Black and White: Reading "Race" in American Literature, 1638–1867* [New York: Oxford Univ. Press, 1994], 105).

20. The passage in which Jefferson prognosticates a likely slave revolt reads, "Indeed I tremble for my country when I reflect that God is just: that his justice cannot sleep for ever: that considering numbers, nature and natural means only, a revolution of the wheel of fortune, an exchange of situation, is among possible events: that it may become probable by supernatural interference!" (*Notes on the State of Virginia*, ed. William Peden [Chapel Hill: Univ. of North Carolina Press, 1982], 163).

21. Emerson, "Address on the Fugitive Slave Law": "Massachusetts is little, but, if true to itself, can be the brain which turns about the behemoth" (*Complete Works* 11: 211).

22. Kennedy's brilliant reading of Poe's 1844 story "Some Words with a Mummy" operates precisely at this critical intersection of the jingoistic expansionist nationalism of the era that elected Polk, and the "Yankee" (as Poe terms it) Anglo-Saxonist assertions of racial superiority that underwrite it.

23. Colin Dayan, "Amorous Bondage: Poe, Ladies, and Slaves," *American Literature* 66, no. 2 (Jun. 1994): 254.

24. Poe joyously reprinted this entire censure of him in the *Broadway Journal*, rejoining that "insanity is a word that the Brook Farm Phalanx should never be brought to mention under any circumstances whatsoever" (*ER*, 1100, 1102–3).

25. In a footnote, Poe sources the cultural imperialism in particular (the "taking away" of the name America "from those regions which employ it at present") back to one of the "Frogpondians" present at his hoax the year before: "Mr. [Benjamin Hazard] Field, in a meeting of 'The New York Historical Society,' proposed that we take the name of 'America,' and bestow 'Columbia' upon the continent" (*ER*, 1415).

26. In a letter to F.W. Thomas in 1849, for instance, he writes that "the Frogpondians . . . are getting worse and worse, and pretend not to be aware that there *are* any literary people out of Boston. . . . It would be the easiest thing in the world to use them up *en masse*. One really well-written satire would accomplish the business" (Poe, *Letters*, ed. John Ward Ostrom [New York: Gordian Press, 1966], 2:427).

27. For a reading of governmental metaphor in the text, see W. C. Harris, "Edgar Allan Poe's *Eureka* and the Poetics of Constitution," *American Literary History* 12, no. 1–2 (2000): 1–40.

28. Emerson, "Editors' Address, *Massachusetts Quarterly Review*, December, 1847" (*Complete Works* 11: 391).

29. Maurice Lee points out that in an 1847 review in Edward Duycknick's *Literary World*, "Bad News of the Transcendental Poets," a critic (whom he takes to be Poe himself) cheers, "The transcendental balloon is rapidly suffering collapse" ("Absolute Poe: His System of Transcendental Racism," *American Literature* 75, no. 4 [December 2003]: 769).

30. Dayan, "Amorous Bondage," 253.

31. Emerson, "West India Emancipation," *Complete Works* 11: 100.

32. Poe makes a marvelously succinct statement of Manifest Destiny ideology here: "[A]

sufficient reason for the Titanic scale, in respect of mere *Space,* on which the Universe of Stars is seen to be constructed . . . [is so t]hat the Universe of Stars might *endure* throughout an æra at all commensurate with the grandeur of its component material proportions and with the high majesty of its spiritual purposes" (1340).

33. In a number of extraordinary fantasias in this ostensible 2848 letter from Pundita, Poe links industrial and slave capitalism, as in the following passage that conflates the production of silk and paper, as well as the exploitation of a laboring body ("worm") raised on watermelon and then destroyed in a factory: "This silk, as he explained it to me, was a fabric composed of the entrails of a species of earth-worm. The worm was carefully fed on mulberries—a kind of fruit resembling a water-melon—and, when sufficiently fat, was crushed in a mill. The paste thus arising was called *papyrus* in its primary state, and went through a variety of presses until it finally became 'silk'" (*PT,* 872).

34. Proposals for *The Stylus, ER,* 1035, 1093.

35. *Complete Works* 11: 383.

36. This is the opening sentence of Poe's 1849 review of James Russell Lowell's *A Fable for Critics,* an essay often cited to evidence Poe's southern sectionalism (*ER,* 814).

37. Poe to Maria W. Clemm, *Letters* 2: 452. Poe earned a total of fourteen dollars for *Eureka.*

III | Plotting Poe's Influence

Cruising (Perversely) for Context

Poe and Murder, Women and Apes

LELAND S. PERSON

In his second review of Hawthorne's *Twice-Told Tales,* Poe famously prescribes the ideal strategy for the "skilful literary artist," who constructs a tale by conceiving, "with deliberate care, a certain unique or single *effect*" and "then combines such events as may best aid him in establishing this preconceived effect." As Poe elaborates this deterministic artistic paradigm, he declares that in the "whole composition there should be no word written, of which the tendency, direct or indirect, is not to the one pre-established design" (572). In emphasizing the writer's "deliberate care" and intense focus on producing a predetermined "effect," Poe seeks control over both the creative process and the reader. As he says, "during the hour of perusal the soul of the reader is at the writer's control" (572). Or as James Machor concludes, "Poe's entire concept of effect and his privileging of it as 'indispensable' to the brief tale were undergirded by the assumption in informed response that the successful author would be a virtual enchanter who controlled the audience with his or her spellbinding artistic performance" ("Mastering," 169). In Machor's view, Poe approached the writer-reader relationship as a "virtual battle for authority, waged as both frontal assault and guerilla warfare" (172).

Poe's view of the writer-reader relationship, as he articulates it in this review, seems almost axiomatic, so it is intriguing to examine a later statement in the Hawthorne review, where Poe seems to give the reader a more creative role—one that anticipates Roland Barthes's concept of the "writerly text" (5). In this reading experience, the reader's soul or mind is not controlled by the writer but participates in the creative process as a kind of co-author. In fact, this shared process seems to produce a higher form of art—what Poe paradoxically calls "true originality."

> [T]he true originality—true in respect of its purposes—is that which, in bringing out the half-formed, the reluctant, or the unexpressed fancies of mankind, or in exciting the more delicate pulses of the heart's passion, or in giving birth to

some universal sentiment or instinct in embryo, thus combines with the pleasurable effect of *apparent* novelty, a real egotistic delight. The reader, in the case first supposed (that of the absolute novelty,) is excited, but embarrassed, disturbed, in some degree even pained at his own want of perception, at his own folly in not having himself hit upon the idea. In the second case, his pleasure is doubled. He is filled with an intrinsic and extrinsic delight. He feels and intensely enjoys the seeming novelty of the thought, enjoys it as really novel, as absolutely original with the writer—*and* himself. They two, he fancies, have, alone of all men, thought thus. They two have, together, created this thing. Henceforward there is a bond of sympathy between them, a sympathy which irradiates every subsequent page of the book. ("Nathaniel Hawthorne," 581)

Of course, if we read carefully, we notice that this feeling of sympathy is only something that the reader "fancies." This is part of Poe's intention. He does not really cede control of the reader's mind or soul. He only seems to do so. He is the master illusionist. The reader contributes to the reading that the author has been aiming at from the beginning. As Machor puts it, "Poe defined this intimate bond with the reader by taking away as much as he gave"; the reader was "induced to feel a bond of achievement that remained an illusion, staged by the writer who has kept the true nature of the accomplishment—the wires controlling the scene—hidden behind the curtain of his or her craft" ("Mastering," 174).

What's a reader to do? Poe always seems one step ahead of us. Even when we think we are producing meaning, he has anticipated the moves we make. I want to explore the work of reading Poe, especially reading Poe historically and bifocally in relation to both the context in which he wrote and the context that motivates our reading and re-reading of his tales. We have been historicizing Poe like mad in recent years, exemplified especially in books by Terence Whalen and Jonathan Elmer, essays by Joan Dayan, Leslie Ginsberg, Teresa Goddu, and others, and in two collections, *The American Face of Edgar Allan Poe* and *Romancing the Shadow: Poe and Race*. Not surprisingly, many historical approaches to Poe's work have been rooted in identity politics, especially those of gender and race. Sponsoring many of these approaches have been contemporary political imperatives. So inspired, we read backwards from our present historical moment and values. I'm not criticizing these contingencies, to play off the title of Barbara Herrnstein Smith's famous essay, "Contingencies of Value," because this is the inevitable way criticism—the critical conversation—works. In fact, I want to emphasize and examine the tension between the contemporary historical imperatives that drive our reading and our desire to honor the integrity of history.

The *Romancing the Shadow* collection, for example, takes its title from Toni Morrison and her challenge to American literary scholars to discover a racial presence even in texts from which race seems absent. There is an assumption in this challenge that we are now in a better position to see what was there all along but presumably hidden for one reason or another from nineteenth-century readers, who may have responded emotionally to embedded racial cues or racial symbols without being able or willing to translate feelings into words. Our own present historical moment inspires us to interrogate or re-interrogate the past for evidence of issues that concern us here and now. We like to think—inspired by what might be called a New Positivism—that we respect the integrity and difference of past historical moments. Of course we run the risk of anachronism—what Valerie Rohy, in a brilliant reading of "Ligeia" as a lesbian text, calls "anachronistic projection" (66). All historical research is "always to some degree ahistorical—or rather, anachronistic," she points out (69). The gap between historical reality—history "as it is"—and our ability to see it is inevitable, but for that very reason not necessarily a barrier to our understanding. We do the best we can. The challenge is to get as close as possible to understanding the past on its own terms, while acknowledging that what prompts the research in the first place are the contemporary issues, perspectives, and terms that make us want to do so. If we expect to recover "all" of a historical moment, "wholly and without a single detail lost," Julian Lethbridge warns, "then of course we cannot have it, and probably do not want it. But that understanding of 'as it really was' is trivial. We do not want the unmediated, undivided, unconceptualized whole—we want bits of it. We want it sorted and divided according to our own needs and purposes; and what these needs and purposes are depends upon ourselves; depends upon what problems we are grappling with. We want what is pertinent to ourselves at the moment, to the questions we ask" (101).

It is especially tricky to historicize readers and reader responses. As James Machor has declared, "what remains elusive finally is a clear sense of what the actual reading experiences were for the numerous nineteenth-century readers whose encounters with literature took place, not in public forums, but alone in the bedrooms of middle-class homes in suburban Boston, or in barn lofts in rural Virginia, or between stolen moments of leisure at factory workbenches in Pittsburgh and Chicago" ("Introduction," xxi). Machor himself has made gallant efforts to fill this gap. One important finding is an idea we now take for granted: the unreliable narrator. Machor has discovered that, by the 1850s, "reviewers were beginning to define narration as a technique in which deliberate unreliability was a legitimate aesthetic strategy and to alert readers to use that interpretive paradigm for making sense of potentially problematic and disruptive texts" ("Poetics" 57). This insight adds another variable to the tension between our present imperatives and the historically embedded text—the possibility that the author deliberately tries to fool us.

Whatever our reading strategies, reading Poe can make us feel as if we are staring at Rorschach blots and being expected to identify the shape as something we recognize—or perhaps as something we sort of know we have projected onto the screen the blot provides. While that kind of personality test has its historical dimension, it feels ahistorical. The ink blots are abstract and lack the sort of particularity that would historicize them. Poe routinely presents us with a similar challenge, either by not identifying the location of his tales or by locating them in a foreign country, a different time and place. Since Poe's tales do not normally provide us with a wealth of historical details, we have to guess at the "real" historical background in which Poe has situated his writing. We observe Poe closely, perhaps scouring the biographical details of his life and the *Poe Log*. We examine his other writings—his reviews and essays. We keep assaying the historical record, hoping that one or more of Poe's tales respond to a historical cue or encourage a historical connection. But in addition, we know that Poe likes to play the hoaxer who reads his reader and gets the reader to produce the reading he wants—as, for example, in the passage from the Hawthorne review. We read the text, but the text in some sense reads us. It provokes us, evoking from us many facets of our personalities—those most appropriate to the text and its meaning. Something in us allows us to recognize something in the text—"cruising" and being cruised by the text, as Eric Savoy and James Creech have termed it. The idea that a writer and a text can "cruise" their readers has a wider application. Cruising and being cruised by a text—an idea that can work for many literary works, not just arguably "gay" ones. The text seduces the reader into revealing important, intimate information about himself. Thereby, the reader produces the reading that the text "wants." Surely, if any literary texts can be said to "wink" at us, it is Poe's that do so.

My title, of course, refers to Poe's "The Imp of the Perverse." In that work, Poe identifies an "innate and primitive principle of human action, a paradoxical something" called *"perverseness,"* through whose "promptings we act, for the reason that we should not" (*Tales* 2: 1220). Applied to reading, such a principle would mean reading against the directions of a narrative—reading what we should not for the very reason that it is discouraged or proscribed. Reading perversely may mean reading against the rhetorical strategies of Poe's first-person narrator, resisting his designs on us. It means reading from other points of view, discovering covert texts that Poe's narrator obscures. It means reading against cultural and legal norms that police and limit our imaginations. It means finding contexts—even contemporary ones—that can serve as new lenses that highlight for us previously obscure facets of a text. Cruising for context means being cruised by context.

READING RACE IN "THE MURDERS IN THE RUE MORGUE"

In a recent essay in MLA's *Approaches to Teaching Poe's Prose and Poetry,* Leonard Cassuto describes the process of leading his students to a historicized interpretation of "The Murders in the Rue Morgue." He begins traditionally by encouraging his students to examine the tale as a "locked-room" mystery. He notes their disappointment when the "ourang-outang" is revealed to be the killer because that discovery forecloses upon moral questions of guilt and innocence. Then comes what he calls the "final pivot" (34)—the historical turn. His goal is to get his students to situate this seemingly ahistorical—and French—tale in its mid-nineteenth-century American moment. He points out that genres become popular "because they respond to collectively held desires." Crime stories especially "open a window onto shared fears of all kinds"; they "channel collective anxieties, so, when we read them, we can see what a culture is worrying about" (35). So, Cassuto asks, "what fears does Poe's violent, escaped orangutan represent?" What were American readers worrying about in 1841? (35). Because his students know "very little" about the 1840s United States, he unlimbers their minds by showing them some old illustrations, including Alfred Kubin's *The Ape* (1909), a picture of a huge black ape (more gorilla than orangutan) holding a white woman, one of his paws between her legs and his fangs poised to bite down on her head. Light bulbs go off—a Eureka! moment—as the class suddenly realizes that "Murders in the Rue Morgue" may have more provocative reference than they had thought—may be more about murders in Southampton County, Virginia, or race riots in Philadelphia than about an improbable killing in Paris.[1]

Cassuto historicizes the image a little further, acknowledging Richard Kopley's research into two probable Poe sources from 1838, one a newspaper account of an escaped orangutan, the other a story of a black man who killed a woman with a razor (36). He also goes on to cite a more recent case of a conservative talk-show host, Bob Lonsberry, who was fired in 2003 for comparing the black mayor of Rochester, New York, to a monkey (37). He stops short at this point, at least in his essay, content, it seems, to have his students recognize that Poe's "Ourang-Outang" is "not just an ape," but a "fraught symbol of sexually charged racial anxiety" (37). Cassuto's account of his students' responses raises several questions. For example, why did his twenty-first-century class need such prompting to make the connection between Poe's orangutan and an African American slave? Cassuto attributes this failure of imagination to their ignorance of nineteenth-century history, but the association is hardly limited to that era.

As I have suggested, I am interested in how readers' imaginations work to make the sorts of connections—especially historical connections—that most of us take for granted. It seems to me very difficult not to recognize the racial signifiers in "The Murders in the Rue Morgue," although readers did so for a long time.[2] And why would contemporary readers fail to make the connections? To construct a genealogy of this racist image—the longstanding identification of apes and black men, especially as that identification becomes triangulated by the presence of a white woman—would require a type of diachronic database to track the material readers at various points in time had available to them, especially in American popular culture, that might have enhanced their ability to make the connection between the murders in Poe's tale and the "sexually charged racial anxiety" that seems to us now so central to the story.[3] "Murders in the Rue Morgue" can be placed into conversation with the popular culture texts that form this ongoing historical context. Historical context helps us read and understand Poe's text in new ways; Poe's text can also help us understand the historical context.

The evolution of scientific racism in the nineteenth century is illustrated in the work of polygenists such as Samuel George Morton, J. C. Nott, George R. Gliddon, and Harvard's Louis Agassiz. As John Haller notes, in the "decades before the American Civil War, the polygenists obtained their most vocal support from the United States." Morton's *Crania Americana* (1839) purports to show by measuring the internal capacity of various skulls in his extensive collection that certain races were mentally superior. The larger the brain, the smarter the individual (and the race). Morton's work was supplemented by physicians J. C. Nott and George R. Gliddon in *Types of Mankind,* a lengthy selection of Morton's papers. A man "must be blind not to be struck by similitudes between some of the lower races of mankind, viewed as connecting links in the animal kingdom," they argued; "nor can it be rationally affirmed, that the Orang-Outan and Chimpanzee are more widely separated from certain African and Oceanic Negroes than are the latter from the Teutonic or Pelasgic types" (457). Nott and Gliddon go on to quote a passage from Dr. Jeffries Wyman, "the very accomplished anatomist of Harvard University," which concludes: "it cannot be denied, however wide the separation, that the Negro and Orang do afford the points where man and the brute, when the totality of their organization is considered, most nearly approach each other" (457). The "truth of these observations becomes popularly apparent," the editors then conclude, "through the following comparative series of likenesses" (457). Even today, if you conduct a Google search for "Blacks" and "Apes," this illustration will pop up:

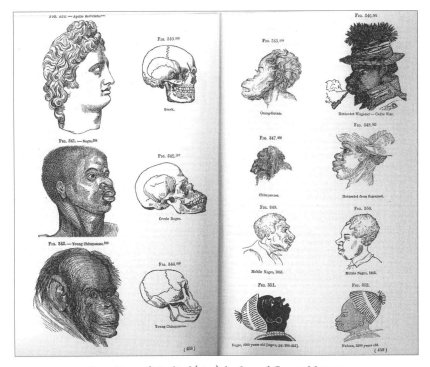

From *Types of Mankind* (1855), by Samuel George Morton.

Nineteenth-century efforts, especially in the South, to read racial differences as species differences seem addressed directly in Poe's tale. Readers or instructors looking for ways to build this scientific context around the story could read it beside the 1932 film version of "Murders," directed by Robert Florey and starring Bela Lugosi as the demonic Dr. Mirakle. They might also examine the original *King Kong* movie (directed by Merian Cooper), which appeared a year later, the same year that Adolf Hitler became chancellor of Germany (Lorenz, 156). The films have some interesting similarities, and they offer interesting lenses through which the violent, triangulated relationship in "Murders" can be viewed. In both, apes are captured and brought by their white captors from their remote native lands to large cities (Paris, New York). Both apes fall for young women, kidnapping them from their bedrooms, carrying them to the rooftops, where they are pursued by the authorities, shot, and killed. The 1932 *Murders* certainly sexualizes the narrative much more explicitly than Poe does.

Posters for the film often featured a sexy, redheaded woman (Camille L'Espanaye, played by Sidney Fox; her hair is red in movie posters) lolling on the bed, her nightgown riding suggestively up her thighs, the ape "gloating" over her unconscious body. An alternative poster substituted Bela Lugosi's leering face for the gorilla, suggesting that there is more than murder in the offing and, presumably, in the imagination of the viewer—and that the ape is a surrogate for its owner.[4] In fact, the film opens with sex and racial violence in the air. At a Paris carnival, scantily clad dancing girls attract the attention of two couples, including Camille and the young medical student, Pierre Dupin. Anticipating the racial theme to follow, the carnival also features "bloodthirsty savages" (Apache Indians) from America, but the main feature of the carnival is Eric, the Ape Man, the "beast with a human soul," according to his keeper, Dr. Mirakle. The film capitalizes on the evolutionary underpinnings of the story and on the fear of amalgamation. Readers seeing the film in 1932 would likely have remembered the Scopes "Monkey Trial" of 1925, which had projected the debate over evolution and, in the popular imagination, man's descent from apes into the public sphere. In the film, Lugosi plays a "mad scientist" inspired by Darwin's evolutionary theories, which are illustrated on the walls of the tent in which Mirakle places Eric on display.[5] "I will prove your kinship with apes," he tells the horrified crowd. "Eric's blood will be mixed with the blood of man." Mirakle is disingenuous in one key respect, for we soon learn that he has been kidnapping women and injecting them with Eric's blood—with deadly results. As soon as Eric sees Camille, he falls in love (or lust). He removes her bonnet, which he crushes in his arms, giving Mirakle an excuse to learn where Camille lives and setting up the later scene in which Eric kidnaps Camille herself.

At the film's climax, Eric enters Camille's second-story apartment, kills her mother (stuffing her body up the chimney, as in the Poe story), and carries Camille to Dr. Mirakle's laboratory. Before Mirakle can inject Camille with Eric's blood, Eric intervenes, overturning a Bunsen burner, killing Mirakle, and escaping with the unconscious Camille, whom he carries across the rooftops of Paris in much the same way that King Kong carries Ann Darrow up the Empire State Building. There are no airplanes in Lugosi's *Murders,* which is set in 1845, but Dupin does take off in hot pursuit and finally succeeds in "treeing" Eric on a rooftop overhanging the Seine. He shoots Eric, who falls into the river, just as Camille awakens.

Despite much less onscreen violence than Poe describes, the film plays to its viewer's fears of amalgamation and evolutionary theory, especially for the implications such a theory has for species and race relations—again, as registered on the bodies of white women. The same can be said of *King Kong,* which raises the possibility of racial and cross-species amalgamation. As the entrepreneurial movie director Carl Denham (Robert Armstrong) says, there is "something on that island that no white man has ever seen." The film explicitly links race and violent sexuality on Skull Island, where Ann Darrow (Fay Wray), identified by the natives as "The Golden Woman," is substituted for a young native woman and offered sacrificially as "The Bride of Kong." Linking Kong with the natives, when the white exploring party first sets foot on the island, they discover some of the natives dressed like gorillas. The most graphically sexual scene (cut from some early versions of the film) shows Kong peeling Ann Darrow's clothes from her body and even sniffing his finger after he does so. (A similar scene appears in the 1976 film, directed by John Guillermin, when Kong puts his finger into Jessica Lange's lap.) Dagmar Lorenz notes that "Kong's interaction with Ann racializes and sexualizes the film" (162), but then concludes that the film ultimately "leaves species boundaries intact. Ann Darrow shows the expected fear and revulsion toward Kong, confirming the rift between human and animal, which implicitly validates the North American racial paradigm, the polarity of Black and White" (167).[6] The 1932 film of *Murders* reaches a similar conclusion, despite its much more explicit testing of racial and species boundaries. Camille is spared the deadly transfusion that kills Mirakle's previous victims and also spared the consequences of the love or lust that Eric feels for her.[7]

Florey subtly injects race into the film through the character of Mirakle's assistant, "Janos, the Black One," played by Noble Johnson, who the next year portrayed the Native Chief on Skull Island in *King Kong.*[8] In an early scene, Mirakle invites members of the sideshow audience to take a closer look at Eric, and he gestures toward the Ape Man's cage, which is outside the frame. Standing at Mirakle's side is Janos, and it is to him that Mirakle seems to be pointing. When Dupin and Camille leave the carnival, moreover, Mirakle orders Janos to follow them in order to discover where Camille lives. Although Eric, not Janos, later enters Camille's apartment and kidnaps her, the characters effectively double one another, thereby reinforcing the black male ape identification.

Even though readers such as Elise Lemire, Lindon Barrett, Leonard Cassuto, and I authorize a racialized interpretation of the story by invoking white fears of slave revolt, murder, and rape, the murders in the Rue Morgue do not have an explicit sexual dimension. Sometimes, a violent murder is just a violent murder. So, what justifies a racialized and sexualized reading of the story? First, it can be argued that such brutal violations of women's bodies inevitably suggest the various forms that violations can take. When women getting ready for bed have their bedrooms invaded by male "animals," we would have to work hard not to think of rape. Second, reading the story within a different context—or in conjunction with a context that included sexual assault—could affect one's understanding. What if readers came to "Murders," for example, after reading Kyle Onstott's *Mandingo* (1957) or seeing the controversial film made twenty years later by Richard Fleischer? Perhaps readers come to "Murders" in a film course that includes *King Kong,* the 1932 *Murders* film as an immediate precursor, *Mandingo,* and the 2005 re-make of *King Kong*? Would such readers create a space for female subjectivity and desire and for the possibility, whether in the characters or readers, of pleasure derived from the ape's presence in the bedroom? This is not to suggest the possibility of pleasure in rape, but only to suggest that the triangulated relationships I have been tracking allow for multiple reader identifications, as well as multiple subject-and-object positions. Nancy Harrowitz, for example, collapses the triangle into a more traditional binary, gendered opposition. "When we consider the orangutan as a double for his master, the sailor in port," she argues, "the meaning of Poe's choice of an orangutan as the perpetrator becomes clearer" and enables us to discover a "hidden story within this story" and "one about which Dupin seems blissfully ignorant" (185). In Harrowitz's hidden story the murderer is really a "garden variety white male pervert": "It is far easier for Dupin to imagine a runaway orangutan, a wild man of the forest, than face the truth about 'sexual' relations at home: the agonistics of violence against women" (188).[9] Poe himself is, arguably, more perceptive—or at least we are.

But let me complicate this reading by examining the film *Mandingo* and the novel on which it is based. The novel, written by Kyle Onstott, was published in 1957, just three years after the Supreme Court's unanimous decision in *Brown v.*

Board of Education declared segregated schools unconstitutional and, arguably, helped launch the civil rights movement of the 1950s and 1960s. The film version of *Mandingo,* which Robin Wood has called the "greatest film about race ever made in Hollywood" (265), appeared in 1975. Most famous for its onscreen depiction of a white woman raping a male slave, the film compares both male and female slaves to apes. When she discovers that her husband, Hammond (Perry King), is spending much of his time with the slave woman Ellen (Brenda Sykes), Blanche Maxwell (Susan George) accuses, "You like that black meat. You might as well have a baboon." Later, after Blanche gives birth to the child fathered by the slave Mede (played by heavyweight champion Ken Norton), her father-in-law (James Mason) reacts bitterly to the idea that Blanche desired the black man: "Blanche never craved that black ape." A gruesome and violent film that depicts the torture and abuse of slaves in graphic detail, *Mandingo* also reveals many of the fault lines in master-slave relationships. As viewers who witness the scene in which Blanche rapes Mede (ironically, by threatening to tell Hammond that Mede raped her), we have no doubt about what Blanche craves. The psychology of that craving is more complicated. Similarly, even though Hammond's relationship with the slave woman Ellen is predicated on his owning her (something he makes explicit when she angers him), it is the closest thing in the film to a loving relationship. As Celine Parreñas Shimzu argues in a brilliant analysis of the film, *Mandingo* "portrays the private sex act between masters and slaves as an intense paradoxical site of sexual pleasure and racial domination" (218). Comparing the film with the novel intensifies the paradoxes even more, as Blanche has a sexual relationship with a second slave, Meg, who witnesses her rape of Mede and threatens to tell her husband. "You goin' to give me whut I wants, anytime I wants, whenever I says," Meg commands her (579). In effect, Blanche rapes Mede by making him play her rapist. Meg than rapes her by threatening to reveal her behavior to her husband. Blanche's bedroom in *Mandingo* has become the site of remarkably—excitingly—diverse sets of desires, subject, and object positions. Is Blanche a rapist or a rape victim or both? What desires are put in play and what pleasures, if any, are derived from the fulfillment of those desires?[10]

At this point, of course, readers may object that we have wandered far afield from the locked bedroom in the Rue Morgue. This is one of the hazards of historicized readings. The context can overwhelm and even take the place of the text. At the same time, contemporary contexts also enable us to read backwards to the source with keener insight and understanding.

World War I recruiting poster

This World War I recruiting poster was much in the news a few years ago when the Annie Leibovitz *Vogue* cover, featuring LeBron James and Gisele Bündchen, hit the newsstands (April 2008). Almost immediately, readers discovered the remarkable similarities among the Leibovitz photograph, the World War I recruiting poster, and also the original *King Kong* movie poster from 1933.[11] (Searching the Internet for the *Vogue* cover will call up the three images side-by-side.) K. R. Kaufman, for example, noted that the "similarities are simply too many to be accidental" in a 3 March 2008 posting on the *Democratic Underground* website.[12] Not surprisingly, commentators claimed that Leibovitz not only intended the allusions, but also was guilty of playing with racist stereotypes associating black males with apes. Rogers Cadenhead, for example, summarized the controversy and the evidence:

Some critics have alleged that the picture, taken by renowned photographer Annie Leibovitz, makes [James] look like King Kong carrying off Fay Wray, a racially loaded simian metaphor. Others don't see it at all, suggesting that James is demonstrating the same intensity he shows on the court and people are trying too hard to be offended. A comparison between the cover and a World War I recruitment poster should settle the argument. Leibovitz was clearly, unmistakeably [sic] using one of the world's most famous black men to portray a ferocious gorilla carrying off a white woman.

Dorothy Snarker went further in arguing that the "symbolism is deeply troubling": "Anyone familiar with our country's terrible history of racism knows the despicable propaganda that once painted black men as frightening, ape-like brutes out to defile the purity of white women. Whether intended or not, this photo hearkens back to that ugly and unconscionable ideology."

Now, there can be little question that the recruiting and movie posters represent strikingly explicit examples of the racial stereotype that "Murders in the Rue Morgue" exploits more subtly. The "mad brute" German gorilla holding a semi-naked white woman, with his feet apparently just recently planted on American soil, reduces the war to a threat against white American women and arguably exploits a racist image familiar to Americans by collapsing distinctions between white German soldiers and American Blacks. (Bringing this racist identification even closer to the present, the "white nationalist" organization Stormfront produced a version of the recruiting poster in which President Obama's face was substituted for the ape's.) Produced between the world wars (in 1933), *King Kong* resurrects that stereotype and, when Kong is captured and transported to New York, also brings it home to American soil. The *Vogue* cover arguably alludes to both the recruiting poster and to *King Kong*. The connection to the recruiting poster is especially noteworthy, as the color of Gisele Bündchen's dress is identical to that of the woman the "mad brute" is holding. Despite the obvious influences, however, the *Vogue* cover does give Gisele Bündchen more status than the woman enjoys in the earlier posters. Almost as tall as James, with her arm around him (not held limply) and with her feet on the ground, Bündchen seems more James's equal, each of them one of the "best bodies" that the issue features. James's pose, especially the open mouth and bared teeth, apes the apes on each of the precursory posters, but Bündchen seems to be enjoying her part in the pantomime. Moreover, if critics of the *Vogue* cover had looked a little further, they might have discovered *Typecasting* (2006), by Stuart Ewen and Elizabeth Ewen, which uses the recruiting poster image on its cover. The Ewens connect the 1933 *King Kong* with the recruiting poster, which they place side-by-side (429), along with a poster for *The Day the Earth Stood Still,* which also features a huge alien holding a beautiful blond woman. The Ewens provide a smart critique of *King Kong,* noting that it was Adolf Hitler's favorite film (437–38).[13] Insofar as Leibovitz's photo points to the Ewens' book, it directs us to an extensive critique of the racist stereotyping that critics of the *Vogue* cover have attributed to her. The *Vogue* cover, like "Murders in the Rue Morgue," must be read more carefully—not just to establish its use of stereotypes but to understand how each text works with that imagery.

As we assess readers' capabilities, of course, these three images figure in much the same way as historical events such as the Nat Turner rebellion and the Philadelphia riots. Readers must have that historical knowledge in order to make the connection. The *Vogue* cover and the controversy surrounding it not only demonstrate the art of cruising for context in our Internet world, but also provide the historical references readers need to recognize the ways that Poe's story can be placed in conversation with many different texts. Contemporary students would be unlikely to know the World War I recruiting poster, although they might know the *King Kong* poster, since the movie regularly appears on television and has been remade in recent years (in 1976 and 2005). Contemporary students would be less likely to make historical connections with the nineteenth-century moment of the tale's composition. They would be more likely to see the orangutan as a black man based on the still-common association of blacks and apes, especially when triangulated through the body of a white woman. Maybe Cassuto's students were simply afraid to say anything, recognizing the racism inherent in the connection—even if one is attributing it to writers and readers in the past. After all, it still comes from your imagination even if you then discover it as a meaning Poe craftily hid in the tale. The Rorschach blot in this case is one of those duck-and-rabbit optical illusions—alternately an orangutan and a black man.

If they had been aware of the controversy over the *Vogue* cover, the authors of a fascinating 2008 laboratory study of the identification of Blacks and apes by undergraduate students might not have concluded that most of them "seem to have forgotten the unpalatable history of Blacks depicted as apes—if they ever knew it to begin with" (Goff, 294). The results of the experiment demonstrate that "U.S. citizens implicitly associate Blacks and apes" and, more important, reveal how this association "influences the extent to which people condone and justify violence against Black suspects," as well as how it affects "the death sentencing decisions of jurors" (294). Overall, the study addresses what the authors call "some of the most extreme, negative outcomes of dehumanization that have captivated social justice research throughout history." Perhaps the most startling finding is that

> Black defendants who were put to death were more likely to have apelike representations in the press than were those whose lives were spared. Though a similar trend was found for Whites, with those sentenced to death more likely to receive apelike representations in the press than those whose lives were spared—perhaps because of the paucity of White death-eligible cases—this pattern was not statistically significant for Whites. Taken together, the results . . . suggest that Black defendants are more likely to be portrayed as apelike in news coverage than White defendants and that this portrayal is associated with a higher probability of state-sponsored executions.[14] (304)

Present-day readers of "The Murders in the Rue Morgue"—indeed, readers from various historical moments since the tale's publication—should have plenty of material in their mental databases to make the connection between the orangutan and a racial/racist context for the story. It is possible, in the absence of historical knowledge (of nineteenth-century examples) that contemporary readers might not think such analogies relevant in an older context—in the same way that contemporary readers often find it surprising that nineteenth-century people had sexual desires. We might call this phenomenon "anachronistic resistance." Readers would not mentally "click" on a link they have in their own minds because the historical distance between their knowledge and the text seems too great to warrant the connection.

What interests me most about the experience of present-day readings of "Murders in the Rue Morgue," then, are the two historical contexts involved—especially the intersection and interplay between the two. In his very smart analysis of the tale, Ed White suggests a "move beyond contextual framing, or some enumeration of historical factors acting on the text, toward some more dialectical approach in which writers assess *themselves* as historical products and try to respond accordingly; but in making reception part of the context, it also demands participation, self-reflection, and evaluation from critical readers (like students) in making the text work historically" (94). Usefully, White eliminates neither the writer nor the reader from the historical transaction. The text is not just some more-or-less blank or passive slate on which history inscribes itself; the writer manages and shapes historical material. Similarly, the reader is not some simple detective agent—in this case, determining that the killer ape might be construed

as a black man. The reader reflects self-consciously on where that insight originated. To what extent does reading in this way draw upon our own deeply en-
grained prejudices? Consider, for example, recent racist associations of apes and
Barack Obama.

Sean Delonas's *New York Post* cartoon (February 18, 2009), based on an incident in Stamford, Connecticut, in which a "pet" chimpanzee escaped from its
owner and mauled one of its owner's friends, identifies Obama with the chimp.
The ape's escape from its owner and violent attack on a woman would resonate
with readers of Poe's tale, and the ending recalls King Kong's shooting and fall to
the New York City pavement, not to mention Eric's killing in the 1932 film of *Murders*. Googling "Obama and Ape" produces similar racist images: Banners showing Curious George eating a banana, but with the caption "Obama in '08" un-
derneath, or the "photograph" of the presidential airplane, labeled "Watermelon
One" and showing a picture of Curious George near the nose and a picture of
President Obama on the tail, each of them eating a slice of watermelon.[15] Not surprisingly, the election of our first African American president evokes such racist
stereotyping as a way of reversing the evolution of racial attitudes.

READING BACKWARDS TO THE SOURCE

Racist imagery associating Blacks and apes provides readers at many different
historical moments with raw material they might bring to bear on their reading
of "The Murders in the Rue Morgue." Such raw material provides a screen or fil-
ter through which Poe's story might be viewed, the obvious danger being that the
contemporary context distorts our vision of the story past a point of plausibil-
ity. The reader's recognition that the orangutan and his behavior can be understood within a context of antebellum slavery and race relations, especially if that
context is prompted or enriched by more contemporary references, represents a
starting point for further discussion. Since that recognition must occur relatively
late in our reading of the story—possibly but not likely before Dupin has identified the orangutan as the perpetrator—"The Murders in the Rue Morgue" must
be re-read. And because of the politically and socially charged triangular relationship I have been exploring, that re-reading could be an unusually self-conscious,
introspective one. It is not just the simple matter of what we know when—but
why we know it.

Once we understand the secret of the orangutan's "identity" (as an encoded
black man), we should circle back through the story, examining what this new

identification means, how it works, what attitudes toward the newly configured relationships—white detective, black man, and white female victims—the story reveals. What does Poe have to say about "sexually charged racial anxiety," the readers who experience it, the symbols that cause it? Once you make the connection Cassuto finally gets his students to make, you read the story differently.

Appreciating the racial connections in this tale restores a particular cultural meaning to the murders, as well as to our solution of the mystery. Given the racist link between apes and Blacks, the murders of two women in "The Murders in the Rue Morgue" ingeniously test the conceptual lines between species and between races. Associations of Blacks and apes are designed, after all, to cover racism with a specious specie-ism. Being of different races implied a common, if distant, ancestor (monogenesis); being of different species implied separate origins (polygenesis). "In the Southern environment," as Adrian Desmond and James Moore put it, "slaves became not only figurative 'others,' but literally another species" (199). Much more explicitly than "Hop-Frog" or "Doctor Tarr and Professor Fether," which also play with human-orangutan comparisons, "Murders" engages in a conversation with pre-Darwinian evolutionary theory, especially polygenetic theories of human development. As Elise Lemire has deftly shown, Poe knew the work of Darwinian precursors such as Frederic Cuvier and Le Comte Georges Buffon.[16]

Offering a "glimpse," in Harry Levin's terms, of an "old Southern bugbear: the fear of exposing a mother or a sister to the suspected brutality of a darker race" (141), the murders seem rooted in white racist fears of black uprisings—especially as those uprisings would register on the bodies of white women. Insofar as Poe engages such ideas, he works some interesting and ironic variations. In depicting the murders in the Rue Morgue as "something *excessively outré*— something altogether irreconcilable with our common notions of human action, even when we suppose the actors most depraved of men" (*Tales* 1: 557)—Poe seems to restore lines of difference and to inscribe the common rationalization of species difference that often buttressed white racism. In this respect, Dupin acts and speaks more like a southern proponent of slavery than like a French detective. He is the consummate voice of reason, the scientist who analyzes and classifies evidence, marking out the categorical differences between the sane and the mad, the human and the animal. John Nickel is certainly right in arguing that the act of reading in this tale "not only exists within power relations but determines them" and in concluding that, in "exhibiting his reading acumen," Dupin "establishes his superiority to his audience—those listening to the account of his interpretation" (43–44). Showing off his superior detecting ability is certainly Dupin's intention. Showing off to the frame narrator, who stands in for the reader, enables Poe to plant an accomplice in the text, much as mind readers plant accomplices in the audience. We have to resist both characters' efforts to influence our reading. In his verbal sketch of the murderer, Dupin combines "the ideas of an agility astounding, a strength superhuman, a ferocity brutal, a butchery without motive, a *grotesquerie* in horror absolutely alien from humanity, and a voice foreign in tone to the ears of men of many nations, and devoid of all distinct or intelligible syllabification" (*Tales* 1: 558). Indeed, only by interpreting the barbarity as the work not of a "madman" or "raving maniac" (the narrator's guess) but of a different species can Dupin solve the crime. The narrator in this respect plays the dupe, just not as obviously as the Prefect G—— does. We may even take some pleasure in seeing the narrator's speculations proven false. We identify with Dupin and his superiority.

Poe seems well aware of what is at stake: the structure and viability of difference in the white imagination. And it is tempting to see Poe the ironist subtly inviting us to resist Dupin's reading of the evidence. Where the narrator posits a madman, Dupin finds an orangutan—both suspects, of course, serving to distance the crime from normative subjectivity and from us. Ostensibly to show the narrator that a mad man could not have committed the murders, Dupin makes a facsimile drawing of the marks found on Mademoiselle L'Espanaye's throat, invites the narrator to place his fingers "in the respective impressions" and then try to wrap the drawing around a "billet" of wood approximately the size of the woman's neck (559). This ironic reenactment places the narrator and the reader in the murderer's position even as it exempts us from occupying that position. The narrator concludes that this "is the mark of no human hand" (559) even as he tries out and thus humanizes the subject position of the murderer. But when Dupin shows him Cuvier's "minute anatomical and generally descriptive account of the large fulvous Ourang-Outang of the East Indian Islands," the narrator says that he "understood the full horrors of the murder at once" (559). Don't we, too, breathe a sigh of relief, now knowing that the vicious murders of the two women were not the work of a human being, not even a madman? Well, not so fast.

"The Murders in the Rue Morgue" turns on the paradox that, in order to solve the crime, the detective, the narrator, and the reader must identify with and thus humanize even the most "*excessively outré*" act of butchery—if only to attribute the crime to some "other" being. Ironically, Poe has already anticipated this rationalization. We cannot so easily write off the orangutan as an inhuman killer and thus remove the tale from the realm of human intentionality. Poe plays with the tendency—certainly still true today—to relegate the most heinous perpetrators, the more heinous the better, to a different category or species altogether. One of Poe's jokes in this tale is that, even though Dupin has been driving the narrative away from the human, the orangutan we finally meet has been at least partially domesticated and humanized by his sailor-owner. The 1932 film, of course, takes this idea to the extreme, eliminating the sailor and making the ape (Eric) the agent of his owner's desires. The film effectively divides male desire among three characters—Dr. Mirakle, Jonas (The Black One), and Eric the ape-man. Aligned interestingly enough with nineteenth-century debates about species and racial differences, the film separates the strands of those debates, representing the role of science in Dr. Mirakle (who comes down on the side of the monogenists) and the tension between race and species in the doubling of the other two characters.

Poe, too, pays attention to these issues. Having established and reinforced lines of difference—between humans and apes and even madmen and apes—he proceeds to break them down. The orangutan's murderous act, we discover, represents a learned behavior. It has learned to imitate its owner, who discovered it one day, "razor in hand, and fully lathered, sitting before a looking-glass, attempting the operation of shaving, in which it had no doubt previously watched its master through the key-hole of the closet" (565). When the sailor attempts to quiet the creature "by the use of a whip" (565), it flees, only to end up in the Rue Morgue and in the bedroom of Madame L'Espanaye and her daughter. "As the sailor looked in, the gigantic animal had seized Madame L'Espanaye by the hair (which was loose, as she had been combing it,) and was flourishing the razor about her face, in imitation of the motions of a barber" (566). Nearly severing the woman's head from her body with "one determined sweep of its muscular arm," "flashing fire from its eyes," and then embedding its "fearful talons" in the daughter's throat, the orangutan happens to notice its master in the window. Suggestively, its "wandering and wild glances fell at this moment upon the head of the bed, over which the face of its master, rigid with horror, was just discernible" (567). This gaze between owner and animal—across the bed (and sexuality) of white womanhood—triangulates desire and violence in a possessive, murderous relationship between master and slave that becomes displaced upon the body of the white woman. The scene reinforces the idea that the orangutan acts in some sense in concert with its master. (The ape's role as its master's agent is even clearer in the 1932 film version of the tale, as Eric clearly acts under Dr. Mirakle's orders when he kidnaps Camille.) Thus triangulated, the narrator (as well as the sailor) finds himself witnessing racially encoded, male-on-female violence. Male power and the male gaze arc between men, Poe suggests, until their inherent violence issues forth in a psycho-logic of violent murder. Ostensibly a spectator at this scene of inhuman, unmotivated violence, the sailor is ultimately revealed to be the source of violence—the orangutan the agent he has set in motion. Thomas Jefferson had noted that

> The whole commerce between master and slave is a perpetual exercise of the most boisterous passions, the most unremitting despotism on the one part, and degrading submissions on the other. Our children see this, and learn to imitate it; for man is an imitative animal. This quality is the germ of all education in him. From the cradle to the grave he is learning to do what he sees others do. If a parent could find no motive either in his philanthropy or his self-love, for restraining the intemperance of passion towards his slave, it should always be a sufficient one that his child is present. But generally it is not sufficient. The parent storms, the child looks on, catches the lineaments of wrath, puts on the same airs in the circle of smaller slaves, gives loose to his worst of passions, and thus nursed, educated, and daily exercised in tyranny, cannot but be stamped by it with odious peculiarities. The man must be a prodigy who can retain his manners and morals undepraved by such circumstances. (162)

Poe goes one obvious step further, tracing the roots of white racist fears to white racist behavior—to the education of slaves, through the "use of a whip," in the possession and murder of women. Under the gaze of its master, Poe notes, "the fury of the beast, *who no doubt bore still in mind the dreaded whip,* was instantly converted into fear" (567; italics added), and it sets about trying to conceal the two women's dead bodies. In that action, as Poe's readers will recognize, the orangutan imitates rational human behavior.

Where does this leave the reader? In an interesting position. If we feel relieved to discover that these brutal murders are not murders at all, that they are "literally meaningless," in Rubin's words, because "there is no motive, no crime, no villain" (142), Poe subverts our feeling of relief by demonstrating that the orangutan acted in recognizably human ways. Poe blurs the hard line between species—and implicitly between races—that scientific racists wished to draw. If we make the ape-human connection and recognize the "sexually charged racial anxiety" that Poe puts in play, we may reveal our own habits of racial stereotyping, but we cannot rest easily in that conclusion either. Orangutan or slave, the killer has learned how to kill from his white master. Either way, Poe suggests, we wouldn't understand the tale at all unless we were capable of acting *"excessively outré"*—which turns out to be human after all.[17]

In his review of Hawthorne's *Twice-Told Tales,* Poe predicated "true originality" on a sympathetic identification between reader and writer so close, as far as the reader is concerned, that they seem to be producing a text together. That sympathetic identification resembles the prerequisite for winning the even-and-odd game that Dupin recounts in "The Purloined Letter." Reading perversely, on the other hand, requires a paradoxical identification and dis-identification with the literary text—a sympathetic engagement that keeps us sympathetically *there* in the text, attentive to every word, but an intellectual and emotional distance that enables us to imagine alternative possibilities. It's as if we have two mental programs running. We are intensely focused on the text, but in the background we have a search engine cruising for contexts that, almost literally, illuminate the text we are reading—as if they were filters that change the color of what we are looking at.

I want to end with a question about an old-fashioned topic—intentionality. In the Hawthorne passage, Poe certainly implies that the reader's sympathetic impression of co-authorship is illusory—that the writer creates and manages that impression as a function of his masterly control of the text. When we cruise for historical contexts we can bring to bear upon Poe's writing—the racial and sexual fears and desires of mid-nineteenth-century America, for example—do we find what Poe has already planted there, like specters in our path? It does not require much perverseness to read Dupin's identification of an orangutan as the murderer in the Rue Morgue as an example of racial panic. But it takes a little. The more important job is not simply to point out the connection between text and context, but, as it has always been, to do something with the connection.

Notes

1. In the most comprehensive effort to historicize Poe's tale, Elise Lemire painstakingly discovers numerous historical influences, many of them associated with Philadelphia, where Poe was living when he wrote the story. I am indebted to Lemire's excellent essay for the many historical connections she makes, including examples of apes being identified with African Americans. One of the worst race riots in Philadelphia, she points out, occurred in May 1838, while the second Anti-Slavery Convention of American Women was taking place (177), and she also notes that a year later a giant ape (either a chimpanzee or orangutan) was put on display to great fanfare (179). In his introduction to the story, Thomas O. Mabbott lists a half-dozen possible sources for the orangutan's behavior, including an article Poe could have seen in which a monkey enters an English woman's bedroom, attacks her, and then is scared off after a violent battle with her husband

(Poe, *Tales* 1: 522–23). David S. Reynolds also cites potential sources for the tale: "The premise of freakish actions by a humanoid orangutan had been introduced in America as early as 1807, with the story of a razor-wielding ape in the *American Magazine of Wonders*, and had been circulating later in works like Joseph Martin's *Select Tales* (1833), an adventure anthology that includes a story about an orangutan who kidnaps a child and suckles it for three months" (246).

2. Paul Woolf has historicized the tale through a different set of signifiers. Noting the early reference to the Palais Royal, which was "internationally renowned" in the mid-nineteenth-century for sex and shopping (9), he makes a cogent case for considering the L'Espanaye women, as well as Dupin himself, as prostitutes.

3. In *Notes on the State of Virginia*, Thomas Jefferson inventories the differences between blacks and whites which, he says, are "fixed in nature." White people are simply more attractive, Jefferson reasons, and as evidence he cites black people's "own judgment in favour of the whites, declared by their preference of them, as uniformly as is the preference of the Oran-ootan for the black women over those of his own species" (138). Winthrop Jordan explains that the "sexual association of apes with Negroes had an inner logic that kept it alive: sexual union seemed to prove a certain affinity without going so far as to indicate actual identity—which was what Englishmen really thought was the case. By forging a sexual link between Negroes and apes, furthermore, Englishmen were able to give vent to their feeling that Negroes were a lewd, lascivious, and wanton people" (18–19).

4. Winthrop Jordan notes that, just as the concept of the Chain of Being "ordered every being on a vertical scale, the association of the Negro with the ape ordered men's deep, unconscious drives into a tightly controlled hierarchy. The association was usually conceived in sexual terms" (107).

5. Lawrence Frank provides the most comprehensive analysis of connections between "Murders" and pre-Darwinian theories, noting that the story appeared "at a time in which both a resurgent evangelicalism and a conservative Natural Theology were confronted by a positivist science that was to have its nineteenth-century culmination in Charles Darwin's *Origin of Species* (1859)" (169–70). The key figure, whom Poe mentions in the text, is Georges Cuvier. When Cuvier wrote up the autopsy report for Saartjie Baartman (aka "The Hottentot Venus") in 1817, he emphasized "the subhumanity, or inferior developmental or evolutionary state, of Africans and their descendants" (Barrett, 168).

6. In contrast, the 2005 version of *King Kong*, directed by Peter Jackson, represents the relationship between Kong and Ann Darrow (Naomi Watts) more progressively. On Skull Island, as Dagmar Lorenz points out, Kong is "carefully modeled after the Silverback Gorilla known from Dian Fosse's studies" (169). Despite a de-emphasis on the cross-species, ape-man identification, Kong and Ann develop genuine, sympathetic feelings for one another. They enjoy a sunset side-by-side. "It's beautiful," she sighs, and then repeats the word "beautiful" for him. He responds by reaching out his hand for her to climb into. She falls asleep in the crook of his elbow. Darrow pleads for Kong's life when the men are trying to capture him. He reaches out his hand to her as he falls unconscious and is captured. Jack Driscoll looks on and notices the feeling between them. When Kong escapes in New York and reunites with Ann, he takes her skating on a pond in Central Park. She laughs. This is date night in New York. On top of the Empire State Building, they reprise the sunset scene on Skull Island. Dying, Kong carefully puts her down (as he did in the 1933 film), but here she touches his face. Crying, she rests her cheek on his arm. He slips away, falling in slow motion to the street below, in a separation scene that recalls the conclusion of *Titanic* (1997).

7. After Mirakle tests Camille's blood, he exclaims, "Her blood is perfect." Suggestively, the only other victim of Mirakle's we see on screen, a streetwalker (played by Arlene Francis), had "black blood" because she had sinned. In the contrast between Camille and the streetwalker, the

film accentuates the racial bifurcation on which the film depends—the dark male animal and the pure white woman.

8. Among the many roles Johnson played in his thirty-five-year career: Queequeg in the 1930 version of *Moby-Dick* and Uncle Tom in *Topsy and Eva* (1927). The Ewens note that, while he was "reduced in the picture [*King Kong*] to a grunting, animalistic savage, Johnson was in fact the founder, in 1916, of the Lincoln Motion Picture Company. It was the first black-owned film studio in the United States" (432).

9. More than twenty years ago, Cynthia Jordan credited Dupin with being unusually sympathetic to the woman's story in "The Murders in the Rue Morgue." Once Dupin realizes that an orangutan killed the two women, she says, he "is then able to recover the entire scenario—the second story—which reveals at last what the women actually suffered. Not surprisingly, that story presents a grim parody of what in Poe's tales constitutes normative masculine behavior. The trained animal had been acting out a masculine script . . ." (147).

10. Unlike the film, which shows Mede stoically enduring Blanche's advances, including the slow process by which she strips off his clothes and her own before he finally feels aroused, Onstott suggests that none of the participants in this strange triangle feel much desire or pleasure. For example, Blanche "resolved that Mede should be at her disposal, that she would enjoy (or pretend to enjoy him) when she would." For his part, Mede "felt no sense of triumph. He was under white domination and did as he was told. . . . To him, woman was woman, female was female. He accepted what was offered, what was prescribed. . . . Even in the most intimate of their embraces, he sensed her scorn of his blackness, her contempt for his race, her loathing for his person, but as well, her satisfaction with his maleness" (581).

11. The connection between the *Vogue* cover and the World War I poster was apparently first made on the Phawker blog site (March 17, 2008). Rogers Cadenhead commented a few days later on *Watching the Watchers,* and Danny Shea followed suit, crediting Cadenhead but not Phawker, on the *Huffington Post* website.

12. Kaufman lists the following similarities: The color of the women's outfits (the same blue in the World War I poster and the *Vogue* photo), LeBron's stance, hunched over and legs apart, his facial expression, a jaw-agape teeth-baring roar, his "weapon" (a basketball) in his right hand, his white-tipped tennis shoes, which match the hairless, lightened toes on the brute, the damsel is in/ on LeBron's left arm, Giselle's stance, with her feet inside LeBron's, but her body angling outward, her dress neckline, revealing as much of her upper torso as possible while remaining G-rated and cover-photo ready, her hairstyle with its wavy curls.

13. "In *King Kong,*" observe the Ewens, "typecasting was once again unified with the global history that stood behind it. The superiority of Western Civilization, the necessity of conquering the savage beast, the lust of dark brutes for fair women, and the heroic account of the white man's burden were combined to present a comprehensive way of seeing" (436–37). Adding the 1932 film version of *Murders in the Rue Morgue* to this rich context has provocative potential for demonstrating the currency of Poe's narrative within a 1930s context—especially the rise of Nazism that would eventually result in the invasion and occupation of Paris.

14. Goff and his colleagues could have cited the Mike Tyson rape trial as an example of such stereotyping. As Jack Lule notes in his extensive analysis of press coverage of the two-week trial, "two portraits of Tyson emerged. He was either a crude, sex-obsessed, violent savage who could barely control his animal instincts or he was a victim of terrible social circumstances, almost saved from the streets by a kindly overseer, but who finally faltered and fell to the connivance of others" (181). "Animal" is the favorite word used to describe Tyson, but other words ("monster," "demon," "rutting beast," "vile creature") also appeared (Lule, 182).

15. For a brief overview of "The Ape in American Bigotry," including the *Vogue* cover controversy, the *New York Post* chimpanzee cartoon, and several other examples involving President Obama, see Brent Staples's essay in the *New York Times*.

16. "Belief in a relationship between blacks and orangutans led to all kinds of comparisons in the nineteenth century between the two and even the insistence that orangutans could be mistaken for blacks" (Lemire, 185). Besides many other books circulating in the mid-nineteenth century, Lemire notes Poe's familiarity with Cuvier when he contributed to *The Conchologist's First Book* (1839) and when he helped write Thomas Wyatt's *Synopsis of Natural History* (1839). She also concludes that "white readers would have read the orangutan's assault as not merely typical of orangutans but as a point of comparison to interracial rape. White women were at risk when in proximity to black men because these men were animals who, like the animal to whom they were supposedly related, had monstrous sexual desires" (195–96).

17. In his provocative psychosexual reading of the story, Leo Lemay argues that Poe "challenges the reader to explain the murders as necessary outcomes of his characters' psychology. Dupin and the narrator, the sailor and the orangutan, and the L'Espanayes, are all the murderers—and the murdered. Indeed, every reader is made imaginatively to feel (and the ideal reader will ultimately perceive) that he is the murderer and the murdered" (180).

Works Cited

Barrett, Lindon. "Presence of Mind: Detection and Racialization in 'The Murders in the Rue Morgue.'" *Romancing the Shadow: Poe and Race.* Ed. J. Gerald Kennedy and Liliane Weissberg. New York: Oxford UP, 2001. 157–76.

Barthes, Roland. *S/Z: An Essay.* Trans. Richard Miller. New York: Farrar, Straus and Giroux, 1974.

Cadenhead, Rogers. "Annie Leibovitz Monkeys Around with LeBron James." *Watching the Watchers.* March 28, 2008. watchingthewatchers.org/news/1378/annie-leibovitz-monkeys-around-lebron (accessed April 19, 2010).

Cassuto, Leonard. "Poe the Crime Writer: Historicizing 'The Murders in the Rue Morgue.'" *Approaches to Teaching Poe's Prose and Poetry.* Ed. Jeffrey Andrew Weinstock and Tony Magistrale. New York: Modern Language Association, 2008. 33–38.

Creech, James. *Closet Writing/Gay Reading: The Case of Melville's Pierre.* Chicago: University of Chicago Press, 1993.

Dayan, Joan. "Amorous Bondage: Poe, Ladies, and Slaves." *The American Face of Edgar Allan Poe.* Ed. Shawn Rosenheim and Stephen Rachman. Baltimore: Johns Hopkins UP, 1995. 179–209.

Desmond, Adrian, and James Moore. *Darwin's Sacred Cause: How a Hatred of Slavery Shaped Darwin's Views on Human Evolution.* Boston: Houghton Mifflin Harcourt, 2009.

Elmer, Jonathan. *Reading at the Social Limit: Affect, Mass Culture, and Edgar Allan Poe.* Palo Alto, CA: Stanford UP, 1995.

Ewen, Stuart, and Elizabeth Ewen. *Typecasting: On the Arts and Sciences of Human Inequality.* Rev. ed. New York: Seven Stories P, 2008.

Frank, Lawrence. "'The Murders in the Rue Morgue': Edgar Allan Poe's Evolutionary Reverie," *Nineteenth-Century Literature* 50, no. 2 (1995): 168–88.

Ginsberg, Lesley. "Slavery and the Gothic Horror of Poe's 'The Black Cat.'" *American Gothic: New Interventions in a National Narrative.* Ed. Robert K. Martin and Eric Savoy. Iowa City: U of Iowa P, 1998. 99–128.

Goddu, Teresa A. "The Ghost of Race: Edgar Allan Poe and the Southern Gothic." *Criticism and the Color Line: Desegregating American Literary Studies.* Ed. Henry B. Wonham. New Brunswick, NJ: Rutgers UP, 1996. 230–50.

———. *Gothic America: Narrative, History, and Nation.* New York: Columbia UP, 1997.

Goff, Philip Atiba, Jennifer Eberhardt, Melissa J. Williams, and Matthew Christian Jackson. "Not Yet Human: Implicit Knowledge, Historical Dehumanization, and Contemporary Consequences." *Journal of Personality and Social Psychology* 94, no. 2 (2008): 292–306.

Haller, John S., Jr. "The Species Problem: Nineteenth-Century Concepts of Racial Inferiority in the Origin of Man Controversy." *American Anthropologist* 72, no. 6 (December 1970): 1319–29.

Harrowitz, Nancy. "Criminality and Poe's Orangutan: The Question of Race in Detection." *Agonistics: Arenas of Creative Contest.* Ed. Janet Lungstrum and Elizabeth Saver. Albany: SUNY P, 1997. 177–95.

Hawthorne, Nathaniel. *The Letters, 1843–1853.* Vol. 16 of *The Centenary Edition of the Works of Nathaniel Hawthorne.* Ed. Thomas Woodson, L. Neal Smith, and Norman Holmes Pearson. Columbus: Ohio State UP, 1985.

Jefferson, Thomas. *Notes on the State of Virginia.* Ed. William Peden. New York: Norton, 1972.

Jordan, Cynthia S. *Second Stories: The Politics of Language, Form, and Gender in Early American Fictions.* Chapel Hill: U of North Carolina P, 1989.

Jordan, Winthrop D. *The White Man's Burden: Historical Origins of Racism in the United States.* New York: Oxford UP, 1974.

Kaufman, K. R. Blog posting. *DemocraticUnderground.com.* March 31, 2008. www.democraticunderground.com/discuss/duboard.php?az=show_mesg&forum=389&topic_id=3082272&mesg_id=3084417 (accessed April 19, 2010).

King Kong. Dir. Merian C. Cooper and Ernest B. Schoedsack. Writ. James Ashmore Creelman and Ruth Rose. Perf. Fay Wray, Robert Armstrong, Bruce Cabot. RKO Radio Pictures, 1933. Two-disc Collector's Edition. Turner Entertainment, 2005.

King Kong. Dir. John Guillermin. Writ. Lorenzo Semple Jr. Perf. Jeff Bridges, Charles Grodin, Jessica Lange. Paramount Pictures, 1976.

King Kong. Dir. Peter Jackson. Writ. Fran Walsh, Phillippa Boyens, and Peter Jackson. Perf. Naomi Watts, Jack Black, Adrien Brody. Universal Pictures, 2005.

Lemay, J. A. Leo. "The Psychology of 'The Murders in the Rue Morgue.'" *American Literature* 54, no. 2 (1982): 165–88.

Lemire, Elise. "'The Murders in the Rue Morgue': Amalgamation Discourses and the Race Riots of 1838 in Poe's Philadelphia." *Romancing the Shadow: Poe and Race.* Ed. J. Gerald Kennedy and Liliane Weissberg. New York: Oxford UP, 2001. 177–204.

Lethbridge, Julian. "The Historian as Detective: Historical Method in Edgar Allan Poe's 'The Murders in the Rue Morgue.'" *Re-Visioning the Past: Historical Self-Reflexivity in*

American Short Fiction. Ed. Bernd Engler and Oliver Scheiding. Trier: WVT, 1998. 87–105.

Levin, Harry. *The Power of Blackness: Hawthorne, Poe, Melville.* New York: Vintage Books, 1958.

Lorenz, Dagmar C. G. "Transatlantic Perspectives on Men, Women, and Other Primates: The Ape Motif in Kafka, Canetti, and Cooper's and Jackson's King Kong Films." *Women in German Yearbook* 23 (2007): 156–78.

Lule, Jack. "The Rape of Mike Tyson: Race, the Press and Symbolic Types." *Critical Studies in Mass Communication* 12, no. 2 (1995): 176–95.

Machor, James L. "Introduction: Readers/Texts/Contexts." *Readers in History: Nineteenth-Century American Literature and the Contexts of Response.* Ed. Machor. Baltimore: Johns Hopkins UP, 1993. vii–xxix.

———. "Mastering Audiences: Poe, Fiction, and Antebellum Reading." *ESQ: A Journal of the American Renaissance* 47 (2001): 163–83.

———. "Poetics as Ideological Hermeneutics: American Fiction and the Historicized Reader of the Early Nineteenth Century." *Reader* 25 (Spring 1991): 49–64.

Mandingo. Dir. Richard Fleischer. Writ. Norman Wexler. Perf. James Mason, Susan George, Perry King, Brenda Sykes, and Ken Norton. Paramount Pictures, 1975.

Morton, Samuel George. *Types of Mankind: or, Ethnological Researches.* Ed. J. C. Nott and George R. Gliddon. 7th ed. Philadelphia: Lippincott, Grambo, 1855.

Morrison, Toni. *Playing in the Dark: Whiteness and the Literary Imagination.* Cambridge, MA: Harvard UP, 1992.

Murders in the Rue Morgue. Dir. Robert Florey. Writ. Tom Reed and Dale Van Every. Perf. Bela Lugosi, Sidney Fox, and Leon Waycoff. Universal Studios, 1932.

Nickel, John. "Reading and the Relations of Power in 'The Murders in the Rue Morgue.'" *Essays in Arts and Sciences* 29 (2000): 43–56.

Onstott, Kyle. *Mandingo.* Uncensored abridgement. Greenwich, CT: Fawcett, 1958.

Person, Leland S. "Poe's Philosophy of Amalgamation: Reading Racism in the Tales," *Romancing the Shadow: Poe and Race.* Ed. J. Gerald Kennedy and Liliane Weissberg. New York: Oxford UP, 2001. 205–24.

Phawker Blog Archive. "Voguing: This Is Progress?" March 30, 2008. www.phawker .com/2008/03/17/voguing-this-is-progress/ (accessed April 19, 2010).

Poe, Edgar Allan. "Nathaniel Hawthorne." *Edgar Allan Poe: Essays and Reviews.* Ed. G. R. Thompson. New York: Library of America, 1984. 568–88.

———. "The Imp of the Perverse." *Tales and Sketches.* Vol. 2: 1843–1844. Ed. Thomas Ollive Mabbott. Urbana: U of Illinois P, 2000. 1217–27.

———. "The Murders in the Rue Morgue." *Tales and Sketches.* Vol. 1: 1831–1842. Ed. Thomas Ollive Mabbott. Urbana: U of Illinois P, 2000. 527–74.

Reynolds, David S. *Beneath the American Renaissance: The Subversive Imagination in the Age of Emerson and Melville.* Cambridge, MA: Harvard UP, 1988.

Rohy, Valerie. "Ahistorical." *GLQ: A Journal of Gay and Lesbian Studies* 12, no. 1 (2006): 61–83.

Rubin, Louis D., Jr. *The Edge of the Swamp: A Study in the Literature and Society of the Old South.* Baton Rouge: Louisiana State UP, 1989.

Savoy, Eric. "Hypocrite Lecteur: Walter Pater, Henry James and Homotextual Politics." *Dalhousie Review* 72, no. 1 (1992): 11–36.

Shea, Danny. "Uncovered: Possible Inspiration for Controversial LeBron James *Vogue* Cover." *The Huffington Post*. March 28, 2008. www.huffingtonpost .com/2008/03/28/uncovered-possible-inspir_n_93944.html. (accessed 19 April 2010).

Shimizu, Celine Parreñas. "Master-Slave Sex Acts: *Mandingo* and the Race/Sex Paradox." *The Persistence of Whiteness: Race and Contemporary Hollywood Cinema*. Ed. Daniel Bernardi. London: Routledge, 2008. 218–32.

Smith, Barbara Herrnstein. "Contingencies of Value." *Critical Inquiry* 10, no. 1 (Sept. 1983): 1–35.

Snarker, Dorothy. "*Vogue* creates controversy with Annie Leibovitz cover shot." *After Ellen* Blog. April 2, 2008. www.afterellen.com/blog/dorothysnarker/vogue-controversy-with-annie-leibovitz-cover (accessed April 19, 2010).

Staples, Brent. "The Ape in American Bigotry, From Thomas Jefferson to 2009." *The New York Times*. February 28, 2009. www.nytimes.com/2009/02/28/opinion/28sat4 .html?_r=1&th=&emc=th (accessed April 20, 2010).

Whalen, Terence. *Edgar Allan Poe and the Masses: The Political Economy of Literature in Antebellum America*. Princeton, NJ: Princeton UP, 1999.

White, Ed. "The Ourang-Outang Situation." *College Literature* 30, no. 3 (Summer 2003): 88–108.

Wood, Robin. *Sexual Politics and Narrative Film: Hollywood and Beyond*. New York: Columbia UP, 1998.

Woolf, Paul. "Prostitutes, Paris and Poe: The Sexual Economy of Edgar Allan Poe's 'The Murders in the Rue Morgue.'" *Clues: A Journal of Detection* 25, no. 1 (Fall 2006): 6–20.

Robert Greenhow, Poe, and the Nineteenth-Century History of Transnational American Studies

ANNA BRICKHOUSE

Throughout the 1840s, Robert Greenhow, a quiet man of letters who loved old books and maps, was suffering periodically from a nervous disorder.[1] Though his official title was "Librarian and Translator," Greenhow was a writer and scholar working in multiple languages and historical periods. He had plenty of reasons to be overwhelmed by the sheer enormity of primary and secondary materials out there in the world, some accessible and some not, with only a limited amount of time to read even a fraction of endlessly proliferating sources—a combination guaranteed to produce a generalized anxiety of interdisciplinarity with which many of us would likely sympathize. Nietzsche might have diagnosed Greenhow with the disease of antiquarianism, the nervous disorder both resulting from and symptomatic of a scrupulous interest in the past for its own sake without regard for its contemporary use-value—an interest that, as Nietzsche saw it, in turn suppresses the health and instinct of youth and the present.[2] But a closer examination of Greenhow's scholarly work suggests, in fact, the opposite: it was the contemporary uses to which history could be put that interested Greenhow—and that, perhaps, left him a nervous wreck. Employed not by a university but by the U.S. Department of State, Greenhow was among the three most highly ranked officials precisely for the services in transnational American historical research that he provided.

Today, however, Greenhow's work has been largely forgotten, overshadowed in historical scholarship by the figure of his far more famous and flamboyant wife, Rose O'Neal Greenhow: "Wild Rose," the "Confederate Spy," as her biographers have dubbed her in telling the story of her larger-than-life career as a secret agent for the South during the Civil War, a decade after her husband's death in 1854. An anxious intellectual, Robert Greenhow does not come off as very interesting or successful compared to Rose. He did not fare particularly well as a diplomat, for example, when President Van Buren sent him to Mexico in 1837 to discuss with the Mexican foreign minister the recent U.S. decision to acknowledge Texas in-dependence. A poor candidate for a Foreign Service career, Greenhow got dys-entery and learned little that would influence future U.S.-Mexican political rela-tions. Rose, on the other hand, was, according to her biographers, a "ravishing and fearless" southern belle who once stitched a tiny silk purse with a coded mes-sage inside, wrapped it into the chignon of one of her female "scouts," and sent it to a Confederate general, thereby (possibly) securing a southern win at Bull Run, and even allegedly changing the "course of the Civil War" itself.[3]

In narratives transparently celebratory of Rose O'Neal Greenhow, Robert Greenhow serves merely as his wife's foil—and the familiar, stock character of the urbane but ineffectual scholar. "More likely to tell a story of the poet Lord Byron, whom he had met in Italy, than rehash the yeas and nays of the last Sen-ate vote," Greenhow was—in accordance with the stereotype—"happiest alone and uninterrupted in his study, deciphering faded, handwritten accounts of ter-ritories and bodies of water in uncharted areas." Disdaining the crude world of politics, he was filled with "enormous pride in his precise translation of docu-ments from their original language into English." But this vision of Greenhow "happiest" in the world of his historical hobbies, pursuing a private passion, is misleading on several counts. It is true that Greenhow was working in a histori-cal moment that precedes the professionalization of American history, as Peter Novick and others have documented it: Greenhow's era can rightly be described as "a time when all historians were 'amateurs' of history," "amateur gentleman-scholar[s]" who used their private funds to support their research and writing.[4] But if Greenhow preceded the advent of the "professional historian" in the late nineteenth century, his institutional affiliations were, by definition, radically dis-tinct from those of his amateur, gentlemanly peers: he was, after all, on the official payroll of the State Department.

The late-nineteenth-century professionalizers of history would famously dis-dain Greenhow's peers—notably Prescott and Bancroft—as "literary historians," hopeless romantics who wrote under the spell of Walter Scott's novels, and mis-construed history as art.[5] This assessment oversimplifies, of course, in its sweep-ing characterization of early nineteenth-century historical sensibilities, which were—as they are now— varied, marked by the generic tensions between litera-ture and history, and dependent on context. The novelist and historian William Gilmore Simms could declare without qualification that "the chief value of his-tory consists in its proper employment for the purposes of art!" The traditional historian was a "mere chronologist," for whom "dates and names . . . are every thing." Simms disdained what he called "that class of modern historians, the professed skeptics," with their "learned ingenuity," "keen and vigilant judgment," "great industry," "vast erudition and sleepless research," and "coldly inquisitive" mode of presentation. Not history but art was "the greatest of all historians": "It is the artist only who is the true historian." But Prescott, later (and still often) known as the chief of the romancers, sided with the "professed skeptics" when he criticized one of his major Spanish sources, the seventeenth-century historian Solís, for putting made-up speeches into the mouths of his historical subjects: "There is something like deception in it," he complained. "The reader is unable to determine what are the sentiments of the characters and what those of the author. History assumes the air of romance, and the bewildered student wanders about in an uncertain light, doubtful whether he is treading on fact or fiction."[6]

Nevertheless, against this range of nineteenth-century Romantic views of the differences between, and relative merits of, history and literature, Greenhow's historical work stands out for its relentless accrual of those dry "dates and names" scorned by Simms—for the sheer weight of accumulated evidence tenaciously resisting the pull of narrative. Greenhow's work seems almost to relish its fetishization of the antiquary's "disinterested love" of the "Facts of History" over and above, indeed at the expense of, any literary appeal.[7] Thus, in the few accounts that reference him today, Greenhow earns the faintly damning praise that might now, in some quarters, be received as a professional kiss of death: he was, ostensibly, "a solid researcher and a clear, objective writer." As I will show here, however, Greenhow was anything but a "solid researcher," at least not in any of the senses in which we currently understand that phrase; he was certainly not objective.[8]

Two pieces of Greenhow's historical scholarship—one written for an explicitly political context and the other for an explicitly antiquarian, and ostensibly neutral one—reveal the oblique and shadowed story of Greenhow's relationship to Edgar Allan Poe. Reading Poe's "Journal of Julius Rodman" alongside Greenhow's work for the U.S. Department of State, I locate these two very different writers within a broad, comparative field that I am, as a kind of provocation, defining as a form of transnational American studies. Taken together, the writings of Greenhow and Poe provide a means of contemplating our field in the wake of the so-called "transnational turn."[9] Ultimately, I hope to raise questions about the contours of particular historical simultaneity—as my title is meant to suggest, between the 1840s and the current disciplinary moment—through which we might consider the transnational trajectory of American studies, its simultaneous proximity to and distance from the state, and its place within a longer disciplinary history than we tend to recognize.

HISTORY VERSUS LITERATURE: GREENHOW, POE, AND THE PRECARIOUS U.S. CLAIM TO THE "OREGON COUNTRY"

In 1811, when Greenhow was a ten-year-old boy, his parents took him to a benefit show in Richmond, a play whose proceeds were to help support a newly orphaned boy named Edgar, son of the late Elizabeth Arnold Poe. A fire broke out in the theater, and Greenhow's mother's last words to her husband were, according to his father's later account, a plea to save her child at all costs. Greenhow and his father barely made it out of the theater alive; Greenhow's mother died in the fire.[10] Greenhow and Poe were thus uncannily connected from their childhoods by a shared tragedy that left Greenhow, like Poe, bereft of a mother. Whether or not they ever met in person is unknown, but their written paths would intersect when the two motherless boys grew up to become writers on opposite sides of a great divide that continues to this day. Greenhow and Poe adopted competing muses, and took opposite sides in the age-old rivalry between Clio and Calliope: a battle between history and literature. Or, to borrow a phrase from Eric Slauter, not so much a battle as a competitive market relationship between history and literature—and marked, in our current moment, by a "trade deficit" on the literary side.[11]

Poe might have agreed that even in the nineteenth century literature imported more from history than it exported to history, and this was, as he saw it, to the detriment, even the destruction, of the latter. "There is no greater error," he wrote, "than dignifying with the name of History a tissue of dates and details, though the dates be ordinarily correct, and the details indisputably true":

> Not even with the aid of acute comment will such a tissue satisfy our individual notions of History. To the effect let us look—to the impression rather than the seal. And how very seldom is any definite impression left upon the mind of the historical reader! [Yet] we shall often discover in Fiction the essential spirit and vitality of Historic Truth—while Truth itself, in many a dull and lumbering archive, shall be found guilty of all the inefficiency of Fiction.

Nineteenth-century readers "very seldom" encountered histories literary enough to merit the name of history, Poe contended. By contrast, readers were "often" treated to the "Historic Truth" in perusing "Fiction." Poe conceded that "Truth itself" might be found through painstaking historical research, but without proper literary elaboration it would remain useless to its readers.[12]

Yet the "dull and lumbering archive," unrefined by literary appeal, is exactly what Greenhow sought to showcase in the first piece of writing I want to examine here, his 1840 "Memoir, Historical and Political, on the Northwest Coast of North America," which he produced after returning from his failed 1837 diplomatic mission in Mexico. As the title's generic designation suggests, this scholarly work was prepared specifically for diplomatic and other official political uses as a learned overview of the existing literatures of European exploration in the Northwest and the competing imperial land claims underpinning the U.S.-British dispute on the "Oregon Question." Greenhow submitted the memoir to the U.S. Senate's Select Committee on the Oregon Territory, which in turn entered the document into the Congressional Record for the Twenty-sixth Congress in February 1840; on February 10, the Senate ordered an immediate printing as well as an additional twenty-five hundred copies to be sent to the Senate itself.[13] To better publicize Greenhow's argument, the Senate would eventually commission and subsidize Greenhow's "revised, corrected, and enlarged" version of the memoir as a book, *The History of Oregon and California and other Territories of the North-West Coast of North America,* published in 1845.[14]

Against the backdrop of Romantic history, Greenhow's work, in both its incarnations, presents itself as the product of the "coldly inquisitive" scholar pursuing facts, uninterested in either the "spirit" or "vitality" of the past. At the same time, however, the history self-consciously circumscribes both the intellectual and political role of the scholar in undertaking the work: "The writer has now completed the task assigned to him," he notes modestly on the final page, "by presenting an exposition of the most important circumstances relative to the discovery and occupation of the northwest coasts and territories of North America, by the people of various civilized nations, and of the pretensions advanced by the Governments of those nations in consequence." There is no aggrandizing of the task of the translator here, no flaunting of the multilingual virtuosity and wide-ranging historical mastery demonstrated by his endeavors in the archives of Spanish, Russian, British, French, and U.S. literatures of exploration. Instead, Greenhow appears to acknowledge the lack of power inhering in his own scholarly performance, which he casts in a humble geographic metaphor: "To indicate farther the course which should be pursued on the part of the United States with regard to their claims," he opines, "lies not within [my] province." But if Greenhow disavows any disciplinary land claim on the "province" of U.S. foreign policy, he unequivocally states the foreign policy upshot of his project: that *"the titles of the United States to the possession of the regions . . . derived from priority of discovery and priority of occupation, are as yet stronger, and more consistent with the principles of national right, than those of any other Power."*[15]

Greenhow constructs this argument for U.S. "titles . . . to the possession" of the Northwest on a framework of transnational research that embraces colonial South America as well as North America, Atlantic as well as Pacific voyages, the East as well as the West. Describing the materials at his disposal, Greenhow develops a method that plays continually on the distinction between literature and history, always taking the side of the latter over the former—and the side of the "modern skeptic" over the Romantic. But Greenhow also works stealthily in the gap between history and literature, manipulating the long-standing battle, or the trade relationship, between them. To do so, he lays out a series of generic specifications that enable him to distinguish between, on the one hand, "true" accounts, characterized by "authenticity and general correctness," and, on the other, three closely related genres: "false" accounts, which have their "origin, generally, in the knavery and the vanity of their authors"; "reported discover[ies]," in which an author deliberately inscribes a "falsehood or amplification" in reporting another's oral statements or written work, usually to "induce" a patron to sponsor "a voyage which [the writer] then projected"; and, finally, the "pretended discovery," comprised of "mere fictions," which are "invented for the purpose of exercising ingenuity, or of testing the credulity of the public."

Greenhow then deftly negotiates these distinctions, highlighting an "exemplary fiction" from the genre of the "pretended voyage," for example, in order to demonstrate the veracity of a different, but equally disputed account. The minute detailing of various discovery narratives often disguises, moreover, the extent to which his argument rests on what we might call pure force of literary-historical assertion: precisely by writing history as a kind of *literary* history, Greenhow can announce that a particular account will be simply "removed from the class of *fictions*," or firmly settled there, through mere attribution of genre.[16] Greenhow thus offers for the reader a purportedly neutral kind of *literary historical* work that he performs in the larger service of *historical* work. The hidden payoff becomes clear only in the larger political context of the history, which is bracketed off until the end of the work: questions of genre allow Greenhow subtly to recast both the weakest forms of evidence supporting what will evolve as his larger argument for U.S. dominion in the "Oregon Country" (as well as the strongest forms of evidence supporting the British case) as a literary history rendered in the service of historical truth: a literary history that allows history finally to triumph over fiction.

To take a particularly compelling example, in turning to what he calls the "most celebrated fiction of the class" of pretended discoveries—those accounts produced "with the view of obtaining emolument or employment"—Greenhow painstakingly details the example of Lorenzo Ferrer Maldonado, a Portuguese explorer who claimed in the sixteenth century to have found the fabled Strait of Anian, a northwest passage from the Pacific to the Atlantic. Ferrer Maldonado's manuscript account of his alleged discovery, "Relation del descubrimiento del Estrecho de Anian en 1588," was copied, circulated, and ultimately printed soon after his return to Spain, and sometimes deemed accurate up through the eighteenth century. By the nineteenth century, of course, the account no longer held up, but Greenhow's lengthy discussion of "Maldonado," as he calls him, provides a prime opportunity for the nineteenth-century linguist to show off his archival and paleographical chops as he describes the "two manuscripts . . . now preserved, the one in the library of the Duke of Infantado, at Madrid, the other in the Ambrosian library, at Milan." Noting that "their contents are nearly the same, except that the Madrid paper is, in some places, more concise than the other, from which it seems to have been, in a manner, abridged," Greenhow delivers his pronouncement that, "[u]pon the whole, there is reason to believe the Madrid document to be a true copy of the history presented by Maldonado" with all the understatement and prudence of a consummate professional. Only if we read the notes do we realize that Greenhow is working from a secondary source, written in English and including full translations of the original Ferrer Maldonado copies, published a mere twenty years earlier.

Greenhow goes on to cite extensive, fantastical passages from this published translation of a copy of the Ferrer Maldonado account, though he acknowledges afterwards that it is "needless to use any arguments to prove that no such voyage could have been ever made." For Greenhow, the larger point is rather the felicitous character of the scholarly transmission of textual histories, even those of "mere fictions" passing as authentic accounts. "So far as is known," Greenhow explains, "the falsehoods of Maldonado have injured no one, and they were ultimately productive of great good": for "it was while engaged, by order of the Spanish government, in examining the archives of the Indies respecting this pretended voyage, that Navarette found those precious documents, relating to the expeditions of Columbus . . . which have thrown so much light on the history of the discovery of the New World." Maldonado's fraud thus becomes the happy occasion of Navarette's unwitting contribution, with his *Viages de Colon,* to nationalist literary history of the U.S.—"a truly acceptable addition," as the *North American Review* characterized Navarette's historical scholarship—"to our literary treasures."[17]

But Greenhow has an additional reason for dwelling on the account of Ferrer Maldonado and the literary context of what he calls the "memoir or narrative," in which "Maldonado" himself is the "hero" of an outlandish romance. Taking up Ferrer Maldonado's account as exemplary fiction from the subgenre of the "pretended voyage" offers Greenhow a strong foil against which to present his ensuing case, this time precisely for the veracity of yet another disputed account: "*A Note made by Michael Lok, the elder touching the Strait of Sea commonly called* Fretum Anian, *in the South Sea, through the North-west Passage of Meta Incognita,*" published in 1625 in Samuel Purchas's *Pilgrims.* Greenhow notes that the account has been "for a long time, considered as less worthy of credit" than that of Ferrer Maldonado—considered, that is, as another "pretended voyage" from the realm of fiction. But "more recent examinations from that part of the world," the Northwest, have, Greenhow avers, "caused [the text] to be removed from the class of fictions." At the outset of his discussion, Greenhow concedes that the account related by Lok "is certainly erroneous as regards the principal circumstance related"—that a "North-west Passage" was discovered. But at the end of his discussion of Lok's account and its central figure—a Greek sailor employed by the Spanish, "called, commonly, Juan de Fuca, but named, properly, Apostolos Valerianos"—Greenhow asserts again that "more recent examinations in [the Northwest] quarter have, however, served to establish a strong presumption in favor of its authenticity and general correctness, so far as the supposed narrator could himself have known." In other words, Greenhow argues, Juan de Fuca told the truth about finding a strait on the northwest coast of North America; his account may thus be placed in the class of authentic but inadvertently "erroneous" narratives: Fuca, that is, is a "supposed narrator" but he is not an unreliable one, for he "could [not] himself have known" that the strait he found was *not* a northwest passage connecting the Pacific and Atlantic. As before, moreover, Greenhow cites no sources for these "recent examinations" demonstrating Fuca's "authenticity"; his argument rests instead on pure force of literary historical assertion: that Fuca's account "has been removed from the class of *fictions.*"[18]

Greenhow's generic designation was not, however, a foregone conclusion for everyone. The English reviewer of Greenhow's book for the London-based *Quarterly Review,* for example, insisted upon the term "fable" for Fuca's account, and placed it in the category of "fables . . . circumstantially and plausibly told," which exacted a particular reader response: they "excited a strong desire to discover the supposed passages." But this disagreement over genre has a subtext that makes Greenhow's literary historical agenda on the subject clear—and that his English reviewer signals through a more specific classification for Fuca's account, when he calls it "an example of *quid Graecia mendax audet*," "what lies Greece dares to tell." The reviewer's allusion to Juvenal's Satire X thus brings a particular historiographical argument to bear on Greenhow's history, for the specific instances that Juvenal cites of "the lies mendacious Greece spun round her history" are both geographical and ideological. The late-Roman historian whom Juvenal (died *ca.* 130 CE) takes to task with the trope of "mendacious Greece" is Herodotus, whose notorious twinned legacy as both "Father of History" and "Father of Lies" evokes Greenhow's discussion of Fuca. Herodotus's uncertain status as either an ancient Greek purveyor of certain inadvertent untruths, or, on the other hand, a knowing author of historical fictions presents the exact historiographical question surrounding Fuca's account of a northwest passage—a question that Greenhow wishes to resolve by simply "remov[ing his text] from the class of fictions" and declaring it merely "erroneous."[19]

Greenhow's reviewer, in other words, has chosen a strangely fitting classical text in which to ground his objections. For unlike Greenhow, Juvenal doesn't seem to care about the difference between fiction and error: he scoffs at Herodotus's image of "sails crowd[ing] through Athos" long ago and other details, taken "from some sweaty-drunk poet's recital"—details, that is, of a supposed, once existent northern passage, a water passage, through the Athos peninsula of Greece. Such "mendacious" writing of history, Juvenal objects, is the result of an always already false imperial desire, as his examples in this section make clear. "One globe seemed all too small for the youthful Alexander," Juvenal observes: "Yet / when he entered the city of brick-walled Babylon, / a coffin was to suffice him." And Hannibal, too, is now reduced to the unimpressive heft of his own decaying bones: "Weigh [him]," warns Juvenal: "How many pounds will you find, now, / in that peerless commander?" But if the lesson here is, in part, that "Death alone reveals / our puny human dimensions," it is also that the writing of imperial histories condemns the future to the same false consciousness. By capturing the victors in an eternal, textual present—"*Now* Spain swells [Hannibal's] empire, *now* he leaps the Pyrenees"—these histories, and the pedagogical structures that circulate them, reproduce imperial desires in each new generation. This is why, in an angry apostrophe to Hannibal, Juvenal urges the centuries-dead general of the Carthaginian empire through the pages of history toward his inevitable imperial afterlife: "On, on, you madman, over your savage Alps, / to thrill schoolboys and supply a theme for future recitations!"[20]

Thus, when Greenhow's English reviewer classifies Juan de Fuca's account as not only a "fable" but an example of "*quid Graecia mendax audet*"—overlaying two accounts, centuries apart but similarly contested, of northern water passages—he brings a specific argument about historiographical imperialism to bear on the seemingly neutral question of genre, as presented in Greenhow. To put it another way, the English reviewer casts a Juvenalian light on Greenhow's history, and specifically on the imperial uses to which he puts his generic classification of Fuca's account. To argue for the veracity of Fuca's account, as Greenhow does, is to deny the priority of the English discovery, by the British captain John Mears, in 1788, of the body of water separating Vancouver and Washington and known today as Juan de Fuca's Strait. This is significant precisely because, according to Greenhow's larger argument for U.S. dominion over the Northwest, the right of "first discovery" is one of the three major criteria by which a nation can secure a territory in accordance with international law. If Fuca's account is "removed from the class of fictions," in other words, then the right of first discovery goes to Spain (for whom Fuca sailed) rather than England, and Spain had, by the time Greenhow was producing his history in the early 1840s, long ago ceded any northwestern land claims to the United States under the Treaty of Adams-Onís. The hidden payoff of Greenhow's ostensibly neutral literary historical work becomes clear in this context: with Fuca securely designated as the first discoverer of the northwestern strait, England lost one crucial piece of its potential case for claims to the land.

By far the most fascinating example of Greenhow's nimble shuttling between literature and history, the fictional and the authentic, occurs in his chapter on the earliest overland claims to the Oregon Country. The U.S. case for priority is not strong at this juncture of the argument, and Greenhow is at pains to contain the threat presented by the 1792 expedition of Alexander Mackenzie, a Scotsman working in the service of the North West Company, who crossed the Rocky Mountains and then reached the Pacific in 1793. Greenhow records the information about this expedition succinctly, without dwelling on details that would prolong the discussion, as he often does in cases where he proposes to move a narrative to or from the "class of fictions"—a manipulation that would be highly unfeasible in the case of Mackenzie's much celebrated and publicized journeys. Just after discussing Mackenzie, however, Greenhow draws the reader's attention to a new source, one whose genre he does specify, describing it only as a "journal

. . . recently discovered in Virginia, and now in course of publication in a periodical magazine at Philadelphia." "It is proper to notice here," Greenhow writes, "an
account of an expedition across the American continent, made between 1791 and
1794 . . . under the direction of Julius Rodman."[21]

"The Journal of Julius Rodman" and Poe's Double Cross

The text to which Greenhow is referring is, of course, Poe's "The Journal of Julius
Rodman," the only other Poe work besides *The Narrative of Arthur Gordon Pym*
that has been considered a novel. Genre proves difficult to determine in the former case, however, given that "Rodman" was never completed. Like *Pym*, "Rodman" presents itself to readers as a nonfiction travel narrative: "Being an Account
of the First Passage Across the Rocky Mountains of North America ever Achieved
by Civilized Man." And like the first chapters of *Pym*, which initially appeared in
the 1837 run of the *Southern Literary Messenger*, "Rodman" too emerged in serial publication—as Greenhow notes in the careful citation in his *Memoir*: "Burton's Magazine and American Monthly Review, edited by William E. Burton and
Edgar A. Poe. Mr. Rodman's journal is commenced in the number for January,
1840, and is continued in those for the next following months." But whereas the
first chapters of *Pym* appeared in the *Messenger* under Poe's own name—and only
in its final, novel form did the text announce itself as a "pretended fiction," with
"the name of Mr. Poe affixed to the articles" "in order that it might certainly be regarded as fiction"—"Rodman" dispenses with the *mise-en-abîme* of novel-as-non-
fiction-disguised-as-fiction and relies instead on the venerable and far simpler
literary device of the found manuscript. It appears in *Burton's Gentleman's Magazine* framed by the ostensible voice of its editor, signed only as "G.M." Moreover,
while *Pym* was received in its own time largely as a bad literary hoax—one early
reviewer complained of its "impudent attempt at humbugging the public"—"The
Journal of Julius Rodman" has maintained a more favorable reputation, if not in
aesthetic terms than as a more convincing literary hoax. The prime evidence supporting this judgment of "Rodman"'s persuasiveness has always been, of course,
its inclusion in Greenhow's official scholarly report regarding U.S. claims to the
Oregon Territory.[22]

    "The Journal of Julius Rodman" announces itself in its first installment as
the printed product of a handwritten diary provided to the editor of the *Gentleman's Magazine* by one James Rodman, the grandson of the diarist and protagonist in question. The subsequent installments, narrated by Julius Rodman with

occasional commentary by the editor, tell in brief the story of Rodman's aristocratic background, his melancholy state after the deaths of his father and sisters, and his decision in 1791 to sell his family property in Kentucky, travel up the Missouri River with a group of fur-trapping expeditionaries, and ultimately to undertake an arduous journey into the great unknown expanses of the "Far North." Never completed, the journal leaves off before describing how Rodman and his party of explorers make their actual crossing of the Rocky Mountains, but readers know from both the subtitle and the opening installment that the crossing has indeed been made and that Rodman long ago returned safely and went on to settle in Virginia, "where most of his descendants now live."[23]

Rodman's route thus fictionally blazes the trail that would fifteen years later be followed by Lewis and Clark, allowing readers to relive that celebrated adventure in the purportedly earlier—indeed, the purportedly original—crossing. In doing so, "The Journal of Julius Rodman" entered quite deliberately into debates over priority in the exploration history of the Northwest, and specifically into an implied conversation about contemporary U.S. claims to the disputed Oregon Territory. In this context, Rodman himself appears to play to contemporary public interest as the sort of rugged explorer associated with a heroic narrative of national expansion; as John Carlos Rowe has pointed out, he transforms over the course of his journal from a melancholic figure suffering from nervous hypochondria (as did Meriwether Lewis) into a vital and energetic frontiersman character who battles ferocious Indians and wild bears in the wilderness. It is no surprise, then, that Greenhow would find it "proper to notice" a text that so brilliantly exploited the prevailing expansionist sentiment of its moment—or that Greenhow's interest in the text would seem to confirm Poe's talents as both a man of letters and a consummate hoaxer.

Indeed, Greenhow's inclusion of this "recently discovered" manuscript in his *Memoir*—a document that was eventually submitted to the Senate and entered into the Senate Record—would constitute the basis for a winking footnote in the annals of Poe reception history. As the eminent Poe scholar David K. Jackson put it in a 1974 note in *Poe Studies,* the strange incident of "Julius Rodman"'s entrance into the Senate record "attests to Poe's contemporary success in imparting verisimilitude to his fictional narrative." "If Poe saw Greenhow's account," Jackson mused, "he must have been highly amused." Furthermore, Jackson observed, because Greenhow had earlier contributed articles to the *Southern Literary Messenger* during the period of Poe's editorial work there, he "must have either met or corresponded with Poe." Yet as the title of the note suggests ("A Poe Hoax Comes

Before the U.S. Senate"), Jackson believed the "hoax" to be Poe's alone; Green-how's participation in the hoax was entirely "unintentional," as Jackson saw it. Poe's literary creation of an ingenious "verisimilitude," in Jackson's view, led to "Robert Greenhow's acceptance of 'Julius Rodman' as a factual and not a fictional account of a journey of exploration."[24]

Certainly, Greenhow's own words about the Rodman account support the scholarly persona of painstaking neutrality and careful moderation that the rest of his *Memoir* cultivates. "From what has been published" thus far in *Burton's Magazine*, Greenhow cautioned,

> it is impossible to form a definitive opinion as to the degree of credit which is due to the narrative, or as to the value of the statements, if they are true; and all that can be here said in addition is, that nothing as yet appears either in the journal or relating to it, calculated to excite suspicions with regard to its authenticity.

Employing a full arsenal of rhetorical strategies of qualification for this commentary on Rodman's "statements"—"if they are true"—Greenhow offers a series of abnegations couched as affirmative propositions: "It is impossible to form"; "Nothing as yet appears." But his careful empiricist acknowledgment of the limits that facticity places on utterability—or "what can be here said"—hardly constitutes an endless deferral of the "definitive." Rather, Greenhow refuses quite specifically to enter into a particular economy of knowledge—that is, to place a wager on, or to invest in either the "degree of credit . . . due" or the gross "value" of Rodman's account. He attempts instead to rig the market from the outside, without risking any of his own scholarly capital, via something like a *rumor* of the text's "authenticity"—a vague assertion that there is nothing "either in the journal or relating to it, calculated to excite suspicions." The latter phrase is in itself ambiguous: it does not state that nothing in the journal excites suspicions; it states rather that nothing "appears . . . *calculated* to excite suspicions"—which raises the question of intentionality in a patently counterintuitive way. Any false account is presumably constructed, for whatever external motivation, precisely to exact belief or faith in its internal veracity; a false account is not, by definition, "calculated to excite suspicions with regard to its authenticity."

This logical impasse, I believe, finally gives Greenhow away. For the "Journal of Julius Rodman" was indeed "calculated to excite suspicions"—and not merely in the overblown racialist sensationalism attending its story of "the first white Man that ever crossed the Western Wilderness," or in the parodic extremes to which it brings the ideology of the sublime.[25] It was also "calculated to excite suspicions" through its blatant textual lifting from authentic accounts of expeditions—including that of Alexander Mackenzie—all of which Greenhow himself had read and even cited in his own *Memoir*, from Nicholas Biddle's *The History of the Expedition under the Command of Lewis and Clark* (1814) to Washington Irving's *Astoria* (1836), an obsequious biographical account of John Jacob Astor's Pacific Fur Company and his establishment of the first American-dominated settlement in the disputed Oregon Territory. In other words, Greenhow *had to have known* that the Rodman account belonged to "the class of fictions," and yet he entered it into his *Memoir* as a text that might well hold up in a test of "its authenticity." And though Greenhow acknowledges that the published part of the account "relates only to the voyage up the Mississippi"—that of the journey beyond this now domestic geography, "no idea is communicated"—he also directs readers' attention to the "editor" of the journal and to its official "Introduction": "where it is stated that they traversed the region 'west of the Rocky Mountains, and north of the 60th parallel, which is still marked upon our maps as unexplored, and which, until this day, has been always so considered.'" Greenhow in effect constructs a definitive reading of the text, mediated through his own scholarly authority in citing from this authoritative reader—one who ostensibly knows the end of the story and can predict the successful outcome of the exploration "north of the 60th parallel," into virgin land.[26]

The historiographical motive for Greenhow's maneuver seems initially odd given that Poe's obvious fiction actually undermines the case for U.S. priority in exploring the West by insisting, almost comically, in the "Introduction," that the "credit" for "the *first* passage across the Rocky Mountains . . . should never have been given" to the far more officially national endeavor of "Lewis and Clark." But the need for Poe's text becomes quite clear by the end of Greenhow's memoir, in his summation of the British case for sovereignty in the Northwest: "The exploration . . . of Lewis and Clark," argue the British, "could not be cited by the United States as strengthening and confirming their claim to that territory, because, '*if not before, at least in the same and subsequent years,* the British Northwest Company had, by means of their agent Mr. Thompson, already established their posts on the head-waters or main branch of the Columbia.'" The Lewis and Clark expedition, in other words, was undermined by the British as too belated to count in favor of a U.S. claim on the Northwest; Greenhow thus stood in danger of losing the primary building block of his argument. The fictional Rodman journey, on the other hand, predated not only Lewis and Clark and "Mr. [David] Thompson," the British explorer, but also the even earlier Mackenzie: as Poe's

"Introduction" states, "Mackenzie succeeded in [crossing the Rockies] in the year 1793," but "Mr. Rodman was the first who overcame those gigantic barriers; crossing them as he did in 1792."[27] Citing from Poe, in other words, Greenhow inserted crucial evidence of U.S. priority in the "Oregon Country" into the official Senate record and, by extension, the official historical record.

No one knows what Poe intended to do with his unfinished "Journal of Julius Rodman" before he abandoned and stopped acknowledging it. But Greenhow's motivations are, to my mind, transparent: he was testing the historiographical waters to see if Poe's narrative—a narrative he must have known was fabricated and, in places, plagiarized—could survive in U.S. history as fact. It must be emphasized that Greenhow swam against the romantic current of his moment in doing so: he was most decidedly not arguing, as would many of his peers, for the higher "Historical Truth" made available by literature. Quite the opposite: Greenhow was taking advantage of a longstanding and still enduring disciplinary antagonism between history and literature—and doing so under cover of the specifically Romantic-inflected and derided figure of the "modern skeptic"—to alter the historical record in a profoundly duplicitous way. He was also protecting his reputation as a distinguished scholar, practitioner of a learned multilingual and transnational form of American studies, by purporting to reserve final judgment on the Poe text's authenticity even as he also encouraged this judgment: indeed, in Greenhow's index, Poe's narrative gets its own, unqualified entry: "Rodman's journey across the continent from the Missouri to the Pacific."[28]

But what was Poe's role in this strange episode? The timing of his publication of the first installment of "Rodman" strongly suggests that Poe—in the midst of financial crisis, on the brink of being fired yet again—made a deal of some kind to write "Rodman" to meet the very demand for which Greenhow used it. After all, Poe could not have failed to notice the example of the leading American man of letters, Irving, who had just a few years earlier reached a quite lucrative agreement with John Jacob Astor to write *Astoria* (from which Rodman's journal would in fact borrow heavily); though Irving's text was neither nonfictional nor published under a manufactured authorial hand, it certainly modeled the crude financial possibilities that could be exploited in the emergent writing of U.S. imperialism, precisely by bringing literary capital and a set of political agendas into a self-conscious but not openly avowed relationship. Indeed, it seems more than coincidental that in the very month before Greenhow submitted his memoir before the Senate's Select Committee on the Oregon Territory, Poe happened to publish a pseudo–travel account of a westerly expedition that ostensibly preceded the British Mackenzie expedition, as the overblown subtitle to the "Journal of Julius Rodman" announces: "Being an account of the *First* Passage Across the Rocky Mountains." The fictional "editors" of Rodman's "Journal" are indeed suspiciously to the point, as we have seen, when they insist that the "credit" for "the *first* passage across the Rocky Mountains . . . should never have been given to Lewis and Clark." Poe appears almost to wink at the fact that he is publishing the Rodman "Journal" just in the nick of time to make it into Greenhow's memoir of the U.S. Senate—much in the same manner as our fictional Rodman makes it across the Rockies just in the nick of time to beat the British Mackenzie to it.

It is certainly possible, of course, that Poe was writing his serialized account partly in hopes of winning the magazine's literary contest (which as assistant editor he was ineligible to enter under his own name). But he was also likely writing this particular northwestern account on a commission from Greenhow or someone else involved in the territorial Oregon dispute. Otherwise, it becomes hard to explain why, if Greenhow didn't believe that he had a deal of some kind with the author of "Rodman," he would take a chance on using something that he had to have known was, if not falsification then fiction, given that its true author might reveal himself at any time. Believing that the author had a vested economic interest in remaining quiet is the only circumstance, to my mind, that adequately explains Greenhow's decision to try to pass off as factual an account so obviously "calculated to excite suspicions." For in producing a text precisely so calculated, I think that Poe in effect reneged on whatever deal he made—that he doublecrossed Greenhow and by extension the State Department by producing an account that not only flaunted its own fictionality and lack of authenticity on every page but also satirized the very context of imperial dispute in which it had been commissioned to intervene.

Indeed, examined in the context of Greenhow's larger body of work, "The Journal of Julius Rodman" reveals an interplay between Rodman's (often plagiarized) voice and the editorial voice that undercuts at every turn the manuscript narrative it purports to present with such gravity and momentousness. The editor continually delights in highlighting the coerciveness of his own particular narrative contract—"We feel assured that all our readers will unite with us," that "our readers will think with us"—while also constantly signposting his own "omissions" and "abridgement" and the "very few liberties" that he has taken with the original manuscript. The discovery of the journal similarly calls into doubt the authenticity of the manuscript itself: Rodman supposedly wrote his journal many years after the fact from an outline diary at the request of Andre Michau, the same French botanist whom Jefferson tried to commission to make a westward exploration. But as the editor notes, the manuscript never reached its intended reader, and while it was "always supposed to have been lost on the road by the young man to whom it was entrusted for delivery," Rodman's journal has not been lost but rather "procured from the messenger [and] concealed," and seemingly by Rodman himself, for it is "discovered years later by his family, after his death, in a secret drawer." So the culpability lies not with the messenger but with the author himself, who has purloined his own missive: as so often with Poe, an allegory of writing, of textual indeterminacy, frames Rodman's journal from the beginning.

More broadly, then, the editorial voice framing Rodman's account reads like a personal taunting of Greenhow at every turn, undercutting the authenticity and therefore the potential usefulness of Rodman's alleged claim to have crossed the Rockies before any civilized man. The editorial narrator also advertises the "romantic fervor" of Rodman's account, which he opposes to the "lukewarm and statistical air which pervades most records of the kind"—an unflattering description that perfectly encapsulates not only his own scholarly voice but Greenhow's. The editor goes out of his way to expose the disingenuousness of the objective neutrality that such tepid, numerically laden prose is meant to convey. The editor claims, for example, that the chief attribute of the journal is its romantic virtue: Rodman's "burning love of Nature"; the "rapture at his heart" as he "stalked through that immense and often terrible wilderness." But these romantic platitudes are revealed as a transparent pretext in the next lines: in an abrupt shift, the editor demands—suddenly all business—that the reader "will turn to a map of North America . . . to follow us in our observations." What follows is a fastidiously dry listing of latitudes, longitudes, parallels, meridians, dates, and explorers' names as the editor plods doggedly through the competitive history of European and Anglo-American expeditions in the Northwest—a historical survey tinged with a faint ridiculousness by the editor's new phrasing for his category: the "earliest travels of any extent made in North America by white people." The shift from the subtitular phrase "civilized man" to "white people" is a subtle one, marking a sort of logical stutter along the trajectory from early modern conquest to nineteenth-century expansionism, and shadowing the whole editorial frame with the oxymoron of imperial "discovery," with the obvious but occluded priority of native peoples.[29]

More importantly, however, Poe's fictionalized editor goes out of his way to put holes in the case for American over European priority in the Northwest by undermining the other American contenders for that title as well as the writings that documented their efforts: Thomas Jefferson is described as "erroneous" in calling John Ledyard the first to attempt northwestern exploration, while Washington Irving "appears to be mistaken" in naming Jonathan Carver's trip as the first overland attempt. Both are supplanted in the editor's account by non-American explorers, particularly those British figures that prove pesky stumbling blocks in Greenhow's legal argument for U.S. priority. And Greenhow must have been furious to discover Poe's hilarious description of Rodman's explorer party, which we only see when the editor finally gets around to presenting the Rodman account itself. For while Greenhow's memoir to the Senate committee promises an account about "an expedition . . . by a party of citizens of the United States, under the direction of Julius Rodman," Poe's Rodman turns out to be an Englishman by birth, and his motley group includes fourteen explorers, six of whom the account defines as "Canadians," five as hailing from the "State" of Kentucky, two as "Virginians," and one as "a negro belonging to" one of the Canadians.[30] Greenhow is thus left in the precarious and indeed foolish position of having to rewrite the group under the patently false sign of U.S. nationalism.

Poe never admitted in print to authoring Rodman, except circuitously in one famous letter that he wrote to Burton, the main editor of *Burton's Gentleman's Magazine*, after Burton had written to Poe apparently complaining that Poe owed him a hundred dollars and that Poe had been sending out a prospectus for a new, competing Philadelphia journal. But Burton also apparently accuses Poe in the letter of something that Poe alludes to but doesn't name specifically. "You do me gross injustice," Poe tells Burton:

> you have wrought yourself into a passion with me on account of some imaginary wrong. . . . As I live, I am utterly unable to say . . . what true grounds of complaint you have against me. . . . I cannot permit myself to suppose that you would say to me in cool blood what you said in your letter of yesterday.

At the end of the letter, though, Poe refers, as so often, to his financial crisis and adds,

> I can give you no definitive answer (respecting the continuation [of] Rodman's Journal,) until I hear from you again. The charge of $100 I shall not admit for an instant. If you persist in it our intercourse is at an end, and I shall refer you to an attorney. But I cannot bring myself to believe that you will. We can each adopt our own measures.

This warning rings distinctly of blackmail. The following year finds Poe working for new editors and writing frantic letters to the Washington writer and government bureaucrat Frederick William Thomas, asking him to entreat various congressmen for a job. Desperate to find a way to insinuate himself into a political appointment, Poe writes, "I mention in particular the Secretary of War, because I have been to W. Point, and this may stand me in some stead. I would be glad to get almost any appointment . . . so that I have *something* independent of letters for a subsistence." Perhaps what we see in Rodman, then, is Poe's attempt at a different kind of government assignment, not from the secretary of war, but from the third-highest-ranking employee of the State Department, Robert Greenhow. Poe was fast approaching what Gerald Kennedy has called the "American turn" in his fictions by the time he wrote "Rodman."[31] Perhaps in this early failed attempt to use letters precisely to "have *something* independent of letters," that inestimable combination of literariness and rage that characterizes so much of his work took him over—and with such force that he double-crossed the Department of State and, like Rodman, effectively purloined his own promised account from its intended receiver.

FROM POLITICS TO ANTIQUARIANISM: THE FIRST DISCOVERY OF THE CHESAPEAKE BAY (BY THE SPANISH)

In the spring of 1848, eight years after Greenhow published his memoir on the "Oregon Country"—and after the "Oregon Question" had been settled with Britain, and the counterpart question of Texas and the Southwest had exploded into the United States' war with Mexico—Greenhow was finishing up another scholarly project, seemingly unrelated to the urgent political matters of the day. If Greenhow had written the 1840 memoir specifically for the U.S. Senate and the Twenty-sixth Congressional record, he produced this later piece of work for an entirely different venue: the Virginia Historical and Philosophical Society, an antiquarian organization founded in 1831. Modeled on the New-York Historical Society and the American Antiquarian Society of Massachusetts, the Virginia Historical and Philosophical Society drew on private funds to carry out its designated mission to preserve books, manuscripts, historic documents, and natural history specimens relating to the state and its history. The antiquarian mission of this society was, as Jonathan P. Cushing put it in his 1833 address, "to procure and preserve whatever relates to the natural, civil, and literary history of this state." Its stated goal of filling the "library [with] all the rare and valuable materials, for a full and correct exposition of the physical resources, and the intellectual power and moral worth of the sons of Virginia" and the "cabinet and museum [with] all those specimens in geology, mineralogy, zoology, and botany, which are necessary to illustrate our natural history," and "to brighten the glory of the commonwealth," seems at first far removed from the legalistic world of international affairs overseen by the Department of State where Greenhow was still employed, and for which he had produced his work on the "Oregon Country." Curiously, however, Greenhow's generic designation for the piece he submitted to the society was the same: he titled it "Memoir on the First Discovery of the Chesapeake Bay" and sent it off that May to Richmond.[32]

The information outlined in the memoir had been, he said, "obtained in the course of researches among the Old Spanish Chroniclers of the New World"—"works [that] have been most lamentably neglected by our historians; few of whom have, indeed, possessed a knowledge of the language in which they are written, sufficient for such investigations." To Greenhow, this was no mere matter of asserting his historiographical and linguistic prowess, however: the Spanish chronicles contain "innumerable . . . facts," "unnoticed, though recorded in full in those venerable volumes"—facts "relating to the countries now included, as well as to those about to be included, within the limits of our republic." Clearly referring in the latter clause to the imminent U.S. territories ceded by Mexico in the Treaty of Guadalupe Hidalgo, signed three months earlier and then ratified by the U.S. Senate in March, Greenhow evokes the larger political context for the strange disclosures presented in his accompanying memoir on the Spanish "discovery" of the Chesapeake Bay. Greenhow avowedly undertook the memoir "with the hope that the Society may succeed . . . in rescuing from destruction the historical monuments and records of our Ancient Dominion, and in bringing to light those which lie in obscurity." Presenting himself as a scrupulous modern historian, sifting through the "dull and lumbering archive" and determined to excavate lost records of the Virginian past, Greenhow begins with a dramatic flourish by dismantling a foundational received truth of Old Dominion history: "The Bay of Chesapeake is usually supposed to have been first seen, and entered by the English . . . who founded the earliest European settlement on its waters in 1607. . . . Accordingly in all our histories, the discovery of the Chesapeake is attributed to the English." But "there is evidence . . . apparently incontrovertible," Greenhow admonishes, "that the Chesapeake was known to the Spaniards, and that an expedition had been made by them for the occupation of its coasts, at least twenty years before any attempt of the English to establish themselves in any part of the American continent."³³

Greenhow cites his eighteenth-century source for this evidence only by its Spanish title, "Ensayo Chronológico para la Historia de la Florida," and notes that the "name . . . given on the title page of the work," "Gabriel de Cardenas Z. Cano," "is fictitious, being an anagram of that of its real author, Andrés González de Barcia." As if word games in Spanish were not intimidating enough to scare off the average U.S. reader of history, Greenhow goes out of his way to discourage future research into González de Barcia's history given its "extreme minuteness on all points, with little regard to their importance" which "render . . . the book intolerable to the general reader." Accordingly, Greenhow offers his own translative services for nineteenth-century U.S. historians in order to narrate the sixteenth-century story of the Spanish in the Chesapeake Bay. As Greenhow tells it, the story begins in good Black Legend style with "the ruthless Adelantado of Florida, Pedro Menendez," who—competing with England—"ordered surveys to be made of the countries farther north" because he "foresaw the absolute necessity of extending the dominion of Spain." Turning here to his source in González de Barcia, Greenhow presents the project of settling the future Virginia: "in the summer of 1566, '[Menendez] dispatched . . . a captain with thirty soldiers and two monks . . . to the Bay of Santa Maria . . . to settle in that region, and to convert its inhabitants to Christianity. [But] The captain . . . was overcome by his crew. . . . So they sailed . . . for Seville, abusing the King and the Adelantado for attempting to settle in that country, of which they spread the worst accounts, though none of them had seen it.'" "Thus it appears," Greenhow concludes from his source, "that the Chesapeake . . . was so well known to the Spaniards in 1566, that an expedition was made for . . . taking possession of the surrounding country. We do not learn that the attempt was repeated."³⁴

For Greenhow, of course, the crucial issue in citing from González de Barcia is settlement: Menendez's dispatch of the monks and soldiers "to settle in that region" and their subsequent "abusing [of] the King and the Adelantado for attempting to settle in that country." Not only do the soldiers' negative accounts of the country constitute legal falsehoods, according to González de Barcia's account, but the very assertion of their fraudulence, based on the premise that "none of them had seen it," undermined any territorial rights potentially deriving from the doctrine of first discovery. As Greenhow explains, in a curious phrasing that evokes his hyper-qualified commentary on the Rodman account: "We do not learn that the attempt was repeated."

Indeed, Greenhow concludes his memoir on an oddly deflating note: "To the utilitarian the question will appear of no importance," he concedes, "nor can any direct advantage be derived from speculations as to the change which might have been made . . . had the Spanish expedition . . . proved successful." Yet in the next sentence, Greenhow employs this very counterfactual to telegraph a dramatic "virtual history" in which the English would not have settled in Virginia because "James the Second of England, would not have readily granted a commission to his subjects to encroach upon territories held" by the Spanish. These are the contingencies of history, Greenhow seems to suggest; in fact, it is precisely the different possible outcome of this colonial moment that underscores the meaning of Greenhow's Anglo-Saxonist present. The "importance" of Greenhow's memoir, then, lies not, contrary to its title, in its establishment of the "First Discovery of the Chesapeake Bay [by the Spanish]"—but in its fully documented, official scholarly pronouncement of a lack of Spanish settlement on the Chesapeake in 1566, or at any subsequent date. As Greenhow puts it, "This is all that Barcia says of the bay of Santa Maria; and nothing has been found with regard to it elsewhere. . . . No allusion to such a bay is made in any account of any voyage . . . by any other Spanish historian except Barcia." In this sense, in his studies of Spanish colonial history, González de Barcia has offered what Greenhow terms a "good service in the cause of American history."[35]

But if any nineteenth-century readers had actually opened the eighteenth-century Spanish history that Greenhow warned was not just hard-going but "intolerable," they would have seen immediately that Greenhow's own translative contribution to "the cause of American history" hinged on a blatant lie. For González de Barcia noted very clearly what today's historians of colonial Virginia know, but Greenhow's nineteenth-century Anglophone readers could not: that the 1566 Spanish attempt to settle in the future Virginia was in fact "repeated," specifically in the year 1570—well before the ill-fated Roanoke voyages, and decades before Jamestown—and this time it resulted in successful arrival on Virginian soil. In the "Year 1570," González de Barcia wrote, a group of Spanish Jesuits, under the direction of "Father Vice Provincial Juan Baptista de Segura . . . tried a method of entering in the Province of Axacan. . . . They walked together until they entered the Province of Axacan, bearing the hardships of the journey, and the hunger . . . in the hope of converting many people to the office of the Church." González de

Barcia's history records not only the arduous journey by land, moreover, but the later interactions with the indigenous, the high hopes of the missionaries, their faith in their native translator, and ultimately, their demise and the end of the settlement. That there was a settlement made by the Spanish in 1570 is never in question. Thus, when Greenhow insisted in his memoir that the failed 1566 voyage to Virginia is "all that Barcia says of the bay of Santa Maria; and nothing has been found with regard to it elsewhere," he was actively committing what we might call a scholarly act of suppression, one entered into the official U.S. historical record over a century after the publication of González de Barcia's history.

In writing about the so-called "First Discovery" of the Chesapeake, then, Greenhow was indeed contributing his "services to the cause of American History." On the one hand, of course, he produced an account of Spanish failure that would bolster a predictably triumphant version of Anglo-American historical success. But even as he outlined the sensational hypothetical possibility of a Spanish Virginia, Greenhow was in a sense also closing up legal loopholes—willfully erasing the historical evidence of a Spanish settlement, however temporary, that preceded the English in Virginia. The Spanish may have had "First Discovery" of the Chesapeake, but Greenhow's memoir was determined to show that the Spanish could not ever claim "First Discovery" of Virginia itself. For as Greenhow knew well from his first-hand experience in supporting the U.S. case during the dispute with Great Britain over the "Oregon Country," the Doctrine of Discovery that had governed the period of European contest for land and resources in the New World held continuing vital importance in the first half of the nineteenth century. During these crucial decades, moreover, the doctrine was both held up to juridical scrutiny and written into federal laws that still apply today.[36]

In the 1823 Supreme Court case *Johnson v. M'Intosh,* Chief Justice John Marshall called the doctrine the "original fundamental principle" governing land rights in the United States and in the territories it hoped to acquire: "that discovery gave title to the government by whose subjects, or by whose authority, it was made, against all other European governments, which title might be consummated by possession"—"that discovery gave exclusive title to those who made it." The Doctrine of Discovery was thus a principle of international law that had governed European powers during the colonial period but that, as the Marshall court laid it out, extended naturally to the new nation:

> The United States, then, have unequivocally acceded to that great and broad rule
> [of discovery] by which its civilized inhabitants now hold this country. They hold,

and assert in themselves, the title by which it was acquired. They maintain, as all others have maintained, that discovery gave an exclusive right to extinguish the Indian title of occupancy, either by purchase or by conquest.

As these last two clauses indicate, the doctrine that allowed the nineteenth-century United States to compete with European powers over disputed territories such as the "Oregon Country" also became the foundational logic of federal Indian policy denying native sovereignty over tribal lands. But if the Doctrine of Discovery was crucial to national expansion on every front, its logic was also particularly fragile during this period. Even those who invoked it to create national policy understood how much it depended on the misrecognition of monarchical rights that had been ostensibly terminated after the American Revolution. As the Marshall court conceded a decade later in *Worcester v. Georgia* (1832), the early modern doctrine appeared, from a nineteenth-century vantage point, "extravagant and absurd": it was "difficult to comprehend" how "feeble settlements made on the sea coast . . . acquired legitimate power by [England] to govern people, or occupy lands from sea to sea"—how discovery "gave the discoverer rights . . . which annulled the pre-existing rights of the ancient possessors."[37] The Marshall court wanted it both ways, in other words: to distance the United States from the "extravagant" doctrine of an early modern, imperial England that was now a competitor for land, and yet also to claim via that same doctrine an aggressive legal foundation for national U.S. expansion that was specifically based in English rights of "First Discovery" that were inherited by, or defaulted to, the people of the former British colonies.

The Doctrine of Discovery was thus indispensable to almost every aspect of U.S. national expansion in the first half of the nineteenth century. No one was in a better position than Greenhow to understand that the spring of 1848, when the discourse of Manifest Destiny rose to a peak following the Mexican War and the incorporation of former Mexican lands into the United States, was not an ideal time to go muddying the ideological and jurisdictional waters of "First Discovery" by announcing the historical irony of Spanish priority in the future state of Virginia, Mother of Presidents, the very birthplace of the nation. This is not necessarily to suggest that Greenhow understood the story of the Spanish settlement as a source of *practical* danger, threatening a potential nineteenth-century Spanish *reconquista* of U.S. land. But the story that Greenhow discovered in González de Barcia *did* endanger U.S. interests in an indirect but powerful way. That Greenhow chose to suppress what he knew to be the truth in his own historiographical endeavors—in the hemispheric scholarship that he produced through the work of translation, through his multilingual proficiencies—is perhaps not surprising, given the exigencies of his work for the State Department. He would perhaps justify his scholarly deceit in the same way he judged the Spanish writer Maldonado and his distortions of the past: "The falsehoods of Maldonado have injured no one, and they were ultimately productive of great good."[38]

TRANSNATIONAL AMERICAN STUDIES AND THE STATE: THE POLITICS OF DUPLICITY

The so-called transnational turn in American studies has generated a great deal of its critical traction out of historicizing itself, undertaking the project of naming the present disciplinary moment through a series of often ominous questions. Might the transnational turn in American studies be simply the most recent incarnation of Western academic imperialism? Is the hidden hand of NAFTA behind all our scholarly efforts, nudging us toward every new formulation? Do we risk reinscribing an aggressive U.S. ideology of expansionism and military interventionism when we seek to expand the purview of American studies from the national to the hemispheric? The case of Greenhow does not answer these questions directly, of course. But it may present a way to reframe them productively. For in its chilling picture of scholarly imperialism, the nineteenth-century example of Greenhow's work presents a kind of critical agency that is potentially salutary in reminding us that scholars can make, and have always made, *conscious* intellectual and political choices alongside the unconscious ones that we are more inclined to worry about these days. This in itself is reason to engage in the act of scholarship rather than simply reflect upon it: though the two endeavors are of course intertwined and at times indistinguishable, the latter often defines the current state of the field—of hemispheric American studies, in particular—more than the former.

Greenhow was clearly disingenuous about the political stakes—the specific influence upon foreign policy—of his scholarship, a rhetorical position that helped shore up his authority as an objective expert, which he then used precisely to political ends. There is sometimes, I think, a similar disingenuousness in the discourse of transnational American studies about the political stakes of contemporary scholarship, though it works in the opposite direction: by insisting upon or simply implying the (often dangerous) political stakes of a scholarship that is always already at risk of becoming coextensive with imperialism. This is not to deny the importance of self-critique in the scholarly realm. What I am suggesting is that the widespread imputing of questionable political motives and effects to contemporary scholarship places a potentially distorting exigency on the act of scholarly production itself: puts a certain pressure on us, that is, to know the end of the stories we tell in advance of finding them through our research, and to rig the game intellectually every bit as much as Greenhow does in the nineteenth century.

The example of Greenhow's scholarship also suggests something about the pitfalls—perhaps especially for literary scholars—of insisting too perfunctorily on the mutually constitutive languages of literature and history, though these have long been the grounds of rich, interdisciplinary work. Today we're accustomed to, even desensitized by, the tropes of history writing, by the idea of finding fiction in the archives. But the outlandish example of Greenhow—a scholar *putting* fiction in the archives, and then re-labeling it as history—provides a reminder to hold all our postmodern skepticism about the stability of historical inquiry in tension with an alternative understanding of the relation between literature and history: an understanding that insists on the differences between the two, even in acknowledging their secret sharing. This is not a roundabout way of suggesting that Greenhow was engaging in a nefarious, postmodern vision of history *avant la lettre*. But he *was* relying on, counting on the very slippery overlap of literature and history that we now routinely assume as if it provided in and of itself a liberatory critical position. He was, moreover, relying on this overlap at a particular historical moment—in the 1840s, when arguments about the divergent historical development of the hemisphere were emerging in full force as a narrative about an anti-democratic, racially amalgamated, and economically deteriorating Spanish America practically begging for U.S. intervention. Perhaps most importantly, Greenhow was insisting—against the prevailing historical romanticism of his day—upon the difference between the history and fiction precisely in order to *dissimulate* the difference between them. Objectivity was his retreat, the alibi for his willful distortion of the relation between history and literature, critically deployed precisely in order to shape the *future* of uneven development in the hemisphere: the U.S. acquisition of the states that made up the "Oregon Country" in 1846 as well as two-thirds of Mexico in 1848.

But the most troubling aspect of Greenhow's work—particularly if we define it, as I have here, as a form of transnational American studies—is its duplicity. Because Greenhow worked for the State Department rather than a university, the problem of his duplicity presents itself in two overlapping contexts: the realms of scholarship and politics. Lying in politics is not new, certainly not surprising, and not even—if we agree with Martin Jay's recent work on the "virtues of mendacity" in political speech—necessarily a problem. Jay's controversial formulation of lying as "democratic fabulation," as a democratic political virtue rather than a vice, depends in part upon a refusal to subordinate international to domestic relations in elaborating a concept of the political. While a domestic "classical liberal version of the political will tends to privilege the trust involved in contractual agreements, which is based on truth-telling," the context of "international relations, the realm of diplomatic compromise and maneuvering," with its "imperatives of raison d'état," has never centered on transparency and truthfulness as absolute virtues. Understood in this way, the point of political speech is to shape the outcome of a particular situation, not to communicate the unvarnished truth to an interlocutor—though mendacity, as Jay points out, also depends by definition on a baseline presumption of truthfulness on the interlocutor's part: "A lie works, after all, only against the horizon of normative veridical practices that make it plausible." Or, to borrow again from Greenhow's language, a false account is not, by definition, "*calculated* to excite suspicions with regard to its authenticity."[39]

The realm of scholarship, on the other hand, is quite different. Located within what Jay somewhat hedgingly calls the "more veridically inclined institution" of the academy, scholarship has always defined truthfulness as a virtue, and it proceeds on the assumption of truthfulness—even when, and perhaps especially when, acknowledging that it is also not what Jay calls "the arena for the triumph of rational argumentation" that it has sometimes been imagined to be. Literary scholarship, in particular, understands itself as inextricably tied to aesthetics in a way that complicates and makes ambiguous the very conceptual interdependence of truth and falsehood, upon which lying depends. Lying is not plausible or even useful when one is most interested in the gaps and nuanced tensions between representation and reality. At the same time, there is no international context for scholarly conversation in which an unexpected duplicitous move is understood as par for the course, part of the tradition of a never-ending process of maneuvering diplomatic alliances and enmities. Lying in politics is different from lying in scholarship on any number of counts.

The case of Greenhow's duplicitous scholarship—produced by a paid political official but presented to the reading public as the work of a "modern historian [and] professed skeptic," an empiricist whose objectivity set him apart from his "literary" historian peers—thus raises a fundamental question about scholarship's relative proximity to and distance from the state. As Jay notes, "However useful it may be to isolate the special circumstances of 'the political,' it is also important to acknowledge that no impermeable firewall can be built between it and other spheres of human endeavor." For the purposes of our contemporary scholarly moment, then, the point that Greenhow's story reinforces is that we need to understand and self-consciously envision the separation of scholarship and the state *not* because scholarship is so weak, so unconscious, and so porous to "the political," as to be always in danger of co-option by its motives and agendas, but because the truth-telling imperatives of politics and scholarship are simply different. And Poe's "Journal of Julius Rodman," with its ineffably literary double-cross of both scholarship *and* the state, reminds us that they need to be different.

At the same time, of course, Poe's work also reminds us that the gap between *literature* and the state remains substantial and significant even when it appears to be deliberately closed, whether by the avowed political sympathies of the author, or by—as likely in the case of "Rodman"—explicit contract for authorial remuneration. Indeed, Poe's life-long attempts to curry favor and financial reward via partisan affiliations and statements of political position could not, in the end, contain the critical force of his literary work as he faced the contradictions and self-serving pieties of nineteenth-century U.S. nationalism. In this sense, too, Poe provides a salutary insight into the current state of our field—which, in its headlong rush to become "transnational," can seem almost to have forgotten the enduring history of U.S. literary nationalism that gave rise to the conceptual necessity of this critical moment in the first place. Over the course of his short career, Poe's imaginative rage directed itself again and again at the progressive version of history that underwrote U.S. expansionism, from the rise of Jacksonian politics and culture through the Polk presidency and the end of the U.S.-Mexican War. Perhaps, then, Poe's quarrel with nationalism may point the way toward a more dialectical mode of transnational American studies, one which does not reflexively toss out the national baby with the bath water.

Notes

1. This essay is adapted from its original appearance as "Scholarship and the State: Robert Greenhow and Transnational American Studies 1848/2008," *American Literary History* 20, no. 4 (Winter 2008): 695–722, and is reprinted by permission of Oxford University Press. Information about Greenhow appears in Ann Blackman, *Wild Rose: The True Story of a Civil War Spy* (New York: Random House, 2006), 141–44. On Greenhow's life and personality more generally, see Blackman, 94–100, and Nash K. Burger, *Confederate Spy: Rose O'Neale Greenhow* (New York: F. Watts, 1967), 14–18.

2. See Friedrich Nietzsche, *On the Use and Abuse of History for Life* (Sioux Falls, SD: Nuvision Publications, 2007), especially section III (25–29) and 75–76.

3. Blackman, 94, 104–7, 6, 305.

4. The description of this historical era is cited from "A Brief History of the American Antiquarian Society," www.americanantiquarian.org/briefhistory.htm. On the advent of history as a profession, see Peter Novick, *That Noble Dream: The "Objectivity Question" and the American Historical Profession* (New York: Cambridge Univ. Press, 1988), especially chapters 1 and 2, "The European Legacy" and "The Professionalization Project" (21–60). On nineteenth-century history and the New World, see John Burrow's *A History of Histories: Epics, Chronicles, Romances, and Inquiries from Herodotus and Thucydides to the Twentieth Century* (New York: Vintage, 2009), chapter 24, pp. 423–52; on U.S. history during the first half of the nineteenth century, especially Romantic history and antiquarianism, see George H. Callcott, *History in the United States, 1800–1860: Its Practice and Purpose* (Baltimore: Johns Hopkins Univ. Press, 1970).

5. Blackman, 98–99; Novick, 45.

6. William Gilmore Simms, *Views and Reviews in American Literature: History and Fiction* (New York: Putnam, 1845), 23–25; William H. Prescott, *History of the Conquest of Mexico*, 3 vols. (London: Bentley, 1843), vol. 3: 294.

7. This characterization of the antiquary comes from Theodore Parker's 1849 review essay, "The Character of Mr. Prescott as an Historian," cited in John Ernest, "Reading the Romantic Past: William H. Prescott's History of the Conquest of Mexico," *American Literary History* 5, no. 2 (1993): 231–49. See Ernest more generally for a brilliant reading of what he calls Prescott's "self-reflexive understanding" and his "demonstration of truth as a perspectival methodology and corresponding mode of representation" in *Conquest of Mexico* (233).

8. Blackman, 99.

9. On the idea of a "transnational turn," see Shelley Fisher Fishkin, "Crossroads of Cultures: The Transnational Turn in American Studies—Presidential Address to the American Studies Association, November 12, 2004," *American Quarterly* 57, no. 1 (March 2005): 17–57.

10. For an account of the fire and Greenhow's near-death, see Blackman, 95–96.

11. Slauter's essay, "History, Literature, and the Atlantic World," *William and Mary Quarterly* 65, no. 1 (2008): 1–36, focuses on the market relationship of scholarship in particular, identifying a "trade deficit" on the literary history side of things. See also Jill Lepore, "Just the Facts, Ma'am: Fake Memoirs, Factual Fictions, and the History of History," *New Yorker*, March 24, 2008, on the long-standing battle between history and literature.

12. Edgar Allan Poe, "Edward Lytton Bulwer," *Essays and Reviews*, ed. G. R. Thompson (New York: Library of America, 1984), 145.

13. U.S. Senate Document of the Twenty-sixth Congress, 1st sess., vol. 4 (1839–40), 140–41. See David K. Jackson, "A Poe Hoax Comes before the U.S. Senate," *Poe Studies* 7, no.2 (1974): 47–48.

14. Throughout the next section, I'll be citing from Robert Greenhow, *The History of Oregon and California and Other Territories of the North-West Coast of North America* (Boston: Little and Brown, 1845), unless otherwise specified. There are some interesting differences between the wording of Greenhow's *Memoir, Historical and Political, on the Northwest Coast of North America* (Washington, DC: Blair and Rives, 1840) and that of the *History*, including greater emphasis on the fictionality of those accounts Greenhow dismisses.

15. Greenhow, *Memoir*, 200.

16. Greenhow, *History*, 78–79, 86.

17. Ibid., 79, 83–84; "New Documents Concerning Columbus," *North American Review* 24, no. 55 (1827): 265.

18. Greenhow, *History*, 86–88.

19. "The Oregon Question," *London Quarterly Review* 153 (Dec. 1845): 310; Greenhow, *History*, 81, 86.

20. Juvenal, *The Sixteen Satires*, 3rd ed., trans. Peter Green (New York: Penguin, 1998), 80–81, my emphasis.

21. Greenhow, *Memoir*, 140. Note that Greenhow eliminated the Rodman account from his 1845 *History*; sometime between the publication of the *Memoir* in 1840 and the "revised, corrected, and enlarged" *History* in 1845, Greenhow evidently decided that the Poe text would not stand up as historical evidence.

22. Edgar Allan Poe, "The Journal of Julius Rodman," *Burton's Gentleman's Magazine* 6 (Jan.–June 1840): 44; Greenhow, *Memoir*, 140n; Poe, *The Narrative of Arthur Gordon Pym of Nantucket*, in *Poetry and Tales*, ed. Patrick F. Quinn (New York: Library of America, 1984), 1008. The "impudent attempt at humbugging the public" comment appears in "Review of New Books," *Burton's Gentleman's Magazine* 3 (July–Dec. 1838): 211.

23. Poe, "The Journal of Julius Rodman," 44.

24. Jackson, "Poe Hoax," 47.

25. Greenhow, *Memoir*, 141. As advertised on the rear cover of the February 1840 installment of "The Journal of Julius Rodman." On "Rodman" as a parody, see John J. Teunissen and Evelyn J. Hinz, "Poe's *Journal of Julius Rodman* as Parody," *Nineteenth-Century Literature* 27, no. 3 (Dec. 1972): 317–38; on "Rodman" and U.S. imperial ideology, see John Carlos Rowe, *Literary Culture and U.S. Imperialism: from the Revolution to World War II* (New York: Oxford Univ. Press, 2000), 55–70.

26. Greenhow, *Memoir*, 141.

27. Poe, "The Journal of Julius Rodman," 47; Greenhow, *Memoir*, 153.

28. Greenhow, *Memoir*, 227.

29. Poe, "The Journal of Julius Rodman," 44–47.

30. Greenhow, *Memoir*, 140; Poe, "The Journal of Julius Rodman," 80–81.

31. Regarding Poe's West Point background, one should bear in mind that he was actually court-martialed and thrown out within six months. For more on the "Rodman"-era changes occurring in Poe's fiction, see J. Gerald Kennedy, *The American Turn of Edgar Allan Poe* (Baltimore: Edgar Allan Poe Society of Baltimore, 2002), as well as Kennedy's "A Mania for Composition: Poe's Annus Mirabilis and the Violence of Nation-building," *American Literary History* 17, no. 1 (Spring 2005): 10.

32. Jonathan P. Cushing, "An Address, Spoken before the Society, 1843," *Collections of the Virginia Historical and Philosophical Society* (Richmond, VA: Thomas W. White, 1833), vol. 1: 13, 33. Greenhow's memoir is collected in Conway Robinson, *An Account of Discoveries in the West Until 1519* (Richmond, VA: Shepherd and Collin, 1848).

33. Robinson, *An Account of Discoveries*, 481–85.

34. Ibid., 486–88.

35. Ibid., 489–91, 486.

36. On the history of the Discovery Doctrine and its far-reaching implication for American Indian law, see Robert J. Miller, *Discovered and Conquered: Thomas Jefferson, Lewis & Clark, and Manifest Destiny* (Lincoln: Univ. of Nebraska Press, 2008).

37. *Johnson & Graham's Lessee v. M'Intosh*, 21 U.S. 543 (1823).

38. Greenhow, *History*, 84.

39. The phrase "democratic fabulation" is from Martin Jay's "Mendacious Flowers," *London Review of Books* 21, no. 15 (July 1999): 16–17; all other Jay citations are from the essay "The Virtues of Mendacity," available at www.polisci.upenn.edu/theoryworkshops/martinjay.pdf.

Poe's Lyrical Media

The Raven's Returns

ELIZA RICHARDS

"The Raven" is usually understood as an exercise in containment. Critics have determined that its repetitive structures hold evidence of psychological trauma: over the loss of beloved women, the death of writing, slavery ("le noir!"), or modernity's impingements, for example.[1] In these readings, the poem's highly elaborated, artificial mechanism evinces a protective response to shock rooted in compulsive repetition: the trauma is rehearsed but never escaped. Poe's echo chamber institutes a clear and impermeable boundary between the poem and the world; there is no mistaking the fact that we have entered a circumscribed linguistic environment, and sometimes it seems that there is no escape: like the speaker, the reader remains under the shadow of the raven. For Daniel Hoffman, the poem transfers the author's affliction to the reader; Poe alleviates his own affective overload "by making of [his] passions an intricate mechanism for the production of the effects of passion in another person's soul—transferring from the Self to the Other both the anguish of self-torture and the sybaritic luxury of a sorrow passive and never-ending." For Debra Fried, "The Raven" dramatizes an even more radical dead end. Building on the closed logic of the epitaph, Poe buries himself alive within his poem: "Becoming his own responding muse, Poe is repeatedly answered with the low and delicious word Death." In Barbara Johnson's reading, "The Raven" stages an encounter with poetic language as such. Because the repetition of clichés evacuates meaning, "The Raven" makes plain that readers cannot tolerate a vacuum: "repetition engenders its own compulsion-to-sense. Poetry works *because* the signifier cannot remain empty—because, not in spite, of the mechanical nature of its artifice." The reader is compelled to make sense precisely because it is not there, in the process understanding a basic fact about the function of poetic language.[2] Broadly differing, these critics agree that "The Raven" operates according to an inevitable logic in which the reader or the speaker or the author, or all three, is forced to confront an ultimate limit. Whether personal or impersonal, psychological or linguistic, the enclosed poetic world of "The Raven" sucks the reader into a tautological encounter with what it contains.

Something strange happens to this presumption of containment, however, when we broaden our interpretive context to include the many copycat poems inspired by "The Raven," for the poem has persistently encouraged not only its own recitative repetition, but also its rewriting, in the form of parodies, imitations, and versions of all kinds. The point these imitations make is not how self-enclosed "The Raven" is, but how permeable, how reproducible, how allusive; how much it is like other forms of linguistic expression; how it is composed of previously existing materials. They demonstrate that it can be expanded upon, rebuilt, rewritten, and that it can be adapted to new visual and acoustic media and different cultural, political, and social circumstances. Considering "The Raven" within the context of the responses it has inspired suggests that its self-enclosed logic, if it exists at all, makes it particularly suited to circulating through and extending open communication networks. Readers and rewriters have long recognized, in other words, that "The Raven" is a medium or a means of communication first, and a record of a particular expression only as a model or example for readers to emulate. In "The Raven," Poe wrote a poem that could circulate through a developing mass-media network, instructing readers about the communications terrain through which it travels. According to Walter Benjamin, the primary function of "art in the age of its technological reproducibility" is "to train human beings in the apperceptions and . . . vast apparatus whose role in their lives is expanding almost daily." Because of this primary function, "to an ever-increasing degree, the work reproduced becomes the reproduction of a work designed for reproducibility."[3] Poe's "Raven" trains readers in mass-media functions and encourages them to internalize that knowledge by rewriting the poem within their own media contexts. The poem's reproducibility, not its originality, underpins its exceptional longevity and vast, self-perpetuating, international literary presence.

Recently critics have developed new ways of reading literary works within the terms of their circulation and reception, displacing the author function as the center of critical practice. In *Reading at the Social Limit: Affect, Mass Culture, and Edgar Allan Poe* (1995), Jonathan Elmer initiated this trend in Poe studies by reading Poe as a "symptom" as well as a theorizer of mass culture. Extending that insight in *American Literature and the Culture of Reprinting* (2003), Meredith McGill tracks and analyzes the ways that Poe's work circulated anonymously and was persistently mistaken for the writings of others. McGill argues that twentieth-century author-centered criticism has obscured "a literary system that places authorship in complex forms of suspension and that trades on the dislocation of texts from their origins." In *Gender and the Poetics of Reception in Poe's Circle* (2004), I explored the ways that Poe forged a transactional poetics in collaboration with his female peers in the pages of newspapers, magazines, and letters; I sought to explain why collective mimetic practices accrued to a single individual, while the other practitioners were forgotten. All three studies show that putting the singular author at the center of Poe studies curtails an analysis of the complex ways he and other writers negotiated the terms of a print culture defined by the circulation of imitable, conventional, and commonly held literary effects and properties that bore a complex relationship to authority and authorship. Jerome McGann builds on this point in his essay in this volume, speculating about the ways digital archives could reflect and assist such insights.[4]

"The Raven" showcases its mechanical properties, and its initial reception registers a fascination with the poem as a reproducible verbal object. Indeed, readers rewrote "The Raven" in order to investigate the properties and functions of this rewritable form. While a number of critics have noted that Walt Whitman's "Out of the Cradle Endlessly Rocking" pays ambivalent tribute to "The Raven" as a negative forerunner of Whitman's positive poetics, Whitman articulates a sense of indebtedness to Poe's recombinatory form because it negotiates an open, adaptable, flexible poetic relationship to a mass readership, one based on effects rather than causes, reading rather than writing, listening rather than speaking. The pessimistic or optimistic valence of the vision is less important than the underlying communicative structure.

A "WONDROUS MECHANISM"

"The Raven" addresses the challenges of a mass readership at mid-century by carrying the terms of its assembly, deconstruction, and reconstruction within it. Poe foregrounds the poem's mechanistic model of construction, encouraging readers to put themselves in the position of writers: for if something has been constructed, it can be taken apart and put together again by others. These new writers assume the speaker's role, adapting the poem to a range of expressive purposes. The poem invites rewriting as a way of engaging a wide, various, and largely anonymous population of readers. The success of this experiment is confirmed by its effects: dozens of adaptations, parodies, versions, imitations, and tributes proliferated upon the poem's publication; they continue multiplying to the present day.[5] Offering readers vast possibilities of recombination, "The Raven" operates under a broad range of circumstances in recognizable but altered forms. Poe draws from earlier collaborative poetic practices and adapts them to altered conditions of reception in the magazine age. By fusing the adaptability and reproducibility of collective forms—especially the ballad—with an idiosyncratic poetic mechanism that carries his authorial signature, Poe crafts a mode of poetic production that can be used in a range of ways but that nevertheless continues to work in his name, which operates as a kind of brand name for a coordinated collection of poetic functions.

Rapidly and widely reprinted, reviewed, rewritten, and discussed, "The Raven" created a sensation upon its publication in January 1845, owing as much or more to its evocative, recombinatory powers as to its originality.[6] The *Town* carried an illustration of a humanized raven, the "portrait of a distinguished poet, critic and writer of tales." The caption foregrounded the irony that a critic so insistent on the importance of originality (the "Little Longfellow War" had been carried out in the previous months) would be acclaimed for works that broadcast their literary indebtedness: "He is remarkable for his great powers of originality which have been evinced in his great work, the 'Raven,' showing no resemblance to an old English ballad or to the 'Ancient Mariner' in its construction" (*PL* 554). Admirers often identified its ability to summon literary lookalikes as the source of its uncanny appeal. Henry Tuckerman recalls a gathering at a New York physician's home where the doctor introduced Poe as

> "The Raven!" and certainly no human physiognomy more resembled that bird than the stranger's, who, without a smile or a word, bowed slightly and slowly; with a fixed, and, it almost seemed, a portentous gaze, as if complacently accepting the character thus thrust upon him. Instantly, the fancy of all present began to conjure up all the ravens they had ever heard of or seen, from those that fed Elijah to the one in "Barnaby Rudge"; and it was not for some minutes that Edgar A. Poe was recognized, in the "fearful guest," to be "evermore" associated in the minds of all present, not with the "lost Lenore," but with that extraordinary presentation of the Doctor's.

Tuckerman sketches a complex series of associations, in which the doctor personifies the Raven in the figure of Poe, who then takes on the qualities of his bird in the guests' imaginations; they in turn summon all the ravens in their literary memories. Those associations then accrue to the man whose famous "Nevermore" converts into an "evermore," consolidating Poe's place in guests' minds as the latest version of a literary symbol at once ancient (Elijah), modern (Rudge), and enduring. It is the act of association itself, first the doctor's and then the guests', that consolidates Poe's name; the guests will remember Poe not because of his "lost Lenore," but because the doctor encouraged, and they pursued, a chain of associations.[7]

Many readers have noted the poem's ability to summon an array of precursors. They do not speak simply in terms of allusiveness; something about "The Raven" strongly suggests that it had already been written, that Poe cobbled together pieces of previous poems in a particularly ingenious way. An unusual number of his contemporaries claimed that Poe stole the poem, in whole or in parts, from them, or that they helped him write it.[8] Candidates for poetic prototypes include Henry Hirst's "To a Ruined Fountain in a Grecian Picture" (in which a "never-dying raven" cannot remember the names of the dead), Thomas Holley Chivers's "To Allegra Florence in Heaven" (with trochaic disyllabic "ing" end rhymes that sound like Poe's: "Holy angels now are bending / To receive thy soul ascending"), Albert Pike's "Isadore" (a poem about the death of a beautiful woman, from the lips of a bereaved lover, with the refrain "Thou art lost to me forever, Isadore"), and Elizabeth Barrett's "Lady Geraldine's Courtship" (with trochaic octameter lines, one of which features a familiar piece of drapery: "With a rushing stir, uncertain, in the air the purple curtain"), to give some of the most prominent examples. Other poems identified as precursors include Coleridge's *Rime of the Ancient Mariner* (another experimental ballad featuring a white rather than a black bird), Shelley's "A Lament" (featuring the refrain "No more—Oh, never more"), and Charles Gardette's "The Demon of the Fire" (which was actually written after "The Raven" as a hoax precursor poem, but was attributed to Poe into the twentieth century). Critics have traced sources for the rhythm, the narrative of lost love, the refrain, the word "nevermore," and the raven, as well as for the synthetic amalgamation. T. O. Mabbott identifies the parrot in Poe's 1829 poem "Romance" as a precursor to the raven; he also notes that in "The Fall of the House of Usher," Jean Baptiste Louis Gresset's poem about a parrot, *Ver-vert,* sits on a library shelf, and that in "The Philosophy of Composition," Poe tells readers that the parrot was his first candidate for the poem. A number of Poe's contemporaries insisted that he first considered the owl for the raven's role; others have suggested that the raven was imported from another literary work, most frequently, Charles Dickens's *Barnaby Rudge.* Far from denying the poem's derivativeness, Poe actively drew attention to its many literary doubles. He wrote a review of Elizabeth Barrett's poems that featured "Lady Geraldine's Courtship" just weeks before he published "The Raven." The first sentence of "The Philosophy of Composition" refers to "an examination I once made of the mechanism of 'Barnaby Rudge,'" encouraging readers to track down his review of Dickens's raven and then find Poe's own bird an improvement over the original mechanism.[9] Poe promoted his poem as an ingenious recombination of existing parts gathered from the works of his contemporaries and predecessors and assembled in "The Raven."[10]

Even without the help of Poe and his critics, "The Raven" flaunts its secondariness, its ability to encourage reproduction by foregrounding its own composite qualities. Barbara Johnson has said that "the poem's status as a mechanical repetition" is advertised in the rhyming, rhythmic, repetitive structure and in its saturation of conventional poetic words and images: "it would be hard to find a poem . . . which is packed with more clichés than 'The Raven': ember, remember, December, midnight, darkness, marble busts—all the bric-a-brac of poetic language is set out in jangling, alliterative trochees to hammer out a kind of ur-background of the gothic encounter."[11] The figure par excellence of this bric-a-brac for Johnson is "the word 'nevermore,'" which "stands in Poe as a figure for poetic language as such." Poe underscores the word's emptiness by putting it into a raven's mouth: "since the bird is not human, the word is proffered as a pure signifier, empty of human intentionality." Critics and reviewers have consistently used the language of mechanics to account for the poem's peculiarity. An 1845 reviewer in the *New York Illustrated Magazine* said that Poe's "'Raven' is more remarkable for its mechanical construction than for its spirit of poetry." Professor H. E. Shepherd observed at Poe's 1877 memorial service that "no poem in our language presents a more graceful grouping of metrical appliances and devices."[12] A critic in the *Southern Quarterly Review* of July 1848 breaks the poem down into its constitutive parts in order to demystify its appeal:

> Mr. Poe deserves much credit for the production of so remarkable a metrical novelty. Much of its peculiarity depends upon the artistical arrangement of its rhymes, which, being movable, and made to fall upon different syllables in different verses, give a pleasing variety which would otherwise be too monotonous.

The "arrangement" of "moveable" rhymes is one of the finite and mundane principles underpinning the reproducible construction of "The Raven."

While the raven's utterance may be void of human intentionality, as Johnson notes, the poetic system that produces and reproduces that utterance is not. Though it may not express the feelings or thoughts or desires of any particular person, the "wondrous mechanism" of "The Raven" had to be assembled by human hands.[13] The poem is a vehicle of expression built by an author who de-clines to speak through it; instead, a bereaved lover enters a lopsided dialogue with a raven in a staging of lyric as melodrama. Poe designed a poem that so ob-viously stages lyric expression that readers never lose sight of the artifice; that design is emblematized by the raven who repeats human speech without com-prehending it. It is left to the poem's narrator to bestow meaning upon a purpose-less utterance; in doing so, he assumes the position of a reader who encourages other readers external to the poem to find meaning in its empty structure, just as he finds meaning in the raven's unmotivated utterance. Following Poe's own ob-servations in "The Philosophy of Composition," Johnson reads the scenario this way. The nevermore's empty repetition offers an opportunity for the bereaved lover to "write his own story around the signifier, letting it seal the letter of his fate until, finally, it utterly incorporates him: 'And my soul from out that shadow that lies floating on the floor / Shall be lifted—nevermore.' Sense has been made by the absorption of the subject by the signifier."[14] As a figure for the reader, Poe's bereaved lover serves as a guide through the poem's process of generating per-sonal causes from impersonal effects. Poe casts the poem as a linguistic machine abandoned by its maker that invites readers to discover its mode of functioning and take over its operations. In doing so, they adapt their own expressive opera-tions to the structure of the poem; under the sign of the raven, they make "sense" via a medium of mass communication. Foregrounding its rewriteability as well as its own rewritten status, "The Raven" generates and consolidates a network of poems that accrue their meaning in relation to one another, a meaning which is held in common.

Poe underscores the reader's instrumental role in the poem's operations in "The Philosophy of Composition," published in *Graham's Magazine* in the wake of the tremendous success of "The Raven."[15] While "The Philosophy of Composi-tion" may or may not accurately describe Poe's compositional process (many crit-ics have debated this question), it certainly does explain how readers might write, or re-write, "The Raven." The essay serves as an instruction manual to the way the poem was "put together" that stresses how easily anyone might do it; Poe's "analysis" demonstrates a "reconstruction" for interested readers. Nowhere does he identify self-expression as a goal, which would limit the poem's adaptability to the purposes of others; to the contrary, Poe dismisses the "fine frenzy" and "ecstatic intuition" of other poets as an emotional hoax. In the place of personal origins, Poe substitutes "effects." In the place of individual achievement, Poe uses the impersonal language of mathematics and mechanics; both discourses are based on a premise or a goal of repeatable outcomes rather than unrepeatable creation. His claims for "originality of combination" in the matter of meter and form likewise depersonalize the results. He chooses a ready-made refrain, the "pivot upon which the whole structure might turn," for its efficiency and functionality, both proven by long-standing use: "the universality of its employment sufficed to assure me of its intrinsic value." The necessity of creating a functional mechanism through the proper combination of parts determined most if not all of his compositional decisions; the central necessity of combining "two ideas, of a lover lamenting his deceased mistress and a Raven continuously repeating the word 'Nevermore'"—determined the way the rest of the poem was put together. The climax was an inevitable result, "forced upon me in the progress of the construction."[16] Poe himself, he suggests, was not the author so much as the assembler who was compelled to follow obvious rules that operate as inflexibly as the laws of physics in order for the poem to work. Poe seeks to demonstrate in "The Philosophy of Composition" that "The Raven" is made to be re-made; it is turned in a way that enables its return, over and over again, in the most unlikely places.

A "construction" designed to convey a universal "effect" that derives from no determinate cause, "The Raven" marks itself as a medium of mass communication, as a vehicle for voices, but for no voice in particular. Welcoming readers to operate its vocal "instrument," the poem encourages recitation—it was quickly added to elocution manuals.[17] And readers persistently rewrote and restaged the poem, putting it to use in a range of communicative circumstances for diverse ends. Johnson argues that the poem's basic insight and lesson is that the genuineness of poetic language derives from its artifice; but if we take the poem's entire print context into account, we might say instead that the effectiveness of the poem as an expressive medium is derived from its mechanical operations. Those operations underwrite its reproducibility, which, in Benjamin's terms, is its cultural work: "the work reproduced becomes the reproduction of a work designed for reproducibility."[18]

The poem's reproducibility and its reproductions were themselves the topic of literary commentary in Poe's time; the editors of *Yale Magazine* expressed mock dismay over its proliferative capabilities:

> We know not how to account for the singular phenomenon exhibited by Mr. Poe's "The Raven." Certainly this is the most remarkable bird of the age. What a patriarch he is getting to be! Not a week passes unmarked by the flight of a new covey from his nest. . . . We have seen, within a day or two, one "owl" and one "whippoorwill," both claiming said "Raven" for their mutual dad.

"The Raven" fathered not just "The Owl" and "The Whippoorwill," but also "The Vulture," "The Dove," "The Parrot," "The Turkey," and "The Goblin Goose." The poem claimed many other progeny in the weeks, months, and years after its own birth: "The Gazelle," "The Black Cat," "The Pole Cat" (which Abraham Lincoln found amusing), "The Tom-Cat," "The Ravenous Bull," "Her Pa's Dog," and "The Bed Bug" all claimed lineages, as did "The Demon of the Mirror," "The Fire-Fiend," and "The Mammoth Squash."[19]

If the work of artistic reproducibility is to train readers "in the apperceptions and vast apparatus whose role in their lives is expanding almost daily," "The Raven" was quite explicitly and self-consciously used to understand and harness the operations of the press as a medium of mass communication. In one of the earliest parodies, for example, "The Craven: by Poh!" Dr. F. Felix Gouraud advertises his soap while accusing other makers of selling inferior copies. Using the logic of counterfeit to counter copies of his soap, Gouraud imitates Poe's critical persona as the plagiarism police in order to warn "the public against purchasing any *imitations* of his fine products":

> Once upon a midnight dreary, while with toil and care quite weary,
> I was pondering on man's proneness to deceitfulness and guile,
> Soon I fell into a seeming state 'twixt wakefulness and dreaming,
> When my mind's eye saw a scheming fellow counterfeiting Soap
> Yes! counterfeiting GOURAUD's matchless *Medicated Soap;*
> *Twisting sand into a rope!*[20]

While it may seem paradoxical or at least counterproductive to imitate an imitative poem by a writer who reputedly abhors imitation in order to warn against counterfeits, Dr. Gouraud understands and practices Poe's doubled position as both the exposer and purveyor of copies: as a master of reproduction. Adopting Poe's highly imitable poem to warn against imitations draws attention to the process of making copies, and the ease with which, in an age of mechanical reproducibility, one can take the recipe of another, make a version of the same thing, and market it as the original; and yet the versions are not identical. One—Gouraud's copy of Poe's poem or the imitation soap—is untransmuted "sand." The other—Poe's poem or Gouraud's matchless medicated soap—is a cohesive, superior product. Just as Gouraud's advertisement lacks the captivating charm of "The Raven" while retaining its form and appropriating its fame, his counterfeiter profits from an inferior product. The difference is that Gouraud admits his imitation, while the deceitful "Craven" who sells false soap hides it. Or so Gouraud argues;

what he demonstrates is a complex interplay between an unoriginal original and its copy, which instructs the reader on the ways that understanding the intricacies of print reproduction can help one discern the difference between legitimate and illegitimate poems, advertisements, and soap; the distinction emphatically does not rely on originality, but on effective and transformative synthesis.

Poe was clearly intrigued by the poem's reproductive possibilities, its capacity to ground and extend a discursive network that mediated a range of cultural conversations via proliferation. Indicating that an aesthetics of reproducibility was in play, Poe discriminated among these versions, critiquing, praising, and republishing excerpts of those he particularly liked in the *Broadway Journal,* which he edited in 1845, the year "The Raven" was published. Though he often accused writers of plagiarism, imitation, and derivativeness, Poe praised "The Gazelle," for instance, written by a "new-found boy-poet of only fifteen," as N. P. Willis described the author in an editorial note that preceded the poem in the May 3, 1845, edition of the *Weekly Mirror;* Poe declared in the *Broadway Journal* that, "although professedly an imitation, [this poem] has a great deal of original power."[21] "The Gazelle"'s trochaic octameter quatrains with an added half-line and the internal disyllabic "ing" rhymes immediately mark an affinity with "The Raven," for this combination of rhythmic and sonic parts defined the poem's signature novelty. Certain words ("murmur") and archaic-sounding syntactic structures ("down flinging," "up springing") also code "The Gazelle" as being "after the manner of Poe's 'Raven,'" as the epigraph tells us. The poem's plot bears distinct structural similarities as well. A young man reading a book thinks he hears a voice repeating the same phrase over and over again, and searches for the source:

> Then my book at once down flinging, from my reverie upspringing,
> Searched I through the forest, striving my vain terror to dispel,
> All things to my search subjecting, not a bush or tree neglecting,
> When behind a rock projecting, saw I there a white gazelle,
> And that soft and silvery murmur, in my ear so slowly fell,
> > Merely whispering "Fare thee well!"

The gazelle gazes at the young man, drops a tear, and repeats the same phrase over and over again, until he begins to believe that the animal has the "dark eyes" of his "long lost Isabel." His intuition is confirmed when the gazelle transforms into "a seraph glowing, with her golden tresses flowing"; she continues to repeat "Fare thee well" while she "fades" back into the animal form.

Clearly signifying its resemblance to "The Raven," "The Gazelle" creatively recombines the "original" poem's elements to different effect. A talking animal's single phrase serves as the "fulcrum" for both poems, but while ravens can mimic human speech, gazelles cannot; a situation potentially explicable in natural terms can only be a product of supernatural intervention or delusion in C.C. Cooke's poem. While both animals serve as a mediating vehicle between the human world and other worlds, the white gazelle is apparently a messenger from holy lands, while the raven hearkens from "Night's Plutonian Shore." Both creatures cause the men in the poems to think of their lost loves, but the raven declines to transmit any message from Lenore, while the gazelle speaks for and then as Isabel. The raven may be unconscious of or oblivious to any message it carries; the gazelle's transmission is fully intentional. The emphatic refusal of anthropomorphosis in "The Raven" becomes adamant personification in "The Gazelle"; that animal's big brown eyes are more suited to the imposition of the human than the bird's "fiery eyes." Taken together, the two poems map a field that spans from the natural to the supernatural, from the demonic to the heavenly, demonstrating that seeming polarities lie along a spectrum of exchange.

What "The Gazelle" shares with "The Raven" is the technical display of creative reproducibility at work. "The Gazelle"'s plastic adaptation of "The Raven" draws attention to both poems' reproductive powers even while identifying their source in a network of relations to other works, particularly by Byron. Cooke's poem draws out, identifies, and creates a relation between "The Raven," "The Gazelle," and Byron's "Fare Thee Well," "To Ianthe," and *The Giaour.*[22] Byron's "Fare Thee Well" circulated with a story that he sent the poem to his wife as a biting tribute to the end of their relationship. By substituting the title phrase from Byron's poem for Poe's "nevermore," Cooke gives his heavenly gazelle a sinister undertone. If the gazelle's "fare thee well" seems to be a reassuring message from the speaker's Isabel that she still loves him in the afterlife, the unmistakable echo of Byron's poem reminds readers that the same phrase is addressed bitterly to a woman who has reneged on her avowal of everlasting love. That a gazelle utters this phrase further underscores the Byronic underpinnings of Cooke's rendition of Poe's poem, because gazelles were a recurring feature of Byron's poems; Byron, like Cooke, evokes the comparison between the eyes of women and gazelles. In *The Giaour,* "Her eye's dark charm 't were vain to tell, / But gaze on that of the Gazelle, / It will assist thy fancy well" (ll. 473–75). And in "To Ianthe," the speaker begs his love to

> let that eye, which, wild as the Gazelle's,
> Now brightly bold or beautifully shy,

> Wins as it wanders, dazzles where it dwells,
> Glance o'er this page; nor to my verse deny
> That smile for which my breast might vainly sigh. (ll. 28–32)

Byron's gazelle similes bring us full circle back to Poe via "Ligeia," whose eyes "were, I must believe, far larger than the ordinary eyes of our own race. They were even far fuller than the fullest of the gazelle eyes of the tribe of the valley of Nour-jahad."[23] These eyes wander over pages, through print media, and from body to body, carrying us from Ligeia to Lady Rowena, from gazelles to spirit-women, from Cooke to Byron to Poe. They signify the mobility of unindividuated atten-tion, the attention of a reader, but of no reader in particular.

The simile all these works hold in common—women's eyes are like gazelles' eyes—shows readers the ways that women circulate as mediums of convertibil-ity through a poetic network, figuring the operations of print culture. The phrase "mediums of convertibility" summons Colin (Joan) Dayan's *Fables of Mind*, a brilliant study of Poe and moral philosophy. Expanding the critical lens to in-clude the communicative networks through which "The Raven" circulated shows us that Dayan's insight, that women served persistently as vehicles of exchange— between body and spirit, eye and idea—holds true for the world outside of Poe's fiction; indeed, it shows that the limit between authors' minds and writings on the one hand, and the vast apparatus of antebellum print culture on the other, is highly permeable, even fluid.[24]

While the exchanges in the poems and stories of Byron, Poe, and Cooke are ostensibly private, emotional, and romantic, the pairs of lovers—in each case a man who in speaking summons the figure of a woman—can be read as figura-tions of the operations of print in the age of mass media. The writers figure these operations as intimate exchanges in order to "train humans in the vast appara-tus of print culture"; they take a clichéd literary scenario and adapt it to the task of teaching readers how to discern and interpret patterns of exchange in this age of print reproducibility. The pedagogical nature of the task is articulated clearly in Willis's note that a "boy poet of fifteen" wrote "The Gazelle." The publishing scenario is one of a young poet apprenticing himself to a master of mimicry; he shows he has learned his lesson by foregrounding Poe's own apprenticeship to Byron, who was himself a pioneer in the manipulation of the poet's self-image via the circulation of poetry in ephemeral print media.

Poe's explicit expression of admiration and encouragement for Cooke's exten-sion of the poetics of reproducibility is not singular; it is strange that critics con-tinue to cast Poe as hostile to mimicry when he is so clearly devoted to exploring,

disseminating, and promoting complex forms of imitation. Poe praised and published "A Tale of Luzon," for example, by Mary Hewitt, in which a white bird
brings Christian solace to an old man:

> Now, a bird swan-white, and shaking drops like diamonds from his plumes,
> Springs from out the glancing fountain, and across the garden brooks,
> Bright as 'twere a heavenly sunbeam, darteth through the open door—
> Swan-white, enters like a spirit from the far Elysian shore.[25]

Like "The Gazelle," "A Tale of Luzon" inverts the raven's dark origins: Hewitt's
"swan-white bird" comes from an "Elysian shore." Instead of transmitting despair
and brooding melancholy, this bird brings "words of comfort" that inspire the
old man's tranquility: "None may know what words of comfort that swan-white
bird could impart, / But joy illumines the old man's visage, and sweet peace is in
his heart." Hewitt explicates her logic of conversion in a letter to Poe that accom-
panied her poem. She explains "the singular coincidence . . . of the simultaneous
appearance of your admirable poem, 'The Raven,' and the receipt of a letter by
myself from a very dear brother resident in Manilla, containing a marvelous history of a 'white bird,' the which, although the very opposite of the 'raven,' struck
me as being so singularly like it in groundwork as to constitute a 'remarkable coincidence.'" Mrs. Hewitt encloses her verse "paraphrase," as well as her brother's
original letter in her letter to Poe. Her materials inspired him not only to write
to her expressing great enthusiasm for the story and the verse "paraphrase," but
also to publish "A Tale of Luzon" in the *Broadway Journal* (it appeared on March
22, 1845):

> The coincidence to which you call my attention is certainly remarkable, and the
> story as narrated by your brother is full of rich interest, no particle of which, most
> assuredly, is lost in your truly admirable paraphrase. I fear, indeed, that my enthusi-
> asm for all that I *feel* to be poetry, has hurried me into some indiscretion touching
> the 'Tale of Luzon.' Immediately upon reading it, I took it to the printer, and it is
> now in type for the *Broadway Journal* of this week.[26]

Mrs. Hewitt responded: "I certainly intended to place the 'Tale of Luzon' quite at
your disposal and beg you to believe that I appreciate highly the kindness that has
prompted your favorable notice of my lines. After the 'RAVEN,' my verse seemed
to me but a broken chime—and since sending it to you, I have wondered at my
own temerity. I shall be proud to see it published in the columns of the *Broadway
Journal.*"

Poe and Hewitt agree that the "coincidence" of the two stories, bound together in opposition, suggests a powerful, impersonal, extensive communicative force at work, one that stretches from the Philippines to New York; the conversions of dark to light, hell to heaven, despair to tranquility make up part of a single system or "groundwork" of which both "The Raven" and "A Tale of Luzon" are a part. Hewitt's refiguration, like Cooke's, also explicates the operations of print circulation; when considered conjointly with "The Raven," the "groundwork" of print culture is clarified, spiritualized, and illuminated. Vehicles of transmission, the mysterious birds come from points of unclear and unlocatable origin, disseminating phrases whose effect depends upon the reader's interpretive needs and desires. The recipients make what they will of the message, which is also a medium. The most powerful message that the birds carry is that their word must be disseminated; Hewitt obeys the call of "The Raven" by converting her brother's story from the Philippines into a version of the poem; and Poe obeys the call of Hewitt's "swan-white bird" by "immediately" converting her manuscript poem to print.

Versions of "The Raven" like "The Gazelle" and "A Tale of Luzon" make clear that Poe's poetic operations depend upon and articulate the communicative potential of a sophisticated and highly developed "reprint culture."[27] That Poe is not alone, and that writers of the period—especially in New York City, the publishing center of the time—were aware of and self-conscious about their role as explicators of the operations and potential of emerging mass print culture is made clear in the work of "Snarles, The Corporation Poet." Even more than Poe, Snarles demonstrates the corporate nature of newspaper and magazine poetry in the period by adopting and amalgamating various poets' styles in his weekly editorial poem in the *New World,* and adapting them to the political, social, or literary happening that he wishes to comment upon. His pseudonym signifies the literary operations he deploys. Francis Quarles was a famous emblem poet; "The Raven" was first published under the signature "Quarles," locating the poem more or less ironically in a tradition of moral allegory. Snarles evokes that tradition while suggesting a certain critical surliness in the author, a tendency to criticize current events: Snarles brings the quarrel out in Quarles. That Snarles, who assumes the role of supreme representative or metafigure of reprint culture, derives some of his operations from Poe's poem is made clear by the ways he uses "The Raven" as one prototype for his commentary. On February 22, for example, "The Raven" serves as the basis for "The Veto," a critique of corruption in local politics: "Once upon an evening dreary, the Council pondered weak and weary, / Over many a long petition which was voted down a bore." Over eighteen stanzas, Snarles charts the course of a Council meeting, exposes the mayor's corruption, and vows that quite soon he will be dethroned from his position of "official trust," to "be lifted 'NEVERMORE.'"[28]

In Snarles's "The Pressgang. A Vision," Poe is just one of many writers figured as periodical mouthpieces; Snarles satirizes "all the City's Press," in which "each paper seemed personified, by goblins strange and tall." "The Pressgang" is a mélange of metered forms in which each newspaper appears as its editor and is glossed in the style of that editor's poetry; N. P. Willis's poetry, for example, serves as the basis of "the MIRROR's manly tread." Also personified are the *Gazette,* the *Courier and Enquirer,* the *Spirit,* the *Native,* and Poe's *Broadway Journal.* This poetic play suggests that the tendency to understand publications as their editors and writings as their writers was widespread, and not an anomalous treatment of Poe inspired by the reception of "The Raven." In Snarles's poem, Poe is identified doubly: the *Broadway Journal* assumes the image of Poe, but it walks with the "step sedate and stately" of his Raven. Snarles notes Poe's reputation as a fearless critic:

> Then with step sedate and stately, as if thrones had borne him lately,
> Came a bold and daring warrior up the distant echoing floor;
> As he passed the COURIER's Colonel, then I saw THE BROADWAY JOURNAL,
> In a character supernal, on his gallant front he bore,
> And with stately step and solemn marched he proudly through the door,
>   As if he pondered, evermore.

> With his keen sardonic smiling, every other care beguiling,
> Right and left he bravely wielded a double-edged and broad claymore,
> And with gallant presence dashing, 'mid his confreres stoutly clashing,
> He unpityingly went slashing, as he keenly scanned them o'er,
> While with eye and mien undaunted, such a gallant presence bore,
>   As might awe them, evermore.

In the world of personified newspapers, Poe's criticism is a gallant knight, "scanning" his enemies and editing or evaluating them without mercy. (Humorously exempting this portrait of himself from his characteristic criticism, Poe extracted and reprinted it in the *Broadway Journal* on April 26, with the title "A Gentle Puff," advertising himself as well as the *New World.*) In "The Pressgang," Snarles shows the way that the author figure serves to connect various literary functions in the press: the critic, the poet, and the editor are combined in the single character Poe (or Poh!), each seemingly discrete function informing the others. Snarles educates readers in the structure of the literary world in this way, encouraging them to make connections and comparisons.

A more-or-less simultaneous web of "Raven"-inspired poems maps out and explicates the operations of print culture in the mid-1840s. But how do "The Raven" and the knowledge it carries adapt and survive across time, and how is that knowledge absorbed and transmitted in a later period, under different conditions of mass communication? Answers might be found through a reading of Walt Whitman's "Out of the Cradle Endlessly Rocking," which first appeared under the title "A Child's Reminiscence" in the New York *Saturday Press* on December 24, 1859.[29] It has long been remarked that "The Raven" haunts "Out of the Cradle," even if no one has gone so far as to claim that Whitman's poem is an adaptation or version of Poe's poem. Joseph DeFalco argues that Whitman delineates and heightens his poetics of optimism in contrast to his pessimistic predecessor: Whitman's "gambit of borrowing critical elements from Poe's poem and deploying them in his own poem at Poe's expense heightened his own themes by way of the dialectic." Extending this idea, Edwin Fussell argues that Whitman embedded references to Poe in order to chart "the triumphant birth of an entire American poetry surpassing the English," a feat Whitman could only accomplish by killing off his unfortunate predecessor, Poe, who was unable to extricate himself from the shadow of British tradition. At the same time, Whitman also "enshrin[ed] Poe as the inarticulate originator of the American poetic tradition."[30] Offering a less stridently nationalistic interpretation, Kerry Larson argues that Whitman relies on Poe's poem as a starting point in his attempt to neutralize the tragedy of death and to harness it to a generative poetic outlook:

> Though each in his way is a harbinger of death, neither mockingbird nor raven attains tragic sublimity: the latter in particular is hardly more than a gothic spook embodying the "human thirst for self-torture"—a hallucinated contrivance whereby the speaker of the poem "takes a phrenzied pleasure in so modelling the questions as to receive the expected *nevermore*." Whitman, oppositely, wishes to eliminate masochism from death, wishes to reclaim for death a meaningfulness that both sacralizes art and retrieves its orphaned castaway.

All three critics agree that Whitman uses Poe's poem as a stepping stone and then moves to a fully original position. In Larson's words, "accepting the full burden of loss so as to leap swiftly beyond it, Whitman prepares for his full transcendence in receiving with grateful recognition the word up from the sea, the synthesizing third term 'neither like the bird nor my child's arous'd heart.'"[31]

But the logic of convertibility that persistently links "The Raven" with its offspring complicates the idea that Whitman leaves one-half of this "dialectic" behind him. That logic is just as apparent in "Out of the Cradle" as in the other poems discussed, and it locks the poems into an inextricable relation, which enables Whitman to acknowledge and absorb Poe's insights about the workings of mass print communication and to adapt it to his own expressive purposes. "Out of the Cradle" charts this adaptation of a formal inheritance that enables a mode of communication in which causes are derived from effects, and the poet is a product of his poem and his readers, rather than the reverse.

It is no coincidence that "Out of the Cradle" was first published in Henry Clapp's *Saturday Press,* a periodical associated with the mid-century Bohemian circle that included Whitman and gathered at Pfaff's pub. "The Vault at Pfaff's," a digital project managed by Edward Whitley at Lehigh University, makes a searchable version of the *Saturday Press* available; that site enables an exploration of the print networks through which Poe's poetical print operations informed poems that explicate the new aesthetic possibilities enabled by later print conditions. Clapp published the first issue of the *Saturday Press* on October 23, 1858, nine years after Poe's death and almost fourteen years after the publication of "The Raven." Though its period of influence was brief, waning with the advent of the Civil War, experimental writers like Walt Whitman benefited enormously from this outlet; Clapp published eleven of Whitman's poems and over twenty reviews of *Leaves of Grass* between December 1859 and December 1860. W. D. Howells said that the *Saturday Press* "embodied the new literary life of the city. It was clever, and full of the wit that tries its teeth upon everything."[32]

The new literary life of the *Saturday Press* took as a touchstone the work of Poe, who is listed on the Vault site as one of the "Pfaffians" even though he had been dead for a decade before this life emerged. Versions of "The Raven" proliferated in the *Press,* giving Poe's voice an afterlife that allowed it to intermingle and inform the works of this new generation of writers. Indeed, on December 15, 1860, the *Press* transcribed and printed spirit-medium Lizzie Doten's posthumous message from Poe in the style of "The Raven," delivered at the end of a lecture in Boston. Like Hewitt's bird and Cooke's gazelle, Poe speaks "From the throne of life eternal, / From the home of love supernal / Where the angel feet make music over all the starry floor."[33] (Directly beneath Doten's poem on the page lies "A Portrait" by Walt Whitman.) On November 19, 1859, Charles Gardette published what he claimed to be a "poem that was written by Mr. Poe, while experimenting toward that wondrous mechanism, 'The Raven'"; Poe discarded the poem, "considering it incomplete," and it somehow made its way into Gardette's hands.[34]

In "The Fire-Fiend: A Nightmare, from an Unpublished Manuscript of the Late Poe," a robin appears that links Poe's raven with Whitman's mocking-bird:

> Through my ivy-fretted casement filtered in a tremulous note
> From a tall and stately linden where a Robin swelled his throat: —
> Querulous, quaker-breasted Robin, calling quaintly for his mate!

The Robin wakes the speaker from his nightmare vision of a fire-bred Demon to a daylight conversion: "The fiendish Fire had smouldered to a white and form-less heap"; in its place was a "Spectral finger" that pointed "To a Bible, massive, golden, on a table carved and olden." The speaker's fear that demons rule the world is checked in the daylight, when the vision confirms "All Power is of God, of God alone!" This is the same sort of conversion enacted in Cooke, Hewitt, Doten, and, a month later, Whitman. Poe's hellish vision becomes one of heav-enly light.

One month after Gardette's Poe poem appeared, Whitman published "A Child's Reminiscence," which features a mockingbird that seems to be a descen-dant of Gardette's Robin as well as Poe's Raven; the marking of a line of descent suggests that Whitman pays tribute not only to Poe or Gardette, but to the entire web of associations that print circulation enables. As in other versions of "The Raven," Whitman fuses the story of the writer with the story of his mocking-bird. Whitman confessed to being as interested in Poe's life story as in his poems: "There is an indescribable magnetism about the poet's life and reminiscences, as well as the poems."[35] Both Poe and the mockingbird come north with their spouses; both lose their beloved mates prematurely, and the loss leaves them both despairing. Just as Poe writes poems about lost women, the mockingbird sings without hope of reply when his mate disappears (Gardette's Robin makes the biographical connection before Whitman does, and Whitman seems to fol-low suit). Identifying Poe with his poetic creation in the figure of the mocking-bird, Whitman expresses allegiance with that "lone singer, wonderful, causing tears," in "A Child's Reminiscence," making the bird his poetic double, his "sad brother," his "dusky demon aroused, the fire, the sweet hell within" (notice the nod to Gardette's "Fire-Fiend": "till the Demon seemed to name me").[36] At the same time, the mockingbird explicitly figures Whitman's own relationship of mimicry with Poe.

Whitman's conversions focus on naturalizing Poe's artificiality, which, in his tribute to Poe, Whitman declared that he himself abhorred: "Poe's verses illus-trate an intense faculty for technical and abstract beauty, with the rhyming art to excess, an incorrigible propensity toward nocturnal themes, a demoniac under-tone behind every page—and, by final judgment, probably belong among the electric lights of imaginative literature, brilliant and dazzling, but with no heat." Whitman, to the contrary, says that he "wanted, and still want[s] for poetry, the clear sun shining, and fresh air blowing—the strength and power of health, not of delirium, even amid the stormiest passions—with always the background of the eternal moralities."[37] Poe's claustrophobic echo chamber becomes the expansive outdoors in Whitman's poem, which looks seaward to a distant horizon. Instead of the raven, a "hallucinated contrivance" that emerges out of the night from a dark, alternative world, "Out of the Cradle" features a perfectly natural mock-ingbird, dwelling on Paumanok's mundane, daylit, windy shore. The raven's soli-tary voyage is countered by the mockingbird's migration north from Alabama with his "she-bird" for nesting season. Whitman's long, "free verse" lines depend upon, even as they unravel, Poe's rigidly metered trochaic octameter. "Ing" end-ings serve as the rhyming and rhythmic base in both poems as prelude and coun-terpoint to "nevermore"; but Whitman dissolves the mechanicity of Poe's meter into an oceanic flow:

> The aria sinking,
> All else continuing—the stars shining,
> The winds blowing the notes of the wondrous bird echoing,
> With angry moans the fierce old mother yet, as ever, incessantly moaning,
> On the sands of Paumanok's shore gray and rustling,
> The yellow half-moon enlarged, sagging down, dropping, the face of the sea
>   almost touching,
> The boy ecstatic—with his bare feet the waves—with his hair the atmosphere
>   dallying.

As the poem approaches the climactic sequence of never mores, the lines get lon-ger and longer, extending, as Poe's do, to unusual lengths, through the repetitive chant of continuous verb forms.

The conversions suggest that Whitman's natural world is a by-product of Poe's unnatural poetic world. Rather than drawing his inspiration directly from nature, Whitman shows how he builds his naturalistic poetics out of and against Poe's mechanistic poetics. Most critical responses to "Out of the Cradle" (and there are many) identify the poem's origins not in previous poetic practices, but in Whit-man's personal experiences and innovative poetic aspirations. In his recent essay on the poem, for example, Howard Nelson contemplates the poem's inspiring moment:

It is entirely probable that Whitman had some such boyhood experience with mockingbirds as described in the poem, but whether it was that experience that turned him into an "outsetting bard," making him conscious of "the sweet hell within," is doubtful. Is he describing something that happened to him, perhaps around puberty? Pretty clearly, this is projection backward of complex emotional experiences on an earlier, and simpler, outward one.[38]

Nelson goes on to speculate that the later, more "complex" emotional experience may be Whitman's conflicted emotions over same-sex love relationships. Whitman's first-person narrative of epiphany, of the moment that a boy becomes a poet, encourages readers to assume that he tells his own story of self-realization. This assumption underpins an ongoing belief in Whitman's originality and exceptionalism; his democratic poetics engage readers on equal terms, but that engagement does not emerge out of an equally democratic engagement with his fellow writers; rather, it is entirely of his own making and on his own terms. Unusual among Whitman critics, Kerry Larson notes the "openness to literary conventions" of "Out of the Cradle"; even more pertinently, he asserts that "this antiphonal design, easily missed in line by line explications of the poem, is important not only as a formal device but for what it implies about Whitman's restructuring of the terms of communicative exchange."[39] I have suggested that Whitman restructures the "terms of communicative exchange" with the materials that Poe provided in "The Raven" and other poems, and that he acknowledged this debt in "Out of the Cradle." In doing so, he, like Poe, allows readers to imagine themselves in the position of the poem's writer, and therefore write the poem in their terms. This direction of inquiry opens Whitman up to the intersubjective and interactive networks of production and reception at mid-century.

Whitman acknowledges his debt to Poe's previous innovations in this field not only in "Out of the Cradle," but also in his comments on Poe towards the end of his life. He begins his essay on "Edgar Poe's Significance" with a meditation on mass culture:

Comprehending artists in a mass, musicians, painters, actors, and so on, and considering each and all of them as radiations or flanges of that furious whirling wheel, poetry, the centre and axis of the whole, where else indeed may we so well investigate the causes, growths, tally-marks of the time—the age's matter and malady?[40]

"Radiations or flanges of that furious wheel," the "mass" of artists are organized, not by their own individual will, or according to their own individual personalities or accomplishments, but by cultural movements that exceed them into a single, inscrutable, forward-moving whole. Whitman calls the "center and axis of the whole" not poets, or any particular poet, but "poetry." Poets themselves are indicators—"tally-marks" of this overwhelming motion. Whitman identifies Poe as one of the key, if personally distasteful, tally-marks of his age. But he also credits Poe with his own insight into the workings of this field, and his own place and function within it. One of the few literary luminaries to attend Poe's reburial in November 1875, Whitman said in an interview (and quoted that interview in his later essay):

> For a long while and lately, I had a distaste for Poe's writings. I wanted, and still want for poetry, the clear sun shining, and fresh air blowing—the strength and power of health, not of delirium, even amid the stormiest passions—with always the background of the eternal moralities. Noncomplying with these requirements, Poe's genius has yet conquer'd a special recognition for itself, and I too have come to fully admit it, and appreciate it and him.[41]

Appreciating both "him" and "it," Whitman stresses that "it"—Poe's "special recognition" outweighs any particular emotional valence in his work. Whitman admired Poe's ability to speak for and to his time. What "The Raven" gave Whitman that the American geography and the "barbaric yawp" of the 1855 *Leaves of Grass* did not provide is the particular poetics of reception I have delineated. The 1860 *Calamus* poems make clear that Whitman had come to find the bard-centered poetics of his earlier poem inadequate to the task of communicating with readers. "Out of the Cradle" works through "The Raven" to reconstruct Whitman's relation to readers and to poetic language, relocating the poet as the recipient rather than the originator of the word.

Just as the bereaved lover in "The Raven" makes his story from the raven's nevermore, Whitman's speaker characterizes himself as a projection of Poe's poem:

> O you demon, singing by yourself! Projecting me!
> O solitary me, listening—never more shall I cease imitating, perpetuating you,
> Never more shall I escape,
> Never more shall the reverberations,
> Never more the cries of unsatisfied love be absent from me,
> Never again leave me to be the peaceful child I was before.

Far from transcending or escaping from the shadow of "The Raven," Whitman finds that he must fully embrace the darkness in order to find a way out of a poetic dead end. He agrees with Poe that romantic lyric expression must be adapted to a mass print culture because it is not capacious enough to express the feelings and thoughts of more than a single individual, no matter how enormously sympathetic with the plights of others. In a mass-media culture, the poet must be expressed by his readers, rather than the reverse. This is the reception-based poetics that Poe dramatized in "The Raven," and it is the one that concludes Whitman's poem as well. Recall that Barbara Johnson argues that the raven's repetition of the word nevermore offers an opportunity for the bereaved lover to "write his own story around the signifier, letting it seal the letter of his fate until, finally, it utterly incorporates him: 'And my soul from out that shadow that lies floating on the floor / Shall be lifted—nevermore.'" Just as "sense has been made by the absorption of the subject by the signifier" in Poe's poem, so Whitman chooses to be spoken, rather than to speak: "The sea whisper'd me." If Poe is, in Fussell's phrase, "the inarticulate originator" of an American tradition, Whitman joins him in that role, assuming the mantle of inarticulacy so that others may speak to him in a voice far more massive than that of a single individual.

Notes

1. I would like to express my gratitude for Sarah Carr's superb research assistance on this project. The Americanist Study Group at UNC, especially Angie Calcaterra, Tim Marr, Kelly Ross, Aaron Shackelford, Matthew Taylor, and Elissa Zellinger offered helpful comments on an earlier draft. Kelly Ross read this essay more than once in its entirety, offering astute insights for improvement each time. The first possibility is suggested by Kenneth Silverman, *Edgar A. Poe: Mournful and Never-Ending Remembrance* (New York: HarperCollins, 1992), and Mutlu Blasing, *American Poetry: The Rhetoric and its Forms* (New Haven, CT: Yale Univ. Press, 1987). The second possibility is raised by J. Gerald Kennedy in *Poe, Death, and the Life of Writing* (New Haven, CT: Yale Univ. Press, 1987). The third is Richard Godden's in "Poe and the Poetics of Opacity: Or, Another Way of Looking at That Black Bird," *ELH* 64, no. 4 (Winter 2000): 993–1009. The fourth is Jonathan Elmer's in "The Jingle Man: Trauma and the Aesthetic," *Fissions and Fusions: Proceedings of the First Conference of the Cape Studies Association,* ed. Lesley Marx et al. (Belville, South Africa: Univ. of the Western Cape, 1997), 131–45.

2. Daniel Hoffman, *Poe Poe Poe Poe Poe Poe Poe* (Garden City, NY: Doubleday, 1972), 91; Debra Fried, "Repetition, Refrain, and Epitaph," *ELH* 53, no. 3 (1986): 615–32, 627; Barbara Johnson, "Strange Fits: Wordsworth and Poe on the Nature of Poetic Language," *A World of Difference* (Baltimore: Johns Hopkins Univ. Press, 1987), 89–99, 98.

3. Walter Benjamin, "The Work of Art in the Age of Its Technological Reproducibility," *The Work of Art in the Age of its Technological Reproducibility and Other Writings,* ed. Michael W. Jennings, Brigid Doherty, and Thomas Y. Levin (Cambridge, MA: Harvard Univ. Press, 2008), 24, 26.

4. Jonathan Elmer, *Reading at the Social Limit: Affect, Mass Culture, and Edgar Allan Poe* (Palo Alto, CA: Stanford Univ. Press, 1995), 21; Meredith McGill, *American Literature and the Culture of Reprinting, 1834–1853* (Philadelphia: Univ. of Pennsylvania Press, 2003), 147; Eliza Richards, *Gender and the Poetics of Reception in Poe's Circle* (New York: Cambridge Univ. Press, 2004).

5. A cursory Google search shows that the Internet is perhaps even more hospitable to the poem and its offspring than mass print media.

6. On the reception of "The Raven," see Silverman, 231–42; *The Collected Works of Edgar Allan Poe* 1: *Poems,* ed. T. O. Mabbott (Cambridge, MA: Harvard Univ. Press, 1969), 359–64 (hereafter cited as *Poems);* Arthur Hobson Quinn, *Edgar Allan Poe: A Critical Biography* (1941; Baltimore: Johns Hopkins Univ. Press, 1998), chap. 14; and Dwight Thomas and David K. Jackson, *The Poe Log: A Documentary Life of Edgar Allan Poe, 1809–1849* (Boston: G. K. Hall, 1987), hereafter cited as *PL. Broadway Journal* editor Charles Briggs wrote James Russell Lowell that "everyone has been raven mad about [Poe's] last poem" (*PL,* 514). Popular writer Elizabeth Oakes Smith recalled in later years that "the Raven became known everywhere, and everyone was saying 'Nevermore'" (*PL,* 497). Months later, the poem was still captivating readers; in April of 1846 Elizabeth Barrett wrote Poe that his "'Raven' has produced a sensation, a 'fit horror,' here in England" (*PL,* 632).

7. *PL,* 497–98. Poe himself was much in demand—the poem made him a literary celebrity— and hosts of literary gatherings all over New York City and beyond invited him to recite the poem to their guests; for the rest of his life he frequently concluded his public lectures and appearances with a recitation of the poem. For a handful of these reports (there are many more), see descriptions of gatherings at the homes of Anne Lynch, Caroline Kirkland, and John Francis (*PL,* 496–99, 551, 616).

8. On this topic, see my "Outsourcing 'The Raven': Retroactive Origins," *Victorian Poetry* 43, no. 2 (2005): 205–21.

9. Edgar Allan Poe, "The Philosophy of Composition," in *Poe: Essays and Reviews,* ed. G. R. Thompson (New York: Library of America, 1984), 13. Hereafter cited as *ER.*

10. See identifications and discussions of these precursors by T. O. Mabbott in *Poems,* 353–59; John Ingram in *The Raven, by Edgar Allan Poe; with Literary and Historical Commentary* (London: George Redway, 1885), especially "Genesis" (1–16; Ingram votes for "Isadore" as the most important precursor poem); and Edmund Clarence Stedman's "Comment on the Poem" in *The Raven* (New York: Harper and Brothers, 1884), 9–14. "The Demon of the Fire" has a complicated history. Stedman thought it was Poe's juvenilia, but it was actually written after his death by a young man pretending to have discovered an early Poe poem. See C. D. Gardette, *The Whole Truth in the Question of "The Fire-Fiend," between Dr. R. Shelton Mackenzie and C.D. Gardette briefly stated by the latter* (Philadelphia, 1864).

11. Johnson, "Strange Fits," 98.

12. *PL,* 602; Sara Sigourney Rice, *Edgar Allan Poe: A Memorial Volume* (Baltimore: Turnbull Bros., 1877), 52.

13. The phrase comes from Charles Gardette's prefatory note to "The Fire-Fiend," when he first published it as an imperfect forerunner of "The Raven," in the *New York Saturday Evening Press* on November 19, 1859: "The following fantastic poem was written by Mr. Poe, while experimenting toward the wondrous mechanism, 'The Raven.'"

14. Johnson, "Strange Fits," 99.

15. Leland Person discusses "The Philosophy of Composition" in terms of reading rather than writing: "Reading the raven no less than reading 'The Raven' means writing, or composing a philosophy." See his "Poe's Composition of Philosophy: Reading and Writing 'The Raven,'" *Arizona Quarterly* 46, no. 3 (Fall 1990): 1–15, 2.

16. *ER,* 14–21.

17. Note in the *Poe Log:* "C. Shepard, Publisher, 191 Broadway, issues the second edition of George Vandenhoff's *A Plain System Of Elocution,* which contains compositions in prose and verse suitable for 'Practice in Oratorical, Poetical, and Dramatic Reading and Recitation.' Among the works selected is 'The Raven,' now printed in a book for the first time" (524).

18. Benjamin, 26.

19. "Editor's Table," *The Yale Literary Magazine,* June 1845, 338. These poems and many others are identified in *Parodies of the Works of English and American Authors,* collected and annotated by Walter Hamilton (London: Reeves and Turner, 1889), vol. 2: 25–95. See also *PL,* Ingram, and *Poems.* My research assistant Sarah Carr and I have identified many others in searches of digital databases, particularly the American Periodical Series Online. Lincoln mentions "the polecat" in a letter, reprinted in Osborne Oldroyd, *The Poet's Lincoln: Tributes in Verse to the Martyred President* (Boston: Chapple Publishing Co., 1915), vi.

20. Published in the March 25, 1845, edition of the *Evening Mirror.* See *PL,* 521.

21. "The Gazelle (After the Manner of Poe's 'Raven')," by C. C. Cooke, was published in the *Evening Mirror* on April 29 and reprinted in the *Weekly Mirror* on May 3, 1845 (*PL,* 528–31); Poe commented on "The Gazelle" in the *Broadway Journal* "Miscellany" on May 10, 1845.

22. Thanks to Jerome McGann for drawing my attention to Byron's gazelles.

23. *Edgar Allan Poe: Tales and Sketches,* ed. Thomas Ollive Mabbott (Urbana: Univ. of Illinois Press, 1978), vol. 1: 313.

24. "Poe wants to push his reader to the point where seeming opposites—what is and is not, man and woman—can be converted into and dismantled or replaced by one another." See Joan Dayan, *Fables of Mind : An Inquiry into Poe's Fiction* (New York: Oxford Univ. Press, 1987), 134.

25. Mary E. Hewitt, *Poems: Sacred, Passionate, and Legendary* (New York: Lamport, Blakeman, and Law, 1853), 168–70. See *PL,* 516–20, for much of the Hewitt-Poe correspondence.

26. The letter is dated March 20, 1845; a copy is at the Edgar Allan Poe Society website: www .eapoe.org/works/letters/p4503201.htm (accessed April 10, 2012).

27. Meredith McGill coined the very useful term "reprint culture."

28. Snarles, the Corporation Poet, also published a poem on March 8 in the *New World* entitled "Songs of the Suburbs," another verse medley, with these lines in "The Raven'"s meter: "Ah distinctly I remember it was in the bleak December / When the Tenth's respected member had possession of the floor," etc.

29. It then became "A Word out of the Sea" and was included in the 1860 *Leaves of Grass.* The final title, "Out of the Cradle Endlessly Rocking," first appeared in 1871. See Walt Whitman, *Selected Poems, 1855–1892,* ed. Gary Schmidgall (New York: St. Martin's, 1999)—especially Schmidgall's note, 497.

30. Joseph DeFalco, "Whitman's Changes in 'Out of the Cradle' and Poe's 'Raven,'" *Walt Whitman Review* 16 (March 1970): 22–27, 24; Edwin Fussell, *Lucifer in Harness: American Meter, Metaphor, and Diction* (Princeton, NJ: Princeton Univ. Press, 1973), 130–31. According to Fussell, Whitman's conversion of Poe's word "nevermore" to the simpler American diction "death" dramatizes the death of the shadow of British tradition under which Poe labored and the birth of the American poet, Whitman, who found a way out from beneath that shadow: "To find the American way of salvation, the American poet had to die to the British tradition, the British way of poetic diction, and to suffer the birth pangs of a wild land noisy with natural and human dissonance and dislocation. And only an earlier American poet could see him through the agonies of death. But now it was accomplished, and American poetry would never be the same again" (134).

31. Kerry C. Larson. *Whitman's Drama of Consensus* (Chicago: Univ. of Chicago Press, 1987), 195.

32. The Vault at Pfaff's can be found at digital.lib.lehigh.edu/pfaffs/about/welcome/ (accessed April 10, 2012). Information in this paragraph is drawn from the "Introduction" to the *Saturday Press* at the site digital.lib.lehigh.edu/pfaffs/sat/press/ (accessed April 10, 2012); and the biographies of Whitman and Poe: digital.lib.lehigh.edu/pfaffs/people/individuals (accessed April 10, 2012).

33. Lizzie Doten, "A 'Medium'-Poem," *New-York Saturday Press,* December 15, 1860: 4. On-line at The Vault: digital.lib.lehigh.edu/pfaffs/works/search/id-2687_start-1_pd2–77/ (accessed April 10, 2012).

34. That hoax poem, "The Fire Fiend: A Nightmare," was attributed to Poe into the twentieth century, despite Gardette having revealed his hoax in 1864. For the complete story, see Gardette's *The Whole Truth in the Question of "The Fire Fiend": Between Dr. R. Shelton Mackenzie and C. D. Gardette; Briefly Stated by the Latter* (Philadelphia: Sherman & Co., 1864). The Fire-Fiend is available through The Vault: digital.lib.lehigh.edu/pfaffs/works/search/id-1209_start-1_pd1–77/ (accessed April 10, 2012).

35. Walt Whitman, "Edgar Poe's Significance," in *Specimen Days.* Reprinted in *Whitman: Complete Poetry and Collected Prose,* ed. Justin Kaplan (New York: Library of America, 1982), 872. A number of critics have noted that Whitman's fiction bears a strong resemblance to Poe's. Younger than Poe, Whitman edited and wrote for many of the same periodicals.

36. I work from the first published version of Whitman's poem, entitled "A Child's Reminiscence," available at the Vault: digital.lib.lehigh.edu/pfaffs/works/search/id-1699_start-1_pd1–47/ (accessed April 10, 2012).

37. Whitman, "Edgar Poe's Significance," 873.

38. Howard Nelson, "Out of the Cradle Endlessly Rocking," *A Companion to Walt Whitman,* ed. Donald D. Cummings (New York: Wiley-Blackwell, 2009), 496–507, 502.

39. Larson, 187–89.

40. Whitman, "Edgar Poe's Significance," 872.

41. Ibid.," 873.

IV | Repositioning Poe in Literary America

Poe by the Numbers

Odd Man Out?

MAURICE S. LEE

Poe has been traditionally seen as an anomaly in nineteenth-century American literary history, though it is not clear how one might precisely define his status outside the critical center. In the first half of the twentieth century, important fig-ures marginalized Poe. D. H. Lawrence damned him with pity; T. S. Eliot could not quite respect him; Van Wyck Brooks and Vernon Parrington largely excluded him from the main currents of American thought. Most influentially, F. O. Mat-thiessen's *American Renaissance* (1941) famously failed to devote a chapter to Poe (though Matthiessen, it should be said, felt defensive enough to justify the omis-sion in a footnote and shift his position in later writings).[1] It is a truism in Poe studies and beyond that Poe was sidelined from the field of the American Renais-sance, reenacting the alienation he experienced in his life as a rejected son, pro-fessional pariah, southerner, aesthete, political reactionary, addict, lunatic, and impoverished genius—a composite stereotype advertised by Rufus Griswold, sketched by Melville in *The Confidence-Man* (1857), and still thriving in popular culture today. Even when Poe in the 1990s became naturalized as a distinctively American writer, the very notion of national identity, representative authorship, and the American Renaissance was coming under duress. As if to add insult to injury (or demonstrate the economics of exclusivity), Poe was admitted into a canon in the very throes of devaluation.[2]

And yet the story of Poe's critical neglect is not as compelling as it once seemed. To take Matthiessen and his minions too readily as metonyms for an-tebellum literary study indulges in the sort of hagiographic master narrative for which American Renaissance scholarship is often criticized. Matthiessen is in-voked less and less today; and when he is, he is usually treated not as a critic with his own interpretations and methods, but rather as something of an author representing an ostensibly dominant tradition that itself has been increasingly marginalized—even if no one really knows what has displaced the American Renaissance at the center of nineteenth-century American literature.[3]

At the risk of fantasizing a simplified past, one might say that mid-twentieth-century Americanists could credibly conceptualize their field: the canon was smaller; scholarly consensus was valued; American literary study sought to define itself intellectually and institutionally; with fewer faculty, fewer venues, and less pressure to publish, scholars could keep up with all the work in their specialty and determine what was central or not. The situation is more complicated today, not only because of greater sensitivity to canon formation, cultural pluralism, and methodological variety, but also because of the sheer quantity of materials that constitute the study of antebellum literature. Ideology by definition may be difficult to see, but a flood of information can also be obscuring when, in the absence of comprehensive maps, centers and margins seem everywhere and nowhere at once. Specialists today certainly have impressions of what is happening in their field, but who can rightfully claim to know the whole terrain? Under such conditions, how can one place Poe within a vast and unorganized scholarly landscape?

Most disciplines address informational excess with quantitative analysis; and so let me turn—as odd as it may seem—to the *MLA International Bibliography* for a thought experiment that ponders how literary centers and margins might be statistically understood.[4] Using authors' names as subject search terms and delimiting date ranges by decade, we get a sense for the amount of scholarly attention major antebellum writers have received over the last eighty years. As suggested by figure 1 (and a subset of it, figure 2), Poe does not seem so marginal at all. Judging by the quantity of publications, Poe was actually the most widely studied antebellum author in the decades immediately before and after the appearance of *American Renaissance* in 1941. His status does slip relative to Matthiessen's main figures (Emerson, Thoreau, Hawthorne, Melville, and Whitman) over the course of the 1950s, but beginning in the 1960s he quickly makes up ground. Poe surpasses Emerson, Thoreau, and then Whitman by the 1970s; and since 1980 he is second only to Melville as a subject of antebellum scholarship. This is not simply because of non-English publications, which might be taken to indicate a kind of marginalization in the field of American literature; for while Poe predictably leads in this category, the quantity of foreign-language scholarship on him is not enough to alter his standing significantly.

Of course, numbers can only say so much and may remind literary scholars of why they went into literature. The primitive data offered here does not distinguish between monographs and shorter pieces, highly and less-circulated publications,

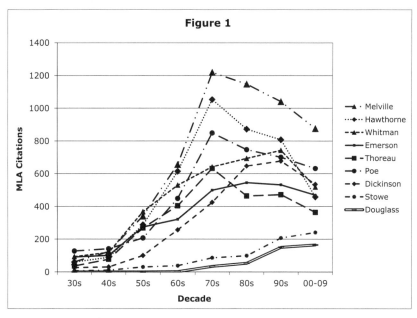

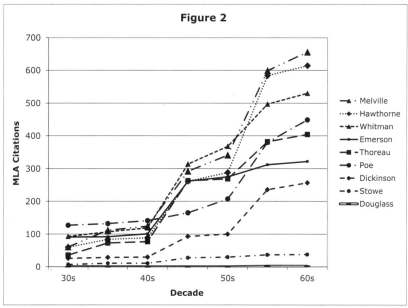

Figs. 1 and 2. Number of MLA citations in each decade by author.

prestigious and lesser-known scholars. Nor does it take into account structural factors—which print sources are included in the MLA bibliography, how subject terms are assigned, what sort of criteria editorial boards use, how sales and financing affect publishing, which author societies publish their own journals, etc. The data say little about the afterlife of specific publications in subsequent scholarship and teaching; and they certainly do not show how Poe is discussed in relation to other American Renaissance authors—whether, for instance, he is treated as a self-standing figure, a representative writer, an interlocutor, or a departure from some norm.

No statistical analysis, howsoever sophisticated, can fully address such issues; and yet the data provided here can be stimulating even if one doubts its explanatory force. To venture a few general impressions: for all the talk (celebratory and apocalyptic) that one used to hear about the multicultural revolution, interest in Douglass and Stowe seems to be reaching a plateau well below that of Poe and Matthiessen's white males. Only Dickinson, the least explicitly political of the "new canon," has broken through the glass ceiling, indicating both the power and limits of three decades of canon revision. Hawthorne is suffering the most precipitous drop, perhaps because of declining interest in the New England Mind, though Emerson and Thoreau are muddling along nicely: in literary history as in their lives, they cross paths and never lose sight of each other as if in endless, intimate competition. Being partial to Melville, I found myself gratified by his abiding popularity, though I was chagrined—and also surprised by my chagrin—to see in stark numerical terms how clearly he and the writers listed here have declined as a percentage of American literary scholarship (figure 3). The field has become more diffuse, but the steady slide over the decades from the mid-teens to 7 percent seems quite steep and irreversible. As with cable and satellite television, there are so many new options that major networks cannot help but lose market share. And as with television or internet news sources, one cannot keep up with everything: though the MLA data for 2000–2009 remain incomplete, current scholars of antebellum literature, when compared to those of the mid-century, face at least seven times the amount of newly printed scholarship, to say nothing of unlisted internet essays, relevant studies not categorized by author, and the aggregative weight of critical history itself.

Again, we should not read too much into statistics. As Hume and our ongoing financial crisis show, correlation should not be mistaken for causality, and past performances do not guarantee future results. Nonetheless, the statistically interested scholar may find it impossible *not* to read meanings into the

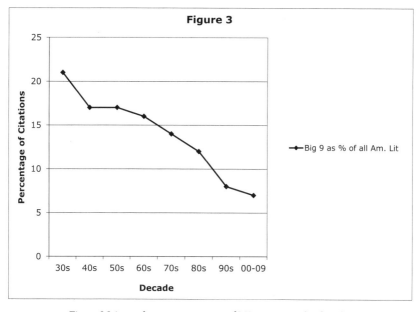

Fig. 3. Major authors as percentage of MLA citations by decade.

bibliographic data at hand, which offer not only positive facts for careful argumentation, but also provocation for speculative analysis and even imaginative play. Surely THERE is where Dickinson rode the feminist tide. THERE is where American high schools finally exhausted *The Scarlet Letter* (1850). THERE is where Cold War scholars blacklisted Poe, and THERE is where French theory redeemed him. Perhaps THERE is where a newly Americanized Poe fought against the field's general loss of market share. Perhaps in thirty years or so, Poe will overtake Melville. Or maybe, using different projection models, Douglass will overtake Poe. Dismal and invigorating, blunt and insightful, objective but also subject to the projections of intuition, habit, and desire, statistics—as Theodore Porter has shown—are a powerful element of modernity: they help us mediate uncertainty but can never quite master the epistemological crisis of superabundant information.[5] They might even be useful, though by no means definitive, in estimating Poe's place in our print culture—and his own.

To return to an earlier point, MLA bibliographic data suggest that Poe's critical marginalization is, numerically speaking, a thing of the past. Poe often does not fit the nationalist narratives of the American Renaissance, but such narratives have been losing momentum for decades; and it turns out that Poe connects powerfully with Matthiessen's five along axes of race, Transcendentalism, Gothicism, transatlanticism, authorship, and more. And yet the sense of Poe's exclusion has proven hard to abjure, especially in a lingering academic climate that tends to valorize critical neglect. The rhetoric of marginalization seems to have crested but is at times deployed by almost everyone—close readers, theorists, and cultural critics; scholars of traditional and emerging texts; and (at a broader cultural level) atheists and Christians, liberals and conservatives, historically oppressed classes and angry white men, underdog teams that sneak into the NCAA basketball tournament and number-one seeds from powerhouse programs that still manage to feel disrespected. This is not to say that there are no margins and centers; rather, the quantity of antebellum literary scholarship, coupled with the conceptual and rhetorical power of projects premised on the reclamation of margins, has created an atmosphere in which few can (or even want to) put their subjects at the center of things. In some ways, the best strategies for gaining attention depend on keeping some distance from the center—not unlike Poe's "Descent into the Maelstrom" (1841) in which the narrator comes tantalizingly close but never quite reaches the destructive eye of the whirlpool.

This tense attitude toward marginality is evident in major antebellum writers, who—like the modern academics who study them—have reasons to be sensitive to print markets. Melville seemed unable to stand his popular success and quarreled with readers, reviewers, and publishers. Thoreau found little profit in the literary marketplace, unsuccessfully trying his hand at journalism and grousing that anything that succeeds with a mass audience is bad. Emerson, too, had hard words for journalists and figured himself as a lone voice in the wilderness, his many followers notwithstanding. Despite much acclaim, Hawthorne also felt isolated from American literary centers, calling himself "the obscurest man of letters in America" and bemoaning his displacement by the scribbling-women mob.[6] Whitman sought his country's approval only to be initially rejected; but even after he outlived his infamy to become a nationally celebrated figure, he continued to insist on his alienation. Dickinson claimed to write letters to a world that never wrote to her, though more accurately she herself chose not to enter print culture, especially given her personal access to powerful editors and influential writers. Douglass's "What to the Slave Is the Fourth of July?" (1852) shows brilliantly how to hold center stage by displaying one's marginalization, while Stowe (somewhat differently) claimed political authority by keeping her distance from the public sphere. Such is the irony of founding a canon on romantic and sentimental writers who are simultaneously attracted to and repelled by what they take to be literary centers.

Something similar can be said of Poe, who presents himself as both a maven and a victim of print culture. On the one hand, he displays an insider's knowledge of the personal habits of writers and editors and the secret practices of the literary establishment. On the other hand, he presents himself as an outsider—objective, independent, and persecuted by "*clique[s]*," "monopol[ies]," "coteries," and the dreaded "Longfellow junto."[7] Poe's ambivalence has a number of potential explanations, none of them mutually exclusive. Demographically, he was both privileged and underprivileged. Professionally, he was connected and painfully itinerant. Psychologically, he struggled to find a stable identity. Romantically, we might as well blame Byron for his urge to be both loved and left alone. Poe's inconsistent views of the press can always be attributed to some mix of aggression, pandering, and irony. Yet Poe, like others in his era, may have suffered very real confusion. During an information revolution in which no one could map the bewildering sprawl of the American and transatlantic press, Poe had no reliable way of gauging whether he was inside or outside the center or whether there were centers at all. In this way, and as is often the case, our problems seem Poe's own. Just as we struggle to locate Poe in the vastness of our field, Poe struggles to know his place within a wildly proliferating press. And just as we might turn to a statistical experiment to manage the overwhelming material on Poe, Poe also turns—with significant skepticism—toward the possibilities of quantifying print culture.

In his "Marginal Notes," published in *Godey's Lady's Book* in September 1845, Poe describes print culture, not so much as a cause of informational excess, but rather as a reaction to it:

> The increase, within a few years, of the magazine literature, is by no means to be regarded as indicating what some critics would suppose it to indicate—a downward tendency in American taste or in American letters. It is but a sign of the times, an indication of an era in which men are forced upon the curt, the condensed, the well-digested in place of the voluminous—in a word, upon journalism in lieu of dissertation.... [Men] have a vast increase in the thinking material; they have more facts, more to think about. For this reason, they are disposed to put the greatest amount of thought in the smallest compass.[8]

For someone who eked out his living in the "Magazine Prison-House" and was punched in the face by at least two editors, Poe in this passage gives a fairly rosy view of antebellum print culture.[9] We need not take Poe's praise as seriously as did William Charvat, who argued in *The Profession of Authorship in America, 1800–1870* (1968) that a more professionalized Poe came to see periodicals as "the appropriate expression of American culture."[10] Poe was in 1845 flirting with American literary nationalism more ardently than ever before; and he probably restrains some of his rage against the press to ingratiate himself with Young America. Yet no matter how politic Poe's occasional lauding of the popular press can be, his vindication of journalistic brevity highlights a crucial dynamic: antebellum print culture participated in the era's information explosion and the concomitant struggle to manage what Poe calls "more facts, more to think about."

Scholars have become increasingly aware that the quality of Poe's writings cannot be separated from the quantity of print that inundated his culture. For Terence Whalen, Poe's relationship to literary production is conditioned by an oversupply of information (economically understood), while Meredith McGill emphasizes how the "decentralized mass-production" of reprinting complicates Poe's sense of authorial control. Though they differ as to the over-determining power of the market, both Whalen and McGill discuss how Poe struggles to master the spread of print materials in an era that saw dramatic advances in literacy, transportation, communications, print technology, and publishing networks.[11] What has not been explored in any sustained way is how Poe—and to some extent, his culture—responded to informational excess by attempting to quantify the period's vast literary landscape. Which is to say that Poe is not only embedded in the material conditions so productively studied by Charvat, Whalen, McGill, Kevin Hayes, Leon Jackson, and others; for Poe, mapping print culture also involves emerging scientific approaches to the challenge of mass facts.

The rise of quantification and what Mary Poovey has called the "modern fact" hardly began in the nineteenth century, though the antebellum era developed powerful new techniques for collecting and processing data. As historians of science have shown, Pierre Laplace, Charles Babbage, and Siméon Denis Poisson used mathematical formulae for the easier and more precise calculations of averages, probabilities, margins of error, and variance distributions. Such advances instigated and ran parallel with progress in a number of fields—astronomy (John Herschel), logic (John Stuart Mill), what we now call game theory (Antoine-Augustin Cournot), and—most influentially—statistical sociology (foremost among its founders, Adolphe Quetelet). Political economy and the natural sciences increasingly relied on quantification, as did disciplines in the humanities such as history (Henry Buckle), political theory (utilitarianism), and postbellum philosophy (pragmatism).[12] In Europe and the United States, quantitative thinking further spread at the level of culture, a shift charted by historians Patricia Cline Cohen and Theodore Porter. Data-driven industries such as insurance and investment expanded; government surveys became more prevalent; educators placed new emphasis on numerical literacy; the ongoing market revolution required calculations in everyday life; and statistics influenced discussions of the weather and trade, politics and crime, birth and death.[13]

Literature, especially romantic literature, is often set against the rise of quantitative science. To speak only of Matthiessen's famous five: Hawthorne's scientists are murderous dissectors; Melville's empiricists are no match for the mysteries of the universe; Emerson recoils from what he called the "terrible tabulation of the French statists" (that is, statisticians); Thoreau mocks the counting of cats in Zanzibar and shuns the "dry docks of science"; Whitman prefers immediate experiences in nature to the tables and charts of astronomy.[14] Poe seems an easy addition to this list. His "Sonnet—to Science" (1829), with its echoes of Keats's "Lamia" (1820), represents science as a "Vulture" of "dull realities" that feeds on the poet's heart, while his scientific hoaxes more satirically subvert the authority of empiricism.[15] This accords with a familiar picture of Poe—the Gothic writer who undermines Enlightenment reason with the grotesque, supernatural, and sensational. And it reinforces a venerable false dualism: romantic skepticism versus scientific positivism.

But Poe, like other American romantics, has a more complicated relationship with science and numbers. John Irwin has shown how Poe's mathematical obsessions drive his tales of ratiocination; and *Eureka* (1848) has been recognized as a sophisticated, if unstable, cosmological text.[16] Poe's scientific imagination generally tends toward the abstract and theoretical. He complained in an 1848 letter of "*merely* scientific men . . . who cultivate the physical sciences to the exclusion . . . of the mathematics, of metaphysics and of logic," a charge that *Eureka* pursues at length in its attack on Baconian scientists (the so-called "Hogites," whom Poe dubs "diggers and pedlers of minute *facts*").[17] That said, Poe never advocates the abandonment of quantification. Dupin may mock the Parisian police for their excessive attention to detail, but Dupin himself remains a careful practitioner of empirical, inductive, and quantitative methods. What most fascinates Poe is how one moves from facts to generalizations, how one turns vast amounts of data into causal laws and comprehensive accounts of reality. When Poe condemns thinkers who "chiefly write the criticisms *against* all efforts at generalization—denouncing these efforts as 'speculative' and 'theoretical,'" he is not denying the importance of facts so much as insisting that facts are not ends in themselves but rather should lead toward conjectures of order.[18] This is the very sort of goal that Poe associates with "the curt, the condensed, the well-digested" work of antebellum print culture, for the distillation and organization of information in the press has affinities with the aims of science in that both aspire to make legible the overwhelming data of the age which they themselves help to generate.

It is worth emphasizing that antebellum print culture played a necessary role in the spread of quantitative thinking. Newspapers and magazines reprinted transactions from London's Royal Society, the American Philosophical Society, and the American Association for the Advancement of Science, as well as from more specialized organizations such as the Statistical Society of London (founded in 1834) and the American Statistical Association (founded in 1839). U.S. government surveys were widely reprinted, and almanacs became more statistically oriented. As with the charts and graphs of today's newspapers, sociological studies by Quetelet and others were reprinted in the antebellum popular press for edification and entertainment alike. Poe himself participated in the ongoing project of popularizing science. He had a hand in *The Conchologist's First Book* (1839); he probably wrote four installments for the *Gentleman's Magazine* series, "Chapter on Science and Art" (1840); and as editor of the *Broadway Journal,* he reprinted material from *Hunt's Commercial Magazine,* whose contents were dominated by statistics. Though Poe's sources are notoriously tricky to trace, he had some knowledge of quantitative pioneers such as Laplace, Mill, Herschel, and Babbage; and as Irwin has demonstrated, Poe had a strong interest and background in mathematical thought.

More metacritically, Poe joined a broader quantitative effort to map print culture itself. Journalistic brevity might help to make sense of "more facts, more to think about," but how can one make sense of the vastness of print culture, especially when print culture itself threatens to increase, not organize, the informational chaos of the age? Antebellum commentators on the popular press frequently refer to its bewildering scope, sometimes trying to represent—and thus contain—print culture through statistics. An 1839 article in the *Baltimore Literary Monument* satirized such efforts by publishing a mock survey of the "5,032 poets" in the United States: "Industriously engaged in useful occupations, 3; neglectful of their appropriate business, 3940; in alms-houses, 75; in states' prisons, etc., 94; in debtors' prisons, 280; street mendicants, 49; ordinary loafers, 225; gentlemanly loafers, 115; uncertain, 251."[19] More seriously, an 1839 piece appearing in *Burton's Gentleman's Magazine* during Poe's stint as assistant editor provided a quantitative assessment of the popular press in France. Under the heading "Statistics of French Periodical Literature," the article begins:

> The number of authors, poets, dramatists, journalists, and literary characters of all descriptions that throng in Paris is incalculable.... Thousands and thousands of individuals depend for their daily bread on papers.... [H]undreds die of hunger.... There is, nevertheless, immense scope in Paris for literary occupation.... There are upwards of twenty-seven daily political journals, of which the circulation is considerable.... There are, moreover, seventy-seven newspapers published once or twice, some even three times, every week.... Each literary society in Paris has its periodical. Le Journal Statistique circulates 13,000 numbers monthly.[20]

The article concludes with a table listing seventeen journals with circulation figures ranging between 1,100 and 13,000. Whether or not Poe wrote or assembled this piece, he was surely interested in the mass of starving writers struggling amidst the numerous opportunities afforded by a large print market. He may also have recognized a telling irony: the sheer number of Parisian writers may be "incalculable," and the "immense scope" of publications may be beyond measure, yet the article still aspires to establish quantitative order, even as its parade of numbers only adds to a sense of confusion that Baudelaire expressed in his 1856 translation of Poe's works: "Who could count [America's] poets? They are innumerable."[21]

One of Poe's impulses, as Whalen and McGill emphasize, is to depict print culture as obfuscating and unknowable. Poe wrote in 1836, "The enormous multiplication of books in every branch of knowledge is one of the greatest evils of the age; since it presents one of the most serious obstacles to the acquisition of correct information."[22] In 1845, Poe referred to the "illimitable" scope of magazines; and he later described the influence of large newspapers as "probably beyond all calculation." Even in "The Literati of New York City" (1846), Poe's most serious attempt to map print culture, he introduces his sketches as "Some Honest Opinions at Random," suggesting an inability to bring any organization or comprehensive perspective to the scene.[23] Just as the deluge of journalistic prose obscures meaning in "'Xing a Paragrab'" (1849), Poe implies that there is simply too much print culture to be properly understood.

Yet Poe's urge to quantify the workings of the literary world remained. Admitting both the power and factitiousness of statistics, Poe cited inflated circulation figures when boasting of his editorial success at the *Southern Literary Messenger.*

There he wrote in his 1836 review of Joseph Rodman Drake and Fitz-Greene Halleck: "[F]rom among ten readers of the *Culprit Fay,* nine would immediately pronounce it a poem betokening the most extraordinary powers of imagination, and of these nine, perhaps five or six . . . would feel embarrassed" by not liking it. Poe elsewhere charged, "ninety-nine . . . out of a hundred" books are puffed, leaving others "utterly overwhelmed and extinguished in the flood"; and in an 1841 review, he complained that popular writers are hacks "ninety-nine times out of a hundred." Poe even mocked the typical editor who claims to review "a flood of publications one tenth of whose title-pages he may possibly have turned over, three fourths of whose contents would be Hebrew to his most desperate efforts at comprehension, and whose entire mass and amount, as might be mathematically demonstrated, would be sufficient to occupy . . . the attention of some ten or twenty readers for a month!"[24] Here the paradox of quantifying print culture is on full display. Acknowledging that no one can keep up with the press, Poe mocks those who pretend to try, but in doing so he himself aspires to a comprehensive critique by turning to numerical representations that, like the very reviewers he deplores, deal in mass generalities that render, not precise analysis, but only estimations.

This dynamic recurs in "The Literati of New York City" when Poe asserts that the "city itself is the focus of American letters," home to "perhaps, one-fourth of all [writers] in America."[25] The large quantity of writers—what makes New York a center—also poses an epistemological and editorial quandary; for while Poe admits, "my limits will not permit me to speak of [the literati] otherwise than in brief," he also insists, "this brevity will be merely consistent with the design." Poe's design is a quantitative one in which explanatory power lies, not in singular or exemplary cases, but in a multitude of well-digested facts. Unlike Emerson's *Representative Men* (1850), a book that dwells on six grand figures, "The Literati of New York City" is more of a survey course. As Gerald Kennedy's essay in this volume emphasizes, Poe tended to expand the canon of American literature. In his "Marginal Notes" for *Godey's Lady's Book,* Poe praises the condensing work that such inclusiveness entails, though in some of his short stories Poe registers serious doubts.

Poe's numerical approach to print culture in his journalism was not unheard of in his time; it may even seem unremarkable to modern readers in an age in which statistical thinking has been largely naturalized.[26] For many antebellum

Americans, however, the emergence of mass facts was profoundly unsettling and led to accusations that the dismal sciences were deterministic, amoral, and dehumanizing. Poe himself expresses similar ambivalence in some of his fictional work, which explores the limits of quantification in general and, more specifically, in regards to print culture.

In "The Mystery of Marie Rogêt" (1842–43), Poe's detective Dupin initially praises quantitative analysis: "[M]odern science has resolved to *calculate upon the unforeseen*. . . . We subject the unlooked for and unimagined to the mathematical *formulae* of the schools." Here Dupin refers to "the Calculus of Probabilities," whose governing logic (sometimes termed frequentism) holds that phenomena, despite variations, in the long run regress to set means. Accordingly, the more data one has on a subject, the more accurately one can predict future outcomes and establish margins of error. In "Rogêt," Dupin notes that young women disappear with "great frequency, in large cities," suggesting how statistical sociology emerges with the rise of urban density and superabundant populations. Using the language of statistical science, Dupin surmises that Rogêt on the day of her disappearance took "a route of more than average diversity from her accustomed one." And he later estimates that "the chances are ten to one" that Rogêt's suitor returned, that "[i]n ninety-nine cases from the hundred" intuition is the best guide, and that the chances are "one thousand to one" that certain evidence would be discovered.[27] Poe, through Dupin, does his quantitative best to sift through the immense amounts of information supplied by the many newspapers covering the case (indeed, quotes from various articles make up a good portion of the story). But if Dupin in "The Murders in the Rue Morgue" (1841) is able to penetrate the cacophony of eyewitness accounts provided by the popular press, in "Rogêt" his quantitative methods fail to solve the murder, marking their analytic limits.

At the end of the tale, Dupin complains of statistical reasoning: "The practice, *in mass*, is . . . philosophical; but it is not the less certain that it engenders vast individual error"—a charge repeated when the story ends by decrying the "mistakes which arise in the path of Reason through her propensity for seeking truth *in detail*."[28] Quetelet also warned in his *Treatise on Man* (1835) not to view subjects (as Dupin later echoes) "too closely." "[W]e must study the masses," Quetelet wrote, "with the view of separating from our observations all that is fortuitous or individual."[29] The problem for Poe is that "Rogêt" is about a single case and that all the data reported in the press, along with Dupin's own quantitative reasoning, figuratively drown the individual victim, who remains brutally effaced (as suggested by the question of whether the mutilated body is even hers). One reason why "Rogêt" is the least popular Dupin tale is that the story, based on the ongoing Mary Rogers case, is so desperately improvised as to make its narrative and logic uneven. Another reason is that the characters, including even Dupin, lack vivid characterization. Young women frequently disappear in great cities, just as individuals were being effaced in the emerging social sciences, an epistemological and aesthetic danger that Poe more self-consciously reflects upon in another tale of urban anonymity.

In "The Man of the Crowd" (1840), the narrator begins as a kind of quantitative sociologist whose observations of a city street take "an abstract and generalizing turn": "I looked at the passengers in masses, and thought of them in their aggregate relations. Even after "descend[ing] to details," the narrator retains sociological categories—different "classes" of businessmen, the "tribe of clerks," "gamblers," "Jew peddlers," and so forth. Not until nightfall does he cease "scrutinizing the mob" and begin an "examination of individual faces," ultimately following an elderly man who has an air of "idiosyncracy." The twist, of course, is that this anomalous man forever seeks out crowds and remains inaccessible, prompting the narrator to call him a "type" and name him *the man of the crowd.* "Type" was a crucial term for Quetelet, a synonym for what he called "the average man"—not a real person but a statistical composite as fictive as the concept of 2.3 children. The narrator of "The Man of the Crowd" has no more success in finding his man than does Dupin in "The Mystery of Marie Rogêt," but "The Man of the Crowd" ultimately succeeds in that the story demonstrates through its lack of characterization the limits of statistical reasoning. Unlike "Rogêt," the purpose of "The Man of the Crowd" is *not* to solve the puzzle at hand. Poe announces from the very start that some "mysteries . . . will not *suffer themselves* to be revealed," just like a book (Poe repeats twice) that "does not permit itself to be read." The narrator of "The Man of the Crowd" can even resemble an urban journalist; but whatever the case, the story shows how quantitative approaches to mass data— in this case, represented by the crowd—lead neither to psychological insight, factual accuracy, or readable literature. Whether used by sociologists or printers, types obscure individual truths, as suggested by the universally famous but ultimately empty selves of the aptly named General John A.B.C. Smith of "The Man That Was Used Up" (1839) and the narrator (and magazine magnate) of "The Literary Life of Thingum Bob, Esq." (1844). As Ronald Zboray argues when referring to the antebellum reading public as a "fictive people," and as Wilkie Collins suggested in his satirical essay, "The Unknown Public" (1858), readerships and even people are impossible to comprehend in an age of mass print culture.[30]

Less abstractly and more personally, "The Man of the Crowd" may also critique a specific editor. In 1837, a long essay appeared in Philadelphia's *Gentleman's Magazine* (later renamed *Burton's Gentleman's Magazine*). William Burton probably wrote "Victor Hugo and the French Drama," which draws at length on statistical reasoning for a theory of verisimilitude:

> Fiction is based on statistics; it has a calculus of its own, and its estimates of probabilities often present problems. . . . [F]iction deals not in the exceptions but the generalities of life[;] it is more or less the estimate of the mean proportional of humanity according to the most approved tables of Quetelet and Babbage.[31]

Just as Quetelet argued in his *Treatise on Man* that statistics can lend "powerful assistance" to artists by keeping them "within due limits," Burton calls for a literature based in realism statistically understood. Poe almost certainly read "Victor Hugo and the French Drama": he seems to have cribbed from it in later comments on Hugo, and he agreed to abide by Burton's aesthetic standards when he became his assistant editor in 1839. Five months after Burton fired him, Poe published "The Man of the Crowd" in the very magazine that Burton had just sold. The story suggests that Burton's statistical approach to literature is misguided, for tales "based on statistics" cannot get at reality, stories using "the tables of Quetelet and Babbage" are unreadable, and observers who dwell too much on mass data miss the lineaments of the individual.

"The Man of the Crowd" may seem to be a romantic dismissal of positive science, but given Poe's interest in quantification, especially in regard to print culture, the story is not so much a rejection as a qualification of statistical analysis. The narrator never knows the man of the crowd as an individual, but sometimes one cannot help but think in terms of "masses" and "aggregate relations." The story points out that such thinking should not be mistaken for a definitive method, for mass data condensed into journalistic brevity do not achieve comprehensiveness. The need for this sort of epistemological modesty is a distinctly modern dilemma that helps to explain how the nineteenth century saw the rise of both quantification and skepticism, not simply in opposition to each other, but also in mutually reinforcing ways. "The Man of the Crowd" can even make a Poe scholar feel like the narrator of the tale; for in trying to place Poe in print culture, we follow him into a literary landscape too sprawling for margins and centers. The paths are winding, the search unending, and, ultimately, recognition is partial at best as historical contexts, constructed mainly from antebellum print materials, threaten to subsume Poe himself.

A final impression. In 1847, *Blackwood's Magazine* reviewed *Tales, by Edgar*

A. Poe (1847) in a larger review of Evert and Edward Duyckinck's *The American Library*. The Duyckinck series was part of a larger nationalist effort to map American literature—one that included Rufus Griswold's many anthologies, the Duyckincks' *Cyclopedia of American Literature* (1855), and Poe's more local "The Literati of New York City." By including a large number of authors, these surveys focused on quantity more than quality, reflecting a longstanding insecurity of American literary criticism. Before *American Renaissance,* most treatments of American literature responded to the intimidating presence of British geniuses by seeking strength in numbers, not comparable great men. The *Blackwood's* review of *The American Library* was quick to draw invidious comparisons between Shakespeare, Milton, and Dickens and what they saw as the relatively motley crew presented by the Duyckincks (including Melville, Hawthorne, Poe, Fuller, Caroline Kirkland, and William Gilmore Simms, whose name *Blackwood's* misspelled as "Sims"). The review also focused on "The Man of the Crowd," admiring aspects of the story but also complaining how it was "difficult to recognise the topography of London" and suggesting that Poe should have consulted "a common guide-book, with its map."[32] One point that Poe and "The Man of the Crowd" make is that there is no accurate map for the observer of large numbers in an information revolution, nor can literary critics armed with statistics finally locate Poe, who remains an ever-circulating figure within—and without—our imagined literary centers.

Notes

1. D. H. Lawrence, *Studies in Classic American Literature* (New York: Doubleday, 1923), 70–88; T. S. Eliot, "From Poe to Valéry" (1948), *To Criticize the Critic and Other Writings* (Lincoln: Univ. of Nebraska Press, 1992), 27–42; Van Wyck Brooks, *America's Coming-of-Age* (New York: B. W. Huebsch, 1915), 59–64; Vernon Louis Parrington, *Main Currents of American Thought* 2: *The Romantic Revolution in America, 1800–1860* (New York: Harcourt, Brace, 1927), 57–59; F. O. Matthiessen, *American Renaissance: Art and Expression in the Age of Emerson and Whitman* (New York: Oxford Univ. Press, 1941), xii. For Poe as marginalized from the American Renaissance, see, for instance, John Carlos Rowe, *At Emerson's Tomb: The Politics of Classic American Literature* (New York: Columbia Univ. Press, 1997), 42–62. The most comprehensive overview of Poe's critical reception is Scott Peeple's *The Afterlife of Edgar Allan Poe* (Rochester, NY: Boydell and Brewer, 2007).

2. For the relatively recent upsurge of work situating Poe in American culture, see *The American Face of Edgar Allan Poe*, ed. Shawn Rosenheim and Stephen Rachman (Baltimore: Johns Hopkins Univ. Press, 1995); and *Romancing the Shadow: Poe and Race*, ed. J. Gerald Kennedy and Liliane Weissberg (New York: Oxford Univ. Press, 2001).

3. Reevaluations of the American Renaissance as a field include David S. Reynolds, *Beneath*

the American Renaissance: The Subversive Imagination in the Age of Emerson and Melville (Cambridge, MA: Harvard Univ. Press, 1988); *The American Renaissance Reconsidered,* ed. Walter Benn Michaels and Donald Pease (Baltimore: Johns Hopkins Univ. Press, 1985); Russell J. Reising, *The Unusable Past: Theory and the Study of American Literature* (New York: Methuen, 1986); and "Re-examining the American Renaissance," a special issue of *ESQ* 49 (2003): 1–3.

4. For similar empirical efforts, see Jay Hubbell, who uses quantitative methods to examine questions of canon in *Who Are the Major American Writers? A Study of the Changing Literary Canon* (Durham, NC: Duke Univ. Press, 1972). Myra Jehlen also uses MLA bibliographic data to track the reputation of Melville in *Herman Melville: A Collection of Critical Essays,* ed. Myra Jehlen (Englewood Cliffs, NJ: Prentice Hall, 1994), 3–4.

5. Theodore Porter, *Trust in Numbers: The Pursuit of Objectivity in Science and Public Life* (Princeton, NJ: Princeton Univ. Press, 1996).

6. Nathaniel Hawthorne, "Preface" to *Twice-Told Tales* (1851), *Nathaniel Hawthorne: Tales and Sketches* (New York: Library of America, 1982), 1150.

7. *Edgar Allan Poe: Essays and Reviews* (New York: Library of America, 1984), 1008, 1010, 1007, 760. Further references to this edition will be cited as *ER.*

8. *ER,* 1377.

9. Poe was hit by John Hill Hewitt, editor of the *Baltimore Saturday Visiter* (sic), and Thomas Dunn English, editor of the *Aristidean.* See Leon Jackson, *The Business of Letters: Authorial Economies in Antebellum America* (Palo Alto, CA: Stanford Univ. Press, 2008), 224; and Kenneth Silverman, *Edgar A. Poe: Mournful and Never-ending Remembrance* (New York: Harper Perennial, 1991), 410.

10. William Charvat, *The Profession of Authorship in America, 1800–1870* (1968; rpt. New York: Columbia Univ. Press, 1992), 85.

11. Terence Whalen, *Edgar Allan Poe and the Masses: The Political Economy of Literature in Antebellum America* (Princeton, NJ: Princeton Univ. Press, 1999); Meredith L. McGill, *American Literature and the Culture of Reprinting, 1834–1854* (Philadelphia: Univ. of Pennsylvania Press, 2003), 3. See also McGill's review of Whalen: "Reading Poe, Reading Capitalism," *American Quarterly* 53, no. 1 (March 2001): 139–47. For an overview of the early American information revolution, see Richard D. Brown, *Knowledge Is Power: The Diffusion of Information in Early America, 1700–1865* (New York: Oxford Univ. Press, 1989); and Ronald J. Zboray, *A Fictive People: Antebellum Economic Development and the American Reading Public* (New York: Oxford Univ. Press, 1993). For a more psychological approach to Poe and mass culture, see Jonathan Elmer, *Reading at the Social Limit: Affect, Mass Culture, and Edgar Allan Poe* (Palo Alto, CA: Stanford Univ. Press, 1995). Catherine Gallagher discusses anxiety about the over-production of Victorian literature in *The Body Economic: Life, Death, and Sensation in Political Economy and the Victorian Novel* (Princeton, NJ: Princeton Univ. Press, 2006), 118–55. For a transatlantic discussion of textual excess, see Andrew Piper, *Dreaming in Books: The Making of the Bibliographic Imagination in the Romantic Age* (Chicago: Univ. of Chicago Press, 2009).

12. Mary Poovey, *A History of the Modern Fact: Problems of Knowledge in the Sciences of Wealth and Society* (Chicago: Univ. of Chicago Press, 1998). Other relevant histories of science include Ian Hacking, *The Taming of Chance* (New York: Cambridge Univ. Press, 1990); Stephen M. Stigler, *The History of Statistics: The Measurement of Uncertainty before 1900* (Cambridge, MA: Harvard Univ. Press, 1986); Lorraine Daston, *Classical Probability in the Enlightenment* (Princeton, NJ: Princeton Univ. Press, 1988); and *The Empire of Chance: How Probability Changed Science and Everyday Life,* ed. Gerd Gigerenzer et al. (New York: Cambridge Univ. Press, 1989).

13. Patricia Cline Cohen, *A Calculating People: The Spread of Numeracy in Early America* (Chicago: Univ. of Chicago Press, 1982); and Theodore M. Porter, *The Rise of Statistical Thinking,*

1820–1900 (Princeton, NJ: Princeton Univ. Press, 1986). See also Jackson Lears, *Something for Nothing: Luck in America* (New York: Penguin, 2003); Oz Frankel, *States of Inquiry: Social Investigations and Print Culture in Nineteenth-Century Britain and the United States* (Baltimore: Johns Hopkins Univ. Press, 2006); Ann Fabian, *Card Sharps, Dream Books, and Bucket Shops: Gambling in Nineteenth-Century America* (Ithaca, NY: Cornell Univ. Press, 1990); and Margo J. Anderson, *The American Census: A Social History* (New Haven, CT: Yale Univ. Press, 1988).

14. Ralph Waldo Emerson, "Representative Men" (1850), *Essays and Lectures* (New York: Library of America, 1983), 670. See also Barbara Packer, "Emerson and the Terrible Tabulations of the French," *Transient and Permanent: The Transcendentalist Movement and Its Contexts*, ed. Charles Capper and Conrad Edick Wright (Boston: Massachusetts Historical Society, 1999), 148–67; Henry David Thoreau, *Walden* (1854), *Walden and Other Writings*, ed. William Howarth (New York: Modern Library, 1981), 260.

15. *Edgar Allan Poe: Poetry and Tales* (New York: Library of America, 1984), 38. Further references to this volume will be cited as *PT*.

16. John T. Irwin, *The Mystery to a Solution: Poe, Borges, and the Analytic Detective Story* (Baltimore, Johns Hopkins Univ. Press, 1994), esp. 318–97.

17. Poe to George Isbell, February 29, 1848, *The Letters of Edgar Allan Poe*, 2 vols., ed. John Ward Ostrom (Cambridge: Harvard Univ. Press, 1948), vol. 2: 363; *Eureka* quoted from *PT*, 1265.

18. Poe to George Isbell, February 29, 1848, *The Letters of Edgar Allan Poe* 2: 363.

19. *Baltimore Literary Monument* 2 (August 1839): 154 (quoted in Jackson, *Business of Letters*, 21).

20. "Statistics of French Periodical Literature," *Burton's Gentleman's Magazine*, February 1839.

21. Quoted in Eliza Richards, *Gender and the Poetics of Reception in Poe's Circle* (New York: Cambridge Univ. Press, 2004), 56.

22. Review of Theodorick Bland's *Reports of Cases Decided in the High Court of Chancery of Maryland*, in *Southern Literary Messenger* 2 (Oct., 1836): 731 (quoted in Whalen, *Poe and the Masses*, 12).

23. *ER*, 1214, 1118.

24. *ER*, 518, 444, 1118, 1008.

25. *ER*, 1120.

26. Sarah Elizabeth Igo, *The Averaged American: Surveys, Citizens, and the Making of a Mass Public* (Cambridge, MA: Harvard Univ. Press, 2007).

27. *PT*, 534, 510, 532, 537, 539, 543. For other studies of "The Mystery of Marie Rogêt" and statistics, see David Van Leer, "Detecting Truth: The World of the Dupin Tales," *New Essays on Poe's Major Tales*, ed. Kenneth Silverman (New York: Cambridge Univ. Press, 1993), 65–88; Mark Seltzer, "The Crime System," *Critical Inquiry* 30 (Spring 2004): 557–83; Leon Chai, *The Romantic Foundations of the American Renaissance* (Ithaca, NY: Cornell Univ. Press, 1987), 116–20.

28. *PT*, 554. See also Poe's "Chapter of Suggestions" (1845): "The theory of chance, or the Calculus of Probabilities, has this remarkable peculiarity, that its truth in general is in direct proportion with its fallacy in particular" (*ER* 1292).

29. Adolphe Quetelet, *A Treatise on Man and the Development of His Faculties*, trans. and ed. Solomon Diamond (1842; Gainesville, FL: Scholars' Facsimiles and Reprints, 1969), 5, 7. (This is the first English translation of Quetelet's book.)

30. *PT*, 389, 390, 392, 396, 388; Zboray, *A Fictive People*.

31. "Victor Hugo and the French Drama," *Gentleman's Magazine* 1 (November 1837): 315–16.

32. "The American Library," *Blackwood's Magazine*, November 1847, 585.

Poe, Decentered Culture, and Critical Method

JEROME McGANN

Some of the most important scholarship in antebellum American literature and culture has emerged in the past fifteen years, much of it examining Poe and his circle of friends and enemies. The work is especially significant because it implicitly—and sometimes explicitly—calls for a distinctively new kind of critical and scholarly methodology. Poe and his American scene provide an illuminating model for studying the issues. But in fact the case is broadly relevant to literary and cultural studies *tout court*. The case of Poe and his contemporary context—the interpretational problems that arise when we try to study that scene and its specific materials—expose a pressing scholarly need that has emerged with the emergence of digital technology.[1]

Here's what happened. Jonathan Elmer's important 1995 study of Poe and mass culture, *Reading at the Social Limit,* began a major reorientation of our critical perspective on the antebellum period in general. This came about because Elmer reconceived Poe less as a self-identical author than as a social "symptom." Elmer's book exposed the codependent relation operating between Poe's reflections of (and on) his world, and the reciprocal ways Poe was "imagined by mass culture."[2] Terence Whalen elaborated this critical procedure in his 1999 book *Edgar Allan Poe and the Masses.* Then followed two books that extended this sociohistorical critical line in more general ways: Timothy Powell offered, in *Ruthless Democracy,* "A Multicultural Interpretation of the American Renaissance" (published in 2000), and Betsy Erkkila cast an even wider net when she set about "Rethinking American Literature from the Revolution to the Culture Wars" (2005). In sharp contrast to previous studies of the antebellum period and the "American Renaissance," these works did not set Poe to the side; rather, they made him a pivotal figure.[3]

Two other books entered that context of sociohistorical work and gave it a decisive focus. These were Meredith McGill's *American Literature and the Culture of Reprinting, 1834–1853* (2003) and Eliza Richards's *Gender and the Poetics of Reception in Poe's Circle* (2004). Proceeding from the vantage of production history in one case (McGill) and reception history in the other (Richards), both demonstrated the necessity of conceiving textual works as social functions. The *ding an sich* of (say) "The Raven" is not a self-identical object, what Stanley Burnshaw—in an influential mid-century formulation—named "The Poem Itself";[4] it is a set of precise but variable relations defined by specific persons and social agents operating in a discourse field (for instance, "antebellum America"). Interpreting "The Raven"—I am choosing it arbitrarily, any work would serve as an example—requires the exposure of as many of those field relations as possible.

Highly significant conclusions follow from this scholarly work, and both McGill and Richards made them explicit. If we are to operate in this kind of critical horizon, Richards observes, we need "a model of literary history that . . . is intersubjective and interactive," because in fact "the poetics of creation are inseparable from the poetics of reception." Or as McGill expresses it: "An author-centered criticism necessarily collapses the range of obscured, withheld, projected, and disavowed forms of authorship" that are always operating in complex discursive fields.[5]

While neither Richards nor McGill synthesizes such "a model of literary history," their work supplies impressive practical instances. But recent antebellum American scholarship is, as I've already suggested, replete with arresting examples. Clearly derivative from the broad New Historicist movement that emerged between 1970 and 1990, this American work gains its special scholarly significance from the extreme volatility of its materials. The dominantly Modernist orientation of the scholarship in that late-twentieth-century moment customarily took revolutionary epochs—most notably the epoch of the French Revolution—as models of historical complexity and contradiction. But those special historical periods tempted scholars to draw maps only of *serious* history, so to speak—history as tragedy. But in antebellum America—or Victorian England for that matter—history comes at once as tragedy and as farce, as Marx saw so clearly. Such historical moments pose a wonderful and difficult challenge, and an opportunity, for scholarship.

As Reynolds and Kennedy have been urging us to remember,[6] antebellum America pivots around multiple centers—Boston where Poe was born, Richmond where he launched his public life, Philadelphia where he failed, New York where he was crucified, Baltimore where he died. Orbiting around those and other less dominant centers, Poe became a measure of his own and their complexities. And so the intensely controversial figure of Poe—three-fifths genius and two-fifths fudge, in Lowell's view—turns out now to be crucial. He is a tragicomic figure, at once master and charlatan, as contradictory as the age in which he lived. The apostle of *poésie pure* is not only, often and always, the *im*purest of authors, he parades his adulterations and mixed messages.

Besides, the impurities run out further and in deeper than the hoaxing dialectics he himself sets in motion. Poe vilifies Longfellow and others for their supposed plagiarisms, but we know he is himself an outrageous plagiarist—borrowing, paraphrasing, imitating with abandon, sometimes signaling or winking to his audience, oftentimes not. His professional irresponsibility can be breathtaking, as when he asked "Frances Sargent Osgood to write a poem 'equal to [his] reputation' that he could present as his own work at [of all places!] the Boston Lyceum" in 1845. "The crisis for Poe," McGill says, is "not that he abandons his critical ideals" but that he "lose[s] control over them."[7]

But this is less a crisis for Poe than the very condition of his modernity. McGill's own work shows that Poe-the-writer accepts and exploits that condition. It's true that Poe the man—Baudelaire's *poète maudit*—suffers dreadfully in the tendentious scene that birthed our celebrated "American Renaissance." His personal life is unbearably painful to read and contemplate. But immersing himself deeply in that scene of complex and often ruthless social and ideological dispute and conflict, Poe gained a unique—a wickedly comic—perspective on his world. That perspective shaped him into the chief critic of his age.

DISLOCATED PERSONS AND EDITORIAL ANALYSTS: THE *BROADWAY JOURNAL* AND OTHER CASES

Like Poe before them, all of these scholars have been connoisseurs of the chaos of antebellum America. One wants to say, thinking of Marianne Moore: "It is a privilege to see so / much confusion" so clearly exposed in such work. Not the least of their scholarly virtues is their dissatisfaction with their own critical tools. Richards tries to imagine "a literary history of multiple narratives," and McGill wonders how to construct "forms of authorship" that are not "author-centered."[8] As they are well aware, our traditional scholarly procedures make it difficult to realize these conceptions. The problems are difficult because they go to the very foundation of literary and cultural studies. Consider that the primary act of scholarship and criticism is editorial—establishing reliable documents, explaining the grounds of their reliability (or lack of it), and then ordering them "authoritatively."

The model of that foundational act is the critical or scholarly edition, and its normative form to date has been the edition of a specific author. That editorial model underpins our investigations, framing the way we perceive and approach the "objects" we will study. Like Laocoön and his children, the scholars I've been discussing all struggle in the coils of that tradition.

As have their distinguished precursors. Burton R. Pollin, one of the two greatest Poe scholars we have had, has recently exposed the issues once again in his effort to produce a complete edition of Poe's works, *The Collected Writings of Edgar Allan Poe.* The basic problem is present in all three of the published volumes, but in volume 3 it appears with greatest clarity. This is Pollin's heroic effort to produce a "Poe edition," as it were, of the *Broadway Journal.* This edition comes in two parts—an editorial volume with scholarly introductions and notes; and a volume of the text—in this case, a photofacsimile of the annotated copy of the journal that Poe gave to Sarah Helen Whitman.

Or I should say a *selected* photofacsimile—a necessary caveat that begins to explain the difficulty. The journal ran from January 4, 1845, through January 3, 1846. Although Poe was contributing from the first issue, he did not become associate editor until March, assuming complete editorial control in July. The journal was published by John Bisco, and its initial chief editor was Charles F. Briggs.

From the outset, Poe was a major contributor to the *Broadway Journal,* and from July he was the chief contributor. The facsimile presentation of the texts supplies a useful bibliographical context for Poe's work. But in going this far to present Poe in his journalistic context, Pollin exposes the deficiencies of his author-centered approach. Two things are especially crucial. First, by giving only those texts that Pollin judges to be Poe's writings, we are left with an expurgated view of Poe's important work as editor. Second, while Poe has annotated his contributions in the Whitman copy of the *Broadway Journal,* the reliability of those identifications is controversial in many ways. Pollin of course discusses the attribution issues— nearly all of them—in excellent detail.[9]

The most notorious of the problematic attributions comes in "The Little Longfellow War" controversy. This event is worth rehearsing in some detail since it illustrates in a relatively brief space the general problem that's at stake. The dispute began with Poe's severe critique of Longfellow in the January 14 issue of the *Evening Mirror,* edited by Nathaniel Willis, at that point a friend and supporter of

Poe. The subsequent controversy included a long "attack" on Poe signed "Outis" ("No Man"). Poe quotes this essay in full when he replies to it in the *Broadway Journal* on March 8, the pseudonymous essay by Outis having been originally published on March 1 in Willis's *Evening Mirror.* Pollin is certain that Poe wrote the "Outis" essay, and he argues his position very well.[10] But others see it differently, and the editorial controversy is not settled. Even more problematic, however, is the critical issue, which Perry Miller long ago outlined with brilliant economy:

> There is reason to suppose that Poe blew [the controversy] up by writing at least one attack on himself (signed "Outis") in order to get the maximum of publicity; he was entirely capable of such a ruse. There is equal likelihood that Briggs entered the game deliberately, writing against Poe with Poe's contrivance [or perhaps without it?] so as to excite further retorts [and thereby promote the circulation of the journal].[11]

Miller writes "at least one attack on himself" because Briggs published another anonymous attack on Poe in the *Broadway Journal* (on February 15). Pollin does not provide us with this text because it was not, in his view, written by Poe; but even so, could it have been written by Briggs? Then various other parties entered the fray, some named, some not, in different periodicals. The whole affair is so interesting in itself that one wants an editorial environment more equal to its complexities—an environment that does not make Poe the pivot point of everything, the "center" determining what we see and how we see it, but only one possible center and "perspective."

The publishing world that enveloped Poe and his contemporaries is replete with these kinds of situations. Poe is so important because he had an acute understanding of the dynamics of his publishing scene, exploiting it—or being exploited by it—repeatedly. McGill's discussion of a publication problem with "Lenore" is arresting. The long-line version of the poem was first published in Willis's *Evening Mirror* on 28 November 1844, the Pindaric version having appeared the previous year in Lowell's periodical *Pioneer.* Although Poe was working in Willis's offices at the time, Willis published the poem as if by an unknown author, stating that it came to him through his correspondence with the Kentucky poet Amelia Welby, who—according to this account—saw it in a badly printed text in the Jackson, Tennessee, *Advocate.* Not only has the latter text never appeared—did it ever exist *in fact*?—Mabbott and others assume its reality in order to infer the existence of another printing of the poem in some New York periodical sometime before October 1844—also a text that has never appeared. Reflecting on the situation McGill rightly wonders:

> Is Poe's presence in [Willis's] office and his penchant for literary deception enough evidence to suggest that the entire correspondence might have been a . . . ruse to generate publicity about a poem to which Poe would soon lay claim in an extended analysis of . . . Welby's poems in the *Democratic Review*? Does the unauthorized circulation of "Lenore" point to reprinting as a problem for Poe, or to Poe's successful manipulation of these conditions of publication? How would we be able to decide without access to Poe's signature?"[12]

Many more questions could justifiably be raised in this context. But McGill's questions expose the key issue: that these textual conditions are marked by radical uncertainties. The surest way to handle the situation, from an editorial point of view, is to provide all of the documents, not just those that an editor, however learned, may judge pertinent. In Pollin's case, "pertinence" is determined in "author-centered" terms: did Poe write the text or didn't he? If Pollin thinks he did, it goes into the edition. If not, it stays out. So the "Outis" review goes in, but the anonymous attack on Poe printed by Briggs in the 15 February issue of the *Broadway Journal* is omitted.

After Poe takes control of the journal in July, the problem grows more pressing because he is responsible for, even if he does not write, the entirety of the journal. Pollin's edition not only removes crucial contextual materials from our attention, it directs us to read in perspectives that are far from certain.

A notable example comes with a series of entries in the 13, 20, and 27 December issues of the *Journal,* all dealing with the veracity of the tale we now know as "The Facts in the Case of M. Valdemar," which Poe had just published in the December issue of the *American Review* under the title "The Facts in Valdemar's Case." In the 13 December issue of the *Broadway Journal,* Poe prints a notice of a review of the *American Review* "article" that had just been published in the *New York Tribune* (10 December). Possibly written by Margaret Fuller, the review condemns Poe's work both for its subject matter and for the misleading "style of giving an air of reality to fictions." In his *Broadway Journal* rejoinder to this review Poe asks: "*Why* cannot a man talk after he is dead?" observing with pertinent if wicked irony that "we find it difficult to understand how any dispassionate transcendentalist can doubt the facts as we state them."

Then in the next issue, 20 December, Poe prints the *American Review* text under a slightly altered title. He heads "The Facts in the Case of M. Valdemar" with a note stating that the reprint comes at a reader's request and in order to let "the article . . . speak for itself." Pollin's edition does not include the *Broadway Journal* reprinted text—an unfortunate omission since Poe mischievously refers to the work as an article, not a story or a tale.[13] The sequence of entries is then completed in the 27 December issue when Poe prints the following: "Mr. Collier, the eminent Mesmerist, has written to us in reference to the extraordinary case of M. Valdemar. We quote a portion of his letter." The quoted letter attests to the veracity of such mesmeric resuscitation, remarking that "I did actually restore to active animation a person who died from excessive drinking of ardent spirits. He was placed in his coffin ready for interment."

If Collyer actually wrote those words, Poe must have found them perversely, comically, gruesomely topical.[14] But the authenticity of this letter has never been corroborated—indeed, its need for corroboration has never been pointed out. Pollin—like Mabbott before him—accepts its veracity.[15] Referring to its author as "Collier" in his headnote, Poe then gives a text dated 16 December 1845 and signed by "Robert H. Collyer." Under the circumstances, we might lift some words from the letter to say of the letter itself: "I have not the least doubt of the *possibility* of such a phenomenon" as the veracity—or the hoax—of this document. Poe had created false documentation for real and living authors before—in "Autography," for example, and "The Balloon Hoax." Whatever the case in *this* case, the management of the entire event is, if not pure poetry, pure Poe.[16]

This example illustrates a salient deficiency in both author-centered and text-centered approaches to literary works and literary history. The *American Review* text of "The Facts in Valdemar's Case" gives only a certain view of that work. The *Broadway Journal* then gives, along with its different title and intercalary texts, an altogether different view. With the publication of those materials we move into a close encounter of a third kind with this work: a view where all the printings—authorized or not, skeptical or otherwise—configure a textual network of remarkable wit and complexity. In publishing his tale, or "article," Poe makes *un coup de dès* that summons the great god chance, who summons in turn various unpremeditated characters. The Valdemar matter gets taken up in the periodical press on both sides of the Atlantic by many readers and reviewers, publishers and editors. All bring their own ideas and dispositions to the event, all contribute to the field of discourse by seeing it in a certain way and letting others know what they see.

The Privilege of Social Dislocation: The Case of *Pym*

The antebellum publishing scene in America and Poe's grasp of its expressive possibilities can be misleading. We must not think of this as a special case. It is not; it simply gives us a graphic picture of the complex nature of every textual condition. Restoration England supplies us with another dramatic case, as we know from the notorious problems of "attribution" that dog the work of Rochester, Dryden, and their respective circles of friends and enemies. Nor is it without reason that D. F. McKenzie focused on Congreve's work in his pursuit of the idea of a "sociology of texts."[17]

But if the case of Poe and his world is not singular in an ontological sense, it is historically notable for two reasons. First, it clearly and (perhaps even more significant) capaciously defines a publishing scene dominated by a volatile mix of periodicals pursuing a variety of different purposes and goals—political, commercial, regional, cultural, religious. Authors and textual works mesh or collide in many different ways under the pressure of conflicted, overlapping, or shared interests. It is a scene ripe for gaming and hoaxing. Second, given the relatively ephemeral character of the principal means of public expression—newspapers and periodicals—the documentary materials that survive from the period are comparatively rich.

For a scholar, these two historical conditions hold out a promise—or is it a temptation?—that new and more comprehensive methods might be developed for studying the complexity of cultural materials and social texts to depths and at ranges not previously possible. Poe's work is crucial in that context because, while it is intensely personal in its perspective, it is not at all subjective, as the work of his celebrated contemporaries—Emerson, Thoreau, and Whitman for instance—so clearly is. To edit Poe adequately we have to locate the work in the full range of its social relations. Poe is a man of that crowd of relations, nor should we imagine that his heart could be laid bare for us. What can be exposed more fully, however, is the network of intersecting interests and relations that comprise antebellum American print culture. An "author-centered" edition will not do. We require an editorial environment where multiple relations can be exposed from a wide range of different perspectives. Some would be individual authors, but others would be centered in a certain time or place, and still others in a particular social agent—for instance, a periodical or a certain social or religious institution. Scholars should be able to shift their focus on the total field at will.

Of course the whole point of the traditional scholarly edition is to supply readers with the means to gain multiple perspectives on the work being edited. Pollin's edition of *The Narrative of Arthur Gordon Pym*—in the first volume of the *Collected Writings*—shows this purpose very clearly. The edition deploys the basic format that has evolved through centuries of development—a format that is, moreover, within the limits of the print medium, flexible and powerful. There is first of all a central reading text—a document that has emerged from the editor's evaluation of the multiple witness texts that make a claim to this central position. All of those witness texts are identified, though only the central text—the so-called "critical text"—is presented *in toto*. Readers are informed in editorial notes where the other witnesses vary from or agree with the critical text, and in many of these cases commentaries are supplied that try to explain the significance of the variations or agreements. The edition also supplies a series of scholarly essays that elucidate—in this particular case—Poe's "Aims and Methods," the work's "Sources," "The Growth of the Text," and an essay on "The Text." Finally, it presents facsimiles of the title pages of the first American book publication (1838) as well as the title pages of the first two English printings (1838, 1841).

The problem in the case of *Pym* is slightly different from what we saw in the case of the material in the *Broadway Journal*—a fact borne out by the presence of Ridgely's important essay, with its discussion—at once learned and speculative—of the work's stages of development over a period of some twenty-two months, and perhaps as long as twenty-eight.[18]

Pym has always been studied in relation to its two initial textual states: the first printing in the *Southern Literary Messenger* (in two installments in January and February 1837) and the much longer book publication by Harper and Brothers in July 1838. These two texts represent completely different—what shall we call them?—works. Because they bear similar titles, and because Poe used the *SLM* materials as the basis for what would become the first four chapters of the Harper book, scholars have commonly approached these works as a problem in bibliography: what is the relation between the *SLM* and the Harper texts—most importantly, what changes were made, and what do they mean? And while these bibliographical issues can scarcely be avoided in any serious study of *Pym*, they serve primarily to bring into focus the complexity of the interpretive questions that populate the *Pym* gravity field.

Here are some of those questions:

1. What is the status of the *SLM* text—which is to ask: why did T. H. White, the editor of *SLM*, publish only two installments? Or, why did he publish any

installments at all, since he had just fired Poe in early January 1837? Or, had Poe written any more of the tale to that point in time? Or, did he have specific plans for further installments? Or, whatever be that case, did Poe make new plans after being cut off from his serial publication? Or, what relation, if any, does the *SLM* text have to the book that Harper and Brothers contracted to publish in the spring of 1837?

2. What is the status of the Harper text—which is to ask: what are the specific textual differences between Harper and *SLM*? And, can we date the changes in any reliable way? And, what are we to make of the gross inconsistencies between the *SLM* and the Harper text, or the hoaxing and bizarre "Preface" and closing editorial Note? And, what are we to make of the "wholesale borrowing" that characterizes so much of the new material in the Harper text? And, what is the relation of the Harper text published in July 1838 and the work contracted in the spring of 1837—for instance, is the "long delay in the publication of *Pym* [due] to Poe's failure to supply copy [or perhaps] to business conditions" and the Panic of 1837? And, since Poe was talking with Harper early in 1836 about publishing a long connected narrative, what, if any, relation does that fact have to the *Pym* materials?

3. What is the status of the non-authoritative printings, i.e., the subsequent dissemination of *Pym* through the culture of reprinting? And, what relation do these texts have to the *SLM* and Harper's texts—other than exhibiting a record of non-authorial readings? And, what is the status of the first two English editions (1838, 1841) and the changes they introduced to the title and the Preface in particular? And, what special status, if any, does the so-called Griswold text (1856) have, considering that it was the most widely disseminated well into the twentieth century?

As Ridgley and Iola Haverstick first showed us in 1966, there are "Many Narratives of Arthur Gordon Pym."[19] Like any good scholarly edition, Pollin's tries to call the salient issues to attention. But the editorial procedure is such that everything pivots around the reading text: justifying it as reliable and authoritative and annotating specific passages so that we can track Poe's intentions, conscious as well as nonconscious. But the fact is that *Pym* has multiple narratives; and while Poe's intentions, conscious or otherwise, are invested in many of them, all are social texts brought into being—that is, into the events that generate their meanings—by multiple agents involved in the work's production and reception histories. A critical edition like Pollin's acknowledges the presence of those many agents and narratives, but it also works to organize them in a stable hierarchy of relations. In doing that, it seriously distorts our access to a comprehensive view of the discourse field—a distortion, ironically enough, that actually moves against the inertia toward social textuality that Poe worked so hard, and so successfully, to gain. When McGill tracks some of those moves, by Poe and others, she says they "chart a progress toward the embattled center of the struggle over a national literature." In fact, it is precisely the kind of "center" that Poe explicates in *Eureka*. It is a field of relations "*of which the centre is everywhere, the circumference nowhere.*"[20]

Concluding Unscientific Prescript (An American Dream)

That kind of field is much less a psychological space of personal expression than a social space of dialogue and dispute. Poe's individual work is exemplary because, more than anyone else in the period, his writings regularly and deliberately make a spectacle of their social relations. The "Longfellow War," the witty theatrics of the "Valdemar Case," the entire record of Poe's multiple publications and subsequent republications and reprintings: through these events we observe Poe's demonstrative explanation and interpretation of the social dynamics of his world and the people who live in it. The work holds a mirror up to that life. The spectacle is framed, at least initially, by something Poe writes and then circulates. Once put in circulation, however, the writing gets seized and reframed by others—eventualities with which Poe may or may not engage again, to give further definition to the complexity of the scene. More than most, Poe's writings demonstrate why a throw of the dice can never abolish chance. Indeed, each throw of the dice only proves the authority of chance.

As Whitman's famous dream of Poe would reveal, Poe's is a stormy, turbulent, and "dislocated" world. Few historians have ever seen the period otherwise. Antebellum America is a virtual byword for a society torn by illusions, conflicts, and extreme violence of many kinds.[21] Poe's first book, *Tamerlane and Other Poems* (1827), was published just before Jackson's first presidential term; and the period of Jackson's "three" administrations (so called) fairly defines the extreme dislocations that made such a fearful turmoil of antebellum America.[22] Coming after Poe, Whitman would famously respond to that dark historic page by trying to see the American world otherwise, by imagining it—representing it—as healthful and harmonious, or rather—as *Democratic Vistas* (1871) shows—as a tormented world dreaming toward health and harmony. But as is clear from the pivotal role

Whitman gives to Poe in "Out of the Cradle Endlessly Rocking,"[23] Whitman's dream of America had first to pass through the strait gate of his dream of Poe.

A great reward awaits the scholar who will also pass through that gate. I have been sketching the volatile character of the discourse field of antebellum America in order to emphasize the significant scholarly and critical opportunity this period holds out for us. Digital environments offer the means for constructing editorial machines that can usefully simulate the complex hyperworld that Poe's work exposes. Fear and Illusion are the watchwords of antebellum America, as Poe more than anyone realized, because its high and conflicted energies were only barely held in control, and often went altogether out of control. The Panic of 1837 is a virtual index of the chaotic energies that were ripping through antebellum America. Poe's comic parodies of Enlightenment, like his quest for a *poésie pure,* are inverted expressions of the signs of the time, the reign of Fear and Illusion.

Scholars have been pursuing machines for editing discourse fields of that kind for some time, the earliest being efforts to design and build different kinds of hypermedia environments. While these are often impressive projects—*The Walt Whitman Archive* for example, or *The Electronic Enlightenment*—we are now beginning to see the serious limitations in their author-centered or thematic approaches. We want more comprehensive textual environments precisely because literary work (and literary work*s*) are only weakly understood if they are understood as self-centered and self-identical.[24]

Some recent digital works that explore integrating timelines, geospatial information, and social software have been provocative—for example, Todd Presner's *Hypercities* project. Even more interesting is Timothy Powell's adventurous *Gibagadinamaagoom: An Ojibwe Digital Archive,* an attempt to construct an online design for a set of cultural materials that do not map to Western Enlightenment design models and, more pertinent to the present discussion, create a special problem for the study of American culture and history.[25] Because Ojibwe "history" is conceived and organized along a "sacred landscape," Ojibwe identities—objects, agents, actions, and locations—are radically discontinuous from the cultural formations that shape the logic of our Western (and American) databases and metadata ontologies. The structural and interpretive demands, and consequences, of this situation are significant, as Powell's description of the project shows.

> The metadata schema and the database structure we have created thus inscribes a
> sacred landscape which allows animikii and other oshkaabewisag ("messengers")

to move freely between the realm of the ancestors and this world. In doing so, we offer a spatio-temporal paradigm that, if acknowledged by Americanists, would perhaps allow us to free ourselves of the deeply problematic concept of periodization and our seemingly endless obsession with nationalism, postnationalism, transnationalism. . . . It is sacred landscape that is distinctly Ojibwe, yet still part of American literary history.

Powell's "Ojibway Digital Archive" points to the general need we have for editorial spaces that would integrate the decentered scholarly present, with its variable critical and cultural interests, with dynamic fields like antebellum America, where multiple agents and relationships have been in play well before scholars in the present thought to investigate them. *NINES* is a project of that kind on *one* end—the present—but its objects of study are not themselves equivalently dynamic. In that respect I think Powell's Ojibway project holds out real promise for passing beyond simply collecting and accessing complex bodies of our still living historical materials.[26] And after all, the critical investigation of these dynamic social texts is what scholarship pursues.

Notes

1. See *The American Literature Scholar in the Digital Age*, ed. Amy Earhart and Andrew Jewell (Ann Arbor: Univ. of Michigan Press, 2010).

2. Jonathan Elmer, *Reading at the Social Limit: Affect, Mass Culture, and Edgar Allan Poe* (Palo Alto, CA: Stanford Univ. Press, 1995), 21.

3. See Terence Whalen, *Edgar Allan Poe and the Masses: The Political Economy of Literature in Antebellum America* (Princeton, NJ: Princeton Univ. Press, 1999); Timothy B. Powell, *Ruthless Democracy: A Multicultural Interpretation of the American Renaissance* (Princeton, NJ: Princeton Univ. Press, 2000); and Betsy Erkkila, *Mixed Bloods and Other Crosses: Rethinking American Literature from the Revolution to the Culture Wars* (Philadelphia: Univ. of Pennsylvania Press, 2005). Earlier work by Donald Pease and others began a move to "rethink" the idea of the American Renaissance, but even in that work Poe remained much more peripheral than in the work of the scholars discussed here. See Pease, *Visionary Compacts: American Renaissance Writings in Cultural Context* (Madison: Univ. of Wisconsin Press, 1987).

4. See Stanley Burnshaw, *The Poem Itself* (New York: Holt, Rinehart, and Winston, 1960).

5. Eliza Richards, *Gender and the Poetics of Reception in Poe's Circle* (New York: Cambridge Univ. Press, 2004), 5, 1. Meredith L. McGill, *American Literature and the Culture of Reprinting, 1834–1853* (Philadelphia: Univ. of Pennsylvania Press, 2007), 147.

6. See, for example, David S. Reynolds, *Beneath the American Renaissance: The Subversive Imagination in the Age of Emerson and Melville* (New York: Knopf, 1988). J. Gerald Kennedy's "'A Mania for Composition': Poe's Annus Mirabilis and the Violence of Nation Building" in *American Literary History* 17, no. 1 (Spring 2005): 1–35, is perhaps his most succinct and penetrating discussion of the key issues.

7. Kenneth Silverman, *Edgar A. Poe: Mournful and Never-ending Remembrance* (New York: HarperCollins, 1992), 286; McGill, 191.

8. Richards, 1. McGill, 147.

9. See Edgar Allan Poe, *Writings in the* Broadway Journal: *The Text,* ed. Burton R. Pollin (New York: Gordian Press, 1986).

10. Burton R. Pollin, *Writings in the* Broadway Journal: *The Annotations* (New York: Gordian Press, 1986), 28–29, 43.

11. Perry Miller, *The Raven and the Whale: Poe, Melville, and the New York Literary Scene* (Baltimore: Johns Hopkins Univ. Press, 1997), 130.

12. McGill, 145.

13. The absence of the text represents Pollin's editorial policy not to print in his edition any Poe texts that are being reprinted from earlier sources. Since the immediate bibliographical context is such a relevant feature of these works, one has to deplore these omissions. Of course the reason for them is plain: Pollin is trying to save paper space.

14. When these materials were being included, the *Broadway Journal* was on the brink of folding. Also, one notes the orthographic difference between "Collier," which is the *Broadway Journal's* spelling of the name, and "Collyer," the spelling given only a few lines below with the printed text of the letter.

15. But see Kent P. Ljungquist, "'Valdemar' and the 'Frogpondians': The Aftermath of Poe's Boston Lyceum Appearance," in *Emersonian Circles: Essays in Honor of Joel Myerson,* ed. Wesley T. Mott and Robert E. Burckholder (Rochester, NY: Univ. of Rochester Press, 1997), 181–206.

16. The fact that Collyer was a living person who could have exposed the letter as a hoax— if it were a hoax—would be a truly exquisite touch. See Pollin's and Ljungquist's commentaries on the tale and the stir it caused in both England and America: Broadway Journal: *Annotations,* 100, and *Emersonian Circles,* 189–96.

17. See D. F. McKenzie, *Bibliography and the Sociology of Texts* (1986; New York: Cambridge Univ. Press, 1999), and *Making Meaning: Printers of the Mind and Other Essays,* ed. Peter D. McDonald and Michael F. Suarez (Amherst: Univ. of Massachusetts Press, 2002). See also David M. Vieth, *Attribution in Restoration Poetry: A Study of Rochester's Poems of 1680* (New Haven, CT: Yale Univ. Press, 1963).

18. Poe was in touch with Harper and Brothers—the eventual book publisher of *Pym*—in March 1836 about publishing "A book-length connected narrative" by Poe. See *The Collected Writings of Edgar Allan Poe,* ed. Burton R. Pollin and J. V. Ridgely (New York: Twayne, 1981), vol. 1: 31.

19. J. V. Ridgeley and Iola S. Haverstick, "Chartless Voyage: The Many Narratives of Arthur Gordon Pym," *Texas Studies in Language and Literature* 6 (Spring 1966): 63–80.

20. See William Conley Harris's discussion of *Eureka* in *E Pluribus Unum: Nineteenth-Century American Literature & the Constitutional Paradox* (Iowa City: Univ. of Iowa Press, 2005), 37–70, and in particular his treatment of the contradictions that are for him the very foundation of "America," 43–61.

21. This historical commonplace is splendidly detailed in Daniel Walker Howe's recent and magisterial study of the period, *What Hath God Wrought: The Transformation of America, 1815–1848* (New York: Oxford Univ. Press, 2007).

22. Historians speak of Jackson's "three administrations" because Van Buren so assiduously—often so disastrously—pursued Jacksonian policies.

23. At lines 144–57. The initial exposure of the Poe allusion was made by Joseph M. DeFalco, "Whitman's Changes in 'Out of the Cradle' and Poe's 'Raven,'" *Walt Whitman Review* 16 (1970): 22–27. Eliza Richards treats this topic in her contribution to this volume.

24. See my essays "Our Literary History," *TLS* 5564 (20 November 2009), 13–15, and "On Creating a Usable Future," *Profession,* 2011: 182–95.

25. See Timothy B. Powell and Larry P. Aitkin, chi-ayy ya ogg (Wisdom Keeper), "Encoding

Culture: Building a Digital Archive Based on Traditional Ojibwe Teachings," in *The American Literature Scholar in the Digital Age,* 250–74.

26. See for instance the "Vision of Britain" project (www.visionofbritain.org.uk [accessed April 14, 2012]) and the "Shaping the West" project (www.stanford.edu/group/spatialhistory/cgi-bin/site/project.php?id=997 [accessed April 14, 2012])—including the interesting discussion of the project "A Data Model for Spatial History: Shaping the West," by Evgenia Schnayder Killeen Hanson, and Mithu Datta (www.stanford.edu/group/spatialhistory/media/images/publication/Railroad_Database_Article.pdf [accessed April 14, 2012]). And for a comprehensive view of some of the most important digital projects now being pursued, see the papers and proceedings of the conference Online Humanities Scholarship, "The Shape of Things to Come": www.shapeofthings.org/ (accessed April 14, 2012). The papers are available print-on-demand: cnx.org/content/col11199/latest/ (accessed April 14, 2012).

Contributors

ANNA BRICKHOUSE, associate professor of English at the University of Virginia, is working on a book about a sixteenth-century indigenous translator from what is now Virginia and his literary afterlife across four centuries. Her book *TransAmerican Literary Relations and the Nineteenth-Century Public Sphere* (2004) won the 2005 Gustave O. Arlt Award.

BETSY ERKKILA is Henry Sanborn Noyes Professor of Literature at Northwestern University. She is the author of *Mixed Bloods and Other Crosses: Rethinking American Literature from the Revolution to the Culture Wars* (2005), *The Wicked Sisters: Women Poets, Literary History, and Discord* (1992), and *Whitman the Political Poet* (1989).

JENNIFER RAE GREESON is associate professor of English at the University of Virginia. She is the author of *Our South: Geographic Fantasy and the Rise of National Literature* (2010) and co-editor of a Norton Critical Edition of Charles W. Chesnutt's *The Conjure Stories* (2012). She has also published many essays on the South and slavery.

LEON JACKSON, associate professor of English at the University of South Carolina, is the author of *The Business of Letters: Authorial Economies in Antebellum America* (2008). He is currently writing a history of blackmail in England and America from the sixteenth century to the present.

J. GERALD KENNEDY is Boyd Professor of English at Louisiana State University and a former chair of the English Department. He is the author of *Poe, Death, and the Life of Writing* (1987) and editor of *The Portable Edgar Allan Poe* (2006), as well as the *Oxford Historical Guide to Edgar Allan Poe* (2001).

MAURICE S. LEE is associate professor of English at Boston University. He is the author of *Uncertain Chances: Science, Skepticism, and Belief in Nineteenth-Century American Literature* (2012) and *Slavery, Philosophy, and American Literature, 1830–1860* (2005). He edited *The Cambridge Companion to Frederick Douglass* (2009).

JEROME McGANN is the John Stewart Bryan University Professor at the University of Virginia. He has authored and edited numerous books, including *Radiant Textuality: Literature after the World Wide Web* and *The Scholar's Art: Literary Studies in a Managed World.* A book of nonsense, *The Invention Tree,* with illustrations by Susan Bee, will be published soon by Chax Press. And forthcoming is his magnum opus on literary theory and method, *Memory Now.*

SCOTT PEEPLES is professor of English at the College of Charleston. He has published numerous essays on nineteenth-century American literature and two books, *The Afterlife of Edgar Allan Poe* (2004) and *Edgar Allan Poe Revisited* (1998). He is co-editor (with Jana Argersinger) of the journal *Poe Studies.*

LELAND S. PERSON, professor of English at the University of Cincinnati, is the author of *The Cambridge Introduction to Nathaniel Hawthorne* (2007) and *Henry James and the Suspense of Masculinity* (2003). He is currently co-editing a volume (*American Novels to 1870*) in the twelve-volume Oxford History of the Novel in English series.

ELIZA RICHARDS is associate professor, Department of English and Comparative Literature, at the University of North Carolina at Chapel Hill, and author of *Gender and the Poetics of Reception in Poe's Circle* (2004). She is completing a book on the relationship between poetry and journalism during the U.S. Civil War.

Index

Adams, John Quincy, 20, 70, 98n28, 179
Adorno, Theodor, 89, 90, 91
Aesthetic Theory (Adorno), 91
Agassiz, Louis, 148
"Al Aaraaf" (Poe), 71
Al Aaraaf, Tamerlane, and Minor Poems (Poe), 70–71
Aldrich, James, 26
Alexander's Weekly Messenger, 6
Allan, John, 40, 49, 72
American Common-Place Book of Poetry (Cheever), 29
American Face of Edgar Allan Poe, The (Rosenheim and Rachman), 3, 144
American literature: first anthologies of, 15, 29, 242; geographical obstacles to, 17, 26, 29; invention of, 1, 15; trends in scholarship of, 227–33, 245–47
American Melodies (Morris), 29
American Monthly Magazine, 44
American Notes for General Circulation (Dickens), 11
American Renaissance (Matthiessen), 2, 228, 242; argument of, 65–66; concept of democracy in, 67–68; exclusion of Poe from, 65–68, 96, 101, 227, 232
"American Scholar, The" (Emerson), 67
American Whig Review, 44, 54, 74
Anderson, Benedict, 2, 14, 51, 104
"Angelic Dialogues" (Poe), 70
antebellum print culture, 3–4; decentralization of, 9, 30, 246–47; mapped via reproductions of "The Raven," 207–15; in New York City, 103–4, 105–7; quantitative thinking and, 236–38; scope of, 4, 233–34, 236–37

anthologies, 7, 15, 29–30
Anthon, Charles, 20, 25
Arcturus, The, 25
Aristotle, 93
Arnold, Benedict, 49
Astor, John Jacob, 183, 184
Astoria (Irving), 6, 183, 184
Authors of the United States, The (Hicks), 31–33
authorship, 3, 13–15; cultural construction of, 26; modern concept of, 14; as profession, 14–15
autograph collecting, 51
"Autography" (Poe), 6, 19–20, 119, 251; as analysis of status, 50–52; authors included in, 20, 22–23, 52; different versions of, 22–24, 51; goals of, 19, 22

Babbage, Charles, 234, 236
Bacon, Francis, 93, 235
"Balloon Hoax, The" (Poe), 6, 105, 108, 251
Bancroft, George, 30, 32, 171
Bank of the United States, 77
Barlow, Thomas Oldham, 31
Barnaby Rudge (Dickens), 204–5
Barnum, P. T., 42, 47, 55
Barrett, Elizabeth, 204, 222n6
Barrett, Lindon, 152
Barthes, Roland, 143
Baudelaire, Charles, 65, 67, 237, 247
Beecher, Henry Ward, 32
Beneath the American Renaissance (Reynolds), 101
Benjamin, Park, 23
Benjamin, Walter, 65, 69, 74–75, 77, 84, 88–91, 201, 207; on "The Man of the Crowd," 92

as King Andrew, 77–78, 81–82, 98n28; Poe's
critique of, 75–85
Jackson, David K., 181–82
Jackson, Leon, 15, 234
Jacobs, Harriet, 119
James, Henry, 65, 96
James, LeBron, 154–55, 165n12
Jay, Martin, 196
Jefferson, Thomas, 70, 79, 129, 139n20, 162,
164n3, 186, 187
Jest Book (Miller), 19
Johnson, Barbara, 200, 205–6, 221
Johnson, Noble, 151, 165n8
Johnson, Richard M., 83
Johnson, Samuel, 14–15
Johnson v. M'Intosh, 192–93
Jones, George, 46
Jones, J. Beauchamp, 23
Jordan, Cynthia, 165n9
Jordan, Winthrop, 164n3–4
"Journal of Julius Rodman, The" (Poe), 6, 8,
172, 180–88, 197; citation by Greenhow of,
179–80, 181–84; critique of imperialism in,
185–87; as hoax, 182–83, 185–86; genre of,
180, 181–82; plot of, 180–81, 185–86; publi-
cation of, 180, 184–85; reception of, 181–82,
187–88
Juvenal, 178

Kaufman, K. R., 154, 165n12
Kazanjian, David, 138n15
Keats, John, 235
Keese, John, 29
Kemble, Fanny, 102
Kennedy, J. Gerald, 83, 137n2, 139n22, 188
Kennedy, John Pendleton, 19, 20, 22, 31, 32,
33, 45
Kepler, Johannes, 93–94
Kettell, Samuel, 15, 29
King Kong (1933), 8, 149–51, 158; movie poster
for, 154–55, 156; *Murders in the Rue Morgue*
(1932) and, 149–51, 165n13; remakes of, 151,
152, 156, 164n6
"King Pest the First" (Poe), 75; critique of
Andrew Jackson in, 81–82; setting of, 81;
themes in, 81–82
Kirkland, Caroline, 6, 25, 33, 242
Klee, Paul, 88

Knickerbocker Magazine, 25, 26
Kopley, Richard, 147
Kubin, Alfred, 147

"Lady Geraldine's Courtship" (Barrett), 204
Lafayette, Marquis de, 40
"Lament, A" (Shelley), 204
Lange, Jessica, 151
Laplace, Pierre, 234, 236
Larson, Kerry, 215
Latrobe, John H. B., 39
Lawrence, D. H., 227
Leaves of Grass (Whitman), 216, 220
Ledyard, John, 187
Lee, Maurice, 137n2, 139n29
Leibovitz, Annie, 154–56
Lemay, Leo, 166n17
Lemire, Elise, 152, 159, 163n1, 166n16
"Lenore" (Poe), 249–50
Lenski, Gerhard, 38
Leslie, Eliza, 20
Lethbridge, Julian, 145
"Letter to Mr. ———" (Poe), 71–72
"Letters from Broadway" (Foster), 116–17, 119
Letters from New York (Child), 119; correspon-
dence genre and, 111; ethnic groups in, 114–
15; images of the city in, 111–14; social re-
form in, 112–14; view of progress in, 115–16
Leverenz, David, 50
Levin, Harry, 159
Lewis and Clark, 6, 181, 183
Liberal Imagination, The (Trilling), 70
Liberator, The (Garrison), 80
Library of American Authors (Duyckinck),
25, 242
"Ligeia" (Poe), 87, 145, 211
Lind, Jenny, 42
"Lionizing" (Poe), 45–46, 47, 48, 81, 82, 98n23
Lippard, George, 106
Literary America (Poe), 2, 27
"Literary Life of Thingum Bob, Esq., The"
(Poe), 240
literati, 1, 6, 13, 16, 30; visual images of, 30–33
Literati, The (Griswold), 30
"Literati of New York City, The" (Poe), 30, 50,
101, 108, 119, 242; American authorship in,
25–27; controversial nature of, 25–26; quan-
titative methods in, 237–38